D1176072

Menstrual Health in Women's Lives

Menstrual Health in Women's Lives

EDITED BY

Alice J. Dan

AND

Linda L. Lewis

UNIVERSITY OF ILLINOIS PRESS

Urbana and Chicago

Publication of this work was supported in part by a grant
from the Society for Menstrual Cycle Research.

©1992 by the Board of Trustees of the University of Illinois
Manufactured in the United States of America
1 2 3 4 5 C P 5 4 3 2 1

This book is printed on acid-free paper.

Library of Congress Cataloging-in-Publication Data

Menstrual health in women's lives / edited by Alice J. Dan and Linda L. Lewis.
   p.   cm.
  Based on work presented at a 1985 conference of the Society for Menstrual Cycle Research
entitled "Menstruation: Clinical Applications and Sociocultural Implications," held at
Galveston, Tex.
  Includes bibliographical references.
  Includes index.
  ISBN 0-252-01784-6 (cloth : alk. paper). — ISBN 0-252-06209-4 (paper : alk. paper)
  1. Menstruation disorders — Congresses. 2. Menstrual cycle — Congresses. 3. Menstruation —
Miscellanea — Congresses. 4. Women — Psychology — Congresses. I. Dan, Alice J. II. Lewis,
Linda L., 1942-   . III. Society for Menstrual Cycle Research.
  [DNLM: 1. Menopause — congresses. 2. Menstrual Cycle — congresses. 3. Menstruation —
congresses. 4. Premenstrual Syndrome — congresses. 5. Women — psychology — congresses.
WP 540 M5484 1985]
RG161.M47 1992
618.1'72 — dc20
DNLM/DLC   90-11178
for Library of Congress   CIP

618.172
M54

92.3617
22006661

Contents

PART THREE

Menopause

PART FOUR
Contextual Issues for
Menstrual Health

Introduction

Alice J. Dan and Linda L. Lewis

Menstrual Health in Women's Lives is a book about building knowledge for menstrual health. Its chapters address some of the most interesting and controversial issues for women today. Based on research from many disciplines, it focuses on the menstrual experience and explores a wide range of topics, including currently popular questions about premenstrual syndrome (PMS), a variety of cultural perspectives on menopause, and broader inquiries into meanings of menstruation and their impact on society.

The menstrual cycle not only is a central aspect of women's lives, but it also offers a model to researchers who want to understand relationships between mind and body, and between social meanings and individual experience. Thus, the authors represented in *Menstrual Health in Women's Lives* come from many fields: psychology, anthropology, nursing, history, sociology, physiology, chronobiology, women's health, theology, primatology, public health, medicine, psychiatry, and education. Characteristic of the new research on women, many of these writers also fall between traditional disciplinary lines. Because they write here not just for colleagues in their discipline but for each other, their work is made accessible to a broad audience of educated lay people. It will be useful not only to health professionals and researchers, but also to women's studies students and others looking for documentation or new ideas for improving understanding of women.

The chapters here are based on work presented in its earlier stages at a 1985 conference in Galveston, Texas, of the Society for Menstrual Cycle Research entitled "Menstruation: Clinical Applications and Sociocultural Implications." The Society celebrated its tenth anniversary in 1989. As the organization matures, it moves past complaints about gaps in research and distortions of women's experience to present serious research attempting to overcome these problems. We know that good health care for women cannot be based on distorted information or inaccurate stereotypes. This volume represents the combined efforts of researchers from many disciplines to create the conditions for menstrual health in women's lives.

Several themes recur throughout the book, including the emphasis on normal experience, the need to recognize interactions among many variables, and the challenge to negative connotations of menstruation. Many chapters emphasize the need for health care providers to be aware of the range of normal menstrual phenomena, to provide a baseline for understanding health deviations. Neither the distortions of cultural stereotypes nor the limitations of clinical situations can provide this context, because both tend to over-emphasize problems in menstrual function. Another aspect of contextual meaning is the recognition of multivariate interactions in menstrual experience. As in other areas of women's studies, information from many sources is needed if menstrual phenomena are to be understood. The meanings of menstruation depend not only on biological variables, but also on social interaction, cultural perspectives, environmental changes, nutrition, fertility patterns, genetic factors, political actions, psychological characteristics, and other sorts of information. Thus, the study of menstrual health is necessarily multidisciplinary in nature. Negative views of menstruation are long standing, and many of the authors of these chapters counter them with positive health meanings. It is crucial for women's well-being that effective methods be found to discredit the use of menstrual phenomena to discriminate against women.

We have written this book for researchers, clinicians, and educators, as well as educated laypersons and students. Researchers will be particularly interested in the clarification of definitions for research, for example, perimenstrual symptoms or normal menopause. Other areas of interest to researchers include the variety of populations represented in these studies, the applications of theories to research, innovations in data-gathering techniques, and new approaches to analysis of data.

Health care providers will be interested in the explication of diagnostic issues, as in the section on PMS. Treatment concerns, such as using progesterone to treat PMS, or biofeedback approaches for menstrual migraines, are also covered. Clinicians are challenged to go beyond studies of pathology, to be aware of normal variations among diverse subcultural groups.

Educators in social sciences, humanities, and health sciences will also find useful materials in this volume. Applications of attribution theory and theories of health-seeking behavior are of particular interest. Some authors suggest original approaches to education, such as in the chapter on menstrual consciousness raising, and others provide examples of the complex interactions among various levels of factors influencing menstrual health.

The book is organized into four major topics: Premenstrual Syndrome (Part 1); Changes Over the Menstrual Cycle (Part 2); Menopause (Part 3), and Contextual Issues for Menstrual Health (Part 4). Each part is preceded by an introduction to give the reader some insight into the contents of the section as a whole. These introductions can guide the reader to specific papers of interest. In addition, the following overview of the book may stimulate readers to go beyond their initial inclinations and broaden their own perspective of menstrual health in women's lives.

Part 1: Premenstrual Syndrome

The volume begins with an exploration of premenstrual syndrome (PMS), one of the most controversial areas of health research for women today. As yet, no consensus exists about the etiology of or treatment for PMS, and these chapters touch on many of the crucial questions to be answered. The first report provides guidelines for improving consensus in PMS research. Three chapters present descriptive findings related to diagnosis of PMS, addressing such questions as: Do women seeking help for PMS show evidence of psychological problems? and How can PMS be viewed in a psychiatric context? Because the American Psychiatric Association has recently placed a diagnosis related to PMS in an experimental category, this work is particularly timely and valuable. The next chapters present theories and evidence about causal factors in PMS. One explores the role of stress in symptomatology. Another examines the notion of circadian desynchrony in relation to premenstrual symptoms, and the last gives a thorough review of the controversy surrounding progesterone as an etiological factor or treatment for PMS.

Part 2: Changes Over the Menstrual Cycle

This section enlarges our view of cyclic change, dealing with the entire cycle and with normal individuals as well as those experiencing symptoms. The section begins with a chapter describing an innovative methodology for recording data representative of real-life events. The next report presents data on changing social interactions, and the following two explore aspects of female sexual change over the cycle, one in women, and one in nonhuman primates. These works are followed by one presenting data on how characteristics of menstrual cycles (such as length and irregularity) are related to personality variables. An outstanding picture of the problem of menstrual migraine headache is given in the next chapter, and the section concludes with the presentation of a model for viewing cyclic symptoms in the context of health-seeking behaviors.

Part 3: Menopause

Menopause has been a severely neglected area of research, and this group of chapters contributes richly to bridging that gap. Several researchers discuss data on the menopausal experience of women from different cultures. The first study, on rural Greek and Mayan Indian women, is fascinating in its depiction of different social meanings. The next two studies present important subcultural groups from our own society, one on black and the other on Hispanic women. A presentation of the difference in perspectives on menopause between gynecologists and their patients follows, using attribution theory to illuminate these meanings. In the next chapter, a measure of attitudes toward menopause is presented which will significantly further these efforts, because the author has specifically designed a measure that can be used cross-culturally. Completing this section is a chapter addressing the need for gathering additional data on the many changes in menstrual cycle patterns as women approach menopause.

Part 4: Contextual Issues for Menstrual Health

The final section of this book deals with varied aspects of the context for menstrual health. An outstanding feminist historian presents an analysis of views of women and menstruation and how they still influence discourse today. A presentation of the meaning of menarche in the family context follows. A frequently overlooked aspect of context is the environment, and two chapters in this section address how environmental factors affect physiological changes related to the menstrual cycle. One chapter reports social effects on menstrual synchrony, and the other reports seasonal effects on menstrual cycles in Alaskan women. Next is a report on a topic of current interest (tampons and toxic shock), raising important questions about tampon safety. The final chapter, by a radical theologian, presents new ways to view menstruation that can support a positive self-concept for women.

There are many settings for menstrual health research, and many levels of investigation. It is as important for individual women to explore and share personal experiences as for researchers to design extensive studies to document the range of normal variation or to conduct controlled trials of health interventions for symptoms related to menstrual function. The negative and distorted images of women's bodies have a long history, and we need to understand how powerfully they are entrenched in social consciousness. To promote menstrual health effectively, many approaches must be tried and evaluated. We must carefully assess situations that need to be changed, systematically plan and implement activities to alter them, and reevaluate the outcomes. Most of all, we must open ourselves to new visions for the future.

A. J. D. and L. L. L.

PART ONE

Premenstrual Syndrome (PMS)

Premenstrual syndrome (PMS) maintains a controversial place in the minds of clinicians, researchers, and scholars. For many women, it means a focus on biology that invites detrimental inferences to all women. For the small but important percentage of women who experience it in severe form, the continuing controversy can mean that someone is listening and someone is searching for a better understanding. The chapters in the first section of this book are by those who are listening, searching, and struggling to honor the issues of women as a group.

Many interested researchers either fail to define PMS or struggle mightily with the issue of defining it, finally arbitrarily selecting a method for use in their particular study. In the first chapter in this section, Mitchell and her colleagues provide a blueprint for the development of normative data which will help define perimenstrual symptoms. The authors take on the difficult task of devising a method that seeks to define high versus low symptom severity, specify symptom clusters, distinguish adequate differences between postmenstrual and premenstrual symptom severity, and illuminate different symptom patterns. Through the use of epidemiological techniques in large community samples, their future work may well provide researchers with much needed standards for defining perimenstrual symptoms. Their goal is that these normative data can then be used for comparison in future studies.

The three chapters that follow contribute to the attempt to understand more about the personality and psychiatric characteristics of women with PMS. Stout and Steege (chap. 2) found a greater frequency of lifetime psychiatric diagnoses (using the Diagnostic Interview Schedule, or DIS) in their sample of women with PMS ($N=223$) compared with a National Institutes of Mental Health matched-age-group sample. However, Baron, MacKenzie, and Wilcox (chap. 3), using just the Somatization scale of the DIS (in a considerably smaller sample), did not find a difference between PMS and non-PMS women. Using the Minnesota Multiphasic Personality Inventory (MMPI), Ostrov, Trupin, and Essex-Sorlie (chap. 4) reported findings that indicated an absence of psychopathology in women with PMS. Whether the methods being used by researchers today are sufficient to answer the questions being posed remains an issue.

In chapter 5, Maddocks and Reid report their examination of the effect of situational stress on the severity of premenstrual symptoms. They concluded that negative life stress does not have a direct influence on severity ratings of premenstrual symptoms. These findings are at odds with other reported studies as well as with the authors' own expectations. They present an interesting discussion of possible reasons for their results, speculating that the symptoms themselves create stress and that the stress in turn breeds symptoms at a time in the cycle when symptoms are expected to be absent. This notion of a possible "carry-over" effect of premenstrual symptoms should prompt a healthy debate among readers.

Dan and her colleagues extend our lines of vision in the search for understanding PMS by postulating a role for the desynchrony of particular aspects of circadian rhythms (such as sleep and body temperature) in premenstrual symptoms (chap. 6). They explore this notion, which grew out of findings in their own research, and conceptualize possible design strategies for this line of study.

In the final chapter of this section, Lewis makes a case for the relevance of continued progesterone-focused research while rejecting the use of progesterone as a therapeutic intervention for PMS (chap. 7). An examination of research findings and discussion of some of the current avenues of progesterone research are used to unscramble this paradox. She takes the position that the controversy, while fraught with problems, has a positive side: It has provided a framework around which women with an important health care concern are being heard.

1

Methodological Issues in the Definition of Premenstrual Syndrome

Ellen S. Mitchell, Martha J. Lentz, Nancy F. Woods,
Kathryn Lee, and Diana Taylor

Menstrual-cycle research currently is hampered by a number of methodologic problems that limit the generalizability of findings, contribute to conflicting results, interfere with the ability to compare and replicate studies, make diagnosis and sample selection difficult, and, overall, restrict the development of a coherent body of literature in the field. These methodological problems are particularly evident in studies of menstrual-cycle symptom experiences such as premenstrual syndrome (PMS). Most definitions of PMS include some reference to a high premenses level of a group of symptoms, with improvement after menses onset. Issues critical to this type of research, which contribute to a lack of consistency among PMS studies, are (a) the description of symptom clusters to form a PMS typology, (b) the definition of appropriate symptom severity levels at postmenses and premenses, (c) the recognition of different patterns of symptom severity across the menstrual cycle, and (d) the definition of an adequate difference between postmenses and premenses symptom severity (i.e., an adequate cycle phase difference). In the following discussion, each of the issues will be addressed: first, in terms of questions raised by the issue; second, by summarizing the different ways investigators have dealt with the issue; and third, by describing how each issue was approached by the research team of Woods, Mitchell, Lentz, Lee, and Taylor. The methods for dealing with each issue are based upon experience with a large ($N=345$) community-based study of perimenstrual symptoms.[1]

Perimenstrual Symptom Clusters

The first issue related to the definition of PMS is that of symptom subtypes. Over 200 different symptoms are reported to be related in some way to the definition of PMS. This issue raises two important questions:

Does the large number of symptoms associated with PMS mean that any combination of symptoms occurring premenstrually is PMS, or is PMS symptom specific? To be labeled PMS must symptoms be present only during the premenses? These questions must be answered before PMS can be specifically defined, consistently diagnosed, and differentiated from other conditions that present with cyclic symptoms. There is growing evidence that PMS is not one specific entity, but is a collection of several specific clusters or groups of related symptoms that occur perimenstrually.

Several different PMS symptom groupings are reported in the literature (Abraham, 1980; Halbreich, Endicott, Schach, & Nee, 1982; Moos, 1968, 1985; Woods, Most, & Dery, 1982). Although this is useful in trying to define PMS, the task is still problematic for the PMS researcher and clinician because there is no agreement yet about which clusters represent PMS and which specific symptoms make up each cluster. One reason for the inconsistency in the content of the symptom clusters is the diversity of samples and methods used to derive the different symptom groups. For example, in the development of his Menstrual Distress Questionnaire (MDQ), Moos (1968) identified eight symptom clusters when he factor analyzed data based on 47 symptoms from 839 healthy women. Seven of these eight clusters he labeled concentration, water retention, negative affect, pain, behavioral change, autonomic reactions, and arousal. The eighth group was used as a control and contained symptoms that supposedly were not part of PMS. Abraham (1980) reported four premenstrual symptom groups composed of 19 symptoms selected from Moos's 47 symptoms based upon clinical relevance. These symptom clusters were labeled anxiety, depression, hydration, and cravings. A fifth cluster, pain, containing three additional symptoms was not included in the PMS definition but became part of a definition of dysmenorrhea. Woods, Most, and Dery (1982), in an attempt to validate the Moos clusters, randomly selected a group of 193 healthy women from the community. They found that of the 47 symptoms used by Moos to define PMS, only 16 had a significant change across the cycle. Using factor analysis of these 16 symptoms, they clustered them into four factors labeled negative affect, water retention, pain, and behavior change. A different and more detailed grouping of symptoms was reported by Halbreich and colleagues (1982). They analyzed a diverse and specific group of 150 symptoms, reduced them to 95 items, and created the Premenstrual Assessment Form (PAF). These 95 symptoms were subdivided into 18 different unipolar scales based on item intercorrelations and alpha coefficients of internal consistency.

Although these four classifications of symptoms attempt to bring clarity out of the PMS symptom chaos, they leave us with unanswered questions. Are symptom clusters sample specific or are there distinct groupings of symptoms that must be present for a diagnosis of PMS, regardless of the sample? Are any symptom clusters unique to premenses and menses when compared with other cycle phases? Which symptoms or clusters of symptoms are a necessary condition for a diagnosis of PMS? It is possible that the inconsistency of symptom clustering found in the literature is due to the use of different types of samples, a different pool of symptoms, and different ways of analyzing and grouping the symptoms into clusters.

To help clarify this issue of symptom occurrence, several approaches seem promising: (a) Test these four different symptom cluster classifications on a community-based sample of healthy women to determine normative patterns of symptom occurrence in menstruating women; (b) obtain symptom intensity data from this normative sample using a symptom pool that includes all symptoms represented within the four existing symptom classifications; (c) collect the symptom data daily for at least two menstrual cycles; (d) factor analyze the symptom severity data by cycle phase on a portion of the sample; (e) confirm the reliability of the analysis on the remaining portion of the sample; (f) test the reliable symptom clusters on a second cycle of data from the same sample; and (g) test the symptom clusters on different samples, including a clinical sample of women with symptoms that increase in severity across the menstrual cycle. These approaches could provide evidence of those symptoms which consistently cluster together in a healthy population and in a clinical population at premenses and at menses. This could be the beginning of the development of a symptom typology that would be a necessary part of a definition of PMS.

In an attempt to address this issue and to answer some of these questions, we tested 57 different symptoms typically associated with PMS and contained in descriptions of the existing PMS symptom clusters. Our sample, a group of 345 menstruating women, completed a 90-day daily diary. The women were selected for the study from computer-generated street segments of census block groups. The women rated the 57 symptoms daily on a scale from *not present* (0) to *extreme* (4). Symptoms with the potential for more than one meaning were kept as separate items. Also, composite items such as insomnia were broken down into their various components (e.g., awakening during the night, early morning awakening, and difficulty getting to sleep can each be labeled insomnia). Finally, because of an interest in symptoms that change in intensity across the menstrual cycle, the wording of those items with bipolar dimensions was altered to indicate specific direction. For example, a change in appetite was specified as increased appetite and decreased appetite rather than a change in eating habits.

To develop a perimenstrual symptom typology, the 57 symptoms were factor analyzed for 226 women for four cycle phases — postmenses, midcycle, premenses, and menses. The factors were tested for reliability on a subsample of 119 women. The first five steps in the development of a perimenstrual symptom typology identified 33 negative symptoms clustering together into five premenstrual symptom groups (Woods, Lentz, Mitchell, Lee, & Taylor, 1986). This collection of 33 symptoms, which is used to classify women into a specific symptom severity pattern, is called the Menstrual Symptom Severity List-Daily (MSSL-D) (Mitchell, Woods, & Lentz, in press). Work is continuing to test the reliability of these five symptom clusters on a second cycle of data and on a different sample of women who fit the PMS symptom severity pattern to determine if they are consistent over time. The goal is to obtain a reliable cluster of perimenstrual symptoms that could be used by other investigators with other types of samples to further test and refine the definition of PMS symptoms. If the typology were used in other PMS studies, it would make comparison of findings across studies more feasible.

Symptom Severity Patterns

A second important issue involved in the definition of PMS is that of symptom severity. This issue has two parts, the level of severity, and the pattern or timing of severity across the menstrual cycle. The issue of symptom severity level raises several questions. How intense must the symptoms be before they are considered at a clinically significant level? If a woman has PMS, how high must her symptom severity be premenstrually? In other words, how high is high, and how low is low? Do all women with high symptom severity premenstrually have PMS?

Studies about premenstrual symptoms do not always account for an absolute level of symptom severity plus a critical amount of change in severity during sample selection. When samples from different PMS studies include women with symptoms of varying intensity, it is difficult to compare findings across such studies. It is also possible that some intervention studies fail to obtain significant changes in severity because the initial intensity level either was not strong enough to detect change or varied so greatly that the effects were masked, creating a Type II error. In other words, some studies base their conclusions on mild symptoms, others on moderate to extreme symptoms, and others on a mix of severity, yet all these samples, regardless of severity, may be labeled as PMS. It is possible that a different underlying mechanism exists for the moderate to extreme versus the mild symptoms, with each requiring different interventions. What is needed is a common method for defining severity level.

In addition to specification of symptom severity level, the pattern or timing of symptom severity is critical for the definition of PMS, that is, the direction and magnitude of change of the symptom intensity across the menstrual cycle from the postmenses to the premenses phase. This severity timing issue is one of symptom exacerbation and raises several questions. To be labeled PMS, is it necessary for symptoms to be of low intensity postmenses and high intensity premenses? Do women with high symptom severity postmenses and even higher intensity premenses have PMS, something else, or some complex mixture? Can PMS be defined without data about postmenses? Findings about PMS are not usually reported in terms of the type of severity pattern they represent. It is often assumed that all high premenses symptoms represent PMS. In studies that do not distinguish patterns of severity, results might be confounded by mixing different patterns into a heterogeneous sample. This also makes it difficult to compare findings across studies.

More frequently, the pattern of low postmenses severity and high premenses severity is labeled as the classic PMS pattern, although low and high severity level usually are not defined. The pattern of high severity postmenses and higher intensity premenses has been referred to as premenstrual magnification (Harrison, 1982). It may be that these two patterns of symptom severity are two subtypes of PMS or two different phenomena. Because of this, when selecting samples and reporting results, it is important that the specific pattern be reported. To define the patterns, a consistent methodology needs to be used.

Approaches that help begin to untangle this issue of symptom severity pattern for both PMS sample selection and clinical diagnosis are those that (a) define low and high severity level postmenses and premenses in a community-based healthy population of women to establish a normative standard; (b) describe patterns of severity across the menstrual cycle in a normative sample based on these criterion levels; and (c) derive postmenses and premenses severity scores for each of the severity patterns in a normative sample.

We addressed this issue by developing specific, systematically derived postmenses and premenses severity level criteria using 327 of our normative sample (Mitchell et al., in press). This manuscript contains a detailed description of the development and application of the cutoff criteria. As a result of this approach, low-, medium-, and high-severity cutoff criteria were identified for both postmenses and premenses based upon the total group mean and standard deviation for Days 6 through 10 postmenses and Days -5 through -1 premenses.

Cycle Phase Difference

An integral part of PMS definition is the issue of the amount of change in symptom intensity across the menstrual cycle. Before it can be said that a woman has PMS, it is necessary first to differentiate the symptom severity level in the premenstrual phase from the level of symptom severity during the postmenses phase, that is, to identify an adequate cycle-phase difference based on the variance of symptom intensity across the cycle. The issue of cycle-phase difference raises an important question that has implications for sample selection and clinical diagnosis. How much change in severity is enough to say that there is cyclicity or an increase across the cycle? That is, what is the minimal angle of the slope representing change in symptom severity?

Some studies define a cycle-phase difference by self-report, as when women are asked whether they have symptoms during the premenstrual week, during menses, and during the remainder of the cycle. Other studies arbitrarily pool all symptoms reported in the premenstrual week and report the mean severity level as evidence of PMS without any comparison with the postmenses phase. Halbreich and colleagues (1982) addressed this issue in their retrospective Premenstrual Assessment Form by asking women to respond to the amount of change in a symptom at premenses compared with the usual nonpremenses state. However, they did not specify any cutoff criteria for adequate change across the cycle. Another approach has been arbitrarily to select a 30% change in symptom severity between postmenses and premenses as evidence of enough change across the cycle (Rubinow & Roy-Byrne, 1984). This approach lacks any empirical basis for the 30% cutoff criterion.

We addressed this issue of defining an adequate cycle-phase difference to demonstrate cyclicity in symptom severity by deriving a cycle-phase difference cutoff score based upon the normative sample of 327 women (Mitchell et al., in press). From the total group mean difference scores and standard deviation, cutoff criteria were developed to define a small, moderate, and large cycle-phase difference. The large cycle-phase difference was considered an adequate amount of change in severity across the menstrual cycle.

The cycle-phase difference and severity level cutoff criteria were applied to the individual 5-day mean postmenses and premenses symptom scores to classify each woman in the sample into one of the symptom severity patterns including PMS, premenstrual magnification, and a low symptom pattern. Those women with a large cycle-phase difference, a low postmenses severity score, and either a medium or high premenses score were labeled as showing the PMS pattern. Those with a large cycle-phase difference, a medium or high postmenses score, and a high premenses score fit into the premenstrual magnification pattern. Finally, those with a small cycle-phase difference and a low severity score both postmenses and premenses were classified into the low-symptom pattern.

Because the source of these cutoff criteria was a population-based sample, these criteria can be used in other studies and by other investigators for PMS sample selection and clinical diagnosis if the same 33 symptoms scaled from 0 to 4 (MSSL-D) are used for data collection. Work by our research team is continuing on the application of these criteria to form PMS, premenstrual magnification, and low symptom subgroups in a different sample and testing for differences between the groups.

Conclusion

By describing the methods currently being used to deal with some of the thorny issues in the area of PMS research, we hope others may be stimulated to use our findings as a normative standard of menstrual cycle symptom experience and to refine our approaches by testing them on different samples. In this manner, the goal of systematically specifying symptom clusters, defining symptom severity patterns, and specifying adequate cycle-phase difference can be achieved. The end result could be more accurate clinical diagnoses to guide therapy, the ability to compare findings from other PMS studies, and a means of replicating PMS studies in order to build a more coherent and meaningful body of knowledge.

NOTE

1. This study, "Prevalence of Perimenstrual Symptoms," was conducted by Nancy F. Woods, principal investigator, and colleagues, and supported by the Division of Nursing, USPHS, DHHS, Grant NU01054.

REFERENCES

Abraham, G. E. (1980). Premenstrual tension. *Current Problems in Obstetrics and Gynecology, 3,* 7–23.

Halbreich, U., Endicott, J., Schach, S., & Nee, J. (1982). The diversity of premenstrual changes as reflected in the Premenstrual Assessment Form. *Acta Psychiatrica Scandinavica, 65,* 46–65.

Harrison, M. (1982). *Self-help for premenstrual syndrome.* New York: Random House.

Mitchell, E. S., Woods, N. F., & Lentz, M. J. (in press). Recognizing PMS when you see it: Criteria for PMS sample selection. In D. Taylor & N. Woods (Eds.), *Menstruation, health and illness.* Washington, DC: Hemisphere.

Moos, R. H. (1968). Psychological aspects of oral contraceptives. *Archives of General Psychiatry, 19,* 87–94.

Moos, R. H. (1985). *Perimenstrual symptoms: A manual and overview of research with the Menstrual Distress Questionnaire.* Palo Alto, CA: Stanford University and Veterans Administration Hospital.

Rubinow, D. R., & Roy-Byrne, P. (1984). Premenstrual syndromes: Overview from a methodologic perspective. *American Journal of Psychiatry, 141,* 163–172.

Woods, N. F., Most, A., & Dery, G. K. (1982). Toward a construct of perimenstrual distress. *Research in Nursing and Health, 5,* 123–136.

Woods, N. F., Lentz, M. J., Mitchell, E. S., Lee, K., & Taylor, D. (1986). *Prevalence of perimenstrual symptoms* (Final Report: NU1054). Division of Nursing, USPHS, DHHS. (Available from N. F. Woods, Department of Parent and Child Nursing, University of Washington, Seattle, WA 98195)

2

Lifetime Psychiatric Diagnoses of Women Seeking Treatment for PMS

Anna L. Stout and John F. Steege

The relationship of premenstrual symptoms to psychiatric disorders has been explored from several perspectives. Smith's (1975) review concluded that psychotic episodes occur premenstrually in women with intermittent psychosis more often than would be expected by chance. Dalton (1959) and Kramp (1968) found a peak in mental hospital admissions in the premenstrual phase. Several studies focusing specifically on the relationship between premenstrual syndrome and affective disorders (Endicott, Halbreich, Schacht, & Nee, 1981; Haskett, Steiner, & Carroll, 1984; Kashiwagi, McClure, & Wetzel, 1976) have suggested that premenstrual symptoms may be a mild manifestation of an affective disorder, particularly when the criterion for symptom duration is reduced. Two studies have reported somewhat contradictory results: Coppen (1965) reported that dysphoric premenstrual symptoms were less prevalent among schizophrenics than controls but that his affective disorders sample was not different from controls except for the depression symptom; Diamond, Rubinstein, Dunner, and Fieve (1976) found no difference in the prevalence of premenstrual depression syndrome in women diagnosed as having primary affective disorder and controls. Clare's (1983) study of British women was the largest scale attempt to examine psychiatric ill-health and premenstrual complaint. Using a brief instrument to detect nonpsychotic psychiatric morbidity and retrospective and prospective symptom recording, Clare found that women with psychiatric ill-health reported more psychiatric and behavioral symptoms, although they did not differ from psychiatrically "healthy" women in their report of physical symptoms premenstrually.

Reports of the association of premenstrual symptoms and psychiatric diagnoses clearly confirm that this interaction is important for further study; however, the relationship is still confused. Conclusions have been limited by the lack of a well-standardized system for assessing psychiatric diagnoses. The development of the National Institute of Mental Health

Diagnostic Interview Schedule (DIS) (Robins, Helzer, Croughan, Williams, & Spitzer, 1981), a highly structured interview designed to make diagnoses using *Diagnostic and Statistical Manual of Mental Disorders* (DSM-III) criteria (American Psychiatric Association, 1980), Research Diagnostic Criteria (RDC) (Spitzer, Endicott, & Robins, 1978), or Feighner criteria (Feighner et al., 1972) allows for standardized assessment of psychiatric diagnoses in conjunction with evaluation of premenstrual symptoms and provides the opportunity for comparison with other samples. The DIS has also been used in a series of large epidemiologic studies performed by independent research teams at five sites in collaboration with the Center for Epidemiologic Studies (CES) of the Division of Biometry and Epidemiology, National Institute of Mental Health (NIMH). This multicenter collaborative project, the Epidemiologic Catchment Area (ECA) Research Program, was designed to investigate the incidence and prevalence of psychiatric disorder, the utilization of general health and mental health services for psychiatric illness, levels of unmet need, and barriers to treatment. The purpose of this investigation was to attempt to learn more about the psychopathological matrix from which premenstrual syndrome (PMS) arises by obtaining information about psychiatric diagnoses at any point in the lifetime of women seeking treatment for PMS. Lifetime psychiatric diagnoses are considered more meaningful than current diagnoses because current diagnoses may be "masked" by PMS symptoms. Data from the clinical sample can then be compared in future studies with data collected from a community sample of women in the same age group.

Method

Setting

The Premenstrual Syndrome Clinic is a component of the Department of Obstetrics and Gynecology at a large private medical center in the Southeast. The clinic is staffed by an interdisciplinary team, including a gynecologist, a clinical psychologist, and a gynecologic nurse practitioner.

Subjects

The first 223 women who completed initial evaluation in the Premenstrual Syndrome Clinic were included in this study. All women had been previously screened by telephone to attempt to determine whether a cyclic symptom pattern existed in association with their menstrual cycle. Women who appeared to complain primarily of other menstrual-cycle-related disorders, such as dysmenorrhea or menopausal symptoms, were eliminated. Women were encouraged at the time of the telephone interview to complete some informal symptom charting before scheduling an assessment appointment, and some women found their perceptions of symptom cyclicity were not confirmed. Women were referred to the Premenstrual Syndrome Clinic by other health care professionals or self-referred on the basis of information obtained through the media or women's self-help groups.

Subjects were 20 to 48 years of age (mean age = 34.0 ± 5.8 years). All except one subject were Caucasian; 27% were nulliparous, 25% had one child, 36% had two children, and 12% had three or more; 73% were married, 14% single, and 13% separated or divorced; 49% had at least a bachelor's degree, and 10% had graduate degrees; 68% were employed outside the home.

As to previous mental health care, 41% reported some contact with outpatient care, with 17% having previous psychiatric admissions. Psychotropic medication had been prescribed in the past for 50% of the women. Psychotropic drugs in that group included antidepressants (30.4%), anxiolytics (34.7%), and antipsychotics (10.3%). The percentages reporting past medication usage overlap, because some women had been prescribed medication in all three categories.

Measure

The National Institute of Mental Health Diagnostic Interview Schedule (DIS) (Robins et al., 1981) is a case-identification instrument that can be used by clinicians and trained lay interviewers. The pattern of DIS questions focuses on the presence, duration, and severity of symptoms that have occurred at any time during an individual's life. The mental disorder diagnostic criteria of the *Diagnostic and Statistical Manual of Mental Disorders* (DSM-III) (American Psychiatric Association, 1980), the Feighner criteria (Feighner et al., 1972), and the Research Diagnostic Criteria (RDC) (Spitzer et al., 1978) can be applied to the information that is elicited. The DIS content and face validity are high (Regier & Burke, 1985) and were certified under contract by the principal authors (J. Williams and R. Spitzer) of the DSM-III diagnostic criteria. Results of the DIS administered by a clinician and a lay interviewer were compared and documented in a pilot study for each diagnosis (Robins, Helzer, Croughan, & Ratcliff, 1981; Robins, Helzer, Ratcliff, & Seyfried, 1982). Another study comparing diagnoses generated by the Schedule for Affective Disorders and Schizophrenia (SADS-L) (Endicott & Spitzer, 1978) shows a high concordance with the DIS in a clinical population (Hesselbrock, Stabenau, Hesselbrock, Mirkin, & Meyer, 1982).

Procedure

Initial assessment visits were all scheduled during the follicular phase (between onset of menstrual flow and ovulation) of the menstrual cycle, and the DIS was administered during that visit. Approximately half of these interviews were administered by the clinic's clinical psychologist and half by a lay interviewer, both of whom were trained in the administration of the DIS. Because the primary purpose of this investigation was to obtain information regarding lifetime psychiatric diagnoses of women with premenstrual complaints, the recency probes regarding symptoms and utilization of health care were modified. The following DIS sections were administered: Manic Episode, Major Depressive Episode, Phobias, Panic Disorder, Obsessive-Compulsive Disorder, Somatization Disorder, Schizophrenia, Antisocial Personality, Alcohol Abuse and Dependence, Drug Abuse and Dependence, and Anorexia. Questions specifically related to assessing Organic Brain Syndrome were eliminated because this disorder was not expected to be as relevant to that age group of the clinical population. The Somatization Disorder section of the DIS of individuals meeting criteria for this diagnosis underwent medical editing by the clinic gynecologist, who followed health symptom coding guidelines (8/8/83) developed by the ECA collaboration project to assure consistency in symptom classification of specific symptoms. In general, a positively reported symptom counts toward Somatization Disorder diagnosis if the symptom reaches severity level and cannot be explained on the basis of physical illness, drug, or alcohol use.

Results and Discussion

Lifetime psychiatric diagnoses were obtained from DIS data using a standardized computer program (3/16/85 version) for DSM-III algorithms developed by the collaborative ECA project. In the version of the program utilized, diagnoses are not excluded because of the presence of other diagnoses. At least one of the DIS/DSM-III lifetime psychiatric diagnoses had been experienced by 81.1% of the women. Prevalence rates are presented in Table 1.

For the relationship between PMS and affective disorders, 0.9% and 2.2% of the sample met DIS/DSM-III criteria for diagnoses of major depressive episode and manic episode, respectively; however, 21% of the sample met criteria for dysthymia. Although criteria for major depression were rarely met, examination of specific items in the affective disorders sections revealed a high frequency of individuals reporting suicidal ideation (63%) and suicide attempts (15%). Criteria were met by 65% of the women for phobia, with none reaching criteria for panic disorder. Of the sample, 16% met criteria for obsessive-compulsive disorder and 8.5% met criteria for somatization disorder. None of the women in this clinical sample reached criteria for schizophrenia or schizophreniform disorders. Of these women, 1.3% met criteria for antisocial personality, 16.1% for a substance abuse disorder, 9.4% for alcohol abuse or

Table 1.
Lifetime Prevalence Rates of DIS/DSM-III Disorders in Women (ages 20–48) Seeking Treatment for PMS (N=223)

Disorder	%
Affective	
Manic episode	2.2
Major depressive episode	.9
Bipolar	.0
Atypical bipolar	.0
Dysthymia	21.0
Anxiety/somatoform	
Phobia	65.0
Panic	.0
Obsessive-compulsive	16.1
Somatization	8.5
Schizophrenic/schizophreniform	
Schizophrenia	.0
Schizophreniform	.0
Personality	
Antisocial personality	1.3
Substance use	
Alcohol abuse/dependence	9.4
Drug abuse/dependence	6.7
Eating	
Anorexia	.4

dependence, 6.7% for drug abuse or dependence, and only 0.4% for anorexia.

Most of the DIS questions eliciting reports of depressive symptoms establish a symptom duration criterion of 2 or more continuous weeks. This duration criterion established by the DSM-III diagnostic system may account for the few women in the PMS clinic sample meeting criteria for major depressive episode. The specific symptoms regarding suicidal ideation and suicidal attempts are considered by the DIS/DSM-III classification to meet criteria if they are reported to have ever occurred. The discrepancy between the low number of women meeting DIS/DSM-III criteria for major depressive episode and the high number of women reporting suicidal ideation and suicide attempts suggests that women seeking treatment for PMS may be more likely to experience shorter periods of depressive symptoms than required to meet criteria for major depressive episode, but that the shorter duration symptoms can be intense and severe. Another explanation may be that women seeking treatment for PMS may be reluctant at the time of initial evaluation to admit to more continuous depression because they are invested in viewing their depressive symptoms as associated with their menstrual cycles. In either case, the number of previous suicide attempts in this group of women whose premenstrual symptoms are disruptive enough to cause them to seek treatment at a clinic specializing in PMS certainly indicates that they constitute a high-risk group. These indices of severity, however, warrant further exploration of premenstrual depressive symptoms and affective disorders despite the small percentages of women meeting criteria for a major depressive disorder.

The largest percentage of women in the PMS clinic sample reached DIS/DSM-III criteria for anxiety/somatoform disorders, followed by affective disorders and substance abuse disorders. Schizophrenia/schizophreniform disorders were not found in this sample. Based on a study by Stout, Steege, Blazer, and George (1986), it appears that the women in this clinic sample met DSM-III criteria for lifetime psychiatric diagnoses of dysthymia, phobia, obsessive-compulsive disorder, somatization disorder, alcohol dependence/abuse, and drug dependence/abuse on the DIS with a much greater frequency than a matched-age-group sample from the ECA program. Further research is needed to investigate whether premenstrual syndrome is strongly associated with specific psychiatric disorders or whether current classification methods are inadequate for differentiation.

REFERENCES

American Psychiatric Association (1980). *Diagnostic and statistical manual of mental disorders* (3d ed.). Washington, DC: Author.

Clare, A. W. (1983). Psychiatric and social aspects of premenstrual complaints. *Psychological Medicine* (Monograph Suppl. 4), pp. 5–49. Cambridge, England: Cambridge University Press.

Coppen, A. (1965). The prevalence of menstrual disorders in psychiatric patients. *British Journal of Psychiatry, 111,* 155–167.

Dalton, K. (1959). Menstruation and acute psychiatric illness. *British Medical Journal, 1,* 148–149.

Diamond, S. B., Rubinstein, A. A., Dunner, D. L., & Fieve, R. R. (1976). Menstrual problems in women with primary affective illness. *Comprehensive Psychiatry, 17,* 541–548.

Endicott, J., Halbreich, U., Schacht, S., & Nee, J. (1981). Premenstrual changes and affective disorders. *Psychosomatic Medicine, 43,* 519–529.

Endicott, J., & Spitzer, R. L. (1978). A diagnostic interview: The Schedule for Affective Disorders and Schizophrenia. *Archives of General Psychiatry, 35,* 837–844.

Feighner, J. P., Robins, E., Guze, S. B., Woodruff, R. A., Winokur, G., & Munoz, R. (1972). Diagnostic criteria for use in psychiatric research. *Archives of General Psychiatry, 26,* 56–63.

Haskett, R. F., Steiner, M., & Carroll, B. J. (1984). Psychoneuroendocrine study of premenstrual tension syndrome. A model for endogenous depression? *Journal of Affective Disorders, 6,* 191–199.

Hesselbrock, V., Stabenau, J., Hesselbrock, M., Mirkin, P., & Meyer, R. (1982). A comparison of two interview schedules: The Schedule for Affective Disorders and Schizophrenia-Lifetime and the National Institute of Mental Health Diagnostic Interview Schedule. *Archives of General Psychiatry, 39,* 674–677.

Kashiwagi, T., McClure, J. H., & Wetzel, R. D. (1976). Premenstrual affective syndrome and psychiatric disorder. *Diseases of the Nervous System, 37,* 116–119.

Kramp, J. L. (1968). Studies of the premenstrual syndrome in relation to psychiatry. *Acta Psychiatrica Scandinavica* (Suppl. *203*), 261–267.

Regier, D. A., & Burke, J. D., Jr. (1985). Epidemiology. In H. I. Kaplan & B. J. Saddock (Eds.), *Comprehensive textbook of psychiatry/IV* (4th ed., Vol. 1, pp. 295–312). Baltimore: Williams & Wilkins.

Robins, L. N., Helzer, J. E., Croughan, J., & Ratcliff, K. S. (1981). National Institute of Mental Health Diagnostic Interview Schedule: Its history, characteristics, and validity. *Archives of General Psychiatry, 38,* 381–389.

Robins, L. N., Helzer, J. E., Croughan, J., Williams, J. B. W., & Spitzer, R. L. (1981). *The NIMH Diagnostic Interview Schedule: Version 111* (DHSS Publication No. ADM-T-42-3; 5-81, 8-81). Washington, DC: U.S. Government Printing Office.

Robins, L. N., Helzer, J. E., Ratcliff, K. S., & Seyfried, W. (1982). Validity of the Diagnostic Interview Schedule: Version II (DSM-III) diagnoses. *Psychological Medicine, 12,* 855–870.

Smith, S. L. (1975). Mood and the menstrual cycle. In E. J. Sachar (Ed.), *Topics in psychoendocrinology (pp. 19–53).* New York: Raven Press.

Spitzer, R. L., Endicott, J., & Robins, E. (1978). Research diagnostic criteria: Rationale and reliability. *Archives of General Psychiatry, 35,* 773–782.

Stout, A. L., Steege, J. F., Blazer, D. G., & George, L. K. (1986). Comparison of lifetime psychiatric diagnoses in premenstrual syndrome clinic and community samples. *Journal of Nervous and Mental Disease, 174,* 517–522.

3

Somatic Symptomatology in Women With Premenstrual or Menstrual Difficulties

Howard I.Baron, Thomas B. MacKenzie,
and Kimerly Wilcox

Psychiatric diagnosis has long been criticized as ambiguous and unreliable. Some diagnostic categories have been based on unverifiable intrapsychic phenomena, and others have been overly inclusive.

The American Psychiatric Association (Williams, 1980) introduced an innovative psychiatric classification scheme known as DSM-III: the third edition of the *Diagnostic and Statistical Manual of Mental Disorders.* This scheme asserts that there are a limited number of identifiable psychiatric disorders. Specific diagnostic criteria are provided for each diagnostic category.

There are two ways in which DSM-III can be used to assign psychiatric diagnoses. The first method is by the clinician, who interviews and examines the patient, looking for signs and symptoms that identify a particular diagnosis. The data gathered in this fashion are subjective at best, as well as being painstakingly slow to obtain. A second way to obtain DSM-III-based psychiatric diagnoses is by use of a structured interview. This has been widely used in epidemiological studies, and the results have been found to be comparable whether the interview is conducted by a psychiatrist or by a trained lay interviewer (Robins, Helzer, Croughan, & Ratcliff, 1981).

One of the most widely used of these DSM-III-based interview formats is the Diagnostic Interview Schedule (DIS) (Robins, Helzer, Croughan, Williams, & Spitzer, 1981), which is used by the National Institute of Mental Health (NIMH). Respondents are asked 259 questions such as the following: "Have you ever had pain in your joints?"; "Have you ever considered yourself a nervous person?"; and "Have you ever had two weeks or more during which you felt sad, blue, depressed, or when you lost all interest and pleasure in things that you usually cared about or enjoyed?" If the subject answers *no,* then the interviewer proceeds to the next question. If the subject answers *yes,* then the interviewer asks a series of follow-up questions beginning with the question, "Did you tell a doctor about (symptoms)?" This algorithm assigns a presumptive etiology to each *yes* response. The possible assignments are psychological symptom (i.e., nerves, stress, anxiety, depression, mental illness); drugs, alcohol, or medication; physical condition; or no definite diagnosis (referring to a doctor's opinion if it was obtained by the patient).

The DIS codes these etiologies as follows: psychological symptom, Code 5; physical condition, Code 4; drugs, etc., Code 3; no definite diagnosis, Code 2, or symptom not experienced, Code 1. A *yes* response that is coded 5 contributes to the evidence for a mental disorder. The number and variety of symptoms coded as 5 are compared with DSM-III criteria, and in this way determine which diagnoses are assigned.

Although this cross-sectional lifetime diagnostic instrument is very useful, it has some limitations. First, for the most part its scoring system does not take into account the duration or cyclicity of the symptoms. This can be especially important when the symptoms are chronologically related to menstruation. Second, the DIS algorithm does not indicate how to score a symptom that is attributed exclusively to the respondent's menses. This leaves the interviewer free to make a choice between scoring the symptom as a physical condition (Code 4) or a psychological symptom (Code 5), and thus the data gathered become less systematic and more subjective.

These limitations raise the possibility that somatic complaints attributable solely to the menstrual cycle will be coded 5 and thus satisfy criteria for DSM-III diagnoses designed to categorize persons preoccupied with somatic dysfunction. This is most likely to occur in somatization disorder, which is thought to affect between 0.2% and 0.3% of all women (Robins et al., 1984) and is entirely based on somatic complaints such as cramps, joint pain, and swelling, symptoms common to the premenstrual syndrome.

The present study was designed to determine whether in women ages 30 to 40, blind to the study purpose, there was a higher incidence of yes answers coded as 5 to questions on the DIS that inquire about somatic symptomatology or somatization disorder in women reporting moderate to severe perimenstrual difficulties compared with women reporting no or mild perimenstrual difficulties.

Second, we sought to determine whether scoring a perimenstrual explanation as a physical condition (Code 4) or as a psychosocial symptom (Code 5) had any effect on the incidence of somatization symptoms or disorders in these populations. We hypothesized that there would be a greater reduction of somatization symptoms in the moderate-severe subjects than in the none-mild subjects if the symptoms associated with their menses were scored as a physical condition rather than as a psychological symptom.

Method

A newspaper advertisement published from May through September 1984 inviting women ages 30 to 40 to participate in a study of "daily changes in health and behavior" drew 175 respondents. Of these women, 148 were reached by telephone, and those who expressed interest ($n = 127$) completed a telephone screening interview at that time. The interviewer sought demographic information and asked screening questions, including the following: "Are you pregnant or nursing?"; "What medications are you taking?"; "Do you now have or have you ever had premenstrual or menstrual difficulties?"; and "Have you ever had any major surgery?" Women who responded affirmatively to the question about perimenstrual difficulties were subsequently asked to rate these as mild, moderate, or severe. Women were excluded ($n = 22$) from the study if they (a) were pregnant or nursing; (b) were taking birth control medication; or (c) had a history of surgery which left them currently anovulatory. The project was at no time presented to the subjects as a study of the premenstruum and menses. The perimenstrual question was the fifth of nine identically phrased questions about the occurrence of diabetes, high blood pressure, allergies, tuberculosis, heart conditions, tumors, thyroid problems, and headaches. Unknown to potential subjects, invitations to participate were issued to balance membership between two groups: none-mild and moderate-severe premenstrual or menstrual difficulties.

Of the 105 eligible responders, 73 reported no or mild perimenstrual difficulties, and 32 reported moderate or severe perimenstrual difficulties. In the none-mild group, 36 were invited to participate, and in the moderate-severe group, all 32 were invited. Of the 68 women given an appointment to take the DIS, 7 in the none-mild group and 3 in the moderate-severe group elected to drop out of the study before the appointment. Therefore, each group had 29 participants; all were Caucasian.

Subjects were interviewed at the University of Minnesota Hospitals by two persons trained in administration of the DIS. Each subject received $15.00. The interview lasted 45 min to 2 hr, 20 min. Interviewers were not blind to either the purpose of the study or the group assignment of each subject interviewed.

The DIS algorithm used to determine etiology was modified by the authors to monitor and record the occurrence of perimenstrual explanations for questions to which the subject answered yes. If a woman spontaneously offered her menstrual cycle or premenstrual syndrome (PMS) as an explanation for the presence of a symptom, her answer was coded 4*. On questions which focused on the menses, a score of 4* was obtained only if the responder offered PMS as an explanation or stated that the symptom was experienced only during her perimenstrual period. Answers to questions referring only to the menses which attributed the symptom to biological (e.g., hormone) or psychological problems not unique to the respondent's menses were not scored as 4*.

Responses to questions from the DIS that comprise DSM-III criteria for somatization disorder were collated (Table 1). The mean number of responses indicative of a somatization disorder for each question was compared across the two groups using a *t* test. This was done for two conditions: (a) a perimenstrual explanation of a somatic symptom (coded 4*) was scored as a physical condition (Code 4); and (b) a perimenstrual explanation of a somatic symptom (coded 4*) was scored as a psychological symptom (Code 5). Statistical significance was considered $p \leq .05$.

Table 1.
Comparison of the Number of Responses Indicative of Somatization Disorder When the Perimenstrually Associated Symptoms (4) Were First Assigned Physical Significance (4*=4) and Then Psychological Significance (4*=5)*

Response	None-mild group		Moderate-severe group	
	4*=4	4*=5	4*=4	4*=5
No. of somatization symptoms	51	51	93	105
Mean no. of symptoms/subject	1.76	1.76	3.21	3.62
SD	1.92	1.92	2.50	3.06

Note. Comparing the none-mild and moderate-severe groups when 4*=4: $t=2.435$, $p=.018$. Comparing the none-mild and moderate-severe groups when 4*=5: $t=2.725$, $p=.009$.

Results

The subjects in the none-mild and the moderate-severe groups had the same mean age (34.9 years) and were similar for mean number of children (1.79 vs. 1.41), percentage married (62% vs. 58%), percentage employed out of the home (62% vs. 72%), and mean years of education (15.1 vs. 14.4), respectively.

In the sample population, no one received the DSM-III diagnosis of somatization disorder whether the perimenstrual symptoms were scored as a physical condition or as a psychological symptom. However, the mean number of somatic symptoms per subject was significantly higher in the moderate-severe group than in the none-mild group (Table 1). This was found both when perimenstrual symptoms were attributed to a physical condition ($t=2.435$, $p=.018$) and when they were considered a psychological symptom ($t=2.725$, $p=.009$).

Women in the moderate-severe group provided the greatest number of Code 5 responses to the questions pertaining to painful menses, irregular menses, excessive bleeding during menses, dyspnea without exertion,

abdominal pain, and joint pain. The difference between Code 5 responses
when perimenstrually associated symptoms were considered a physical
condition versus a psychological symptom was narrow for every question.
Among women in the none-mild group, the highest number of Code 5
responses was obtained on questions pertaining to painful menses and lack
of importance of sex life. There was never a difference in this group
between number of Code 5 responses when perimenstrually associated
symptoms were considered a physical condition versus a psychological
symptom. Therefore, only for women who reported moderate to severe
perimenstrual difficulties did the change in scoring affect total number of
psychological symptoms.

Discussion

In this study, none of the subjects endorsed enough of the DSM-III criteria to obtain a diagnosis of somatization disorder. To assign this diagnosis, the criteria require at least 14 somatic symptoms. The highest individual number of somatic symptoms in the entire study population was
9. The disorder usually has its onset late in adolescence or in the third
decade, and thus our age range should cover the peak incidence of the
disorder (Tomb, 1984). However, because the incidence of somatization
disorder has been found to be 0.2% to 0.3%, it would not be unusual
to find no one with the disorder in a study population of only 58 women
(Robins et al., 1984).

However, a significantly greater incidence of symptoms characteristic
of somatization disorder was found for women in the moderate-severe
group than women in the none-mild group. Because endorsement of
somatic symptoms can contribute to the assignment of a specific psychiatric
diagnosis, this finding has important implications for accurate diagnoses
in women with perimenstrual disturbances. If women with moderate-severe
perimenstrual difficulties endorse an average of 1.45 to 1.86 more
symptoms than women rated none-mild, they would have a higher risk
of satisfying criteria for somatization disorder in large-scale epidemiological
studies. This would be a threshold phenomenon, in that the somatic complaints found to be most commonly associated with the menses could serve
to push some women over the diagnostic threshold.

We found that scoring the perimenstrual somatic symptoms first as a
physical condition and then as a psychological symptom affected only the
DIS scoring of women reporting moderate to severe perimenstrual difficulties. No change in total number of symptoms was seen in the group
with no or mild perimenstrual difficulties. This supports our contention
that the way in which perimenstrually associated somatic complaints are
scored on the DIS is especially important for women with perimenstrual

symptomatology, because by the current scoring system, women with such symptoms are at increased risk of receiving the diagnosis of somatization disorder.

On the actual DIS questionnaire, the only somatic question that specifically asks the responder to consider the perimenstruum is the one concerning abdominal pain (Question 16). The probe reads: "Have you ever had a lot of trouble with abdominal or belly pain, not counting times when you were menstruating?" Here the responder is guided to consider only those times when she is not experiencing active menstrual flow. Even with this exclusionary condition, several of the subjects (5 in the moderate-severe group, 2 in the none-mild group) responded positively. Because none of the other questions pertaining to somatization disorder contain an exclusion of the menses, it is uncertain how many of the somatic complaints elicited would have been scored negatively if the perimenstrual occurrence had been explicitly discounted as in Question 16. In addition, since No. 16 is the first somatic question in the DIS, some responders might incorrectly apply the exclusion of the menstrual period to subsequent questions. The relatively narrow gap in scoring when perimenstrually associated symptoms were assigned physical significance versus psychological significance supports this interpretation. In other words, the phrasing of Question 16 may have biased most women against offering a menstrual explanation for their somatic complaints. Because the DIS does not inquire about cyclic variation in symptomatology, data on whether somatic complaints occur with any chronological relation to the menses are not available. Had the women been asked to consider their menses when answering each question, our independent variable would have been disclosed. Awareness of the purpose of the study might have resulted in a lower number of positive responses, because women who believe they have a physical basis for perimenstrual complaints might purposely answer the probing questions so that a score of 4 (physical condition) would be obtained (AuBuchon & Calhoun, 1985).

In addition to the placement of Question 16, the DIS has another operational shortcoming—its bias with respect to gender. The DIS algorithm assumes the gender of the respondent's physician to be male ("What was *his* diagnosis?"; "What did *he* say was causing. . . ?"; "Did *he* find anything abnormal . . . ?"). Although the effect of this bias in the algorithm may be important, our study did not set out to investigate such a possibility, and thus our modified version was not made gender neutral.

Women in the moderate-severe group provided the greatest number of positive responses on the questions pertaining to painful menses, irregular menses, excessive bleeding during menses, dyspnea without exertion, abdominal pain, and joint pain. Because the initial screening question that categorized these women as moderate to severe was "Have you ever had premenstrual or menstrual difficulties?", the preponderance of somatic complaints centered around the menses is no surprise. In addition, the symptoms of abdominal pain (not during menses), joint pain, and dyspnea have all been associated with premenstrual syndrome, and it is not surprising that they should appear with increased frequency in women who self-report moderate to severe perimenstrual difficulties. Ten of the women in the moderate-severe group even met criteria set by Endicott, Halbreich, Schacht, and Nee (1981) for generalized discomfort syndrome, which is a perimenstrually associated complex of somatic symptoms.

The greatest number of positive responses from the none-mild group was found on questions asking about painful menses and lack of importance of sex life. However, unlike the women in the moderate-severe group in which 41% or 55% (depending on assignment of physical vs. psychological significance) reported painful menses, only 20% of the none-mild group had this complaint. The DIS is strictly a cross-sectional instrument, so it is impossible to conclude whether the women who responded positively in the none-mild group experienced painful menses more or less frequently than positive responders in the moderate-severe group. However, there does seem to be a greater prevalence of experiencing pain with the menses for women self-reporting moderate to severe perimenstrual difficulties.

It is an interesting finding that women in the none-mild group had a greater number of positive responses than did women in the moderate-severe group to the question asking about importance of their sex lives. The question asked, "Would you say that your sex life has been important to you, or could you have gotten along as well without it?" In the none-mild group, 28% answered that they could have gotten along as well without their sex lives, compared with 10% in the moderate-severe group. One explanation may be the increase in libido premenstrually that the moderate-severe group reported, compared with the none-mild group. This question was asked of 47 of the 58 study participants, who later filled out a Premenstrual Assessment Form (Halbreich & Endicott, 1982). These women were asked to rate on a 6-point scale (1 being no change or not present, 6 being extreme) whether they experience increased sexual activity or interest during the premenstruum. The mean score for the moderate-severe group ($n=25$) was 2.60, compared with the none-mild group ($n=22$) mean of 1.95.

In conclusion, we could not establish that the prevalence of somatization disorder is higher among women with moderate to severe perimenstrual difficulties. However, the symptoms of this disorder are more prevalent in this group than in women with no or mild perimenstrual difficulties. We have also discussed the significance of considering the perimenstruum in scoring the DIS. Certainly, the possibility exists of an incorrect assignment of a diagnosis of somatization disorder for women with perimenstrual difficulties, and future epidemiological studies should be cognizant of this when using any cross-sectional diagnostic instrument such as the DIS.

We have addressed somatization disorder here. Similar questions could be raised about affective disorders. How often does a perimenstrual affective syndrome satisfy DSM-III criteria for recurrent depression? A group of healthy women with perimenstrual symptoms would need to be prospectively followed for the occurrence of affective disorders. In future studies of psychiatric diagnosis in women with perimenstrual difficulties, the greatest promise lies in longitudinal symptom ascertainment, so that chronology of the symptoms can be charted. This will clarify the relationship, if any, between symptoms (be they somatic or other) and the menstrual cycle.

REFERENCES

AuBuchon, P. G., & Calhoun, K. S. (1985). Menstrual cycle symptomatology: The role of social expectancy and experimental demand characteristics. *Psychosomatic Medicine, 47,* 35–45.

Endicott, J., Halbreich, U., Schacht, S., & Nee, J. (1981). Premenstrual changes and affective disorders. *Psychosomatic Medicine, 43,* 519–529.

Halbreich, U., & Endicott, J. (1982). Classification of premenstrual syndromes. In R. Friedman (Ed.), *Behavior and the menstrual cycle* (pp. 243–265). New York: Marcel Dekker.

Robins, L. N., Helzer, J. E., Croughan, J., & Ratcliff, K. S. (1981). The NIMH diagnostic interview schedule: Its history, characteristics, and validity. *Archives of General Psychiatry, 38,* 381–389.

Robins, L. N., Helzer, J. E., Croughan, J., Williams, J. B. W., & Spitzer, R. L. (1981). NIMH diagnostic interview schedule: Version III (DHHS Publication No. ADM-T-42-3). Washington, DC: U.S. Government Printing Office.

Robins, L. N., Helzer, J. E., Weissman, M. M., Orvaschel, H., Gruenberg, E., Burke, J. D., & Regnier, D. A. (1984). Lifetime prevalence of specific psychiatric disorders in three sites. *Archives of General Psychiatry, 41,* 949–958.

Tomb, D. A. (1984). *Psychiatry for the house officer* (2d ed.). Baltimore, MD: Williams and Wilkins.

Williams, J. B. W. (Ed.) (1980). *Diagnostic and statistical manual of mental disorders* (3d ed.). Washington, DC: American Psychiatric Association.

4

Psychological Evaluation and Intervention With PMS Women

Karen Ostrov, Suzanne Trupin, and Diane Essex-Sorlie

Many investigators have sought to determine if a relationship exists between premenstrual syndrome (PMS) and personality functioning. Both PMS and personality functioning have been defined in various ways and measured using a variety of instruments. The findings from previous investigations have been contradictory, with some researchers finding a strong positive relationship between PMS and impaired personality functioning and others identifying no significant association. For example, Coppen and Kessel (1963) found that women with severe premenstrual irritability or depression showed more psychopathology on the Maudsely Personality Inventory Scale than did unaffected women. Hain, Linton, Eber, and Chapman (1970), in their study of first-year nursing students, found a positive correlation between psychological maladjustment, as assessed by the Minnesota Multiphasic Personality Inventory (MMPI), and specific premenstrual symptoms. Further, Gruba and Rohrbaugh (1975) reported that significant relationships existed between MMPI scores and premenstrual affective and somatic symptoms. Steege, Stout, and Rupp (1985, p. 399) found that the severity of PMS symptoms correlated positively with increasing dysmenorrhea; however, they did not find MMPI relationships with these symptoms. Taylor (1979) identified a strong association between PMS and certain personality characteristics as measured by Catell's 16 Personality Factor Questionnaire (16 PF), the Eysenck Personality Inventory, and a daily symptom-rating scale. Watts, Dennerstein, and De La Horne (1980) noted that women who suffered premenstrual symptoms could be differentiated from women who did not on the basis of chronic anxiety (trait, rather than state, anxiety), neuroticism, and negative attitudes toward their sexuality. In contrast, Seagull (1974), using the Moos Menstrual Distress Questionnaire (MDQ) to select premenstrual groups with high or low tension and the Rorschach and Thematic Apperception Test (TAT) to describe personality functioning, concluded that no differences existed between women high and low in premenstrual tension on the dimension of neuroticism and personality functioning. Additionally, Kleinhauser (1975) found no relationship between premenstrual symptoms and personality characteristics as measured by the MDQ and Bernreuter Personality Inventory.

As one reviews the literature, particularly in terms of conflicting results, several potential factors emerge which may account, in part, for the absence of a consistent relationship between PMS and personality functioning. For example, Sampson and Prescott (1981) commented that reliance on retrospective accounts to determine periodicity and severity of symptoms confounds many studies. Such accounts are highly vulnerable to decay (forgetting) and on-stage effects, that is, patients reporting "their symptoms as they feel they 'should' occur" (Sampson & Prescott, 1981, p. 400). Unless such retrospective self-report data is supplemented with more reliable and valid measurements, the picture obtained may not be a reasonably true reflection of the occurrence and impact of premenstrual symptoms. Additionally, examining the effects of PMS at different phases of the menstrual cycle may contribute to the discrepant findings reported by various researchers. Further, in some studies, personality functioning was assessed with an investigator-designed instrument for which no data pertaining to validity and reliability were presented or with instruments that lacked a significant history of clinical application and interpretation. In other research, no criteria for the identification of the PMS woman were specified. Consequently, the definition of the PMS woman may vary considerably from study to study.

Thus, the present investigation, which was designed to explore the relationship between PMS and personality functioning, relied on a personality instrument with a long and respected history of clinical use to assess personality functioning; further, the diagnosis of PMS was made by an obstetrician/gynecologist on the basis of four criteria that are thought to represent a consensus among obstetricians/gynecologists in terms of defining PMS (Reid & Yen, 1981; Rubinow & Roy-Byrne, 1984). The particular goal of the study was to ascertain whether certain personality characteristics distinguished premenstrual tension sufferers from other women.

Method

Subjects
Twenty-two women, 23 to 51 years of age, participated. Of these, 12 were identified as having PMS according to four criteria described below, and 10 were not. None of the patients in either group had any other active gynecologic disease; no PMS patient was perimenopausal. Further, except for one patient who had begun progesterone therapy less than one month prior to the evaluation of personality functioning, none of the remaining women had received hormonal treatments prior to the assessment of per-

sonality functioning. No standardization for day of the menstrual cycle was attempted in relation to personality assessment.

Instrument

The MMPI was administered to both groups of women. For a thorough description of the MMPI see Greene (1980) and Graham (1977).

Procedure

Patients seen in a private practice office by a board-certified obstetrician/gynecologist were defined as having PMS if they met four criteria: (a) a symptom complex that related to the luteal phase of the menstrual cycle in a defined pattern; (b) symptoms that had been charted in a log by the patients for at least 3 consecutive months prior to establishing the diagnosis; (c) symptoms that were manifested by somatic, psychological, and behavioral components; and (d) a symptom-free interval lasting at least one week each month for at least 3 consecutive months.

Patients were evaluated initially by a nurse practitioner trained specifically to work with PMS patients and a board-certified obstetrician/gynecologist. The MMPI was administered individually to PMS and non-PMS women by a licensed psychologist under uniform conditions as described in the test manual.

Analyses

Quantitative, as well as qualitative, methods were used to examine data from the 10 basic clinical scales. Quantitative procedures included the construction of frequency distributions, determination of means and standard deviations, examination of mean differences on the 10 basic clinical MMPI scales (Student's t test for independent groups), and scrutiny of the personality profiles of PMS and non-PMS (discriminant analysis) to determine if the profile with which the PMS women presented differed significantly from that of the non-PMS women. It is recognized that extreme caution must be used when the inferential results (t tests and discriminant analysis) are reviewed because sample sizes in the PMS ($n=12$) and non-PMS ($n=10$) group are small. Qualitative analysis focused on clinical interpretations of responses on the 10 basic clinical scales. Content analysis was employed to determine if different clinical themes characterized PMS and non-PMS women, particularly in terms of symptoms, interpersonal relationships, behavioral stability, and diagnostic implications. The clinical interpretations were examined by a psychologist blind to the subjects' group.

In addition, quantitative methods and qualitative description were used to characterize group differences and similarities on the supplementary scales and subscales. It was thought that because scores on 8 of the 10 basic clinical scales represent composite scores from subscales, information may be obscured when the subscale scores are aggregated to form the basic clinical scale score. No inferential analyses were performed because the number of variables was too large in relation to the number of patients studied.

Results

Quantitative Analyses of the Clinical Scales

Results from the quantitative analyses are presented in Table 1 and Figure 1. No significant differences in age, years of education, or marital status were found. More PMS women (83%) had children than did non-PMS women (40%).

Table 1.
Age and Years of Education of the PMS and Non-PMS Women

Index	Age (years)		Education (years)	
	Non-PMS	PMS	Non-PMS	PMS
Mean	33.50	33.25	16.20	15.08
SD	8.59	6.14	2.39	2.02
Range	23–51	23–43	12–20	12–18
n	10	12	10	12

The MMPI scores on 10 basic clinical scales are displayed in Figure 1. The profiles of the PMS and non-PMS women were very similar; in fact,

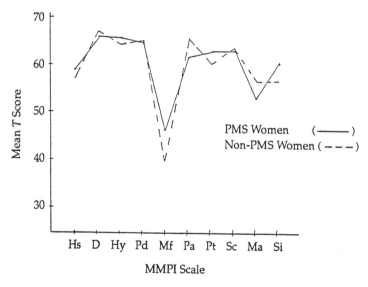

Figure 1. Mean *T* Scores on 10 Minnesota Multiphasic Personality Inventory (MMPI) Scales. PMS (*n*=12) and non-PMS (*n*=10). Scales: HS, hypochondriasis; D, depression; Hy, conversion hysteria; Pd, psychopathic deviate; Mf, masculinity-femininity; Pa, paranoia; Pt, psychasthenia; Sc, schizophrenia; Ma, hypomania; Si, social introversion.

when these profiles were examined statistically using discriminant analysis, no differences were identified ($p > .05$). As noted previously, the statistical analysis must be viewed cautiously because of the small sample sizes in each group. For this reason, it was thought that a qualitative analysis of the clinical narrative interpretations might reveal similarities or differences between the two groups.

Qualitative Analysis of the Clinical Narrative
  The clinical interpretations provided for each subject by the scoring service were analyzed to determine if consistent themes appeared for either the PMS or non-PMS women in each of four categories: symptoms, interpersonal relationships, behavioral stability, and diagnostic implications. Within each of the four categories, no descriptors were found to be used more frequently than others to characterize either PMS or non-PMS women. For example, symptomatic phrases such as "low energy level," "loss of appetite," "unable to sleep," "overly sensitive," "preoccupied with physical symptoms," or "irritable" were not used more frequently to describe PMS women. Similar observations were recorded for the remaining categories (interpersonal relationships, behavioral stability, and diagnostic implications).

  Therefore, based on both quantitative and qualitative analyses of the 10 basic clinical scales, it appears that in our sample the overall personality profiles presented by PMS women are similar to those of the non-PMS women. Thus, the symptoms experienced by PMS women are not associated with identifiable personality alterations as measured on the global clinical scales of the MMPI. Our results indicate that the PMS woman is no more likely than the non-PMS woman to present with psychopathology.

Descriptive Analyses of Supplemental Scales and Subscales
  A variety of additional subscales can be derived from the MMPI, and these were analyzed descriptively for differences between PMS and non-PMS women. No differences were found on the supplementary scales of dependency (Dy), manifest anxiety (MAS), and overcontrolled hostility (O-H). Subscale differences of more than 3 T-score units were noted on 8 of the 40 subscales (Table 2). Except for the higher scores of non-PMS women on the hypomania subscale of "amorality," all of these differences reflected higher scores among PMS women. It appears that information not gleaned from the 10 basic clinical scales would have been overlooked if the subscales had not been scrutinized. Although the mean differences noted have not been identified as statistically significant, they may have implications for therapists and physicians who work with PMS women, particularly in relation to feelings of alienation, lack of ego mastery, personal discomfort, mental dullness, and physical-somatic concerns. As yet,

though, no statements can be made about these feelings being etiological or consequential.

Table 2.
Comparison of PMS and Non-PMS Women on Eight Minnesota Multiphase Personality Inventory (MMPI) Subscales With Differences of More Than Three T-score Units

Subscales	Comparison
5 Depression	PMS women higher on "mental dullness"
5 Hysteria	PMS women higher on "somatic complaints"
5 Psychopathic Deviate	PMS women higher on "social alienation"
6 Masculinity-Femininity	PMS women higher on "denial of stereotypic masculine interests" and "introspective critical"
3 Paranoia	No differences
6 Schizophrenia	PMS women higher on "lack of ego mastery, cognitive" and "lack of ego mastery, conative"
4 Hypomania	Non-PMS women higher on "amorality"
6 Social Introversion	PMS women higher on "inferiority," "discomfort with others," and "physical-somatic concerns"

Conclusions and Discussion

The pathophysiology of PMS is poorly understood, and few therapeutic guidelines exist for the evaluation and treatment of these patients. If the evaluation and treatment of the PMS patient is to be complete and effective, patients who present with symptoms thought to be associated with PMS require a detailed history, thorough physical examination to rule out concomitant gynecologic disease, and a detailed psychologic evaluation of the affective, behavioral, and cognitive manifestations of PMS.

On the basis of data collected in our investigation of PMS and non-PMS women, patients with a clinical diagnosis of PMS present with very stable global personality profiles that are similar to those of women who do not manifest somatic symptoms. But, even though PMS women presented with a stable personality profile, they did evidence elevated mean scores on subscales relating to physical-somatic concerns, personal discomfort, social alienation, emotional alienation, self-alienation, self-criticality, malaise, and mental dullness. However, given the overall stable personality profile of the PMS women, it appears that these women can be managed with medical treatment and with supportive counseling when appropriate.

Relative to treatment, the PMS patient may be reassured that her general personality functioning is within normal limits and that elevations on certain subscales, such as self-criticality or mental dullness, do not reflect a lack of overall stability. Further, the therapist can help the PMS woman understand that such feelings are associated with her premenstrual syndrome, and with appropriate counseling, she can learn to deal with and manage them more effectively.

It is recommended that future research assess personality functioning at the same point in the menstrual cycle for all women. Information from the subscales of the MMPI may contribute to the description of real differences between PMS and non-PMS women, which may be masked when the subscale scores are aggregated into (composite) basic clinical scales. Further, these subscale scores may be useful in the treatment planning for the PMS patient.

In summary, the MMPI has been used in the present study to describe the personality functioning of the patient with a clinical diagnosis of PMS and to compare her functioning with that of a non-PMS woman to determine if certain personality characteristics distinguish them. It was found that the PMS women present with a global personality profile similar to that of non-PMS women. However, elevations in subscale scores pertaining to malaise, alienation, criticality, and mental dullness were observed for PMS women. Such information may provide important indicators for health care professionals involved in the diagnosis and treatment of PMS women.

REFERENCES

Coppen, A., & Kessel, N. (1963). Menstruation and personality. *British Journal of Psychiatry, 109*, 711–721.

Graham, J. R. (1977). *The MMPI: A practical guide.* New York: Oxford University Press.

Greene, R. L. (1980). *The MMPI: An interpretative manual.* New York: Grune and Stratton.

Gruba, G. H., & Rohrbaugh, M. (1975). MMPI correlates of menstrual distress. *Psychosomatic Medicine, 37*, 265–268.

Hain, J. D., Linton, P. H., Eber, H. W., & Chapman, M. M. (1970). Menstrual irregularity, symptoms and personality. *Journal of Psychosomatic Research, 14*, 81–87.

Kleinhauser, J. E. (1976). The pre-menstrual syndrome and its correlation to personality characteristics (Doctoral dissertation, University of South Dakota). *Dissertation Abstracts International, 36*, 8A, 5152.

Reid, R. L., & Yen, S. C. C. (1981). Premenstrual syndrome. *American Journal of Obstetrics and Gynecology, 139*, 85–104.

Rubinow, D. R., & Roy-Byrne, R. (1984). Premenstrual syndromes: Overview from a methodological perspective. *American Journal of Psychiatry, 141*, 163–172.

Sampson, G., & Prescott, P. (1981). The assessment of the symptoms of premenstrual syndrome and their response to therapy. *British Journal of Psychiatry, 138*, 399–405.

Seagull, E. A. (1974). An investigation of personality differences between women with high and low premenstrual tension (Doctoral dissertation, Michigan State University). *Dissertation Abstracts International, 34*, 9B, 4675.

Steege, J., Stout, A., & Rupp, S. (1985). Relationship among premenstrual symptoms and menstrual cycle characteristics. *Obstetrics & Gynecology, 65*, 398–402.

Taylor, J. W. (1979). Psychological factors in the aetiology of premenstrual symptoms. *Australian and New Zealand Journal of Psychiatry, 35*, 34–41.

Watts, S., Dennerstein, L., & De La Horne, D. (1980). The premenstrual syndrome: A psychologcial evaluation. *Journal of Affective Disorders, 2*, 257–266.

5

The Role of Negative Life Stress and PMS: Some Preliminary Findings

Sarah E. Maddocks and Robert L. Reid

Premenstrual syndrome (PMS) describes a heterogeneous group of psychological, behavioral, and physical symptoms that may be experienced during the premenstrual phase of the menstrual cycle. Women who suffer from repeated and severe PMS have reported serious life-style disruption with wide-ranging psychological, social, legal, and political implications. Perhaps because of the heterogeneity of symptom experience, research has typically been fraught with methodological problems. Failure to delineate precisely the essential features of the disorder (Aplanalp, Haskett, & Rose, 1980; Haskett & Aplanalp, 1983) and a disregard for recording the severity of symptoms experienced (Maddocks, 1983) exemplify the problems found in early studies. More recent research has attempted to define the disorder operationally using diagnostic criteria and severity ratings. For instance, Steiner, Haskett, and Carroll (1980) and Haskett, Steiner, Osmun, and Carroll (1980) developed diagnostic criteria for PMS based on methods used by Spitzer, Endicott, and Robins (1978) to define research diagnostic criteria (RDC) for the *Diagnostic and Statistical Manual* (DSM-III) of the American Psychiatric Association (1980). Steiner et al. (1980) employed inclusion and exclusion criteria for the selection of subjects with moderate to severe PMS. New premenstrual tension syndrome (PMTS) rating scales were subsequently developed by Steiner and associates to assess the severity of premenstrual symptoms.

One aspect of the disorder that has not been extensively studied, however, is the role of stress as a moderating variable on premenstrual disturbance. Koeske (1980) asserted that menstrual cycle research has frequently failed to acknowledge the potential influences of environmental variables such as stress on the data reported in the literature. Notable exceptions are studies by Wilcoxon, Schrader, and Sherif (1976), Siegel, Johnson, and Sarason (1979), and Woods, Dery, and Most (1982) who provided limited evidence to suggest that negative life experiences may be associated with the experience of menstrual cycle symptoms.

Wilcoxon et al. (1976) examined 33 subjects, consisting of 11 females taking oral contraceptives, 11 females not taking oral contraceptives, and 11 males in a study of mood and body awareness. Daily questionnaires were completed by each subject for 35 consecutive days concerning daily activities, stressful life events, moods, and somatic changes. Male subjects were assigned a pseudo-cycle by randomly selecting one of the 35 study days as their first "premenstrual" day and constructing a 28-day cycle around this. The results indicated that, overall, the three groups did not differ in their reports of negative affect, impaired concentration, and stressful events during the premenstrual and menstrual phases. However, the more interesting observation was that the experience of stressful life events in this sample accounted for more variance than the phase of cycle for the negative mood factors but not the somatic factors such as pain and water retention.

Siegel et al. (1979) subsequently differentiated the effects of positive and negative life experiences and the use of oral contraceptives on a sample of 244 female undergraduates. These subjects were required to fill out a stress questionnaire, relating experiences occurring in the preceding 12 months as positive or negative, and a menstrual questionnaire concerning the regularity and discomfort experienced during the cycle. A regression analysis examined the relative contribution of oral contraceptive use and the experience of life stress (positive and negative) on factors derived from the menstrual questionnaire. Overall, the relationship between the accumulation of negative life stress and the experience of menstrual discomfort was supported.

Woods et al. (1982) examined the social context in which premenstrual and menstrual symptoms were reported. A stress inventory and the Moos (1968) Menstrual Distress Questionnaire were used to obtain the pertinent information from a sample of 179 women between 18 and 35 years of age. The results of a regression analysis supported the general relationship between life stress and the menstrual cycle previously demonstrated by Wilcoxon et al. (1976) and Siegel et al. (1979).

Taken together, these findings suggest that stressful life experiences to some extent do influence reporting of premenstrual discomfort. Problems exist related to the use of different measures of stress, and the implementation of general menstrual rather than premenstrual inventories. Furthermore, studies have reported on samples of normal women rather than women with demonstrable premenstrual life-style disruption. These factors make it difficult to ascertain the effect of stress on specific premenstrual dysfunction.

An important question, then, is whether stress moderates the experience of premenstrual symptoms in women meeting diagnostic criteria for moderate or severe PMS. We addressed this question by examining the possible moderating effects of situational stress on the severity of premenstrual symptoms. In addition, trait anxiety and social self-esteem were measured to assess the association of these more stable mood variables and the experience of PMS.

Method

Subjects

For inclusion in the study, subjects had to meet these eight criteria: (a) premenstrual dysphoric symptoms for at least six preceding cycles, (b) moderate to severe physical and psychological premenstrual symptoms (i.e., a score of 18 or more on the PMTS observer-rating scale, Steiner et al., 1980), (c) symptoms only during the premenstrual period with marked relief at the onset of menses, (d) age between 18 and 45 years, (e) not pregnant, (f) no hormonal contraception, (g) regular menses for six previous cycles, (h) no psychiatric disorder (from Steiner et al., 1980).

Forty-four women met these criteria and agreed to participate. The subjects were 20 to 45 years of age ($M = 35.02$ years), 72% were married, and 86% had children.

Procedure

Each subject attended a hospital outpatient clinic for an initial interview. A menstrual history and current premenstrual symptoms were documented. Separate ratings of the severity of each subject's premenstrual symptoms according to the Steiner et al. (1980) PMTS observer-rating scale were made by the primary investigator (S. M.) and the gynecologist involved in the study (R. R.). Two ratings were obtained to ensure that the assessment of the subjects' symptoms by the interviewers was reliable.

To rule out any other significant medical illness, the gynecologist obtained a complete medical history from the subject and conducted a physical examination. Each subject then was asked to complete a battery of self-report questionnaires to assess social self-esteem, trait anxiety, and the accumulation of life stresses in the preceding 12 months.

Further self-report measures were collected from each subject every 3 days during her next menstrual cycle to record individual experiences of current menstrual cycle symptoms, feelings of depression, state anxiety, and irritability. Subjects were given envelopes containing the questionnaires to be completed and instructed to begin filling them out on Day 3 of the next menstrual cycle. Day 1 represented the first day of menstruation. The cycle was divided into four phases: early follicular (Days 1–7), late follicular (Days 8–14), early luteal (Days 15–22), and late luteal or premenstrual (Days 23–27). Questionnaires were completed for each of the four phases (i.e., on Days 3, 6, 9, 12, 15, 18, 21, 24, and 27). A telephone answering service was utilized so that the subjects could telephone to report the time of questionnaire completion. At the end of their cycles, subjects delivered the completed questionnaires to the outpatient clinic.

Measures

1. *Life Experiences Survey (LES)* (Sarason, Johnson, & Siegel, 1978)

Subjects responded to this 57-item self-report questionnaire by endorsing those events they had experienced in the past year. The subjects then rated each event endorsed by indicating whether the event exerted a desirable or undesirable impact on their lives at the time of occurrence together with the magnitude of this impact (0 to 3). The LES yields a positive change score, calculated by summing the impact ratings of events designated as positive by the subject, and a negative life change score, calculated for negative ratings.

2. *The Social Self-Esteem Inventory* (Lawson, Marshall, & McGrath, 1979)

This 30-item self-rating scale was developed for the assessment of feelings of self-worth. Items are rated on a 6-point scale from *completely unlike me* (1) to *exactly like me* (6).

3. *The Self-Evaluation Questionnaire (X-2) Trait Anxiety* (Spielberger, Gorsuch, & Lushene, 1970)

This 20-item self-report scale asks subjects how they generally feel. It is designed to measure trait anxiety, or anxiety proneness, a relatively stable, baseline personality characteristic. Items are rated on a 4-point scale from *almost never* (1) to *almost always* (4). Spielberger et al. (1970) have demonstrated that State-Trait Anxiety Inventory (STAI) scores reflect relatively stable individual differences that are unresponsive to situational stress. This scale was used to provide an index of each subject's habitual anxiety.

4. *The Beck Depression Inventory (BDI)* (Beck, Ward, Mendelson, Mock, & Erbaugh, 1961)

The BDI is a 21-item self-report questionnaire designed to assess a subject's current intensity of depression. Items are rated on a 4-point scale (0 to 3). Scores may range from 0 to 63, with 0–9 categorized by Beck as not depressed, 10–15 as mildly depressed, 16–23 as moderately depressed, and 24–63 as severely depressed. Bumberry, Oliver, and McClure (1978) suggest that this inventory appears to be a valid measure of depression only for the day on which it is administered. This inventory was instituted as a repeated measure throughout the menstrual cycle to record fluctuations in each subject's feelings of depression.

5. *The Menstrual Distress Questionnaire Form-T (MDQ-T)* (Moos, 1968)

This questionnaire, containing 47 items, is designed for the assessment of menstrual symptoms as they are experienced "today." Each item is accompanied by a 6-point rating scale ranging from *no experience of symptom* (1) to *acute or partially disabling* (6). Moos (1977) reported that there was little or no evidence of instrument deterioration over consecutive cycles, indicating that Form T is suitable for repeated administrations.

6. *Scales for Rating the Severity of Premenstrual Tension Syndrome (PMTS)* (Steiner et al., 1980)

Two scales, a 36-item self-report questionnaire and a 10-item scale for use by a therapist/researcher, were developed by Steiner et al. (1980) in an attempt to provide valid criteria and instruments that accurately reflect the severity of specific PMS features. The items were derived from the Moos (1968) Menstrual Distress Questionnaire (MDQ), clinical observations, and subjects' descriptions of their feelings and symptoms. The items are designed to reflect the core emotional, behavioral, and physical symptoms of PMS and are organized in 10 categories: irritability-hostility; tension; efficiency; dysphoria; motor coordination; mental cognitive functioning; eating habits; sexual drive and activity; physical symptoms; and social impairment. The PMTS self-rating scale requires *yes-no* responses denoting fluctuations in symptoms. The observer-rating scale requires a rater to circle the most appropriate score for each item on a scale ranging from *no disturbance* (0) to *severe* (4).

7. *The Irritability Scale*

A measure of irritability was included in the study to assess the clinical observation that women with PMS typically complain of intense irritability that is associated with feelings of hostility. A subscale from the Hostility-Guilt Inventory (Buss & Durkee, 1957) was used for this purpose. The full scale was originally designed for the clinical assessment of the various aspects of hostility. The authors state that the 11-item irritability subscale measures "a readiness to explode with negative affect at the slightest provocation" and as such corresponds with the clinical reports of the irritability experienced premenstrually. The original scale was found to be robust against social desirability and to have satisfactory internal consistency reliability.

8. *Self-Evaluation Questionnaire (X-1) State Anxiety* (Spielberger et al., 1970)

This 20-item self-report scale is designed to measure state anxiety, a transitory emotional state characterized by conscious feelings of tension and subjective awareness of heightened autonomic nervous system activity. The subject is asked to report how she feels "right now." Items are rated on a 4-point scale from *not at all* (1) to *very much* (4).

Results

Initial Interview

The ratings made by the two observers for each subject on the PMS observer-rating scale were assessed and found to be reliable ($r = .69$). Mean scores and standard deviations were then calculated for each measure administered at the initial interview. The mean PMS observer-rating was found to be higher than the criterion severity score of 18 ($M = 24.82$, $SD \pm 3.49$), indicating the presence of moderate to severe PMS. Average scores for the Life Experiences Survey (LES) were 6.98 (± 8.98), 7.50 (± 7.87), and 14.45 (± 14.02) for the positive, negative, and total life stress recorded. The negative LES score was slightly higher than the norm of 5.64 achieved by Sarason et al. (1978) for a sample of female undergraduates. The mean Social Self-Esteem Inventory score (SSI) was 128.16 (± 20.4), slightly lower than the norm of 132 published by Lawson et al. (1979) for a female undergraduate sample. The mean trait anxiety was 42.14 (± 9.78) which corresponds to the norm of 41 published by Spielberger et al. (1970) for general medical and surgical patients, and is lower than that of 45 given for psychiatric patients.

Analysis of Menstrual Cycle Data

We defined three menstrual cycle phases most salient to the study. Observations ranged from 21 to 36 days ($M = 27.41$, $SD \pm 3.27$), indicating that some subjects had longer cycles than others. A procedure to obtain a uniform number of observations for each subject was implemented as follows: Data from Day 3 and Day 6 of each cycle were averaged to represent the early follicular phase (designated menstrual). The late luteal phase (designated premenstrual) consisted of the average of the last two questionnaire days in each cycle, thus spanning the 4 to 6 days prior to the onset of menstruation. The third phase (designated intermenstrual) constituted the average of three midcycle questionnaires.

Each of the five measures (MDQ-T, BDI, PMTS Self-rating, State Anxiety, and Irritability scale) was then subjected to an analysis of variance (ANOVA) for repeated measures. The independent variable was phase of cycle (premenstrual, menstrual, and intermenstrual). Significant main effects ($p < .0001$) were obtained for all five measures. Post hoc comparisons using Bonferroni's criterion were subsequently computed so as to

44   Menstrual Health in Women's Lives

examine differences between cycle phases. The pattern of responding appeared to be the same for each measure. All responses were most elevated during the premenstrual phase and were significantly decreased ($p < .05$) during the intermenstrual phase. The menstrual phase responses were found to fall between the premenstrual and intermenstrual scores (see Table 1).

Table 1.
Mean Scores and Standard Deviations (in parentheses) Across Cycle Phases for Beck Depression Inventory (BDI), State-Trait Anxiety Inventory (STAI), Irritability Scale, Menstrual Distress Questionnaire Form T (MDQ-T), and Premenstrual Tension Syndrome Self-Rating Scale (PMTS)

| | F ratio ANOVA | | Cycle phase | | |
Scale	$F(2, 43)$	p	Premenstrual	Menstrual	Intermenstrual
BDI	31.41*	<.0001	16.69 (10.29)	10.35 (8.34)	5.73 (6.44)
STAI	30.26**	<.0001	56.68 (12.47)	45.17 (14.49)	40.33 (12.60)
Irritability	34.94*	<.0001	6.59 (2.79)	4.39 (2.97)	2.81 (2.20)
MDQ-T	44.51*	<.0001	115.77 (31.46)	86.14 (31.92)	71.54 (19.51)
PMTS	51.77*	<.0001	20.50 (7.62)	13.14 (9.14)	9.28 (6.64)

Note: $N=44$.
*Scores for each cycle phase significantly different at $p<.05$. **Premenstrual scores significantly different from menstrual and intermenstrual scores at $p<.05$.

Correlations Between the Menstrual Cycle Data and Measures of Stressful Life Events, Trait Anxiety, and Social Self-Esteem

Stressful life events. Significant positive correlations were found between the LES negative scores and MDQ-T and PMTS scores for all three menstrual cycle phases. This finding suggested that those women recording higher menstrual cycle symptoms also had a higher number of negative life events. The most consistent associations were found during the intermenstrual phase with all five measures correlating positively with LES negative scores ($r=.35$, $p<.05$ to $r=.64$, $p<.0001$).

An interesting observation was that the positive LES scores were negatively correlated with the intermenstrual and premenstrual phase scores, but were not statistically significant (see Table 2).

Trait anxiety. Trait anxiety scores were found to be positively correlated with state anxiety and irritability scores through all three cycle phases ($r=.30$, $p<.05$ to $r=.50$, $p<.0001$). The intermenstrual scores on all the measures were significantly positively correlated with trait anxiety, suggesting that those in the sample with higher trait anxiety were likely to report a higher level of symptomatology at a time in the cycle when symptoms should be at a minimum (see Table 3).

Social self-esteem. As expected, scores on the SSI were negatively correlated with all five menstrual cycle measures. Similar to the LES negative and trait anxiety scores, the intermenstrual phase data revealed significant correlations ($r = -.32$, $p < .05$ to $r = -.39$, $p < .001$) (see Table 4).

Table 2.
*Correlations (Pearson r) Between Menstrual Cycle Scores and the Life Events
Survey (LES) Negative (N) and Positive (P) Scores*

Cycle phase	LES score	Scale				
		BDI	MDQ-T	PMTS	State-Anxiety	Irritability
Premenstrual	N	.18	.35*	.38**	.28	.25
	P	−.08	−.04	−.04	−.04	−.10
Menstrual	N	.51**	.60****	.39**	.55****	.36**
	P	.30*	.39**	.26	.26	.17
Intermenstrual	N	.37**	.64****	.52***	.49***	.35*
	P	−.11	−.04	−.14	−.16	−.17

Note. Scale abbreviations: BDI, Beck Depression Inventory; MDQ-T, Menstrual Distress
Questionnaire Form-T; PMTS, Premenstrual Tension Syndrome Self-Rating Scale.
*$p < .05$. **$p < .07$. ***$p < .001$. ****$p < .0001$.

Table 3.
*Correlations (Pearson r) Between the Menstrual Cycle Scores and Trait Anxiety
Scores*

Cycle phase	Scale				
	BDI	MDQ-T	PMTS	State-Anxiety	Irritability
Premenstrual	.24	.11	.25	.31*	.45***
Menstrual	.28	.23	.19	.30*	.34*
Intermenstrual	.43**	.48***	.39**	.42**	.50***

Note. Scale abbreviations: BDI, Beck Depression Inventory; MDQ-T, Menstrual Distress
Questionnaire Form-T; PMTS, Premenstrual Tension Syndrome Self-Rating Scale.
*$p < .05$. **$p < .01$. ***$p < .001$.

Table 4.
Correlations (Pearson r) Between the Menstrual Cycle Scores and Social Self-Esteem

Cycle phase	Scale				
	BDI	MDQ-T	PMTS	State-Anxiety	Irritability
Premenstrual	−.18	−.09	−.23	−.26*	−.31*
Menstrual	−.09	−.02	−.08	−.08	−.19
Intermenstrual	−.37**	−.36**	−.38**	−.32*	−.39**

Note. Scale abbreviations: BDI, Beck Depression Inventory; MDQ-T, Menstrual Distress
Questionnaire Form-T; PMTS, Premenstrual Tension Syndrome Self-Rating Scale.
*$p < .05$. **$p < .01$.

Association Between Life Stress, Social Self-Esteem, Trait Anxiety,
and Menstrual Cycle Response Patterns

The most interesting findings thus far were the significant correlations
between the intermenstrual recordings and scores on the LES (negative),
Trait Anxiety, and SSI. To explore this association, we examined the data
to investigate the possibility of individual differences within the sample
on indices of negative life events, social self-esteem, and trait anxiety. We
hypothesized that subjects who reported more negative life events, higher
trait anxiety, and lower social self-esteem would also record more menstrual cycle symptoms in general throughout the cycle than subjects with
lower scores on these measures.

An important definitional aspect of PMS is the "on-off" nature of the
symptoms. The criterion used to investigate possible within-sample variation was an intermenstrual score on the MDQ-T of 70 or above. Steiner
et al. (1980) used this cutoff score on a similar sample of subjects with
severe PMS. In the present study, a subgroup was identified in which 18
women reported an MDQ-T score greater than 70 ($M=91.02$). The mean
intermenstrual phase MDQ-T score for the remaining 26 subjects was
56.06. Subsequent ANOVAS for unbalanced data (independent variables
were Groups 1, 2; cycle phase) revealed nonsignificant interaction effects
but significant main effects for groups and cycle phase ($p<.0001$). The
two groups revealed the same pattern of responding that was previously
demonstrated for the full sample. The premenstrual phase scores were
highest, and the intermenstrual phase scores lowest. Group 1 ($n=18$)
revealed higher scores on each of the measures at each cycle phase. The
major finding was the discrepancy in scores during the intermenstrual
phase. Group 2 appeared to return to "normal" levels of menstrual symptomatology, but the scores for Group 1 remained elevated above the expected
minimal symptom experience. For example, depression scores during the
premenstrual phase revealed Group 1 to be moderately depressed
($M=20.61$) and Group 2 to be mildly depressed ($M=13.98$). The intermenstrual phase recordings showed Group 1 to be mildly depressed
($M=10.46$), whereas subjects in Group 2 were definitely not depressed
at this time ($M=2.46$). Similar findings were obtained on the other symptom measures, with Group 1 revealing elevated scores during the intermenstrual phase (see Figures 1 and 2).

Difference scores to assess the degree of change between premenstrual
and intermenstrual phase recordings for the two groups were not found
to be significantly different, indicating that subjects in both groups experienced similar magnitudes of symptom fluctuation. Significant differences
were found, however, between the two groups on indices of negative life
events, trait anxiety, and social self-esteem. Group 1 had higher LES nega-

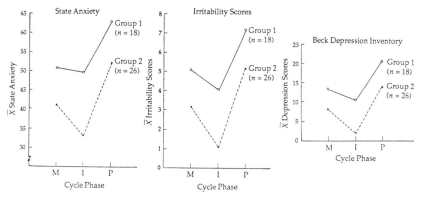

Figure 1. Mean scores for Group 1 (MDQ > 70) and Group 2 (MDQ ≤ 70) on State Anxiety Scale, Irritability Scale, and Beck Depression Inventory (BDI) as a function of cycle phase (M = menstrual; I = intermenstrual; P = premenstrual).

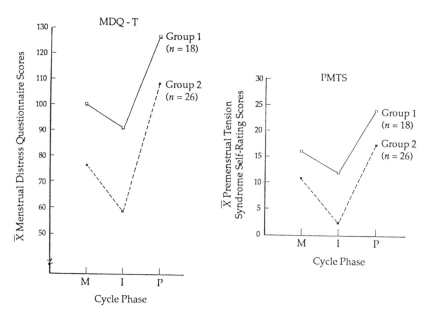

Figure 2. Mean scores for Group 1 (MDQ > 70) and Group 2 (MDQ ≤ 70) Menstrual Distress Questionnaire Form-T (MDQ-T) and Premenstrual Tension Syndrome Self-Rating Scale (PMTS) as a function of cycle phase (M = menstrual; I = intermenstrual; P = premenstrual).

tive scores ($p < .001$), a higher level of trait anxiety ($p < .01$), and lower social self-esteem ($p < .02$) than the subjects in the larger group (see Table 5).

Table 5.
Mean Scores Group 1 (n=18) and Group 2 (n=26) on Life Events Survey (Negative), Social Self-Esteem Inventory, and Trait Anxiety Scale

Instruments administered at initial interview	Group 1	Group 2
Life Events Survey (Negative)***	11.78	4.5
Social Self-Esteem Inventory*	119.78	133.96
Trait Anxiety**	46.39	39.19

$*p<.02$. $**p<.01$. $***p<.001$.

In summary, all the subjects were seen to complain of severe premenstrual symptoms with a significant lessening of symptoms midcycle. Two major aspects of the results are as follows:

1. The intermenstrual phase was most sensitive for measuring associations between negative life stress, trait anxiety, and social self-esteem and menstrual cycle symptomatology.

2. Scores on the LES negative, Trait Anxiety, and Social Self-Esteem scales seem to differentiate between two styles of responding: Those women who have elevated scores throughout the cycle also have higher scores on these measures than do women who report a discrete, time-limited experience of premenstrual symptoms.

Discussion

The main implication of these results seems to be that negative life stress influenced only some members of the sample — the subgroup of 18 women. Although all subjects suffered from severe PMS, this smaller group of 18 subjects reported the most severe premenstrual symptoms and also experienced significantly more negative life changes in the preceding 12 months. Increased trait anxiety and low social self-esteem were both associated with the higher life stress reported by the subgroup.

One possible confound may have been the designation/organization of the data for the intermenstrual phase. Some data included for the analysis of intermenstrual phase may have actually been observations from the early luteal phase. If this were the case, then the elevated scores in the intermenstrual phase may have been attributable to premenstrual symptoms. The raised intermenstrual scores in effect for the subgroup could be accounted for by premenstrual symptoms. However, although this possibility cannot be entirely ruled out, it cannot explain the marked differences between the two groups on severity of symptoms or indices of negative life events, trait anxiety, and social self-esteem.

These preliminary findings do not allow us to infer that negative life stress had a direct influence on the severity ratings of premenstrual symptoms. The limitations of the correlational data confine the interpretation of these results to a more speculative kind of reasoning. Two hypotheses concerning these results will be discussed.

The first hypothesis comes from Steiner et al. (1980) who postulated that women selected according to the diagnostic criteria but who subsequently revealed intermenstrual symptoms constitute a less "pure" sample of PMS sufferers. These authors stated that the raised intermenstrual symptom responses reflect subclinical characteristics, neurotic or reactive disturbances that are exacerbated during the premenstrual phase. In contrast, primary or "pure" PMS sufferers reveal a definite "on-off" pattern of symptoms with an asymptomatic period following the onset of menstruation. Steiner et al. recommended that future research investigating the nature of the disorder should eliminate women who reported the experience of symptoms during the intermenstrual phase. These researchers did not, however, consider the role of stress and its possible influence on symptoms during the intermenstrual phase of the cycle.

Reid (1985) discussed the issue of continuing premenstrual symptoms during the postmenstrual week. Although acknowledging the diagnostic importance of a symptom-free period in differentiating PMS from other chronic psychopathological conditions, Reid argued that "it would not be surprising to see tension or anxiety persist following menstruation in the situation where severe PMS has resulted in substantial deterioration of interpersonal relationships" (p. 6).

To continue this line of reasoning, a second hypothesis is possible to explain the results obtained in the present study. Prolonged recurrent premenstrual disruption that has led to a vicious cycle of events may be responsible for the increase in negative life stress, trait anxiety, and decrease in social self-esteem demonstrated by the 18 women in this sample. The experience of depression, anxiety, and associated symptoms intermenstrually may be a carryover effect of severe PMS, which in turn has caused considerable life-style disruption. For instance, a woman who has repeatedly suffered disabling premenstrual symptoms may experience an increase of negative life events such as marital disharmony, family breakdown, separation, change of employment, etc. The negative aspect of the social and professional disruption may also lead to lowered social self-esteem and an increase in anxiety.

Rather than constituting a less "pure" sample of PMS sufferers, the women with higher negative life stress, trait anxiety, and lower social self-esteem could have suffered from a more pervasive form of PMS in that their social, professional, and domestic lives may have been more vulnerable to disruption. The notion of vulnerability, however, is not easily tested. In addition, the concept of negative life stress as a consequence and not a precursor of PMS means that the precise association of stress in relation to the exact time span of the disabling symptoms needs to be investigated. The criteria used for the selection of subjects in the present study were too limited to allow for a more long-term investigation of the symptom-stress relationship. It is hoped that future research efforts will examine the question of whether stress is an antecedent or consequence of the disorder.

REFERENCES

American Psychiatric Association. (1980). *Diagnostic and statistical manual* (3d ed.). Washington, DC: Author.

Aplanalp, J. M., Haskett, R. F., & Rose, R. M. (1980). The premenstrual syndrome. *Psychiatric Clinics of North America, 3,* 327–347.

Beck, A. T., Ward, C. H., Mendelson, M., Mock, J., & Erbaugh, J. (1961). An inventory for measuring depression. *Archives of General Psychiatry, 4,* 561–571.

Bumberry, W., Oliver, J. M., & McClure, J. N. (1978). Validation of the Beck Depression Inventory in a university population using psychiatric estimate as the criterion. *Journal of Consulting and Clinical Psychology, 46,* 150–155.

Buss, A. H., & Durkee, A. (1957). An inventory for assessing different kinds of hostility. *Journal of Consulting Psychology, 21,* 343–349.

Haskett, R. F., & Aplanalp, J. M. (1983). Premenstrual tension syndrome: Diagnostic criteria and selection of research subjects. *Psychiatric Research, 9,* 125–138.

Haskett, R. F., Steiner, M., Osmun, J. N., & Carroll, B. J. (1980). Severe premenstrual tension: Delineation of the syndrome. *Biological Psychiatry, 15,* 121–139.

Koeske, R. (1980). Theoretical perspectives on menstrual cycle research. In A. J. Dan, E. A. Graham, & C. P. Beecher (Eds.), *The menstrual cycle.* New York: Springer.

Lawson, J. S., Marshall, W. L., & Mcgrath, P. (1979). The social self-esteem inventory. *Educational and Psychological Measurement, 39,* 803–811.

Maddocks, S. E. (1983). *The investigation of symptom response patterns on a sample of women with severe premenstrual syndrome.* Unpublished master's thesis, Queens University at Kingston, Canada.

Moos, R. (1977). *Menstrual distress questionnaire manual.* Unpublished manuscript, Stanford University, CA.

Moos, R. H. (1968). The development of a menstrual distress questionnaire. *Psychosomatic Medicine, 30,* 853–867.

Reid, R. L. (1985). Premenstrual syndrome. In J. M. Leventhal (Ed.), *Current Problems in Obstetrics, Gynecology and Fertility* (Vol. 3, pp. 345–353). Chicago: Year Book Medical Publishers.

Sarason, I. G., Johnson, J. H., & Siegel, J. M. (1978). Assessing the impact of life changes: Development of the life experiences survey. *Journal of Consulting and Clinical Psychology, 45,* 932–946.

Siegel, J. M., Johnson, J. H., & Sarason, I. G. (1979). Life changes and menstrual discomfort. *Journal of Human Stress, 5,* 41–46.

Spielberger, C. D., Gorsuch, R. L., & Lushene, R. E. (1970). *STAI manual for the State-Trait Anxiety Inventory.* Palo Alto, CA: Consulting Psychologists Press.

Spitzer, R. L., Endicott, J., & Robins, E. (1978). Research diagnostic criteria: Rationale and reliability. *Archives of General Psychiatry, 35,* 773–782.

Steiner, M., Haskett, R. E., & Carroll, B. J. (1980). Premenstrual tension syndrome: The development of research diagnostic criteria and new rating scales. *Acta Psychiatrica Scandinavica, 62,* 177–190.

Wilcoxon, L. A., Schrader, S. L., & Sherif, C. W. (1976). Daily self-reports on activities, life events, moods and somatic changes during the menstrual cycle. *Psychosomatic Medicine, 38,* 399–417.

Woods, N. F., Dery, G. K., & Most, A. (1982). Stressful life events and premenstrual symptoms. *Journal of Human Stress, 8,* 23–31.

6

Rationale and Evidence for the Role of Circadian Desynchrony in Premenstrual Symptoms

Alice J. Dan, Robert T. Chatterton, Jr., Frank A. DeLeon-Jones, and Gerald A. Hudgens

This chapter reviews aspects of circadian (or daily 24-hour) rhythms and desynchronization of these biological rhythms as they may relate to premenstrual symptoms and presents some data relevant to these relationships. Several lines of thought have recently led investigators to consider the possibility that disruption in the usual patterns of daily rhythms (or circadian desynchrony) may be a factor in premenstrual symptoms (e.g., Hamilton, Parry, Alagna, Blumenthal, & Herz, 1984). These include similarities in the nature of symptoms occurring premenstrually and those in desynchrony; desynchrony as a mechanism underlying the linkage of stress and symptoms; and the central role of body temperature as a circadian synchronizer. Despite the attention focused on premenstrual symptoms during the last 15 years, premenstrual syndrome (PMS) remains controversial and eludes systematic description. This chapter suggests that a model based on aspects of temporal structure may provide new insights and new directions for research on premenstrual symptoms.

The nature of premenstrual symptoms has presented many difficulties for definitive identification. Although there is general agreement that symptoms occur during the late luteal phase of the menstrual cycle, symptom duration can range from 1 or 2 days to 2 weeks or more. This variability in timing occurs within individuals from one cycle to the next, as well as between individuals. Further, the actual symptoms reported to occur premenstrually constitute a nonspecific cluster of common complaints, all of which may also occur at other times in the menstrual cycle. A superficial similarity can be seen between typical premenstrual symptoms and those related to circadian desynchrony, as found in studies of jet lag, for example, which include malaise, headache, minor digestive upsets, sleep disruptions, irritability, emotional lability, fatigue, appetite changes, and decreased tolerance to stress (Winget, Deroshia, Markley, & Holley, 1984).

Although many physiological parameters have been found to be unrelated to premenstrual symptoms (Reid, 1987), stress has been associated in both retrospective and prospective studies (Dan, Chatterton, Hudgens, & DeLeon-Jones, 1986; Siegel, Johnson & Sarason, 1979; Woods, Most, & Longenecker, 1985). However, the mechanism for this effect is unclear. Stress responses might directly or indirectly affect endocrine variables, through interactions on the molecular level or through behavioral changes related to stress. Recently (Dan et al., 1986; Parry & Wehr, 1987), sleep changes have been related to premenstrual symptoms, and caffeine intake has also shown an association with reported premenstrual symptoms (Rossignol, 1985). Stress, sleep, and caffeine have in common the ability to serve as synchronizers for circadian rhythms (Scheving & Halberg, 1980).

The circadian system has been characterized as "a biological clock that serves to schedule biological events at ecologically appropriate times during the day" (Johnson & Hastings, 1986, p. 29). Rather than a single clock, however, the notion of a "clockshop" has been used (Winfree, 1980) to suggest multiple rhythms, each with the tendency to synchronize with other rhythms and therefore to reinforce the appropriate timing of internal physiological processes. This circadian system is linked, or entrained, to external environmental events, like light and dark or work schedules, but is not caused by them. In the absence of such external phase regulators, circadian rhythms continue free-running, with periods usually slightly different from 24 hours (in the range of 22 to 26 hours).

Entrainment of the endogenous rhythms to the solar day is accomplished on a daily basis by various periodic signals, most prominently the cycle of light and dark (Czeisler et al., 1986). In humans, these signals also include temperature, noise, mealtimes, social interaction, and other behavioral, physiological, and social cycles. Different internal parameters, such as body temperature and sleep patterns, show differences in susceptibility to these signals (also called pacemakers, or *zeitgebers*). Inappropriate signals, like caffeine at the wrong time of day, can lead to transient internal desynchrony (Wever, 1980; Winget et al., 1984). Many rhythms are internally synchronized by body temperature; daily variations in performance efficiency have also been shown to be related to the body temperature rhythm. Further, decoupling of the sleep and temperature rhythms produces impairment in mood and performance independent of total amount of sleep (Taub & Berger, 1974).

In humans, the circadian system is thought by many observers to be controlled by a nonhierarchically coupled dual-oscillator mechanism (Kronauer, Czeisler, Pilato, Moore-Ede, & Weitzman, 1982; Winget et al., 1984) in which the sleep/wake cycle and the body temperature rhythm are linked. Sleep onset and duration have been found to depend on the phase of body temperature rhythm, rather than on how long a person had previously been awake (Czeisler, Weitzman, Moore-Ede, Zimmerman, & Knauer, 1980). The uncoupling of these two rhythms occurs because they respond with different lag times to a phase change requiring resynchronization (Johnson & Hastings, 1986). The sleep/wake rhythm is relatively labile, but the temperature cycle is more stable and takes longer to readjust. This is why shift work rotation or traveling across time zones results in a transient disturbance (desynchrony) of the relative phase relationships among rhythmic functions. Body temperature is also characterized by a circamensual or monthly rhythm (Smolensky, 1980), which may interact with the circadian cycle.

Interactions between circadian and menstrual rhythms have been reported in both directions. Hormonal changes over the monthly cycle can affect circadian rhythms: Estradiol was shown to shorten circadian periods in ovariectomized hamsters (Morin, Fitzgerald, & Zucker, 1977). Menstrual cycles of different lengths affect circadian rhythms, with longer cycles leading to phase advances and shorter cycles leading to phase delays (Engel & Hildebrandt, 1974).

Some hormonal rhythms important to regulating menstrual function are easily shifted when the circadian sleep/wake cycle is shifted (e.g., luteinizing hormone [LH], prolactin, growth hormone), whereas others take up to 2 weeks to resynchronize, similar to body temperature (Weitzman & Hellman, 1974; Winget et al., 1984). One would expect, therefore, that circadian desynchrony would affect menstrual function. Preston, Bateman, Short, and Wilkinson (1974) reported that 28% of airline stewardesses flying transmeridian routes had irregular menstrual cycles. They suggest that the best predictor for the effects of circadian desynchrony is disruption of the body temperature cycle.

A particularly interesting view of the interaction between circadian and menstrual rhythms of body temperature was given in Simpson and Halberg's 1974 study of eight consecutive menstrual cycles in one woman, with 550 measures of body temperature. As shown in Figure 1, significant periodicities of 24 hours, and 26 days were found. The midcycle shift in daily mean temperature ("mesor," see Smolensky, 1980) is clear, but differences in amplitude and phasing are also seen between the follicular and luteal halves of the cycle. Amplitude was greatest when the mesor was high; thus, the daily variation was least around the time of ovulation, and greatest as menses approached. Further, a phase delay of 4 hours appeared in the peak (or "acrophase") during the luteal phase. During the follicular phase, the peak temperature occurred at 8 P.M., but from Days 16 to 24 temperature peaked at 12 midnight. The midcycle temperature shift, then, may be the result of both a change in setpoint and a phase shift of 4 hours.

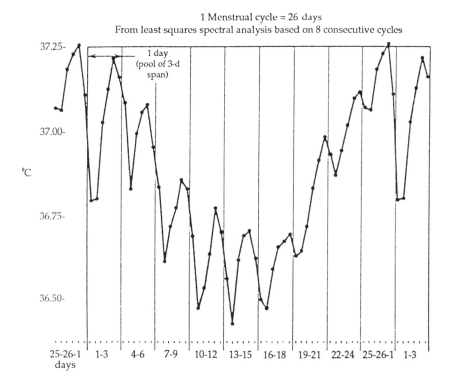

1 Menstrual cycle = 26 days
From least squares spectral analysis based on 8 consecutive cycles

Figure 1. Menstrual changes of circadian temperature rhythm. Idealized menstrual cycle constructed by superimposing eight menstrual cycles, and averaging 3-day spans.

Note. From Simpson and Halberg (1974). Copyright 1974 by John Wiley & Sons. Adapted by permission of the publisher.

In a recent study (Lee, 1988), the dampening of circadian temperature amplitude during the postovulatory phase was confirmed. Lee did not find a phase difference in the temperature peak between follicular and luteal phases. Her study suggests, though, that women show smaller amplitudes and earlier circadian peak temperatures than men.

Neither amplitude nor phase of the temperature cycle has been fully explored as a variable in menstrual functioning. Individuals whose temperature exhibits large daily excursions tend to take longer to adjust to phase shifts, according to Winfree (1982). Furthermore, desynchrony is characterized by a depression of temperature rhythm amplitude for several days (Winget et al., 1984). These findings suggest that amplitude should be investigated. Does the lower amplitude during the postovulatory phase represent a period of vulnerability to desynchronizing effects of stress, sleep loss, or caffeine? Are cycles with greater amplitude in temperature rhythms more susceptible to effects of desynchrony, and more vulnerable to premenstrual distress? Some preliminary data relevant to this latter question are presented here.

We have found no data in the literature directly relating temperature rhythm amplitude with premenstrual symptoms. Many circadian rhythms, including body temperature, show a decline in amplitude with age; this has been interpreted to suggest that there is a tendency for increased desynchrony with age (Hartshorn, 1985). A tendency for increased premenstrual symptoms with age has also been reported (Dalton, 1987).

In our research on stress and menstrual function, we have reported finding links between amount of sleep and incidence of ovulation, between ovulatory characteristics and reports of stress, and among stress, sleep, and symptoms (Chatterton et al., 1985; Dan et al., 1986). Premenstrual symptoms were found to be related to decreased sleep, particularly in the phase immediately following ovulation (Dan et al., 1986). If it can be postulated that women with greater temperature amplitude are more likely to show a clear basal body temperature (BBT) shift, then the presence of the BBT shift could be indicative of susceptibility to the effects of desynchrony. We examined the relationship between ovulatory characteristics (including BBT shift, LH surge, and luteal phase pregnanediol levels) and the occurrence of premenstrual symptoms.

Method

To assess the impact of stress on the menstrual cycle, subjects were recruited from among female students and staff at a large medical center campus. All volunteers reported regular menstrual cycles of 26 to 33 days during the previous year. They denied having used oral contraceptives or other drugs chronically during the previous 3 months. Fifty-one women (aged 19 to 38, $M = 24.5$ years) were followed for one to three menstrual cycles with daily recordings of BBT, hours of sleep, life events, subjectively experienced stress, anxiety, and physical or emotional symptoms. Subjects also collected first morning urine specimens daily for radioimmunoassay (RIA) analysis of LH and pregnanediol (Chatterton, Dan et al., 1985; Chatterton, DeLeon-Jones, Hudgens, Dan, & Cheesman, 1985).

We used all three indicators of ovulation to identify four types of cycle: (a) ovulatory by LH, BBT, and pregnanediol; (b) ovulatory by LH and pregnanediol, but not by BBT; (c) ovulatory by LH and BBT, but not by sustained postovulatory pregnanediol rise; and (d) anovulatory by all measures. Symptoms were reported in response to an open-ended question on the daily form. Premenstrual symptoms were assessed by examining the 7 days prior to menstruation and counting the number of days in which symptoms were reported.

Results

Complete data were available on 82 cycles from 51 women. As frequently found, there was considerable intraindividual variability in both symptom reports and cycle characteristics. Subjects could not be classified into a single group if their cycles differed on occurrence of any of the ovulatory characteristics, so we decided to explore these relationships using cycle as the unit of analysis. Of the 82 cycles, 50 (61%) included at least one premenstrual day with a symptom report. Table 1 shows the variation among different types of cycle in symptomatic and symptom-free premenstrual weeks. Both of the groups showing clear ovulatory BBT shifts reported greater proportions of symptomatic cycles than the other groups (χ^2 for Groups 1 and 3 vs. Groups 2 and 4 = 4.577, $df=1$, $p < .05$). The mean number of premenstrual days on which symptoms were reported shows a similar pattern (see Table 2), but the results did not reach significance ($F=1.927$, $df=3$, 78; $p=.13$).

Table 1.

Number and Percent of Cycles With and Without Premenstrual Symptoms by Ovulatory Criteria (N=82 Cycles)

Type of cycle	With symptoms		Without symptoms	
	n	%	n	%
Ovulatory				
LH peak + elevated				
Pregnanediol + BBT	22	71.0	9	29.0
Pregnanediol only	8	40.0	12	60.0
BBT only	7	87.5	1	12.5
Anovulatory				
No LH peak	13	56.4	10	43.5

Table 2.

Mean Premenstrual Symptom-Days by Ovulatory Criteria (N=82 Cycles)

Type of cycle	Premenstrual symptom-days		
	n	Mean	SD
Ovulatory			
LH peak + elevated			
Pregnanediol + BBT	31	2.87	3.00
Pregnanediol only	20	1.35	2.35
BBT only	8	3.50	2.78
Anovulatory			
No LH peak	23	1.87	2.72

Discussion

Although these findings are suggestive enough to encourage further research on the time structure of temperature rhythms in relation to premenstrual symptoms, their limitations must also be noted. First, although these subjects were gynecologically normal, they were not assessed for premenstrual syndrome. Thus, one might find different patterns in women selected for the presence of premenstrual syndrome. Second, the temperature data do not directly include circadian amplitude information. Furthermore, individual factors might have influenced both cycle and symptom variables, in various ways not controlled for in this analysis. Because both temperature recording and symptom reporting were dependent on subject cooperation, it is possible that the less distinct temperature shifts were associated with fewer symptom reports through negligence, rather than through mechanisms of circadian desynchrony.

To assess fully the impact of circadian temperature variables, including amplitude, mesor shift, and phase shift, on premenstrual symptoms, studies must gather multiple daily measures of temperature in women diagnosed with premenstrual syndrome, as well as in controls. Recording not just hours of sleep but approximate hours of retiring and rising as well would add another important dimension to exploring desynchrony. Parry and Wehr's (1987) report that sleep deprivation lessened premenstrual depressive symptoms is consistent with circadian rhythm literature, in that a phase advance (or "late sleep deprivation") is more effective than a phase delay (or "early sleep deprivation") (Winget et al., 1984).

In addition to altering sleep/wake cycles, other therapeutic approaches suggested by research on desynchrony include exercise, altering the timing of meals, diet planning, and using caffeine at appropriate times to aid in resynchronizing (Ehret, Groh, & Meinert, 1980; Winget et al., 1984). However, an interesting question is whether maintenance of a strict rhythmicity would provide the best physiological background for preventing symptoms, or whether a "stress inoculation" approach of loosening up the schedule would be more effective. Further research relating circadian synchrony and desynchrony to premenstrual symptoms contains rich possibilities.

REFERENCES

Chatterton, R. T., Dan, A. J., DeLeon-Jones, F. A., Hudgens, G. A., Haan, J. N., Cheesman, S. D., & Cheesman, K. L. (1985). Relationships between the amount of sleep, stress, and ovarian function in women. In K. W. McKerns & V. Pantic (Eds.), *Neuroendocrine correlates of stress* (pp. 111–124). New York: Plenum.

Chatterton, R. T., DeLeon-Jones, F. A., Hudgens, G. A., Dan, A. J., & Cheesman, K. L. (1985). Hormonal responses to exercise in non-athletic women. In K. W. McKerns & V. Pantic (Eds.), *Neuroendocrine correlates of stress* (pp. 125–137). New York: Plenum.

Czeisler, C. A., Allen, J. S., Strogatz, S. H., Ronda, J. M., Sanchez, R., Rios, C. D., Freitag, W. O., Richardson, G. S., & Kronauer, R. E. (1986). Bright light resets the human circadian pacemaker independent of the timing of the sleep-wake cycle. *Science, 233,* 667–671.

Czeisler, C. A., Weitzman, E. D., Moore-Ede, M. C., Zimmerman, J. C., Knauer, R. S. (1980). Human sleep: Its duration and organization depend on its circadian phase. *Science, 210,* 1264–1267.

Dalton, K. (1987). Should premenstrual syndrome be a legal defense? In B. E. Ginsberg & B. F. Carter (Eds.), *Premenstrual syndrome: Ethical and legal implications in a biomedical perspective* (pp. 287–300). New York: Plenum.

Dan, A. J., Chatterton, R. T., Hudgens, G. A., & DeLeon-Jones, F. A. (1986, August). *Indicants of stress in relation to menstrual cycle events and symptoms.* Paper presented at the meeting of the American Psychological Association, Washington, DC.

Ehret, C. F., Groh, K. R., & Meinert, J. C. (1980). Considerations of diet in alleviating jet lag. In L. E. Scheving & F. Halberg (Eds.), *Chronobiology: Principles and applications to shifts in schedules* (pp. 393–402). Rockville, MD: Sijthoff and Noordhoff.

Engel, P., & Hildebrandt, G. (1974). Rhythmic variations in reaction time, heart rate, and blood pressure at different durations of the menstrual cycle. In M. Ferin, F. Halberg, R. M. Richart, & R. L. VandeWiele (Eds.), *Biorhythms and human reproduction* (pp. 325–333). New York: Wiley.

Hamilton, J., Parry, B., Alagna, S., Blumenthal, S., & Herz, E. (1984). Premenstrual mood changes: A guide to evaluation and treatment. *Psychiatric Annals, 14,* 426–435.

Hartshorn, J. (1985). *Development of the synchrony desynchrony scale for nursing.* Unpublished doctoral dissertation, University of Texas at Austin.

Johnson, C. H., & Hastings, J. W. (1986). The elusive mechanism of the circadian clock. *American Scientist, 74,* 29–36.

Kronauer, R. E., Czeisler, C. A., Pilato, S., Moore-Ede, M. C., & Weitzman, E. D. (1982). Mathematical model of the human circadian system with two interacting oscillators. *American Journal of Physiology, 242,* 3–17.

Lee, K. A. (1988). Circadian temperature rhythms in relation to menstrual cycle phase. *Journal of Biological Rhythms, 3,* 255–263.

Morin, L. P., Fitzgerald, K. M., & Zucker, I. (1977). Estradiol shortens the period of hamster circadian rhythms. *Science, 196,* 305–306.

Parry, B. L., & Wehr, T. A. (1987). Therapeutic effect of sleep deprivation in patients with premenstrual syndrome. *American Journal of Psychiatry, 144,* 808–810.

Preston, F. S., Bateman, S. C., Short, R. V., & Wilkinson, R. T. (1974). The effects of flying and of time changes on menstrual cycle length and on performance in airline stewardesses. In M. Ferin, F. Halberg, R. M. Richart, & R. L.

VandeWiele (Eds.), *Biorhythms and human reproduction* (pp. 501–512). New York: Wiley.

Reid, R. (1987). Pathophysiology and treatment of premenstrual syndrome. In B. E. Ginsberg & B. F. Carter (Eds.), *Premenstrual syndrome: Ethical and legal implications in a biomedical perspective* (pp. 329–350). New York: Plenum.

Rossignol, A. M. (1985). Caffeine-containing beverages and premenstrual syndrome in young women. *American Journal of Public Health, 75,* 1335–1337.

Scheving, L. E., & Halberg, F. (1980). *Chronobiology: Principles and applications to shifts in schedules.* Rockville, MD: Sijthoff and Noordhoff.

Siegel, J., Johnson, J., & Sarason, I. (1979). Life changes and menstrual discomfort. *Journal of Human Stress, 5,* 41–46.

Simpson, H. W., & Halberg, E. E. (1974). Menstrual changes of the circadian temperature rhythm in women. In M. Ferin, F. Halberg, R. M. Richart, & R. L. VandeWiele (Eds.), *Biorhythms and human reproduction* (pp. 549–556). New York: Wiley.

Smolensky, M. H. (1980). Chronobiologic considerations in the investigation and interpretation of circamensual rhythms in women. In A. J. Dan, E. A. Graham, & C. P. Beecher (Eds.), *The menstrual cycle: A synthesis of interdisciplinary research* (pp. 76–90). New York: Springer.

Taub, J. M., & Berger, R. J. (1974). Effects of acute shifts in circadian rhythms of sleep and wakefulness on performance and mood. In L. E. Scheving, F. Halberg, & J. Pauly (Eds.), *Chronobiology* (pp. 571–575). Tokyo: Igaku Shoin.

Weitzman, E. D., & Hellman, L. (1974). Temporal organization of the 24-hour pattern of the hypothalamic-pituitary axis. In M. Ferin, F. Halberg, R. M. Richart, & R. L. VandeWiele (Eds.), *Biorhythms and human reproduction* (pp. 371–396). New York: Wiley.

Wever, R. A. (1980). Phase shifts of human circadian rhythms due to shifts of artificial *zeitgebers. Chronobiology, 7,* 303–327.

Winfree, A. T. (1980). *The geometry of biological time.* Springer-Verlag.

Winfree, A. T. (1982). Human body clocks and the timing of sleep. *Nature, 297,* 23–27.

Winget, C. M., Deroshia, C. W., Markley, C. L., & Holley, D. C. (1984). A review of human physiological and performance changes associated with desynchronosis of biological rhythms. *Aviation, Space and Environmental Medicine, 55,* 1085–1096.

Woods, N. F., Most, A., & Longenecker, G. D. (1985). Major life events, daily stressors, and perimenstrual symptoms. *Nursing Research, 34,* 263–267.

7

PMS and the Progesterone Controversy

Linda L. Lewis

Premenstrual syndrome (PMS) and progesterone have become linked in the minds of many women experiencing PMS, as well as in the minds of health-care providers and researchers. Why does the controversial subject of progesterone in relation to PMS continue to engage our attention? Is there a rationale for a persistent focus on progesterone in research strategies and its continued use as a therapeutic agent?

There does appear to be a rationale for such research. Current knowledge of neuroendocrine physiology points to an important role for progesterone in normal ovarian cyclicity, and through its effects on the brain, a possible role in PMS. The physiologic rationale for a therapeutic use of progesterone in PMS is fragile, however, and double-blind, controlled studies do not support its effectiveness (over a placebo) in diminishing the symptoms of PMS (Keith, 1985; Maddocks, Hahn, Moller, & Reid, 1986; Sampson, 1979; Smith, 1975; Taylor, 1979; van der Meer, Benedek-Jaszmann, & Van Loenan, 1983). Women who request and physicians who prescribe progesterone either do not know about or choose not to heed these findings. The controversial linking of PMS and progesterone is nurtured by the probability that progesterone has an involvement in PMS etiology, but this involvement does not lead to progesterone replacement therapy as a logical solution. This chapter explores this interesting paradox, looking first at PMS and progesterone etiologic research and then at PMS and progesterone therapy research.

PMS and Progesterone Etiologic Research

The orchestration of the menstrual cycle is most dependent upon estrogen and progesterone signaling. Primate studies indicate that the menstrual cycle is related to the intrinsic lifespan of the cyclic ovarian-dominant structures and is not the result of timed changes dictated by the brain (hypothalamus) or pituitary (Ross & Schreiber, 1986). The developing follicle and the corpus luteum (which produce estrogen and progesterone) determine the length of the menstrual cycle.

In the normal menstrual cycle, the drop in progesterone and estrogen (prior to the onset of menstruation) signals the hypothalamus to secrete gonadotropin releasing hormone (GnRH); GnRH signals the pituitary to release follicle stimulating hormone (FSH) and luteinizing hormone (LH), which in turn prompt the ovary to begin the development of follicles and the release of one mature ovum. The structure left behind after the ovum is released, the corpus luteum, then produces progesterone and estrogen. With the demise of the corpus luteum, the flow of these hormones subsides and the cycle begins again (Ferin, 1982; Yen, 1986).

Neuroendocrine Pathways Involving Progesterone

Researchers are intently interested in the ways in which the fluxes in ovarian-produced progesterone modulate GnRH. Studies point to hypothalamic beta-endorphin (bE) as the intermediary, responding to progesterone, and in turn regulating GnRH. In their work with rhesus monkeys (a good animal model for the human menstrual cycle), Wardlaw, Wehrenberg, Ferin, Antunes, and Frantz (1982) and Wehrenberg, Wardlaw, Frantz, and Ferin (1982) suggest that cyclic changes in ovarian progesterone and estrogen are necessary for the release of hypothalamic bE into the hypothalamic portal-blood. Specifically, they and others (Yen, 1986) believe that progesterone or a combination of progesterone and estrogen can increase central bE activity. Endorphin activity at central nervous system sites reaches peak levels when progesterone and estrogen levels are highest (luteal phase) and falls markedly when these steroid levels decrease (follicular phase) (Facchinetti, Nappi, Petraglia, Volpe, & Genazzani, 1983; Peck, 1982).

The bE-GnRH pathways are becoming more clear: Beta-endorphin neurons interconnect with dopamine (DA) neurons and norepinephrine (NE) neurons, both of which connect with GnRH neurons. The specific functions in DA and NE transmission that bE mediates are unknown, but they are suspected to be involved in the regulation of GnRH neuron activities (Reame, Sauder, Kelch, & Marshall, 1984; Vrbicky et al., 1982; Yen, 1980).

The secretion patterns of GnRH are different in the follicular phase and the luteal phase of the menstrual cycle, reflecting the putative role of progesterone in the bE-GnRH chain of events (Marshall & Kelch, 1986; Soules et al., 1984). Figure 1 diagrams these postulated luteal phase neuroendocrine relationships.

Naloxone challenge studies in normal, cycling women have provided evidence that the frequency of LH pulses (and thus, inferentially, GnRH pulsing) is lower in the latter half of the menstrual cycle (luteal phase) than in the first half (follicular phase) and that this difference is modulated by bE (Quigley & Yen, 1980; Ropert, Quigley, & Yen, 1981; Rossmanith & Yen, 1987). Naloxone, an endorphin receptor antagonist, does not allow bE to bind to presynaptic neurons. When naloxone is given during the follicular phase (to prevent the endorphin-inhibiting effects on GnRH), no increase in LH pulsatile frequency is seen. But when naloxone is given during the luteal phase (removing the inhibiting effect of bE on GnRH), LH pulsatile frequency dramatically increases.

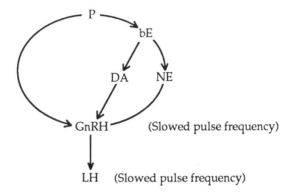

Figure 1. Luteal phase neuroendocrine pathways. P (progesterone); bE (beta-endorphin); DA (dopamine); NE (norepinephrine); GnRH (gonadotropin releasing hormone); LH (luteinizing hormone).

Progesterone, bE, and PMS

Evidence has been presented that points to the ovarian hormones as a pivotal element in PMS etiology. Muse, Cetel, Futterman, and Yen (1984) suspended ovarian cycling (by administering a GnRH agonist) in eight carefully selected women with PMS, stopping the occurrence of physical and behavioral symptoms. The symptoms resumed when ovarian cycling was restored.

Reid and Yen (1981, 1983) have been the primary proponents of a role for bE in the psychobiology of PMS; their interests have been echoed by many other researchers (Chuong, Coulam, Kao, Bergstahl, & Go, 1985; Fritz & Speroff, 1983; Halbreich & Endicott, 1981; Labrum, 1983; Vargyas, Lobo, & Mishell, 1984). Studies suggesting that the bE system is fundamentally involved in the functions of the brain that affect mood, emotion, and behavior (Guillemin, 1980) reinforce an interest in progesterone-bE mechanisms in women with PMS.

Reid (1985) proposed that the progression of bE concentrations across the menstrual cycle paralleled the symptom pattern of many women with PMS. He postulated the presence of specific symptoms (depression, withdrawal, low energy, sleepiness, increased appetite, abdominal bloating, and constipation) as luteal bE increased (possibly driven by rising progesterone) and the presence of other specific symptoms (irritability, tension, anxiety, hostility, aggression, and diarrhea) as bE decreased (possibly in relation to the progesterone decrease) in the days just before the onset of menstruation. However, results of a study of 29 carefully selected women with PMS that examined the temporal patterns of symptoms in relation to Reid's proposed bE pattern did not support this notion (Lewis, 1987). This lack of relationship was similar to work by Hamilton, Parry, Alagna, Blumenthal, and Herz (1984).

Some researchers postulate that the levels or influence of bE may be different in women with PMS. Facchinetti and colleagues (1983) and Vargyas and coworkers (1984) found that women with PMS had blunted or absent LH pulsatile responses to naloxone in the luteal phase compared with women without PMS, suggesting a deficiency or withdrawal of endorphins at a time in the cycle when endorphins are expected to be enhanced. Chuong and associates (1985) found significantly lower luteal phase bE levels in 20 women with PMS compared with 20 nonsymptomatic women. Interpretation of these results, however, must be tempered by the knowledge that only one luteal blood sample was analyzed, and the use of peripheral circulation levels of bE to infer brain levels of bE is questionable. In contrast to Chuong's work, Reame is investigating the relationships between LH pulsatility (as a reflection of bE activity) and symptoms in women with PMS. In a preliminary report (partial sample), Reame, Marshall, Kelch, and Stein (1987) found normal midluteal LH pulsatility patterns in 3 women with PMS, a trend in the data that does not support a role for bE in PMS.

Influenced by Reame's work, Lewis examined both LH pulsatile patterns and progesterone pulsatile patterns in a study of 6 women with PMS (prospectively assessed) and their 6 age-matched controls (unpublished data). Hormone pulsatile characteristics were studied in relation to the symptom-onset pattern of each woman. Three luteal days were selected for blood sampling in each woman: Sampling Day 1 (presymptom onset), and Sampling Days 2 and 3 (during symptoms). Blood was collected every 10 min for 10 hr on the 3 sampling days. The study explored the possibility of synchronous patterns between LH and progesterone pulsatile release that have been suggested in studies by Filicori, Butler, and Crowley (1984) and by Soules et al. (1984), among others. Coincident pulsing between LH and progesterone was found in both groups, with a systematically increasing coupling interval as the luteal phase progressed. However, in women with PMS a significantly tighter than expected coupling occurred (compared with controls) during the blood-sampling time frame that coincided with symptom onset (Sampling Day 2). This altered synchrony between LH and progesterone seen at the time of symptom onset raises the speculation that the corpus luteum is more reactive and may be releasing progesterone at a faster rate. The physiological difference this may make at the level of the hypothalamus remains to be elucidated.

Researchers are currently devising endocrine intervention strategies (removing or adding specific hormones) which are designed to examine further the roles of progesterone and bE in LH pulsatile patterns in women with PMS. Progress in these research approaches may serve to illuminate the putative role of progesterone in the etiology of PMS.

PMS and Progesterone Therapy Research

Many of the "progesterone deficiency" studies were prompted by the postulates of Dalton (1984), a British physician who advocates natural progesterone replacement therapy. Her work has been largely anecdotal. Researchers looking for deviations from normal in the daily luteal phase peripheral concentrations of progesterone in women with PMS, however, have reached no definitive conclusions. Studies have reported low levels (Abraham, Elsner, & Lucas, 1978; Backstrom & Carstensen, 1974; Backstrom, Wide, Sodergard, & Carstensen, 1976; Munday, 1977; Munday, Brush, & Taylor, 1981; Smith, 1975), high levels (O'Brien, Selby, & Symonds, 1980), and no difference in levels (Andersch, Abrahamsson, Wendestam, & Hahn, 1979; Andersen, Larsen, Steenshrup, Svendstrup, & Nielsen, 1977; Taylor, 1979). Interpretation of the results of these studies has been further hampered by PMS research methodological weaknesses, especially those that relate to defining the syndrome, the selection of subjects, and the need for prospective studies (Rubinow & Roy-Byrne, 1984). Most important (as mentioned earlier), progesterone is now known to secrete in a pulsatile fashion (Backstrom, McNeilley, Leak, & Baird, 1982; Steele & Judd, 1986). One study (Filicori, Butler, & Crowley, 1984) found midluteal phase progesterone concentrations that ranged from 4.1 ng/ml to 40.1 ng/ml in a 24-hr period. Clearly, future progesterone concentration studies that do not account for pulsatile progesterone secretion are of limited value.

The use of any therapeutic regime for PMS (progesterone or otherwise) also must take into account the placebo response. Beecher (1955) found that 30%–40% of the general population react to a placebo as if it were an actual drug. Estimates of a placebo response in PMS (as in affective disorders) are even higher: 40%–60% (Rubinow & Roy-Byrne, 1984). Progesterone/placebo double-blind studies have not supported Dalton's emphasis on progesterone replacement (Keith, 1985; Maddocks et al., 1986; Sampson, 1979; Smith, 1975; Taylor, 1979; van der Meer et al., 1983). One study reported a beneficial effect using oral micronized progesterone

(Dennerstein et al., 1985); however, the statistical approach they used (multiple *t* tests) places serious doubts on the validity of the study conclusions.

Progesterone at Pharmacologic Levels
    The physiologic reasoning behind the use of progesterone replacement bears challenging. There is no scientific consensus regarding the presence of abnormal levels of progesterone in women with PMS. Thus, simple replacement of progesterone to physiologic levels is not indicated. If progesterone levels in women with PMS are adequate, administering exogenous progesterone may be moving beyond the actions of normal (physiologic) levels of progesterone, creating pharmacologic effects.
    The theoretical possibility that pharmacologic levels of progesterone would bring about positive results in women with PMS has not been borne out in the progesterone/placebo, double-blind studies mentioned above. Progesterone's anti-aldosterone action, an increase in sodium and water excretion (Landau & Lugibihl, 1958), did not consistently relieve abdominal bloating or breast tenderness in these studies. The relaxant effects of progesterone on smooth muscle and the inhibition of muscular activity in the intestine by endorphins (which are increased when progesterone is increased) may in fact worsen such symptoms as constipation and abdominal bloating (Reid, 1985).
    Progesterone given at pharmacologic doses may be altering PMS symptoms through its analgesic/sedative action. Investigators believe that pregnanolone, a metabolite of progesterone, acts directly on cell metabolism in the hypothalamus, enhancing monoamine oxidase (MAO, the enzyme that metabolizes catecholamines) activity (Bengtsson, 1971; Mauvis-Jarvis, 1983). MAO increases in the presence of progesterone, resulting in less available catecholamines (norepinephrine and dopamine) in the synaptic cleft. When this occurs, synaptic activity (transmission of nerve impulses) is reduced (Jones, 1981; Whitehead, Siddle, Townsend, Lane, & King, 1981; Yen, 1980). Schildkraut (1965) and others believe that altering MAO activity influences brain thresholds related to mood and behavior (Maugh, 1981; Prange, 1982). The effect of decreasing catecholamines in an organism is to decrease its arousal state—in essence, to sedate (Klaiber, Broverman, Vogel, & Kobayashi, 1974; McEwen et al., 1983). Pharmacologic doses of progesterone administered to animals have resulted in profound analgesia (Jones, 1981; Mauvis-Jarvis, 1983). In humans, intravenous infusion of progesterone has induced sleep (Merryman, Boiman, & Barnes, 1954). The anecdotal reporting by some women that natural progesterone "works" for them (aside from or in combination with a placebo effect?) may be the result of a sedative action of progesterone. This should merit

caution in prescribing natural progesterone for women whose predominant symptoms are depressive (Klaiber et al., 1974).

The likelihood that progesterone therapy may be acting as a hormonal tranquilizer is reason for caution. Tranquilizers are not a definitive therapy for PMS. The scientifically unsupported use of a hormone (with unknown long-term side effects) may not be appropriate. This is especially true if one presumes that most women contemplating the use of progesterone are not told of its sedative properties nor warned about the lack of knowledge related to long-term effects.

Some Consequences of the Controversy

The promotion of the use of progesterone therapy for PMS has had several consequences. The subject of PMS has become highly publicized — with mixed blessings (Allen, 1982; Eagan, 1983; Henig, 1982; Parlee, 1982; Rome, 1986; Switzer, 1983; Vaitukaitis, 1984). An important consequence, however, is that more women voicing premenstrual-change concerns are being listened to. Before the media attention given to PMS, many women were reluctant to discuss menstrual cycle changes. Anecdotal evidence exists that when they did, they were often treated with disdain or disinterest by their physicians. This notion is supported by the work of Armitage, Schneiderman, and Bass (1979) who found significantly poorer physician responses to specific complaints (not menstrual-cycle related) made by women compared with *the same* complaints voiced by men.

Improved research methodologies have exerted a moderating effect on the inappropriate emphasis of PMS as an issue for *all* women. In the experience of one respected PMS researcher (Yen, 1986), no more than 10% of cycling women have PMS, whereas Hamilton et al. (1984) cite a 20%–50% incidence; both estimates are considerably smaller than the media initially heralded. For women with PMS, however, the flurry of interest in PMS and the debate about progesterone therapy have been important. Perhaps because of the controversy about progesterone, the public, health care professionals, and researchers have been sensitized to the importance of taking PMS issues seriously and seeking solutions to them (Hopson & Rosenfeld, 1984).

Summary

The evolution of neuroendocrine research in PMS is leading us away from the simpler notion that abnormal concentrations of hormones in the peripheral circulation exist or provide etiological information. Current neuroendocrine research methodologies emphasize examining symptom-related temporal patterns of (pulsatile) hormonal and neurotransmitter changes, looking for asynchronous patterns in the established changes, and studying the effects of various interventions on these neuroendocrine pathways. A major avenue of current investigation is focusing on bE-related changes and the role of progesterone. An exponential step in study design will have been taken when neuroendocrine researchers include the tandem evaluation of environmental circumstances and events in the lives of the women being studied, thus acknowledging the interactive nature of the internal and the external milieu.

A knowledge of the actions of progesterone at physiologic and pharmacologic levels and the results of double-blind progesterone studies do not support progesterone therapy for PMS. However, these elements of the PMS/progesterone controversy have provided a platform from which women have made themselves heard. Partially as a result of the controversy, more women with PMS are being listened to by their health care providers and more researchers are paying serious attention.

REFERENCES

Abraham, G. E., Elsner, C. W., & Lucas, L. A. (1978). Hormonal and behavioral changes during the menstrual cycle. *Senologia, 3,* 33–38.

Allen, J. (1982, November). Premenstrual frenzy. *New York Magazine,* pp. 37–42.

Andersch, B., Abrahamsson, L., Wendestam, R. O., & Hahn, L. (1979). Hormone profile in premenstrual tension: Effects of bromocriptine and diuretics. *Clinical Endocrinology, 11,* 657–664.

Andersen, A. N., Larsen, J. F., Steenshrup, O. R., Svendstrup, B., & Nielsen, J. (1977). Effect of bromocriptine on the premenstrual syndrome: A double-blind clinical trial. *British Journal of Obstetrics and Gynaecology, 84,* 370–374.

Armitage, K. J., Schneiderman, L. J., & Bass, M. A. (1979). Response of physicians to medical complaints in men and women. *Journal of the American Medical Association, 241,* 2186–2187.

Backstrom, T. L., & Carstensen, H. (1974). Estrogen and progesterone in plasma in relation to premenstrual tension. *Journal of Steroid Biochemistry, 5,* 257–260.

Backstrom, T. L., McNeilly, A. S., Leak, R. M., & Baird, D. T. (1982). Pulsatile secretion of LH, FSH, prolactin, oestradiol, and progesterone in the human menstrual cycle. *Clinical Endocrinology, 17,* 29–42.

Backstrom, T. L., Wide, L., Sodergard, R., & Carstensen, H. (1976). FSH, LH, TeBG capacity, oestrogen and progesterone in women with premenstrual tension in the luteal phase. *Journal of Steroid Biochemistry, 6,* 473–485.

Beecher, H. K. (1955). The powerful placebo effect. *Journal of the American Medical Association, 159,* 1602–1606.

Bengtsson, L. P. (1971). Progesterone and its metabolites in blood and urine. In G. Peters and M. Tausk (Eds.), *Pharmacology of the endocrine system and related drugs: Progesterone, progestational drugs and antifertility agents* (Vol. 1, pp. 413–440). New York: Pergamon Press.

Chuong, C. J., Coulam, C. B., Kao, P. C., Bergstahl, E. J., & Go, V. L. (1985).

Neuropeptide levels in premenstrual syndrome. *Fertility and Sterility, 44,* 760–765.

Dalton, K. (1984). *The premenstrual syndrome and progesterone therapy.* Chicago: Year Book Medical Publishers.

Dennerstein, L., Spencer-Gardner, C., Gotts, G., Brown, J. B., Smith, M. A., & Burrows, G. D. (1985). Progesterone and the premenstrual syndrome: A double-blind crossover trial. *British Medical Journal, 290,* 1617–1621.

Eagan, A. (1983, October). The selling of PMS. *Ms.,* pp. 26, 28, 29.

Facchinetti, F., Nappi, G., Petraglia, F., Volpe, A., & Genazzani, A. R. (1983). Estradiol/progesterone imbalances and the premenstrual syndrome. *Lancet, 2,* 1302.

Ferin, M. (1982). The neuroendocrinologic control of the menstrual cycle. In R. C. Friedman (Ed.), *Behavior and the menstrual cycle* (pp. 23–42). New York: Marcel Dekker.

Filicori, M., Butler, J. P., & Crowley, W. F. (1984). Neuroendocrine regulation of the corpus luteum in the human. Evidence for pulsatile progesterone secretion. *Journal of Clinical Investigation, 73,* 1638–1647.

Fritz, M. A., & Speroff, L. (1983). Current concepts of the endocrine characteristics of normal menstrual function: The key to diagnosis and management of disorders. *Clinical Obstetrics and Gynecology, 26,* 647–689.

Guillemin, R. (1980). Beta-lipotropin and endorphins: Implications of current knowledge. In D. T. Krieger & J. C. Hughes (Eds.), *Neuroendocrinology* (pp. 67–74). Sunderland, MA: Sinauer.

Halbreich, U., & Endicott, J. (1981). Possible involvement of endorphin withdrawal or imbalance in specific premenstrual syndromes and postpartal depression. *Medical Hypotheses, 8,* 1045–1058.

Hamilton, J. A., Parry, B., Alagna, S., Blumenthal, S., & Herz, E. (1984). Premenstrual mood changes: A guide to evaluation and treatment. *Psychiatric Annals, 14,* 426–435.

Henig, R. M. (1982, March). Dispelling menstrual myths. *New York Times Magazine, 7,* pp. 64, 65, 68, 70, 71, 74, 75, 78, 79.

Hopson, J., & Rosenfeld, A. (1984, August). PMS: Puzzling monthly symptoms. *Psychology Today,* pp. 30–35.

Jones, G. S. (1981). The historic review of the clinical use of progesterone and progestins. In C. W. Bardin, E. Milgram, & J. P. Mauvais-Jarvis (Eds.), *Progesterone and progestins* (pp. 189–202). New York: Raven Press.

Keith, G. K. (1985). *A study of the premenstrual syndrome and progesterone/placebo therapy.* Unpublished doctoral dissertation, Walden University, San Diego, CA.

Klaiber, E. L., Broverman, D. M., Vogel, W., & Kobayashi, Y. (1974). The use of steroid hormones in depression. In T. M. Itil, G. Laudahn, & W. M. Herrmann (Eds.), *Psychotropic action of hormones* (pp. 135–154). New York: Spectrum.

Labrum, A. H. (1983). Hypothalamic, pineal and pituitary factors in the premenstrual syndrome. *Journal of Reproductive Medicine, 28,* 438–445.

Landau, R. I., & Lugibihl, K. (1958). Inhibition of the sodium-retaining influence of aldosterone by progesterone. *Journal of Clinical Endocrinology and Metabolism, 18,* 1237.

Lewis, L. L. (1987). *Premenstrual syndrome: Endocrine and psychosocial variables in relation to symptom severity.* Unpublished doctoral dissertation, University of Illinois at Chicago.

Maddocks, S., Hahn, P., Moller, F., & Reid, R. L. (1986). A double-blind controlled trial of progesterone vaginal suppositories in the treatment of premenstrual syndrome. *American Journal of Obstetrics and Gynecology, 154,* 573–581.

Marshall, J. C., & Kelch, R. P. (1986). Gonadotropin-releasing hormone: Role of pulsatile secretion in the regulation of reproduction. *New England Journal of Medicine, 315,* 1459–1468.

Maugh, T. H. (1981). Biochemical markers identify mental states. *Science, 214,* 39–41.

Mauvais-Jarvis, P. (1983). Progesterone and progestins: A general overview. In C. W. Bardin, E. Milgram, & P. Mauvais-Jarvis (Eds.), *Progesterone and progestins* (pp. 1–15). New York: Raven Press.

McEwen, B. S., Davis, P. G., Gerlach, J. L., Krey, L. C., MacLusky, N. J., McGinnis, M. Y., Parsons, B., & Rainbow, T. C. (1983). Progestin receptors in the brain and pituitary gland. In C. W. Bardin, E. Milgram, & J. P. Mauvais-Jarvis (Eds.), *Progesterone and progestins* (pp. 59–76). New York: Raven Press.

Merryman, W., Boiman, R., & Barnes, L. (1954). Progesterone anesthesia in human subjects. *Journal of Clinical Endocrinology and Metabolism, 14,* 1567.

Munday, M. (1977). Hormone levels in severe premenstrual tension. *Current Medical Research Opinion, 4* (Suppl. 4), 16.

Munday, M., Brush, M. S., & Taylor, R. W. (1981). Correlations between progesterone, estradiol and aldosterone levels in the premenstrual syndrome. *Clinical Endocrinology, 14,* 1–9.

Muse, K. N., Cetel, N. S., Futterman, L. A., & Yen, S. S. C. (1984). The premenstrual syndrome: Effect of "medical ovariectomy." *New England Journal of Medicine, 311,* 1345–1349.

O'Brien, P. M., Selby, C., & Symonds, E. M. (1980, May 10). Progesterone, fluid and electrolytes in premenstrual syndrome. *British Medical Journal,* 1161–1163.

Parlee, M. B. (1982, September). New findings: Menstrual cycle and behavior. *Ms.,* pp. 126–128.

Peck, S. D. (1982). Can increased beta-endorphins explain the etiology of premenstrual syndrome? *Journal of the American Osteopathic Association, 83,* 192–197.

Prange, A. J. (1982). Hormone therapy in depressive diseases. *Advanced Biochemical Psychopharmacolgy, 32,* 289–296.

Quigley, M. E., & Yen, S. S. C. (1980). The role of the endogenous opiates in LH secretion during the menstrual cycle. *Journal of Clinical Endocrinology and Metabolism, 51,* 179–181.

Reame, N. E., Marshall, J. C., Kelch, R. P., & Stein, K. S. (1987, September). Pulsatile secretion of LH and progesterone (Abstract). *Proceedings of the 2d International Symposium on Premenstrual, Postpartum, and Menopausal Mood Disorders* (p. 22).

Reame, N. E., Sauder, S. E., Kelch, R. P., & Marshall, J. C. (1984). Pulsatile gonadotropin secretion during the human menstrual cycle: Evidence of altered frequency of gonadotropin-releasing hormone secretion. *Journal of Clinical Endocrinology and Metabolism, 59,* 328–337.

Reid, R. (1985). The endocrinology of premenstrual syndrome. In M. Y. Dawood, J. L. McGuire, & L. H. Demers (Eds.), *Premenstrual syndrome and dysmenorrhea* (pp. 51–66). Baltimore: Urban and Schwarzenberg.

Reid, R. L., & Yen, S. S. C. (1981). Premenstrual syndrome. *American Journal of Obstetrics and Gynecology, 139,* 85–104.

Reid, R. L., & Yen, S. S. C. (1983). The premenstrual syndrome. *Clinical Obstetrics and Gynecology, 26,* 710–718.

Rome, E. (1986). Premenstrual syndrome examined through a feminist lens. In V. L. Olesen & N. F. Woods (Eds.), *Culture, society, and menstruation* (pp. 145–151). Washington, DC: Hemisphere.

Ropert, J. F., Quigley, M. E., & Yen, S. S. C. (1981). Endogenous opiates modulate pulsatile luteinizing hormone release in humans. *Journal of Clinical Endocrinology and Metabolism, 52,* 583–585.

Ross, G. T., & Schreiber, J. R. (1986). The ovary. In S. S. C. Yen & R. Jaffe (Eds.), *Reproductive endocrinology* (pp. 115–139). Philadelphia: Saunders.

Rossmanith, W. G., & Yen, S. S. C. (1987). Sleep-associated decrease in luteinizing hormone pulse frequency during the early follicular phase of the menstrual cycle: Evidence for an opioidergic mechanism. *Journal of Clinical Endocrinology and Metabolism, 65,* 715–800.

Rubinow, D. R., & Roy-Byrne, R. (1984). Premenstrual syndromes: Overview from a methodologic perspective. *American Journal of Psychiatry, 141,* 163–172.

Sampson, G. A. (1979). Premenstrual syndrome: A double-blind controlled trial of progesterone and placebo. *British Journal of Psychiatry, 135,* 209–215.

Schildkraut, J. J. (1965). The catecholamine hypothesis of affective disorders. *American Journal of Psychiatry, 122,* 509–522.

Smith, S. L. (1975). Mood and the menstrual cycle. In J. Sachar (Ed.), *Topics in psychoendocrinology* (pp. 19–59). New York: Raven Press.

Soules, M. R., Steiner, R. A., Clifton, D. K., Cohen, N. L., Aksel, S., & Bremner, W. J. (1984). Progesterone modulation of pulsatile luteinizing hormone secretion in normal women. *Journal of Clinical Endocrinology and Metabolism, 58,* 378–383.

Steele, P. A., & Judd, S. J. (1986). Role of endogenous opioids in reducing the frequency of pulsatile LH secretion induced by progesterone in normal women. *Clinical Endocrinology, 25,* 669–674.

Switzer, E. (1983, October). Premenstrual syndrome: The return of the raging hormones. *Working Woman,* pp. 123–127.

Taylor, J. W. (1979). Plasma progesterone, oestradiol 17B and premenstrual symptoms. *Acta Psychiatrica Scandinavica, 60,* 76–86.

Vaitukaitis, J. L. (1984). Premenstrual syndrome. *New England Journal of Medicine, 311,* 1371–1373.

van der Meer, Y. G., Benedek-Jaszmann, L. J., & Van Loenan, A. C. (1983). Effect of high dose progesterone on the premenstrual syndrome: A double-blind crossover trial. *Journal of Psychosomatic Obstetrics and Gynaecology, 2,* 220–223.

Vargyas, J., Lobo, R., & Mishell, D. (1984). Brain opioid activity in the premenstrual syndrome. *Fertility and Sterility, 42,* 324.

Vrbicky, K. W., Baumstark, J. S., Wells, I. C., Hilgers, T. W., Kable, W. T., & Elias, C. J. (1982). Evidence for the involvement of beta-endorphin in the human menstrual cycle. *Fertility and Sterility, 38,* 701–704.

Wardlaw, S. L., Wehrenberg, W. B., Ferin, M., Antunes, J. L., & Frantz, A. G. (1982). Effect of sex steroids on beta-endorphins in hypophyseal portal blood. *Journal of Clinical Endocrinological Metabolism, 55,* 877.

Wehrenberg, W. B., Wardlaw, S. L., Frantz, A. G., & Ferin, M. (1982). Beta-endorphin in hypophyseal portal blood: Variations throughout the menstrual cycle. *Endocrinology, 111,* 879–881.

Whitehead, M. I., Siddle, N. C., Townsend, P. T., Lane, G., & King, R. J. (1981). The use of progestins and progesterone in the treatment of climacteric and post-menopausal symptoms. In C. W. Bardin, E. Milgram, & J. P. Mauvais-Jarvis (Eds.), *Progesterone and progestins* (pp. 277–294). New York: Raven Press.

Yen, S. S. C. (1980). Neuroendocrine regulation of the menstrual cycle. In D. T. Krieger & J. C. Hughes (Eds.), *Neuroendocrinology.* Sunderland, MA: Sinauer.

Yen, S. S. C. (1986). The human menstrual cycle. In S. S. C. Yen & R. B. Jaffe (Eds.), *Reproductive endocrinology* (2d ed., pp. 200–236). Philadelphia: Saunders.

PART TWO

Changes Over the Menstrual Cycle

Menstrual cycle researchers have been urged to look at changes across the menstrual cycle of "normal" women. Each study reported in this section evaluated women who had not been identified as having menstrual cycle problems. Frequently, the subjects were blind to the purpose of the study. The researchers sought to identify changes across the menstrual cycle in a variety of factors: the effect of environment and context on behavior and feelings, sexuality, cycle length variability, migraine headaches, and "perimenstrual changes."

LeFevre and her colleagues (chap. 8) employed a unique system to examine the relationships between psychological state, environment, and menstrual cycle phase during the course of everyday life, using an "on-the-spot" method of data collection. In this project, the ubiquitous pager (a beeper device) was used to signal subjects' data-collection activity at various times during the day. This interesting approach is carefully described and the results are judiciously interpreted (in light of the very small sample). The study presents an intriguing research paradigm which bears replication with larger samples.

The question of whether social context or menstrual cycle phase affects behavior is the focus of Hood's chapter (9). In a normal population, behavior changes were examined through direct observation of social interactions and compared with self-reports of moods and activities, along with menstrual cycle phase.

In the next two chapters, the topic of human sexuality is explored from diverse vantage points. Both authors grapple with the difficult issue of appropriate methodologies for studying human sexuality. Henrik and Sanders (chap. 10) examined daily sexual behavior and arousability in women by giving them a specific stimulus (descriptions of sexual activities), with the aim of assessing a pattern of sexual arousal across the menstrual cycle. Wallis and Englander-Golden (chap. 11) provide a comparative review of research methodologies and findings on human and non-human female primate sexuality. A direct cross-species interpretation between monkey and human is not intended. Rather, the author seeks to provide information with which researchers may create alternative frameworks for thinking about human sexuality research.

What is behind the differing menstrual cycle lengths among women, and the variability of cycle length within an individual woman? Eschewing the 28-day cycle as the actual "normal" cycle length for all women, Sanders and Reinisch (chap. 12) examined cycle length and relative variability in 78 women between the ages of 17 and 21 years. In particular, they wanted to know if psychological correlates existed in relation to these menstrual cycle parameters. Their results indicated that cycle length was related to trait (or physiological) parameters, while the relative variability of cycle length was related to state (or environmental) parameters.

Solbach's work (chap. 13) centers on the problem of migraine headaches and their temporal relationship to the menstrual cycle. It is an area of study that few researchers have pursued. Of particular interest is the indication that menstrual-related migraines are different and respond to therapy differently than do nonmenstrual-related migraines. Two studies of women with menstrual migraines are presented, one in which biofeedback was used and one in which drug therapy was implemented.

The final chapter in this section avoids a disease-entity paradigm and focuses instead on increasing our understanding of women's experiences of symptoms. Woods and her colleagues (chap. 14) elaborate a model for perimenstrual-symptoms research which links symptom experiences to social and cultural context. Their results are most interesting and are further enriched by the use of a large ($N=225$), multiethnic sample of Asian, black, white, Native American, and Hispanic women. Their work provides us with a much needed view of women from a health perspective.

8

Psychological and Social Behavior of Couples Over a Menstrual Cycle: "On-the-Spot" Sampling From Everyday Life

Judith LeFevre, Cynthia Hedricks, Ruth B. Church, and Martha McClintock

Some studies of the relationships between the menstrual cycle, psychological state, and behavior have not found an effect of menstrual cycle phase. One explanation for these negative findings is that factors other than the menstrual cycle also influence psychological state and behavior. For example, women's moods can be influenced by the different environments of everyday life as well as by the menstrual cycle phase (Dan, 1976; Koeske & Koeske, 1973). However, few studies have investigated the influence of the environment, perhaps because the complexity of everyday life precludes direct experimental control.

In our study, we investigated the relationships between psychological state, behavior, and the menstrual cycle as they occur in the course of everyday life. To sample psychological states and behavior in the different contexts in everyday life, we used an "on-the-spot" method of data collection. In this chapter presenting our "work in progress," we describe how this method has been used to date and illustrate its use with a preliminary analysis of the relative influence of the environment and menstrual cycle phase on the psychological state. We focus on two psychological states, mood and activation (a motivational variable), and two types of environment, the social context and location. We compare women with their male partners and also explore individual differences among women in response to the menstrual cycle.

Method

Subject Selection and Description
Study presentation. Knowing the purpose of a study can bias a subject's response, particularly when the menstrual cycle is being investigated (Ruble, 1977). Therefore, this study was presented as an investigation of

biological rhythms in couples. To maintain this general impression, comparable measures were taken from both couple members. At the end of the study, none of the subjects had detected a focus on the menstrual cycle.

Screening procedure. Nine couples expressed interest in the study in response to advertisements and word-of-mouth recruitment. Seven were selected after an initial screening to ensure that they were (a) between 20 and 35 years of age, when women have the most stable menstrual cycles (Treloar, Boynton, Behn, & Brown, 1967); (b) living together or married for at least one year, so that they had an established relationship; (c) childless and heterosexual, so that the family context and couple interactions were similar across subjects; (d) using birth control which did not alter endogenous hormonal cycles; and (e) in good physical and mental health, because health may independently affect psychological state and behavior. Furthermore, women were asked if they had regular menstrual cycles. One couple did not complete the study, leaving a final sample of six couples.

Assessing subject characteristics. Couples who met the screening criteria were scheduled for an initial interview used for assessing subject characteristics. During the interview, each member responded separately to both verbal and written questionnaires on personal history, life style, and health. Several standardized inventories were included to verify that the subjects were normal and to measure individual differences. Because personality can mediate menstrual cycle effects (Englander-Golden, Chang, Whitmore, & Dienstbier, 1980; Ruble, 1977), subjects were asked to complete the SCL-90 (a psychiatric rating scale; Derogatis, Lipman, & Covi, 1973). Furthermore, because couple interaction was a focus of the study, they were asked to complete the Spanier Dyadic Adjustment Scale (a measure of adjustment in couples who are married or living together; Spanier, 1976). All subjects were also asked to complete an Inventory of Stressful Life Events (a revised version of the Holmes-Rahe Schedule of Recent Experience; Holmes & Rahe, 1967), which assesses recent stressful events that might affect the subjects' current psychological state or behavior. Finally, women were asked to complete the Self-Rating Scale for Premenstrual Tension Syndrome (Steiner, Haskett, & Carroll, 1980), which required them to describe how their menstrual cycles affect their psychological and physical states, particularly during the premenstrual phase. This allowed us to assess a woman's expectation of menstrual cycle effects on psychological state and compare this expectation with changes that actually occurred during the menstrual cycle.

At the completion of the study, the subjects participated in a final interview. To provide reliability, they answered the same questionnaires that were given during the initial interview. We asked questions on sexual preference, sexual involvement with others beside the partner, and drug use. These questions were asked only in the final interview.

Subject characteristics. All 12 subjects were Caucasian and between 24 and 35 years of age, except for one man who was 36. Subjects were either working ($n=9$) or full-time students ($n=3$), and most had completed some graduate education ($n=8$). All of the couples had been living together for at least 2 years, and all but one were married.

In general, the subjects had scores within normal ranges on the SCL-90, the Spanier Dyadic Adjustment Scale, and the Inventory of Stressful Life Events. However, one couple had recently experienced the death of the husband's father. The husband had high ratings on psychiatric symptomatology (SCL-90), and the couple had low scores on marital adjustment. In addition, the wife in a second couple was having an extramarital affair, and this couple also had low scores on marital adjustment.

All of the subjects were in good physical health. None of the women had ever been pregnant, and all used birth control other than the pill or I.U.D. Their menstrual cycles were between 27 and 35 days long. In addition, all of the women had scores within the normal range on the Self-Rating Scale for Premenstrual Tension.

Although the women had normal scores on the Self-Rating Scale for Premenstrual Tension and the SCL-90, the variation in their scores could be used to assess sources of individual differences. For example, a woman's personal or cultural expectations of menstrual cycle effects (Englander-Golden et al., 1980; Ruble, 1977) or her personality (Englander-Golden, 1977; Kleinhauser, 1975) may influence her psychological state during the menstrual cycle.

Collecting "On-the-Spot" and Daily Data

Procedure. Psychological state, behavior, and physical symptoms were sampled in both partners in the couple for 30 consecutive days, to obtain data in all phases of the woman's menstrual cycle. The procedures for data collection were explained to the subjects during the initial interview. To increase the likelihood of independent responses in members of the couple, each partner was trained separately in the methods for data collection. Both partners were also asked not to discuss the study until it was completed and to mail their data to us daily to prevent the partner from seeing it.

Psychological state and behavior were sampled for 30 days with the Experience Sampling Method, an "on-the-spot" method of data collection (Larson & Csikszentmihalyi, 1983). Subjects carried electronic pagers and were paged randomly throughout the day. Immediately upon being paged, they completed a pager questionnaire which took 1–2 min to complete. In addition, subjects filled out daily questionnaires to record menstrual cycle information, physical symptoms, sexual behavior, and unusual events.

Subjects were paged three times a day, once during the morning, afternoon, and evening at randomly selected times; thus, they were asked to complete 90 pager questionnaires. Because we were concerned that the length of the study might affect the subjects' later responses, and thereby confound the interpretation of menstrual cycle effects, couples began the study during different phases of the menstrual cycle.

Compliance was excellent, although it decreased during the last week of data collection. Subjects completed most of the questionnaires ($M=88\%$). All but one couple said they would participate again in a similar study. Nonetheless, the study was demanding, and the results must be interpreted in light of potential biases due to the method.

Measures of psychological state and environment. The items on the pager questionnaire were used to measure subjects' psychological state and immediate environment at the moment they were paged. The questionnaire covered a variety of emotional, motivational, and cognitive states, including mood, sexuality, feelings about their partner, concentration, and sense of control. It also asked what the subject was doing and thinking about, to determine whether activity or thoughts covaried with menstrual cycle phase. To identify the context of the response, the questionnaire also asked who the subject was with and where she or he was.

Measures of menstrual cycle phase and physical symptoms. All subjects completed daily questionnaires which included items for identifying menstrual cycle phase and recording physical symptoms. To mask our interest in the menstrual cycle, both men and women were trained to measure their basal body temperature (BBT) and assess their physical symptoms (e.g., abdominal pain, nausea, hunger pangs, skin disorders, backaches, headaches, fatigue, etc.). Women were also trained in the Billings method for monitoring changes in cervical and vaginal secretions (Hilgers, Abraham, & Cavanagh, 1978; Hilgers & Bailey, 1980).

Preliminary Analysis

A brief report of our preliminary analysis of data collected to date follows to illustrate our use of the "on-the-spot" method. This particular analysis compared the effects of the environment and the woman's menstrual cycle phase on the psychological state of both members of a couple. Specifically, it focused on two psychological states, mood and activation (a motivational variable) and two types of environments, the social context and location.

Assessing Mood and Activation

Two aspects of psychological state were identified by factor analysis of items on the pager questionnaire: mood and activation. Although mood is frequently measured in studies of the menstrual cycle, activation or arousal is less commonly assessed. We measured *both* mood and activation to determine if the environment had different effects on different psychological states. Positive and negative mood and the degree of activation were assessed by responses to the scaled items that composed each factor. Table 1 lists the factor items. The means of the items were used for analysis.

Table 1.
Psychological State Factors

Factor			
Mood		Activation	
Happy	Sad	Active	Passive
Cheerful	Irritable	Alert	Drowsy
Elated	Depressed	Strong	Vulnerable
Friendly	Hostile	Outgoing	Withdrawn

Assessing Social Context and Location

To assess the effects of the environment on psychological state, we focused on two contexts: the social context and location. The social context of the subject at the time she or he was paged was determined from the response to the open-ended question, "Who were you with?" Similarly, the location of the subject was determined from the response to the question, "Where are you?" Later, each response was coded in terms of general categories for social context and location (see Table 2).

Table 2.
Environmental Context

Context
Social
Friends
Partner
Others (colleagues, coworkers, teachers, strangers, etc.)
Alone
Location
Public places (restaurants, stores, parks, museums, etc.)
Work (work or school)
Home

Assessing Menstrual Cycle Phase

The day of ovulation was estimated from the concordance of several measures: the thermal shift of a biphasic BBT, the presence of *Spinnbarkeit* in the cervical mucus, *Mittleschmertz*, and counting backwards from the onset of menses assuming a 14-day luteal phase (Hilgers et al., 1978; Hilgers

& Bailey, 1980). In all women, several of these measures could be used to estimate the day of ovulation.

After identifying the estimated day of ovulation and the onset of menstruation, menstrual cycles were divided into six phases: (a) Menses 1 (the first 3 days of menses when menstrual discomfort is highest (McCance, Luff, & Widowson, 1937); (b) Menses 2 (the remaining days of menses); (c) the follicular phase (the days between Menses 2 and the periovulatory phase); (d) the periovulatory phase (the estimated day of ovulation ± 1 day); (e) the luteal phase (the days between the periovulatory phase and the premenstrual phase); and (f) the premenstrual phase (the 3 days prior to menses).

Preliminary Results

In our preliminary analysis, we began to address questions such as these: What is the relative influence of the environment and menstrual cycle phase on the psychological state and behavior of women? Do they have a similar influence on the male partners? And finally, can individual variation in the strength of menstrual cycle effects be attributed to personality differences among women or to their personal expectations about their menstrual cycle? Because our sample size was very small ($N=6$ couples), we investigated these questions by identifying consistent patterns among our subjects (characteristic of $\geq 80\%$ of either women or men) and by testing for correlations. Thus, the following preliminary results need to be confirmed on a larger sample.

Influences on psychological state. The menstrual cycle had a detectable effect on both mood and activation in the course of everyday life. Women were happiest in the periovulatory and early menstrual phases, and their activation was lowest premenstrually. However, women's moods were affected less by the menstrual cycle or location than by variation in the social environment. Activation, on the other hand, was affected equally by the menstrual cycle and by variation in the social environment and location.

Men were as variable in their moods as women were. However, in contrast to their moods, men's activation varied more across different social environments and locations than it did in women. In addition, their activation varied with their partner's menstrual cycle; it was highest when their partners were premenstrual.

Individual differences. Half (3) of the women had a drop in mood premenstrually. Individual differences in the magnitude of premenstrual mood changes were better explained by personality than by personal expectations about the premenstrual phase. That is, women who were more generally depressed experienced a greater drop in mood premenstrually. On the other hand, women who expected premenstrual distress did not necessarily experience a drop in mood (Church, Marquette, Lefevre, Hedricks, & McClintock, 1986).

Summary

In this study we used an "on-the-spot" method of data collection, the Experience Sampling Method (ESM), to tap the psychological experiences of individuals at the moment that they occur during the menstrual cycle. Although this method has frequently been used to assess the effects of nonbiological factors such as social and physical context on psychological state, it has rarely been used to assess the effects of a biological factor, such as the menstrual cycle. Using this method, we found that the psychological states of both partners in a couple change as a function of the woman's menstrual cycle phase. Furthermore, psychological state changes even more as a function of the environment. Finally, individual differences in women's premenstrual psychological state are associated with personality differences, rather than expectations. Although these findings need to be replicated on a larger sample, they suggest that psychological state reflects the interaction of biology, the environmental context, and personality. The study methods also establish a research paradigm for the investigation of biological determinants of human behavior in the context of everyday life.

REFERENCES

Church, R. B., Marquette, L. D., LeFevre, J. A., Hedricks, C., & McClintock, M. K. (1986). Changes in psychological state during the human menstrual cycle. In F. Massimini & P. Inghilleri (Eds.), *The daily experience: Theory and method of analysis* (pp. 359–368). Milan, Italy: Franco Angeli s.r.l.

Dan, A. (1976). *Patterns of behavioral and mood variation in men and women: Variability and the menstrual cycle.* Unpublished doctoral dissertation, The University of Chicago.

Derogatis, L. R., Lipman, R. S., & Covi, L. (1973). SCL-90: An outpatient psychiatric rating scale—preliminary report. *Psychopharmacology Bulletin, 9,* 13–28.

Englander-Golden, P. (1977). *A longitudinal study of cyclical variations in mood and behavior as a function of repression.* Unpublished doctoral dissertation, University of Nebraska, Lincoln.

Englander-Golden, P., Chang, H., Whitmore, M. R., & Dienstbier, R. A. (1980). Female sexual arousal and the menstrual cycle. *Journal of Human Stress, 6,* 42–48.

Hilgers, T. W., Abraham, G. E., & Cavanagh, D. (1978). Natural family planning: I. The peak symptom and estimated time of ovulation. *Obstetrics and Gynecology, 52,* 575–582.

Hilgers, T. W., & Bailey, A. J. (1980). Natural family planning: II. Basal body temperature and estimated time of ovulation. *Obstetrics and Gynecology, 55,* 333–339.

Holmes, T. H., & Rahe, R. H. (1967). The Social Readjustment Rating Scale. *Journal of Psychosomatic Research, 11,* 213–218.

Kleinhauser, J. E. (1975). *The premenstrual syndrome and its correlation to personality characteristics.* Unpublished doctoral dissertation, University of South Dakota.

Koeske, R. K., & Koeske, G. F. (1973). An attributional approach to moods and the menstrual cycle. *Journal of Personality and Social Psychiatry, 31,* 473–478.

Larson, R. & Csikszentmihalyi, M. (1983). The experience sampling method. In H. T. Reis (Ed.), *Naturalistic approaches to studying social interaction: New directions for methodology of social and behavioral science* (pp. 41–56). San Francisco: Jossey-Bass.

McCance, R. A., Luff, M. C., & Widowson, E. E. (1937). Physical and emotional periodicities in women. *Journal of Hygiene, 37,* 571–605.

Ruble, D. N. (1977). Premenstrual symptoms: A reinterpretation. *Science, 197,* 291–292.

Spanier, G. B. (1976). Measuring dyadic adjustment: New scales for assessing the quality of marriage and similar dyads. *Journal of Marriage and the Family, 38,* 15–28.

Steiner, M., Haskett, R. F., & Carroll, B. J. (1980). Premenstrual tension syndrome: The development of research diagnostic criteria and new rating scales. *Acta Psychiatrica Scandinavica, 62,* 177–190.

Treloar, A. E., Boynton, R. E., Behn, B. G., & Brown, B. W. (1967). Variation of the human menstrual cycle through reproductive life. *International Journal of Fertility, 12,* 77–126.

9

Contextual Determinants of Menstrual Cycle Effects in Observations of Social Interactions

Kathryn E. Hood

The ovulatory cycle is the primary character that defines the female sex. Accordingly, the study of sex differences in social behavior includes a central focus on the behavioral changes that might be related to the cyclic pattern of menstrual phases. From the perspective of comparative developmental psychology, this relationship is important for understanding the social ecology of sex, the evolution of reproductive patterns, and the nature of sex differentiation in social development. There is another perspective, equally compelling, that frames this issue: the contemporary perspective of women's emancipation from the historical restrictions on female social roles. The possible existence of behavioral changes associated with the menstrual cycle has been viewed by some as a factor that limits women's choices in work, family, and personal expression. Whether this concern is well directed in social policy and practical decision making depends on a critical understanding of the methods of discovery and findings that are current in the field.

The study of self-reported changes in mood and activities during the menstrual cycle is well advanced (for example, see Abplanalp, Donnelly, & Rose, 1979; Mansfield, Hood, & Henderson, 1989; Parlee, 1982a; Rossi & Rossi, 1977; Udry & Morris, 1968; Wilcoxon, Schrader, & Sherif, 1976; for a review, see Logue & Moos, 1986), but only a few studies have directly assessed actual changes in behavior in nonclinical samples (see Alagna & Hamilton, 1986; Doty & Silverthorne, 1975; Morris & Udry, 1970) and even fewer have directly assessed social interactions (Sanders, 1978). This relative lack of evidence stands in sharp contrast to one focus of public speculation, which is about premenstrual changes in social behavior and interactional style.

This chapter presents a summary of some new research findings from the study of a normal or unselected sample. These findings bear on the central question of whether actual behavioral change occurs during the menstrual cycle. They are uniquely relevant because they are based on direct observations of social interactions, and because the study was designed to vary the demand characteristics of the social context of interactions, to take into account not simply whether there are cycle-related changes in social behavior, but also when and under what conditions these changes are likely to occur.

Models of Menstrual-Related Behavior Change

Clinical Origins and Scientific Status

The early conception of perimenstrual impairment or disability, derived from clinical research, is now reified in an appendix of the *Diagnostic and Statistical Manual of Mental Disorders* (DSM III-R) as Late Luteal Phase Dysphoric Disorder (American Psychiatric Association, 1987). The recently proposed establishment of this diagnostic clinical syndrome was accompanied by considerable controversy. It was opposed by the Association for Women in Psychology (Chrisler, 1986) and by high-achieving professionals who regard it as potentially discriminatory, and as an ill-formulated account of women's abilities (for example, New York District Attorney Elizabeth Holtzman, 1984). It was questioned by scientists who find the temporal definition of the syndrome and the lack of clearly specified symptomatic content to be problematic (Abplanalp, 1983; Janowsky & Rausch, 1985; Parlee, 1973, 1982b; Rubinow & Roy-Byrne, 1984; for a general methodological critique, see Koeske, 1983). However, it was welcomed by clinical practitioners as a guide for the psychotherapeutic and pharmacological interventions implemented to relieve the persistent suffering of their clients.

The ongoing and lively debate about the scientific status of this exclusively female disorder reflects a research literature marked by inconsistent findings. Underlying various views in the PMS debate is a theoretical divide, well expressed in the critiques of Parlee (1973, 1982b; also see Brooks-Gunn, 1986). Much of the clinical research in menstrual-behavior change has been problem oriented, focused on psychopathology, and often formulated within a medical model of hormone-mediated effects.

An Energy Model of the Menstrual Cycle in Context

Scientists interested in normative development have proposed a biopsychosocial model of menstrual-behavior relationships that includes the interaction of different levels of factors, societal values, self-attributions, immediate context, and expectations about future life circumstances (AuBuchon & Calhoun, 1985; Berdy, 1979; Brooks-Gunn, 1986; Koeske & Koeske, 1975; Olasov & Jackson, 1987; Rodin, 1976; also see the "Menstrual Joy Questionnaire" in Delaney, Lupton, & Toth, 1976). Figure 1 portrays such a model, with only one such factor included: social context.

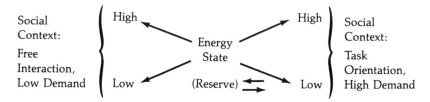

Figure 1. An energy model of context effects. In the context of unstructured free interaction, individuals in a low-energy state may be less active than individuals in a high-energy state. In the context of a task orientation, individuals in a low-energy state may compensate by calling up energy reserves.

The basic assumption of this partial model is that the changes produced by menstrual cycle phase shifts are essentially changes in energy state or arousal: high or low, in this simple version. These changes in energy state are proposed to be affectively neutral; depending on the context, one can be distressed in a high-energy state or in a low-energy state, and one can be happy in either state (e.g., Schachter & Singer, 1962). The physiological changes that occur during the menstrual cycle significantly alter basic energy functions such as carbohydrate metabolism, and iron availability for hemoglobin-based oxygen transport in blood (Southam & Gonzaga, 1965).

Which energy states are associated with which menstrual cycle phases? Part of the answer to this question may come from a sensitivity to the phenomenology of presenting symptoms in menstrual-related experiences: for example, distinguishing agitated or irritable depression (high energy) from lethargic depression (low energy), distinguishing problems in concentration due to unorganized and distractible activity (high energy) from problems due to lack of initiative (low energy). The late premenstrual phase may be associated with a high-energy state, perhaps mediated by decreased levels of progesterone. (Progesterone is a mild tranquilizer, and at pharmacological levels, a hypnotic agent; see the references in Lahmeyer, Miller, & DeLeon-Jones, 1982; Rausch & Janowsky, 1982.) This late premenstrual high-energy state may be positive (elation, extraversion, productivity) or it may be negative (agitation, irritability, distractibility), depending on the current circumstances and personal history of each individual. Several research reports concur in finding enhanced energy among some women in the late premenstrual phase (Alagna & Hamilton, 1986; Backstrom et al., 1983; Moos & Leiderman, 1978; Parlee, 1982a) and decreased energy in the period of menstruation (e.g., Abplanalp et al., 1979).

The focus on social context in this partial model represents the main research issue in this investigation: the effects of social context on menstrual-behavior changes in a nonclinical sample. Most notably, there is in the model a central energy state, which may vary with menstrual cycle phases, in some individuals, in some cycles; also, there is an additional "energy reserve," which may be drawn upon under demand or stress. This theoretical construct bears some relationship to the physical substrate of energy metabolism (e.g., the quick energy burst available from anaerobic glycolysis), but it is meant to refer also to more general psychological energy, concentration, or social interest/extraversion. This notion may be useful as a heuristic in beginning to analyze the complex of factors that influence social interactions.

Observations of Social Interactions During the Menstrual Cycle in Two Contexts

In comparative research on the ovulatory cycle and aggressive behavior, female rodents show increased attacks on other females when in the postovulatory phase of low circulating progesterone (Hood, 1984, 1985). To assess the generality of this finding across species, a prospective longitudinal observational study of female college students was implemented in a setting which was designed to first allow unstructured social interaction, and then to provoke active social participation in an intellectual discussion (Hood, 1986).

To provide a context in which aggressive or assertive behavior might be appropriate, discussion sessions were organized to call forth the subjects' own opinions on controversial topics. Each subject first completed an opinion questionnaire containing items like these: "In our country, the sentences handed out to criminals are usually too light. . . . Teenagers should be allowed to decide most things for themselves. . . . There will always be wars, no matter how hard people try to prevent them. . . . It is insulting to women to have the 'obey' clause remain in the marriage ceremony." These items were then presented for discussion during the weekly meetings. For each meeting, the experimenter chose three topics for discussion so that each subject disagreed with the other 2 in the group for one topic, which is called the "challenge" topic for that subject. Subjects were instructed to "discuss their own opinions and feelings about the topic, to discuss the underlying issues, and why people might agree or disagree about this topic."

Subjects were all students in an introductory psychology course, and earned credit for participation in research. No subject was on medication. To avoid bias, subjects were not informed about the purpose of this study (AuBuchon & Calhoun, 1985; Englander-Golden, Whitmore, & Dienstbier, 1978; Koeske, 1980; Ruble, 1977); they were told that the study assessed health and mood states.

The study used a short-term longitudinal design with four videotaped weekly meetings for each subject. Each of the 10 discussion groups had the same 3 participants at each meeting; the 3 were relatively unfamiliar to each other. At each 30-min meeting, the 3 subjects were asked to wait in the meeting room for 5 min; this was designated the "free interaction" period. They were then asked to discuss one topic. Discussion was terminated by the subjects, or by the experimenter if it exceeded 5 min. The second topic was introduced for discussion, and after that topic was completed, a third topic was presented. In this manner each subject received one challenge topic for discussion at each of the four weekly meetings.

The menstrual cycle stage of 28 regularly cycling subjects was determined in a separate procedure. All subjects returned a daily questionnaire during this 40-day period. This self-report form contained 14 items about moods and activities, along with five health-related questions, including the question, "Did you have menstrual flow today?" The self-report forms were collected daily by the experimenter. Assignment to menstrual cycle stages was based on a 28-day scheme (Figure 2). With the first day of

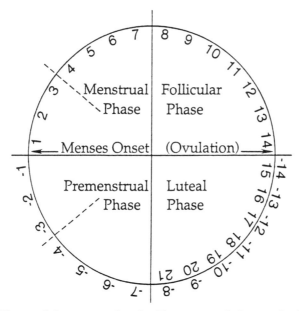

Figure 2. Phases of the menstrual cycle. The menstrual phase is the first 3 days of menstrual flow. Premenstrual I is the 3 days preceding menses onset. Premenstrual II is the 4 days preceding the Premenstrual I phase, and is considered separately from the Premenstrual I phase. The "midcycle" includes both the follicular and the luteal phases.

reported menstrual flow counted as Day 1, the menstrual stage included Days 1 to 3, the follicular stage Days 8 to 14, and the luteal stage Days 15 to 21. If one counted backward from Day 1, the luteal stage included Days –8 to –14, and the premenstrual stage I included Days –1 to –3. Additional analyses were carried out with the menstrual stage defined as Days 1 to 7, and with the premenstrual stage II defined as Days –4 to –7. These daily self-reports, along with retrospective self-reports and responses to the Moos Menstrual Distress Questionnaire (collected at the end of the experiment), are currently being analyzed, and will be compared with behaviors observed during these described menstrual cycle stages (Hood, 1986).

Videotapes of interactions during the meetings were coded in three different methods, with one method focused on content analysis, one method focused on social participation style, and one including only nonverbal behavior. All coding was carried out by observers blind to the menstrual cycle phase of subjects. For all three coding schemes, interrater agreement was acceptable ($r = .80$ to $.90$).

Changes in Assertive Statements

The popular conception of menstrual changes in social behavior is that women are more irritable, more aroused, or more assertive during the premenstrual phase. To test this hypothesis, it was proposed that in the premenstrual stage more than in the follicular stage, women would assert her own position during discussions of their challenge topic (the topic on which they disagreed with the two other group members). During the discussion of each subject's challenge topic, statements by that subject were coded as congruent with her own position, or alternatively, as incongruent, irrelevant, neutral, or uncategorizable. The results of analysis of variance (ANOVA), with repeated measures for individuals (28 levels) and menstrual cycle stage (4 levels) as factors, showed no change in assertiveness, as measured by the frequency of stating one's own opinion during discussions of each person's four challenge topics.

Changes in Participation Style

The second hypothesis tested was that subjects' style of participation in intellectual social tasks would change during the menstrual cycle. Each statement or verbal turn by each subject was classified as either assertive-style participation or as responsive-style participation. Assertive participation included these behaviors: initiate a discussion, disagree with someone, request information, assert an opinion, or share a personal story. Responsive participation included these behaviors: agree with someone, and respond to someone. A multivariate ANOVA indicates that there was no effect of menstrual cycle stage on the frequency of assertive and responsive participation during the challenge question. However, when the period of unstructured or free interaction (the 5-min period which began each meeting) was considered separately, there was a significant cycle effect, and it was not a premenstrual change. Rather, it was a menstrual phase effect; the frequency of assertive participation during the menstrual phase was lower than during the midcycle phase (follicular plus luteal, i.e., Days 8–21). The frequency of assertive participation during the premenstrual phase was not different from the midcycle phase. Responsive participation showed no change during the free-interaction period.

Changes in Nonverbal Behavior

In the third set of behavioral analyses, the duration of several nonverbal acts was coded during the free interaction and challenge topic periods, and two a priori dependent measures were formed: a measure of positive social interest (the sum of scores for smile, nod, and seating position, with scores for look-away, arms-folded, and legs-crossed subtracted) and an activity measure (the sum of self-manipulation, arm movement, leg movement, and foot movement). For the social interest scores, ANOVAS for menstrual cycle phase showed no cycle effects and no context effects. For the activity scores, the outcomes were quite differentiated: Mean activity scores were elevated during the challenge topic periods, compared with the free interaction periods, with significantly higher activity in the luteal and premenstrual phases than in the follicular phase. The effects of the relatively demanding social context were found, not in social behaviors, but rather in nonspecific movement patterns, which increased, particularly in the postovulatory phases of the cycle. In this case, the effect of social context was reversed: Menstrual phase effects were found under the high demand condition, and not in the unstructured period of low demand.

Testing Models of Menstrual-Related Change

The expectation that premenstrual behavior changes would resemble PMS, with increased assertive statements, assertive-style interactions, and nonverbal signs of social withdrawal, was not met (Table 1). The expectations derived from a neutral energy-change model (Figure 1), that the premenstrual phase would include increased assertive statements, assertive-style interactions, responsive-style interactions, and increased nonverbal positive social interest and activity, were only weakly met. Assertive-style participation was decreased during menses, a hypothetical low-energy state. Nonverbal activity was high during the premenstrual phase, but also high during the luteal phase. This finding addressed one aspect of the proposed energy model: that the premenstrual period is a relatively high energy state. The interpretation of the elevated activity score in the luteal

Table 1.
*Contextual Determinants of Menstrual Cycle Effects in Observations
of Social Interactions*

	Outcome by context	
Observed behaviors	Free interaction	Task orientation
Assertive style	Menstrual phase < midcycle	No change
Responsive style	No change	No change
Efficacy		No change
Nonverbal-social	No change	No change
Nonverbal-activity	No change	Luteal > follicular
		Premenstrual > follicular

Note. Midcycle = Days 8–14 (follicular phase) plus Days 15–21 (luteal phase).

phase was more problematic. Because progesterone levels are high during the luteal phase, this finding seemed to preclude a simple model of progesterone-mediated behavioral inhibition. Finally, the expectation that menstrual-behavioral changes depend on characteristics of the social context was met. When behavioral changes were found, they were context specific. The demanding social context of controversial discussions may be construed as having two effects in interaction with cycle phase: (a) elevating assertive-style participation by subjects in a low-energy state (menstrual phase) by stimulating subjects to draw on their hypothetical energy reserves, and (b) amplifying the expression of raw, undirected, nonverbal energy of subjects already in a high-energy state (luteal and premenstrual phase).

Changes in Daily Self-Reports and Contextual Analysis

The preliminary analyses of subjects' concurrent daily self-reports offered an intriguing counterpoint to the behavioral findings (Hood, 1986). In brief, these 7-point rating scales include a complex of items that might be elevated in the premenstrual phase if impairment from PMS is evident: feeling aggressive, sad, having difficulty in coping, and in concentrating, as well as items that might be low, such as feeling physically well, capable, friendly, happy. One neutral item was analyzed: feeling active. In preliminary analyses, only two items showed significant effects of menstrual phase: coping, and feeling physically well. However, these effects were in the opposite direction to that predicted by a PMS-impairment hypothesis: Subjects found it *easier* to cope in premenstrual phase II (Days –4 to –7), and showed no difference from the follicular phase in premenstrual phase I (Days –1 to –3). Subjects felt *more* physically well in premenstrual phase I than in the follicular phase.

The patterns of self-reports of mood states reported here replicated those found in several other investigations. These include no psychological change over the cycle (Lahmeyer et al., 1982; Mansfield et al., 1989; Sanders, Warner, Backstrom, & Bancroft, 1983; Slade, 1984), no PMS-like change (Abplanalp et al., 1979), and finding of a "premenstrual elation syndrome" (Parlee, 1982a), perhaps a state similar to our subjects' reports of feeling physically more well and finding it "easier to cope" in the premenstrual phase (also see Endicott, Halbreich, Schact, & Nee, 1981; Rossi & Rossi, 1977).

The daily self-report scales were also set in the context of what Rossi and Rossi (1977) call "social time" — the effect of day of the week as social context. Our results mirrored their report in that the power of social context effects far exceeds the power of menstrual cycle effects (what they call "body time"). The day-of-the-week effect was significant for 10 of the 13 items in a repeated measures ANOVA. When day of the week was entered as a covariate, there was no significant menstrual cycle effect. This pattern of results suggests a strong interaction, with some subjects more sensitive to both day-of-the-week and menstrual cycle effects.

Changes in Retrospective Self-Reports and Contextual Analysis
One other aspect of the study describes the effects of another contextual determinant of menstrual cycle effects. To show the influence on retrospective self-reports of the social structure of the context, two kinds of retrospective self-reports were collected at the end of the study period. First, one was collected based on naive subjects' recollected experiences of the weeks around an event from the public domain, a socially salient basketball game. One week later, a retrospective account was collected based on a private, salient event, the onset of menses. In each case, the same 14-item questionnaire was used, and subjects were asked to report how they felt the week before the event, the week of the event, and the week after the event. The comparison of daily self-reports with these two types of retrospective reports may provide insight on the effects of the two different contexts for retrospection about the same time period.

In a first examination of the retrospective data, self-reports of "feeling aggressive" during the weeks around menses showed a PMS-like pattern: significantly higher levels in the premenstrual week. However, no corresponding effect was found in the daily scores of "feeling aggressive" in naive subjects, and no corresponding behavior change was noted in the weekly observations of social interactions. This suggests that the context of recollection helps to organize the contents of that recollection, yielding information specific to a certain emotional or cognitive set, for example, about PMS, or about previous menstrual cycle experiences.

Changes — Yes, But Not Premenstrual Syndrome
The results of this investigation demonstrated that social context is a

critical determinant of menstrual cycle effects. There is no effect of menstrual phase on social behavior when the context demands a task orientation. On the other hand, when the context is unstructured, with no task defined, then menstrual cycle effects do become evident, during, not before, the period of menstruation. The finding of context-dependent effects suggests an extension of the prevailing model of biological determinants of behavioral change. By expanding the model to include an array of social, cognitive, attitudinal, interactional, and developmental factors in menstrual cycle reseach, theory will progressively approach the goal of "lifting the curse of menstruation" (Golub, 1983), embracing and respecting the complexity of social exchange.

Why no evidence for late luteal phase dysphoric disorder, or premenstrual syndrome, in these behavior samples? The women were young (18 to 22 years), they were not a clinical sample (by design), they were assessed in interactions with relatively unfamiliar peers in a semi-public setting (again by design), and the analysis included only one cycle. Any of these factors might explain the lack of a premenstrual change. However, these findings do represent an examination of the prevalence of PMS in a normal sample of women, in a context designed to simulate a school or work setting. Behaviors in intimate relationships, at home, or in long-term stressful contexts may present a different pattern of menstrual-behavior change. However that turns out, it remains that private-domain phenomena may not predict public-domain behavior. To understand social behavior in the public domain, at school and at work, the best approach is to study that domain directly.

The study of social-contextual influences has been fruitful in a variety of approaches to the study of human development, in areas as diverse as child development and individual temperament in different family contexts (Thomas, Chess, Sillan, & Mendez, 1974), dating patterns and pubertal development in ballet dancers (Gargiulo, Attie, Brooks-Gunn, & Warren, 1987), sex differences in social and aggressive behaviors (Eagly & Steffen, 1986; Frodi, Maccaulay, & Thome, 1977; LaNouie & Curtis, 1985), family work-parenting adaptations (Crouter, Perry-Jenkins, Huston, & McHale, 1987), and in the larger social context, chronic ecologic stress in particular neighborhoods and in women's lives (Caspi, Bolger, & Eckenrode, 1987). Furthermore, when stressful life events are considered in relation to menstrual cycle phase effects, they are relatively more powerful in accounting for negative mood states (Abplanalp et al., 1979; Wilcoxon et al., 1976; Woods, Dery, & Most, 1982; on this score, also see Purifoy & Koopmans, 1980; Sanders et al., 1983; Sherif, 1980). These investigations share a theoretical perspective of developmental contextualism (Bronfenbrenner & Crouter, 1983; Lerner, 1985, 1989; Lerner, Skinner, & Sorrell, 1980) that can substantially inform the study of biological/

psychological/social factors interwoven in multiple levels of interactions. Striving for a biopsychosocial synthesis can stimulate new perspectives on theory, sometimes even setting dogma on its head (for example, Petersen & Hood, 1988).

These research areas directly address some of the challenges faced by women in the public domain. Although menstrual-related psychological changes may represent a legitimate health care issue for some women, some of the time (see Hart, Coleman, & Russell, 1987), there is little evidence that women typically suffer in public performance because of private physiological factors. Women are equally capable in task-related social interaction and problem solving at any stage of the menstrual cycle (also see Graham & Glasser, 1985; Sommer, 1982). This reinterpretation of menstrual cycle effects offers a sharp contrast to the persuasive advertising that, under the bold heading, "Now they'll have to come up with a new reason to keep us out of the White House," advises women to medicate themselves so that "the irritability and the body aches that come the week before your period . . . should not prevent a woman from being as responsible, reasonable, or emotionally capable as she is the rest of the month. . . . Premenstrual tension is not a political problem, it is a physical one." In this scenario, not only is the personal political, but the physical is political, too. To imagine any universal limits imposed by female physiology is premature. Placing the issue of menstrual cycle effects on behavior in an appropriate context may help to ensure the goal of full participation by all citizens in the body politic.

NOTE

This research was funded by a postdoctoral fellowship from NICHD (F32-HD06348) during which Robert B. Cairns, at the University of North Carolina at Chapel Hill, gave generous advice and support; by an NIH Biomedical Research Support Grant (RR07082-20); and by an Interdisciplinary Research Grant from the College of Health and Human Development, The Pennsylvania State University.

REFERENCES

Abplanalp, J. M. (1983). Psychologic components of the premenstrual syndrome. *Journal of Reproductive Medicine, 28,* 517–524.

Abplanalp, J. J., Donnelly, B. A., & Rose, R. M. (1979). Psychoendocrinology of the menstrual cycle: I. Enjoyment of daily activities and moods. *Psychosomatic Medicine, 41,* 587–604.

Alagna, S. W., & Hamilton, J. A. (1986). Social stimulus perception and self-evaluation: Effects of menstrual cycle phase. *Psychology of Women Quarterly, 10,* 327–338.

American Psychiatric Association. (1987). *Diagnostic and statistical manual of mental disorders* (3d ed., rev.). Washington, DC: Author.

AuBuchon, P. B., & Calhoun, K. S. (1985). Menstrual cycle symptomatology: The role of social expectancy and experimental demand characteristics. *Psychosomatic Medicine, 47,* 35–45.

Backstrom, T., Sanders, D., Leask, R., Davidson, D., Warner, P., & Bancroft, J. (1983). Mood, sexuality, hormones, and the menstrual cycle: II. Hormone levels and their relationship to the premenstrual syndrome. *Psychosomatic Medicine, 45,* 503–507.

Berdy, M. (1979). *Towards an attributional theory of menstrual distress.* Unpublished doctoral dissertation, Temple University, Philadelphia, PA.

Bronfenbrenner, U., & Crouter, A. C. (1983). The evolution of environmental models in developmental research. In P. H. Mussen (Ed.), *Handbook of child psychology* (Vol. 1, pp. 357–414). New York: Wiley.

Brooks-Gunn, J. (1986). Differentiating premenstrual symptoms and syndromes. *Psychosomatic Medicine, 48,* 385–387.

Caspi, A., Bolger, N., & Eckenrode, J. (1987). Linking person and context in the daily stress process. *Journal of Personality and Social Psychology, 52,* 184–195.

Chrisler, J. C. (1986, May). [Letter to the editor]. *APA Monitor.*

Crouter, A. C., Perry-Jenkins, M., Huston, T. L., & McHale, S. M. (1987). Processes underlying father involvement in dual-earner and single-earner families. *Developmental Psychology, 23,* 431–440.

Delaney, J., Lupton, M. J., & Toth, E. (1976). *The curse: A cultural history of menstruation.* New York: Signet. [Rev. ed., Urbana: University of Illinois Press, 1988]

Doty, R., & Silverthorne, C. (1975). Influence of menstrual cycles on volunteering behavior. *Nature, 254,* 139–140.

Eagly, A. H., & Steffen, V. J. (1986). Gender and aggressive behavior: A meta-analytic review of the social psychological literature. *Psychological Bulletin, 100,* 309–330.

Endicott, J., Halbreich, U., Schact, S., & Nee, J. (1981). Premenstrual changes and affective disorders. *Psychosomatic Medicine, 43,* 519–530.

Englander-Golden, P., Whitmore, M. R., & Dienstbier, R. A. (1978). Menstrual cycle as focus of study and self-reports of moods and behaviors. *Motivation and Emotion, 2,* 75–86.

Frodi, A., Maccaulay, J., & Thome, P. R. (1977). Are women always less aggressive than men? A review of the experimental literature. *Psychological Bulletin, 84,* 634–660.

Gargiulo, I., Attie, I., Brooks-Gunn, J., & Warren, M. P. (1987). Girls' dating behavior as a function of social context and maturation. *Developmental Psychology, 23,* 730–737.

Golub, S. (1983). *Lifting the curse of menstruation: A feminist appraisal of the influence of menstruation on women's lives.* New York: Haworth Press.

Graham, E. A., & Glasser, M. G. (1985). Relationship of pregnanediol level to behavior and mood. *Psychosomatic Medicine, 47,* 26–34.

Hart, W. G., Coleman, G. J., & Russell, J. W. (1987). Assessment of premenstrual symptomatology: A re-evaluation of the predictive validity of self-report. *Journal of Psychosomatic Research, 31*, 185-190.

Holtzman, E. (1984, October). *Premenstrual changes as a legal defense.* Paper presented at the conference, Premenstrual Syndrome: New Findings and Controversies, Mt. Sinai School of Medicine, City University of New York.

Hood, K. E. (1984). Aggression among female rats during the estrus cycle. In K. J. Flanelly, R. J. Blanchard, & D. C. Blanchard (Eds.), *Biological perspectives on aggression.* New York: Allan Liss.

Hood, K. E. (1985, June). *Patterns of aggression among female mice during the estrus cycle.* Paper presented at the annual meeting of the Animal Behavior Society, Raleigh, NC.

Hood, K. E. (1986, July). *Human aggressive and assertive behavior changes during the menstrual cycle.* Paper presented at the biennial meeting of the International Society for Research on Aggression, Chicago, IL.

Janowsky, D. S., & Rausch, J. (1985). Biochemical hypotheses of premenstrual tension syndrome. *Psychological Medicine, 15*, 3-8.

Koeske, R. D. (1980). Theoretical perspectives for menstrual cycle research: The relevance of attributional approaches for the perception and explanation of premenstrual emotionality. In A. Dan, E. Graham, & C. Beecher (Eds.), *The menstrual cycle: A synthesis of interdisciplinary research* (pp. 8-25). New York: Springer.

Koeske, R. D. (1983). Lifting the curse of menstruation: Toward a feminist perspective on the menstrual cycle. In S. Golub (Ed.), *Lifting the curse of menstruation: A feminist appraisal of the influence of menstruation in women's lives* (pp. 1-16). New York: Haworth Press.

Koeske, R. D., & Koeske, G. (1975). An attributional approach to moods and the menstrual cycle. *Journal of Personality and Social Psychology, 31*, 473-478.

Lahmeyer, H. W., Miller, M., & DeLeon-Jones, F. (1982). Anxiety and mood fluctuation during the normal menstrual cycle. *Psychosomatic Medicine, 44*, 183-194.

LaNouie, J. B., & Curtis, R. C. (1985). Improving women's performance in mixed-sex situations by effort attributions. *Psychology of Women Quarterly, 9*, 337-356.

Lerner, R. M. (1985). Individual and context in developmental psychology: Conceptual and theoretical issues. In J. R. Nesselroade & A. von Eye (Eds.), *Individual development and social change: Explanatory analyses* (pp. 155-187). New York: Academic Press.

Lerner, R. M. (1989). Developmental contextualism and the life-span view of person-context interaction. In M. Bornstein & J. S. Bruner (Eds.), *Interaction in human development* (pp. 217-239). Hillsdale, NJ: Erlbaum.

Lerner, R. M., Skinner, E. A., & Sorrell, G. T. (1980). Methodological implications of contextual/dialectic theories of development. *Human Development, 23*, 225-235.

Logue, C. M., & Moos, R. H. (1986). Perimenstrual symptoms: Prevalence and risk factors. *Psychosomatic Medicine, 48*, 388-414.

Mansfield, P. K., Hood, K. E., & Henderson, J. (1989). Women and their husbands: Mood and arousal fluctuations across the menstrual cycle and days of the week. *Psychosomatic Medicine, 51,* 66–80.

Moos, R. H., & Leiderman, N. B. (1978). Toward a menstrual cycle symptom typology. *Journal of Psychosomatic Research, 22,* 31–40.

Morris, N. M., & Udry, J. R. (1970). Variations in pedometer activity during the menstrual cycle. *Obstetrics and Gynecology, 35,* 199–201.

Olasov, B., & Jackson, J. (1987). Effects of expectancies on women's reports of moods during the menstrual cycle. *Psychosomatic Medicine, 49,* 65–78.

Parlee, M. B. (1973). The premenstrual syndrome. *Psychological Bulletin, 80,* 454–465.

Parlee, M. B. (1982a). Changes in mood and activation levels during the menstrual cycle in experimentally naive subjects. *Psychology of Women Quarterly, 7,* 119–131.

Parlee, M. B. (1982b). The psychology of the menstrual cycle: Biological and psychological perspectives. In R. C. Freeman (Ed.), *Behavior and the menstrual cycle* (pp. 77–100). New York: Dekker.

Petersen, A. C., & Hood, K. E. (1988). The role of experience in cognitive performance and brain development. In G. M. Vroman, D. Burnham, S. G. Gordon, & E. Tobach (Eds.), *Genes and gender V: Women at work: Socialization toward inequality* (pp. 52–77). New York: Gordian.

Purifoy, F. E., & Koopmans, L. H. (1980). Androstenedione, testosterone, and free testosterone concentration in women of various occupations. *Social Biology, 26,* 179–188.

Rausch, J. L., & Janowsky, D. S. (1982). Premenstrual tension: Etiology. In R. C. Freeman (Ed.), *Behavior and the menstrual cycle* (pp. 397–427). New York: Dekker.

Rodin, J. (1976). Menstruation, reattribution, and competence. *Journal of Personality and Social Psychology, 33,* 345–353.

Rossi, A. S., & Rossi, P. E. (1977). Body time and social time: Mood patterns by menstrual cycle phase and day of week. *Social Science Research, 6,* 273–308. [Reprinted in J. E. Parsons (Ed.), *The psychobiology of sex differences and sex roles,* 1980, New York: McGraw-Hill.]

Rubinow, D. R., & Roy-Byrne, P. (1984). Premenstrual syndromes: Overview from a methodologic perspective. *American Journal of Psychiatry, 41,* 163–172.

Ruble, D. N. (1977). Premenstrual syndromes: A reinterpretation. *Science, 197,* 291–292.

Sanders, D., Warner, P., Backstrom, T., and Bancroft, J. (1983). Mood, sexuality, hormones, and the menstrual cycle. I. Changes in mood and physical state: Description of subjects and method. *Psychosomatic Medicine, 45,* 487–581.

Sanders, J. J. (1978). Relation of personal space to the human menstrual cycle. *Journal of Psychology, 100,* 275–278.

Schachter, S., & Singer, J. E. (1962). Cognitive, social, and physiological determinants of emotional state. *Psychological Review, 64,* 379–399.

Sherif, C. (1980). A social psychological perspective on the menstrual cycle. In J. E. Parsons (Ed.), *The psychobiology of sex differences and sex roles* (pp. 245–268). New York: McGraw-Hill.

Slade, P. (1984). Premenstrual emotional changes in normal women: Fact or fiction? *Journal of Psychosomatic Research, 28,* 1–7.

Sommer, B. (1982). Cognitive behavior and the menstrual cycle. In R. C. Friedman (Ed.), *Behavior and the menstrual cycle* (pp. 101–127). New York: Dekker.

Southam, A. L., & Gonzaga, F. P. (1965). Systemic changes during the menstrual cycle. *American Journal of Obstetrics and Gynecology, 91,* 142–165.

Thomas, A., Chess, S., Sillan, J., & Mendez, O. (1974). Cross-cultural study of behavior in children with special vulnerabilities to stress. In D. F. Ricks, A. Thomas, & M. Roff (Eds.), *Life history research in psychopathology* (pp. 53–67). Minneapolis: University of Minnesota Press.

Udry, J. R., & Morris, N. M. (1968). Distribution of coitus in the menstrual cycle. *Nature, 220,* 593–596.

Wilcoxon, L. A., Schrader, S. J., & Sherif, C. W. (1976). Daily self-reports on activities, life-events, moods, and somatic changes during the menstrual cycle. *Psychosomatic Medicine, 38,* 399–417.

Woods, N. F., Dery, E. K., & Most, A. (1982). Stressful life events and perimenstrual symptoms. *Journal of Human Stress, 8,* 23–31.

10

Sexual Arousability During the Menstrual Cycle in Response to Daily Sexual Stimuli

Elizabeth Henrik and Susan Sanders

The relation between female sexual motivation and the hormonal events of the menstrual cycle has so far escaped our understanding. This chapter begins by presenting some of the contradictory findings in this area and shows how they may have stemmed from various methodological weaknesses. Preliminary data are then presented from a project designed to reexamine the issue of women's sexual arousal during the menstrual cycle on the basis of a more precise methodology. We intend to show that this methodology, addressed here to research on sexual behavior and arousal, is equally relevant to other areas of research on the menstrual cycle, in particular to research on the premenstrual syndrome.

The understanding of how endocrine factors may influence women's sexual motivation has interested researchers since the early part of this century (Cavanagh, 1969). However, only during the past two decades has extensive experimental literature been accumulated on the topic. Evidence now seems to indicate that overall blood plasma levels of estrogen and androgen affect, to some extent, the sexual responding both of normally cycling women and of women who receive gonadal steroids (Dennerstein, Burrows, Wood, & Hyman, 1980; Persky, Lief, Strauss, Miller, & O'Brien, 1978; Schreiner-Engel, Schiave, Smith, & White, 1981; Sherwin, Gelfand, & Brender, 1985). In general, estrogen and androgen have been linked to an increase in sexual responding and progesterone to a decrease in responding. The research for a cyclic control of sexual motivation by gonadal steroids of the menstrual cycle, however, has not borne fruit or produced unequivocal results. The findings of numerous studies have varied enormously and, in general, have conflicted with one another. In such studies, it was hypothesized that increased sexual activity will occur when estrogen and androgen levels are high, around the time of ovulation. Conversely, a decrease in responding is expected to occur when progesterone levels are high, during the luteal phase (Morris & Udry, 1971; Udry & Morris, 1968, 1970). Thus, one would predict that in women who do not use contraceptive pills, levels of sexual behaviors and arousal would fluctuate according to cyclic fluctuations in hormone levels, whereas behavioral fluctuations would be absent in women whose cycles are regulated by the high doses of estrogen and progesterone found in oral contraceptives. These hypotheses were tested by examining the sexual behavior of normally cycling women and comparing it with that of a control group consisting of women taking oral contraceptives. Some studies did indeed find the expected fluctuations in the responding of normally cycling women and the predicted stable, unfluctuating rates of responding in oral contraceptive users. The results of many other studies, however, have not corroborated these findings with women not on the pill. Schreiner-Engel et al. (1981) reported the results of their review of the literature, in which they identified 32 studies, all of which had found at least one increase in sexual behavior at some point during the cycle. Four studies found increases during menstruation, 18 after menstruation, 8 during ovulation, and 17 at premenses. Some of the studies found increases at more than one phase of the cycle.

Before one could conclude from these diverse findings that women's sexual behavior does not show any lawful relation to reproductive cycles, that human female sexual motivation is free of hormonal control, the general methodologies of menstrual cycle studies require some reconsideration. The central problem of all menstrual cycle research may be the inherent limitation of research with human subjects, that is, the lack of adequate control over the input variables and over the measurement of the output variables. This limitation may nowhere be more prevalent than in the studies of sexual behavior and mood changes during the menstrual cycle. For sexual behavior, most of the studies focused on intercourse or on a combination of intercourse and arousal, and only occasionally on the initiation of sexual interaction. These behaviors were measured through daily self-reports, usually without the aid of a rating scale (Adams, Gold, & Burt, 1978; Cutler, Garcia, & Krieger, 1979; Cutler, Preti, Huggins, Erickson, & Garcia, 1985; Englander-Golden, Chang, Whitmore, & Dienstbier, 1980; Harvey, 1987; Markowitz & Brender, 1976; Matteo & Rissman, 1984; McCollough, 1973; Spitz, Gold, & Adams, 1975; Udry & Morris, 1968, 1970, 1977). In this paradigm, neither the input or stimulus variables, nor the output or response variables are under experimental control. Therefore, different studies may have measured somewhat different behaviors and under a variety of stimulus conditions unknown to the researchers. The discrepancies in results reported by Schreiner-Engel et al. (1981) may therefore not be unexpected, nor is it surprising that the understanding of the cyclicity of female sexual motivation has been elusive.

In contrast to human research, the findings and methods of animal studies may be informative at this point. In several mammalian species, it has been clearly established that reproductive cycles regulate the sexual behavior of the female. Changes in the levels of ovarian hormones during estrous and menstrual cycles bring about predictable changes in sexual activity (Lisk, 1978). These findings have been established with methodologies that are precise both in measuring behavior and in identifying a stimulus to which the behavior is a response. Both are under the control of the experimenter. Studies most relevant to the human menstrual cycle are those conducted with nonhuman primates. With rhesus monkeys, for example, researchers established a procedure whereby the female had to perform a certain number of bar presses every day to gain access to a male, thereby indicating her daily sexual motivation during the cycle. In this paradigm, the experimenters have recorded a precisely measurable behavior, bar presses, as a response to a stimulus under control, a particular conspecific. An important part of this procedure is that the animals are tested *daily* during the cycle. In one version of this paradigm, ovariectomized females served as subjects and were given daily injections of gonadal steroids in dosages and combinations that mimicked the steroid levels of the normal cycle (Michael, Zumpe, & Bonsall, 1982). Under the above paradigms and in this strictly controlled setting, a lawful relation between cycles and female sexual motivation could be established.

The kind of full control of variables present in such animal experiments is not available to human menstrual cycle researchers, but some amount of control may be accessible such as the use of a particular stimulus to which women respond. Indeed, the introduction of a clearly identifiable, stable stimulus may be of primary importance in this area of work. Without it, there is no reference point against which some type of behavior can be assessed. This is particularly the case when responses to a given stimulus may fluctuate due to internal states. The particular purpose of some menstrual cycle research is to detect fluctuations in behaviors that are induced by fluctuations in endocrine states. However, when the external stimulus is unknown, when there is a multitude of potential sexual stimuli, and when these stimuli themselves may vary from day to day, then it is impossible to evaluate endocrine-related changes in sexual behavior because that behavior may reflect varying stimulus conditions.

In a small number of studies investigating human sexual arousal, experimental controls have been introduced. These studies, conducted in a laboratory setting, presented specific stimuli to women in the form of erotic films, auditory tapes, or written stories (Abramson, Repczynski, & Merrill, 1976; Griffith & Walker, 1975; Hoon, Bruce, & Kinchloe, 1982; Morrell, Dixen, Carter, & Davidson, 1984; Shreiner-Engel et al., 1981). The experiments also used an objective, quantifiable behavioral measure, vaginal blood flow and volume measured by photoplethysmography, along with self-reported arousal. Of these studies, only the one conducted by Schreiner-Engel and colleagues reported that significant changes occurred in sexual responding at different phases of the cycle. These changes were manifested in plethysmograph-recorded measures but not in the self-reported measures in response to auditory tapes.

The other studies did not detect differential responding during the various phases of the cycle under either subjective or objective assessment of arousal. Two studies (Schreiner-Engel et al., 1981; Morrell et al., 1984) that assayed blood levels of estradiol, progesterone, and testosterone did not find significant correlations between steroid levels and either subjective or objective measures of arousal.

One feature common to these studies is the periodical testing of women, yet the behavioral and hormonal tests were performed on each subject no more than one to five times, once in each phase of the cycle, the day for testing in a particular phase having been estimated and determined in advance. This relatively infrequent and predetermined behavior testing raises a number of questions. It may be, for instance, that behavioral changes during the cycle have such magnitude or are of such a nature that more frequent samplings are necessary if reliable patterns are to be detected. It is also not yet known for humans what the time relationship is between hormonal and behavioral changes, how soon behavior modifications follow changes in the hormone level, or how long such behavior modifications remain at a particular level. Because the latencies between hormone/behavior relations are not known, steroid and behavioral measures that are sampled concurrently but at spaced intervals may miss the true temporal relations and patterns.

Given the methodological problems of the menstrual cycle research outlined above, it was decided to assess sexual arousal in women on a daily basis, by giving them a specific stimulus to which they can respond. For practical reasons, it was not possible to conduct a daily laboratory study. We provided our subjects, therefore, with a set of descriptions of sexual activities and asked them to assess their arousal in relation to these activities. This exercise was to be carried out at home.

In the sample studied, we included both celibates and women with partners. Several investigators have reported that sexual motivation in women is strongly influenced by the presence of a partner and the interaction with that partner. Furthermore, Spitz et al. (1975) found that the self-reported arousal of women on any particular day was more influenced by the occurrence of intercourse on that day than by the relevant phase of the cycle. For this reason, it was decided to include in the study a group of celibate women who were not expected to be influenced by interaction with a partner. Only two studies, by Cavanagh (1969) and by Cutler et al. (1985), have reported on this population. Cavanagh found that sexual feelings and dreams in a clinical group of celibate women were high during the first half of the cycle, peaked on Day 13, and dropped for the remainder of the cycle. Cutler et al. (1985) studied celibate women in the context of sexual behavior frequency and ovulatory-type menstrual cycles. These investigators found that celibate women, who had no incidence of coital behavior, presented the lowest incidence of ovulatory-type menstrual cycles.

The present study reassesses the pattern of sexual arousal during the menstrual cycle by using a daily stimulus. Women with natural menstrual cycles were recruited as well as women with cycles regulated by contraceptive pills who served as a control group for hormonal fluctuations. The normally cycling women included a group of celibate women. All the other women, whether or not on the pill, were either married or cohabiting, thus providing a stable condition of availability of a sexual partner.

Method

Subjects

The initial group consisted of 38 women, and 35 completed the study. Of these, 27, aged 20–37 years, contributed the 28 cycles reported. The relevant demographic characteristics of these subjects are presented in Table 1.

Table 1.
Demographic Characteristics of the 27 Subjects

	Group		
Demographic variable	Celibate ($n=8$)	No pill, married or cohabiting ($n=11$)	Pill, married or cohabiting ($n=8$)
Years of age			
Mean	24	26.25	24.25
Range	20–34	23–37	21–30
Occupation	7 students	7 students	5 students
	1 employed	1 unemployed	3 employed
		3 employed	
Months married or cohabiting			
Mean		24.75	34.5
Range		2–60	1–108
Birth control method		6 condom	8 combination
		1 tubal ligation	estrogen and
		2 intrauterine	progesterone oral
		device	contraceptive pill
		1 cervical cap	
		1 none (♀ partner)	

Women were recruited through notices on bulletin boards and in local and campus newspapers. Applicants were first interviewed by telephone to determine their suitability for participation. Acceptable applicants had to be in good health, not taking any medication, free of gynecological problems, and not pregnant. They had to have regularly occurring menstrual cycles of 24–32 days length, with menses no longer than 5 days as determined by past records. If applicants were using oral contraceptives, they had to have been taking the pill for at least 3 months prior to the beginning of the study and to continue taking it while participating. Subjects were not to use the sympto-thermo method of contraception. It was required that the participants fall into one of two groups: those who were either married or cohabiting with their sexual partner, and those who were celibate, that is, with no sexual partner and committed to avoiding a partner while in the study.

Materials

A questionnaire containing three sections was designed. The first section contained items for recording basal body temperature (BBT), menstruation, vaginal discharge, abdominal pain, and breast changes. The second section had items on routine events, such as body weight, the type and quantity of food consumed, the amount and quality of sleep, as well as items for recording any unusual occurrence taking place during the day. The primary function of this section was to reduce the saliency of the fact that the subject was participating in a menstrual cycle study. The third section of the questionnaire contained instruments to measure levels of self-rated sexual arousal and physical sensations in response to written sexual stimuli and to record the frequency of sexual activity.

The instrument to measure sexual arousal was adapted from the Sexual Arousability Inventory (SAI) developed by Hoon, Hoon, and Wincze (1976). The SAI is composed of a list of 28 statements describing sexual activities and situations: for example, "When you see a loved one nude." The inventory is divided into two interchangeable forms, A and B, each containing 14 items. The items are read by the subject, and the typical level of sexual arousal reached while experiencing each activity is reported on a 9-point Likert-type scale that ranges from –1 to 7. An SAI score is determined by adding the positive and negative responses. Hoon et al. (1976) reported that the SAI had a split-half reliability of .92, a test-retest reliability of .69, and concurrent validity with physiological sensations of arousal.

For the present study, the SAI was modified and adapted for daily use. First, the instructions for completing the daily forms were altered so that the subjects were asked to imagine themselves in each situation and to rate the level of arousal they would feel if they were to experience the situation that day. Second, a change in the wording of items was introduced to facilitate imagining each situation with any preferred sexual partner. Thus all references to "loved one" and to gender were deleted and the word "partner" was uniformly used. Furthermore, the rating scale was extended in the negative direction to allow more flexibility in describing the degree of negative responses toward any particular item. The scale contained 11 points, ranging from +5, through 0, to –5. The 14-item forms were assembled into a package so as to reduce the development of a response set which would be expected to occur if identical items, in identical order, were presented every day. For this reason, the split-half forms, A and B, were presented on alternate days, and the order of the 14 items was randomized daily.

The other instrument in this section was a physical sensation scale for reporting the level of sensations experienced while imaging the sexual situations described in the SAI. The physical sensations of general excitement, breast and genital sensations, and vaginal dampness were rated on a 4-point scale, ranging from 0 to 3. The final item of this section concerned sexual activity that had occurred during the previous 24 hours. The frequency of masturbation, necking, petting, intercourse, intense sexual activity with a partner not including intercourse (e.g., oral sex, mutual masturbation), and finally orgasm was recorded on a 4-point scale, ranging from zero sexual activity to activity four or more times per day.

Ovu-Therm Basal Thermometers (supplied by Mansfield Medical Distributors Ltd., Montreal) were used for measuring BBT. The thermometer scale ranged from 35.5°C to 38.0°C and was marked in gradients of 0.05°C.

Procedure

At the time of a personal interview, full instructions were provided to the participants and they were asked to sign an informed consent form. Before beginning the study, all participants had practiced recording their BBT and vaginal mucus characteristics for approximately one week. Participants were then given questionnaires to be completed every day and to be returned in person to the experimenter once a week. Some of the women also participated in a physiological study of breast temperature recording. These subjects returned their completed questionnaire when reporting to the lab. Some of the subjects started on the first day of the cycle, others on random days. Data were collected for 5–8 weeks.

Data Analysis

Monthly charts of BBT and vaginal mucus were evaluated by one of the experimenters and by two gynecologists working in family planning. Forty-five cycles of BBT and data on mucus were charted from 35 women. Of these, 17 cycles were excluded for the following reasons: 6 cycles were judged to be anovulatory; the evaluators did not agree on another 6 cycles; the BBT chart of one woman on the pill showed an ovulatory pattern; one cycle was more than 45 days long; one cycle from a pill-taking woman was only 20 days long; and the data from one subject were judged to be unreliable because of irregularities in completing and returning the questionnaire. Finally, only 29 cycles were acceptable and met the selection criterion of an agreement between at least two of the judges. The data from one other woman was not considered because she had broken up with her partner during the study. The data presented below are based on 28 cycles. One menstrual cycle was defined as the time period starting with the first day of menses and ending with the day preceding the onset of the next menstrual bleeding.

The day of ovulation was estimated from the BBT charts; reverse cycle Day 14 was designated as the day of ovulation for women on the pill. The day of ovulation and the menses occurring at the beginning and at the end of the cycle were used to divide the cycle into eight phases: the menstrual (MNS), the early, middle, and late follicular (FOL), the ovulatory (OVU), and the early, middle, and late luteal (LUT). The menstrual phase included the days of bleeding and spotting. The ovulatory phase included the estimated day of ovulation and 2 days before and one day after. The remaining days were divided into three equal portions of the follicular and the luteal phases. The mean score per day for each phase was calculated and was used in the analysis of variance (ANOVA) of a 3×8, Groups $\times$ Phases mixed design (BMDP 2V). Pairwise comparisons were made by the Newman-Keuls test.

Results

In this chapter, only the sexual arousal (SAI) and physical sensation data are reported. The overall mean SAI scores of the three groups of women [celibates (CELIB), not on the pill married (NPMAR), and pill-taking married (PILLM)] did not differ significantly from each other. As shown in Figure 1, the pill group had the highest scores followed by the married group, and the celibates reported the lowest scores, but the main effect of Groups was not significant. The main effect of Phases also was not significant. However, there was a significant Groups $\times$ Phases interaction, $F(14, 175) = 1.86$, $p = .034$, indicating differences in the pattern of responding among the three groups, all of whom reported an increase in arousal from the menses to the early follicular phase. Thereafter, however, they differed. The NPMAR group reported a second increase during the ovulatory phase, and then the mean scores of both the CELIB and NPMAR women declined during the luteal phase. The pattern of the PILLM group was characterized by a drop in mean arousal levels during

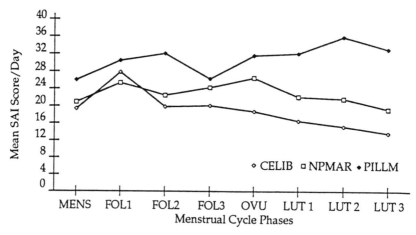

Figure 1. Mean daily sexual arousability (SAI) scores of three groups of women (CELIB, celibates; NPMAR, married, not taking the pill; PILLM, pill-taking, married) during eight phases of the menstrual cycle (MENS, menses; FOL, follicular; OVU, ovulatory; LUT, luteal).

the late follicular phase and an increase during the luteal phases. The Newman-Keuls test, however, detected reliable differences among the phases within the CELIB group only. Their mean scores of arousal declined significantly, $p < .05$, during the three luteal phases, 16.40, 15.24, and 13.60, respectively, compared with their highest mean score of 27.80 in the early follicular phase.

Similar to the SAI scores, the mean physical sensation scores did not differentiate between the three groups. However, there were reliable changes in responding across the various phases, giving a significant main effect of phases, $F(7, 175) = 2.66$, $p = .012$. In addition, the three groups manifested different patterns of physical sensation during the cycle as indicated by a significant Groups × Phases interaction, $F(14, 175) = 1.94$, $p = .025$. As shown in Figure 2, both the CELIB and NPMAR groups reported more sensations during the follicular and ovulatory phases than at other times. Both groups reported a decline in sensations after ovulation; however, the CELIB group clearly demonstrated a luteal trough. The Newman-Keuls test, however, did not identify these mean phase differences as significant. Compared with the no-pill subjects, the pill subjects reported a sharp drop during the late follicular phase and an increase thereafter. These women experienced significantly more physical sensations during the middle luteal phase than during the menses or during the late follicular phase, at the time when the drop occurred. The means were 5.66, 3.47, and 3.26, respectively. The mean score of 3.26 during this drop was

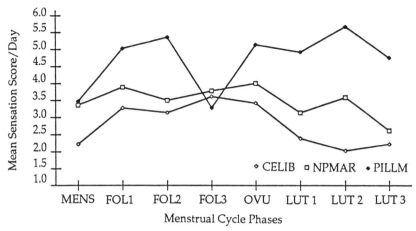

Figure 2. Mean daily bodily sensation scores of three groups of women (CELIB, celibates; NPMAR, married, not taking the pill; PILLM, pill-taking, married) during eight phases of the menstrual cycle (MENS, menses; FOL, follicular; OVU, ovulatory; LUT, luteal).

also significantly different from 5.35, the one reported in the middle follicular phase, which preceded the drop. The decline in the group score may have been partially caused by the consistent zero scores of 2 subjects during the days constituting that phase.

Discussion

The two groups of women, who lived under different conditions of sexual partnership but who were cycling naturally, seemed to be more similar to each other in their pattern of responding on both variables than they were to the women who were taking contraceptive pills. The common feature in sexual arousal and physical sensations of the naturally cycling women was an enhanced responding during the follicular and ovulatory phases when levels of estrogen would be expected to increase. This is in agreement with earlier findings on sexual behavior (Adams et al., 1978; Englander-Golden et al., 1980; Harvey, 1987; Udry & Morris, 1970; Udry, Morris, & Waller, 1973). The luteal trough seen in the present study has also been observed in other studies at times when progesterone levels are expected to be elevated (Udry & Morris, 1970; Udry, Morris, & Waller, 1973).

The response pattern of women taking the pill, in contrast to that of women not on the pill, was characterized by a gradual increase both in arousal and physical sensations throughout the cycle. There was no luteal trough on either measure. Similar findings were reported by Englander-Golden et al. (1980), Udry and Morris (1970), and Udry, Morris, and Waller (1973). The cumulative effect of steroids in contraceptive pills may account for the more sustained level of sexual arousal in the pill-taking women.

The comparison of individual phases yielded reliable differences in only a few cases. A power analysis done subsequently indicated that a sample size of $N=50$/group would be required to allow the reliable detection of differences among the phases of all the groups for a moderate effect. A significant Groups×Phases interaction and the different patterns of responding seem to warrant a replication with a larger number of subjects. Although the results may be interpreted as indicating that endocrine factors are more important in determining the women's sexual responsiveness than are marital factors, further investigation is needed to substantiate this point.

The present findings differ from those of other studies concerning sexual arousal (Abramson et al., 1976; Griffith & Walker, 1975; Hoon et al., 1982; Morrell et al., 1984). These investigators did not find different responding by women at different times of the cycle. In the present study, the celibates and pill-taking women changed their arousal responses reliably throughout the cycle, although in opposite directions. On the other hand, married women not on the pill showed a nonsignificant trend similar to that of the celibates. The discrepancy between the previous studies and the current one may be attributed to our testing arousal daily, whereas in the other studies tests were conducted only one to five times during the cycle on predetermined days representing a particular phase. Continuous testing throughout the cycle may allow a more accurate determination of patterns than does infrequent testing. Because it is not known how changes in endocrine background create changes in behavior, nor is it known what the response delay between endocrine and behavioral events might be, an infrequent sampling may miss the detection of slight changes. Indeed, the recent work of Hedricks, Piccinino, Udry, and Chimbira (1987) indicates that the detection of significant changes in sexual behavior in relation to hormonal changes requires a precise timing between the measurement of the behavior and the underlying endocrine events.

NOTE

This work was supported by a grant from Concordia University, FCAC and Rector's General Research Fund to Elizabeth Henrik. Data from the first 15 subjects were reported in the master's thesis, Concordia University, of Susan Sanders. The authors wish to thank A. Gardiner of Montreal and S. Parenteau-Carreau from SERENA Montreal for their contribution in evaluating the BBT charts.

Requests for information about the instruments used in the study may be made to Elizabeth Henrik, Department of Psychology, Concordia University, Sir George Williams Campus, 1455 de Maisonneuve Boulevard West, Montreal, Quebec H3G 1M8, Canada.

REFERENCES

Abramson, P. R., Repczynski, C. A., & Merrill, L. R. (1976). The menstrual cycle and response to erotic literature. *Journal of Clinical and Consulting Psychology, 44,* 1018–1019.

Adams, D. B., Gold, A. R., & Burt, A. D. (1978). Rise in female-initiated sexual activity at ovulation and its suppression by oral contraceptives. *New England Journal of Medicine, 299,* 1145–1150.

Cavanagh, J. R. (1969). Rhythm of sexual desire in women. *Medical Aspects of Human Sexuality, 3,* 29–39.

Cutler, W. B., Garcia, C. R., & Krieger, A. M. (1979). Sexual behavior frequency and menstrual cycle length in mature premenopausal women. *Psychoneuroendocrinology, 4,* 297–310.

Cutler, W. B., Preti, G., Huggins, G. R., Erickson, B., & Garcia, C. R. (1985). Sexual behavior frequency and biphasic ovulatory cycles. *Physiology and Behavior, 34,* 805–810.

Dennerstein, L., Burrows, G. D., Wood, C., & Hyman, G. (1980). Hormones and sexuality: Effect of estrogen and progesterone. *Obstetrics & Gynecology, 56,* 316–322.

Englander-Golden, P., Chang, H. S., Whitmore, M. R., & Dienstbier, R. A. (1980). Female sexual arousal and the menstrual cycle. *Journal of Human Stress, 6,* 42–48.

Griffith, M., & Walker, E. C. (1975). Menstrual cycle phases and personality variables as related to response to erotic stimuli. *Archives of Sexual Behavior, 4,* 599–603.

Harvey, M. S. (1987). Female sexual behavior: Fluctuations during the menstrual cycle. *Journal of Psychomatic Research, 31,* 101–110.

Hedricks, C., Piccinino, L. J., Udry, J. R., & Chimbira, T. H. K. (1987). Peak coital rate coincides with onset of luteinizing hormone surge. *Fertility and Sterility, 48,* 234–238.

Hoon, P. W., Bruce, K., & Kinchloe, B. (1982). Does the menstrual cycle play a role in sexual arousal? *Psychophysiology, 19,* 21–26.

Hoon, E. R., Hoon, P. W., & Wincze, J. P. (1976). An inventory for the measurement of female sexual arousability: The SAI. *Archives of Sexual Behavior, 5,* 291–300.

Lisk, R. D. (1978). The regulation of sexual "heat." In J. B. Hutchison (Ed.), *Biological determinants of sexual behavior* (pp. 424–466). New York: Wiley.

Markowitz, H., & Brender, W. (1976). Patterns of sexual responsiveness during the menstrual cycle. In R. Gemme & C. C. Wheeler (Eds.), *Progress in sexology* (pp. 329–334). New York: Plenum Press.

Matteo, S., & Rissman, E. F. (1984). Increased sexual activity during the middle portion of the human menstrual cycle. *Hormones and Behavior, 18,* 249–255.

McCollough, R. C. (1973). *Rhythms of sexual desire and sexual activity in the human female* (Doctoral dissertation, University of Oregon, 1973). *Dissertation Abstracts International, 34,* 4669B–4670B.

Michael, R. P., Zumpe, D., & Bonsall, R. W. (1982). Behavior of rhesus monkeys during artificial menstrual cycles. *Journal of Comparative and Physiological Psychology, 96,* 875–885.

Morrell, M. J., Dixen, J. M., Carter, C. S., & Davidson, J. M. (1984). The influence of age and cycling status on sexual arousability in women. *American Journal of Obstetrics and Gynecology, 148,* 66–78.

Morris, N. M., & Udry, J. R. (1971). Sexual frequency and contraceptive pills. *Social Biology, 18,* 40–45.

Persky, H., Lief, H. I., Strauss, D., Miller, W. R., & O'Brien, C. P. (1978). Plasma testosterone level and sexual behavior of couples. *Archives of Sexual Behavior, 7,* 157–173.

Schreiner-Engel, P., Schiave, R. C., Smith, H., & White, D. (1981). Sexual arousability and the menstrual cycle. *Psychosomatic Medicine, 43,* 199–214.

Sherwin, B. B., Gelfand, M. M., & Brender, W. (1985). Androgen enhances sexual motivation in females: A prospective, crossover study of sex steroid administration in the surgical menopause. *Psychosomatic Medicine, 4,* 339–351.

Spitz, C. J., Gold, A. R., & Adams, D. B. (1975). Cognitive and hormonal factors affecting coital frequency. *Archives of Sexual Behavior, 4,* 249–263.

Udry, J. R., & Morris, N. M. (1968). Distribution of coitus in the menstrual cycle. *Nature, 220,* 593–596.

Udry, J. R., & Morris, N. M. (1970). Effect of contraceptive pills on the distribution of sexual activity in the menstrual cycle. *Nature, 227,* 502–503.

Udry, J. R., & Morris, N. M. (1977). The distribution of events in the menstrual cycle. *Journal of Reproduction and Fertility, 51,* 419–425.

Udry, J. R., Morris, N. M., & Waller, L. (1973). Effect of contraceptive pills on sexual activity in the luteal phase of the human menstrual cycle. *Archives of Sexual Behavior, 2,* 205–213.

11

A Comparative Review of Primate Sexuality Across the Menstrual Cycle

Janette Wallis and Paula Englander-Golden

The investigation of human female sexuality is confounded by personal and cultural influences and the difficulties associated with a meaningful assessment of thoughts and feelings. It is not accurate to make direct interpretations of data from nonhumans to humans regarding sexuality. We can, however, gain insight into human sexuality research by examining nonhuman sexuality research methods and findings.

This chapter examines sexuality in female primates with special emphasis on three species: rhesus monkey (*Macaca mulatta*), chimpanzee (*Pan troglodytes*), and human (*Homo sapiens*). This comparative review illustrates the striking similarities and discusses the significance of differences among these species. (For a thorough review of human sexuality research, see Sanders and Bancroft, 1982.)

Numerous studies have presented findings on human female sexuality across the menstrual cycle. The results are frustratingly varied, some showing midcycle peaks in sexual behavior, others presenting a premenstrual increase, and still others indicating no observable cyclicity in human female sexuality (Table 1). Not only are the results of these studies inconsistent, the methods used differ in two major ways. First, the reports use different criteria to measure female sexuality. Patterns of sexual arousal, orgasm, sexual fantasies, self- versus partner-initiated intercourse, or total sexual encounters are all important considerations in assessing sexuality, and their differences may be more real than apparent. Second, the conditions under which information is obtained vary from study to study. Englander-Golden, Chang, Whitmore, and Dienstbier (1980) found that when women were unaware of the purpose of the study, their self-reports of sexual arousal showed significant peaks near midcycle, premenstrually, and on late menstrual Day 4. However, the same study indicated that women who were aware of the study's purpose tended to give conflicting reports of sexual arousal.

Most studies have used frequency of intercourse as a measure of female sexuality. The investigation of coitus in humans is inherently problematic

Table 1.
Occurrence of Various Measures of Human Female Sexuality Throughout the Menstrual Cycle

Measure/source	Phase of cycle/peak						
	Mid follicular	Late follicular/ovulation	Early/mid luteal	Premenstrual	Menstrual	Postmenstrual	No peak
Coitus-total							
Abplanalp, Rose, Donnelly, & Livingston-Vaughn (1979)							X
Bancroft, Sanders, Davidson, & Warner (1983)	X						
Hart (1960)				X			
James (1971)						X	
Kinsey, Pomeroy, Martin, & Gebhard (1948)							X
Palmer, Udry, & Morris (1982)			X				
Persky, Lief, Strauss, Miller, & O'Brien (1978)				X			X
Udry & Morris (1968)		X		X			

Female initiated						
Adams, Burt, & Gold (1978)					X	
Bancroft et al. (1983)						X
Matteo & Rissman (1984)					X	
Masturbation						
Bancroft et al. (1983)			X			
Matteo & Rissman (1984)	X				X	
Orgasm, sexual gratification						
Abplanalp et al. (1979)				X		
Matteo & Rissman (1984)	X					
Persky et al. (1978)	X					
Arousal, feelings, fantasies						
Bancroft et al. (1983)						X
Englander-Golden, Chang, Whitmore, & Dienstbier (1980)			X		X	
Matteo & Rissman (1984)		X				
Schreiner-Engel, Schiavi, Smith, & White (1981)	X					

because of a variety of confounding cultural, personal, and interpersonal variables. Contemporary couples often find that their sex lives take secondary priority to work schedules as reflected in reports of diurnal and weekly variation in copulatory frequency (Palmer, Udry, & Morris, 1982). Many studies report that there is a tendency to abstain from intercourse during menstruation, perhaps resulting in a pre- and/or postmenstruation increase in sexual activity. To control for such an effect, Matteo and Rissman (1984) sought to investigate this phenomenon in couples who may be less likely to allow menstruation to interfere with sexual activity; they studied the activity of 14 lesbian couples and, indeed, found no decline of sexual encounters during menstruation and no resulting pre- or postmenstrual peaks.

Another confounding variable, which Matteo and Rissman (1984) were able to avoid, is the fear of pregnancy. Although most studies either omit subjects using oral contraceptives, or consider them separately, the risk of conception can still be a deciding factor in the frequency of coitus. Women wishing to avoid pregnancy may abstain during unsafe days, especially if their form of contraception is relatively inconvenient (or nonexistent). Conversely, those couples hoping to conceive may artificially skew the results of a study with peak midcycle copulation.

For the above reasons, and for a variety of interpersonal difficulties that can arise at any given time, it may be most accurate to investigate human female sexuality in terms of solitary, individual sexual arousal. Although frequency of masturbation is a tangible, easily measured behavior, our society still has not developed an open attitude for discussing autogenital stimulation, suggesting that studies of masturbatory behavior may lead to biased results. We are, therefore, left with measuring thoughts, feelings, fantasies, etc., as the most valid — if abstract — measure of human female sexuality. Because cultural and personal influences can only be minimized but not eliminated for human subjects and an accurate (or adequate) record of thoughts and feelings is difficult to obtain, it is of interest and importance to look to other female primates in our investigation of sexuality.

Defining Female Primate Sexuality
Because it is virtually impossible to record feelings in nonhuman mammals, we investigate female sexuality by recording physical changes in the female and the resulting or concurrent behaviors that she, her male partner, or both exhibit. Beach (1976) defined three indicators of sexuality in female mammals that have proven to be valuable tools in the comparative study of primate sexuality: *Attractivity* refers to the female's stimulus value as indicated by male sexual response; *proceptivity* indicates the female's initiative in establishing sexual interaction; and *receptivity* is

defined in terms of the female's response to the male and her actions to facilitate intromission.

An endocrine-controlled mechanism within female primates operates during the menstrual cycle to maximize the chance of conception; McCauley and Erhardt (1976) postulated that hormonal control may work via any or all of the following paths: (a) the mechanism of control may act directly on the brain and indirectly influence female sexual behavior, (b) it may act directly on the genitalia and trigger an increase in genital swelling, leading to an increase in sexual response, or (c) it may work by enhancing the sexual attractiveness of females for males. These hormonally controlled behavioral and physical changes can be subcategorized to aid the investigation of female attractivity, proceptivity, and receptivity. Figure 1 illustrates the relationship of these parameters as they apply to female sexuality.

Hormonal Effects on Female Sexuality

Primate species exhibit differences in cycle length and breeding season, although the basic profiles of gonadotrophins, estrogens, and progesterone are very similar across species (rhesus, Hess & Resko, 1973; Wallen, Winston, Gaventa, Davis-DaSilver, & Collins, 1984; chimpanzee, Graham, 1981; Reyes, Winter, Faiman, & Hobson, 1975; human, Guerraro et al., 1976; Kling & Westfahl, 1978; Persky, Lief, O'Brien, Strauss, & Miller, 1977).

Though traditionally labeled the "male hormone," testosterone is found in higher concentrations than estrogen in female primates, although usually far below male levels. Whereas testosterone in males is produced primarily in the testes, only one-third of all testosterone in females originates from the gonads; the rest is secreted by the adrenals. Testosterone increases near midcycle, either concurrent with (rhesus, Wallen et al., 1984; human, Persky et al., 1977) or just after (chimpanzee, Nadler, Graham, Gosselin, & Collins, 1985; human, Guerraro et al., 1976; Kling & Westfahl, 1978) the estradiol peak.

The following sections review recent primate literature describing the hormonal effects on female sexuality, as diagrammed in Figure 1. Two major points of hormonal action, as noted by Herbert (1974), are (a) somatic, relating to the tissue on which it is acting to produce its behavioral effects; and (b) brain, relating to particular components of behavior of this or another individual that are altered in consequence.

Physiological Effects of Hormonal Action on the Genitalia

In a review of nonhuman primate behavior, Baum, Everitt, Herbert, & Keverne (1977) noted that most hormone-dependent changes in sexuality

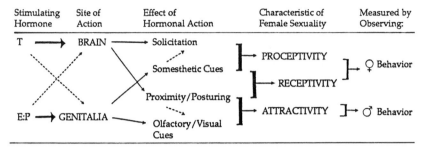

Figure 1. Proposed scheme of the hormonal effects on the brain and genitalia, resulting in behavioral and physiological changes associated with female sexuality. T, testosterone; E, estrogen; P, progesterone; proceptivity, female initiative in establishing sexual interaction; receptivity, female response to male sexual initiation; attractivity, female's value as a sexual stimulus to the male.

result from fluctuations in nonbehavioral attributes of female sexual attractiveness, specifically those related to changes in and around the vagina. He further noted that the primary hormones responsible for stimulating the vagina are estrogens, whereas progesterone appears to have a disruptive effect on sex by way of suppressing estrogenic response. Changes in the female pelvic region and genitalia result in two types of signals: (a) those received by the female (somesthetic cues), and (b) those received by other individuals (olfactory and visual cues).

Vasocongestion and Somesthetic Cues

Several nonhuman primate species exhibit a cyclical swelling of the anogenital area which is often accompanied by changes in color and skin texture (Figure 2) (see review by Dixson, 1983). Sexual behavior is most frequently observed during the periods of swelling (discussed below). This "sexual swelling" is due to accumulation of interstitial fluid (other than blood) and is hormonally regulated. As follicular estrogen levels rise, the swelling increases; the tissue remains fully swollen for several days, then swelling decreases with falling estrogen and increasing progesterone levels (pigtail monkey, *Macaca nemestrina*, Bullock, Paris, & Goy, 1972; chacma baboon, *Papio ursinus*, Gillman & Gilbert, 1946; olive baboon, *Papio cynocephalus*, Kling & Westfahl, 1978; chimpanzee, *Pan troglodytes*, Graham, 1976). Ovulation occurs during the last 1 or 2 days of maximum swelling (chimpanzee, Graham, 1982). Clark and Birch (1948) and Graham, Collins, Robinson and Preedy (1972) found that although progesterone administration alone inhibits the estrogen-induced swelling, an adequate ratio of estrogen to progesterone is required for the maintenance of genital swelling.

As the primate genital swelling progresses, it literally engulfs the clitoral shaft and creates pressure from all sides (Figure 2C). Zuckerman (1932)

A

B

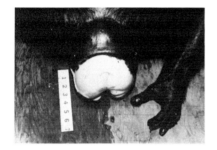

C

Figure 2. Genital swelling of an adult female chimpanzee (*Pan troglodytes*). Note that the clitoris, which is visible during phases of no swelling (A) and partial swelling (B), is completely engulfed during maximum swelling (C).

speculated that when the chimpanzee sexual skin is swollen, its sensory nerve endings may be stimulated by pressure that reflexly motivates the animal to sexual behavior. It is interesting to note that in baboons and chimpanzees, increased sexual initiative occurs not at swelling onset but when the increased swelling reaches, and includes, the clitoral area (Scott, 1984; Wallis, 1986).

In women, there is no apparent cyclical engorgement of the external genitalia, per se; however, the entire pelvic region goes through fluctuating states of congestion. Unlike the nonhuman primate sexual swelling that consists of water build-up in the perineum, the engorgement in women is due to changes in blood volume in the pelvic area, resulting in increased venous congestion. Sherfey (1972) and McCauley and Erhardt (1976) suggest that one reason for a premenstrual peak in sexual activity, reported frequently in human studies, may be pelvic vasocongestion which contributes to more genital sensitivity. The hormonal events concurrent with premenstrual vasocongestion indicate a rapid fall in progesterone and estrogen, resulting in an estrogen:progesterone ratio that allows estrogenic stimulation and produces an increase in vascularity.

Olfactory and Visual Cues

The cyclical swelling of the genital area of some female primates, described above, not only provides a stimulus for the female, but also serves to attract males. Clutton-Brock and Harvey (1976) noted that most of the species showing this prominent midcycle sexual swelling live in multi-male groups. Increased inter-male competition and ability of females to exercise partner choice make it advantageous for a female to exhibit a dramatic visual indicator of sexual receptivity several days before ovulation occurs (see Clutton-Brock & Harvey, 1976; Harcourt, 1981; Hrdy & Whitten, 1987).

Although the visual stimulus of a swollen perineum is highly correlated with male sexual arousal (baboons, Bielert & Anderson, 1985; chimpanzees, Tinklepaugh, 1933; Tutin & McGinnis, 1981; van Lawick-Goodall, 1968; Wallis, 1982, 1986), some studies have found that olfactory cues may outweigh visual changes in some species. Herbert (1966) applied estrogen to the perineum of female rhesus monkeys and noted a color change, but no change in male behavior. When estrogen was placed inside the vagina, however, the color change was accompanied by increased mounting by males. Herbert (1970) emphasized that the effect of estrogen treatment was an increase in attractivity alone, that is, there was an increased frequency of male mounting but no increase in female presentations. Removal of the ovaries, in fact, produces a decrease in male copulatory behavior (Michael, Herbert, & Welegalla, 1967).

Girolami (1985) found that estrogen treatment in vervet monkeys produced a slight increase in olfactory genital investigation. Genital inspection in a pair of moustached monkeys (*Cercopithecus cephus*) is illustrated in Figure 3. Similarly, chimpanzee males show an increased rate of genital inspection at the onset of sexual swelling in the female (van Lawick-Goodall, 1969; Wallis, 1986). The occurrence of synchronized onset of menstrual cycles in group-housed chimpanzees suggests a hormonally controlled olfactory signal operating between females as well (Wallis, 1985).

The quantity of vaginal secretion increases during the periovulatory period, suggesting a relationship to estrogen content (crab-eating monkeys, *Macaca fascicularis*, Wallis, King, & Roth-Meyer, 1986; rhesus and baboons, Hafez, 1971; humans, Billings & Billings, 1973). In fact, Utian (1972) found that the problem of vaginal dryness in postmenopausal women is reduced after estrogen treatment. Several behavioral studies have focused on this correlation between vaginal secretions and the timing of estrogen increase and ovulation. Certain components of rhesus vaginal secretions may affect the sexual behavior of males (Jensen & Sassenrath, 1977; Michael & Keverne, 1970), although experience and maturity are key factors in male rhesus sexual response (Goldfoot, Kravetz, Goy, & Freeman, 1976).

Keith, Stromberg, Krotoszynsk, Shah, and Dravniecks (1975) found a midcycle peak in reports of pleasant and mild odor of human vaginal

Figure 3. Male-to-female genital inspection in the moustached monkey (*Cerco-pithecus cephus*).

secretions in conjunction with maximum concentrations of certain aliphatic acids. Although Doty, Ford, Preti, and Huggins (1975) also found changes in the pleasantness and the intensity of vaginal odors, they report it is unlikely that humans can consciously use odors as cues to the time of ovulation. Morris and Udry (1978) supported this theory with the finding that vaginal smears have no apparent stimulating or attractive effect on males when applied to human female subjects.

Behavioral Effects of Hormonal Action on the Brain

In "lower" mammals, the periodic occurrence of sexual activity and the exact time of ovulation are so highly correlated that reference to an "estrous cycle" or "estrous behavior" correctly implies a strict relationship between sex and procreation. However, in some primate species (especially humans), sexual activity also serves to strengthen social bonds and satisfy individual pleasure. Loy (1987), in fact, has published a thorough and compelling essay arguing that Old World monkeys and apes do not exhibit true "estrous" cycles. The added functions of coitus have accompanied a tendency for sexual behavior to occur outside of the periovulatory period in some primates (see Hrdy, 1988, for review).

Solicitation

Most female nonhuman primates indicate interest in a male by presenting the hindquarters, often looking back at the male, and arching the tail (if one exists) out of the way. In some species, the only postural difference between presentation for genital inspection (Figure 4) and presentation for copulation (Figure 5) is that the latter may involve crouching or bending the legs. Various other proceptive behaviors have been noted. For example, female chimpanzees have been observed to actually grasp the male's penis, inserting it into the vagina (Wallis, 1982). A review of most nonhuman primate species indicates that females tend to show higher sexual initiative around the periovulatory period (Nadler, Herndon, & Wallis, 1986).

Removal of the adrenals in females (i.e, removal of the main source of androgens) results in a decrease in proceptive behavior in rhesus females which can be restored with testosterone treatment (Baum, Everitt, Herbert, & Keverne, 1977; Everitt & Herbert, 1971). Everitt and Herbert (1975) found no observable change in the rhesus vagina and clitoris when testosterone was administered (i.e., no change in somesthetic cues was noted with testosterone treatment). Therefore, Baum et al. speculated that testosterone's effects on female sexuality are by way of stimulating the central nervous system, specifically the anterior hypothalamus.

Proximity Maintenance and Receptive Posturing

A female may copulate several times during her cycle without actually soliciting a sexual bout herself; other behavioral actions such as proximity maintenance and appropriate posturing may prove her receptive to male sexual invitations (Figure 6). In this case, the term "proximity maintenance" refers to a female's tendency to change travel patterns and generally maintain social contact with males, rather than the more overt (proceptive) behavior of "approaching." For example, a wild champanzee exhibiting a sexual swelling is frequently seen in the company of many males, traveling, foraging, and grooming with them. In contrast, an anestrous female rarely maintains close physical or social proximity to males (Goodall, 1986; Nishida, 1979; van Lawick-Goodall, 1968). Obviously, a female cannot receive a sexual invitation if she is not near males. The majority of all chimpanzee copulations in the wild and in captivity are initiated by males, although females have the option of responding favorably or refusing to receive males, and a high level of partner preference has been reported (Coe, Connolly, Kraemer, & Levine, 1979; Nishida, 1979; Tutin, 1980; van Lawick-Goodall, 1969; Wallis, 1982, 1986).

As diagrammed in Figure 1, a change in the testosterone level in the female can result in behavioral changes in both the female and the male. Herbert (1974) found that decreased levels of testosterone in female rhesus monkeys resulted in lower mounting response by the males, because the

Figure 4. A female spot-nosed monkey (*Cercopithecus nictitans*) presents for genital inspection (cf. Figure 5).

Figure 5. A female spot-nosed monkey presents for copulation. Note that for copulatory presentation, as opposed to genital inspection (Figure 4), the female assumes a crouching position.

Figure 6. Copulatory attempt by two adolescent chimpanzees. While the male attempts intromission, the female patiently maintains a receptive posture.

female was less receptive to his initiations; she affected his behavior by refusing to maintain the receptive posture required for intromission and subsequent ejaculation. Everitt, Herbert, and Hamer (1971) removed the ovaries and adrenals of monkeys and found a dramatic decrease in receptivity. When these animals received testosterone treatment, receptivity was restored, but estrogen treatment had no significant effect.

These behavioral aspects of female sexuality (solicitation and proximity maintenance/receptivity posturing) are most easily examined in nonhuman primate species; the behavioral mechanisms involved when a female chimpanzee adjusts her ranging pattern to travel with a group of males are not comparable to any easily measured behavior in women. Perhaps the term "libido," usually discussed in relation to human sexual drive, must incorporate both "solicitation" and "proximity maintenance."

As in monkeys, adrenalectomy is found to decrease libido in women (Waxenberg, Drellich, & Sutherland, 1959). This loss of sexual drive may be restored with androgen (testosterone) treatment (Money, 1961; Waxenberg et al., 1959). Studd et al. (1977), in fact, found that androgen treatment increased libido, even when normal levels of androgens already existed. Salmon and Geist (1943) credited androgens with creating emotional receptivity to excitation and increasing sensitivity to the stimulating effects of estrogen on the genitalia.

Measuring Female Sexuality in Primates

Most detailed studies of female sexuality in nonhuman primates have focused on captive populations. Results from the often-used "pair-test" studies, in which animals that live separately are placed together daily for 30- or 60-min tests, have proven to differ from the patterns of sexual behavior seen in group-living subjects (for a discussion of these two approaches, see Gordon, 1981; Wallen et al., 1984). Because the group-caged situation resembles natural living conditions more closely, we present data from studies of group-living nonhuman primates.

Female rhesus monkeys show a sexual behavior profile that is highly correlated to the female's ovarian cycle. Estrogen and progesterone changes in the female have a direct effect on attractivity, changing the ability to stimulate mounting behavior by the male (Herbert, 1974). There is also a positive correlation between proceptive behavior (approach) and a rise in estradiol (Cochran, 1979; Wallen et al., 1984). Wallen et al. proposed that the cyclic changes in the behavior of females, although not related to fluctuations in testosterone level, may require normal levels of testosterone to set a basal level of female sexual interest that increases by estradiol stimulation.

The occurrence of sexual behavior exhibited by adult chimpanzees is closely correlated to the follicular increase in estrogen and the resultant change in genital swelling. Not only is sexual activity highest during maximum genital swelling, but there is a gradual increase as swelling progresses (Hasegawa & Hiraiwa-Hasegawa, 1990; Wallis, 1986). Wallis (1986) found that, although receptivity (successful male attempts) did not vary with cycle phase, both attractivity and proceptivity peaked a few days prior to detumescence of the sex skin. Rather than coinciding with the last day of maximum swelling (ovulation), these measures peaked more closely to the probable time of the estrogen and testosterone peaks. Because sexual behavior does not increase with the luteal rise in estradiol, and progesterone inhibits sexual swelling at that time, it appears that progesterone has an inhibitory effect on sexual behavior as well.

As discussed in the introduction, human sexual initiative is difficult to measure. To date, no reports have offered comparable information of proceptivity, attractivity, and receptivity in women. Many studies of human sexuality have been conducted, and the results are as varied as the study techniques (Table 1). The striking difference in the profile of sexuality in women as opposed to sexuality in rhesus and chimpanzee females is that there are virtually no periods of total abstinence; the increased period of estrus seen in higher nonhuman primates has evolved into a tendency toward continual receptivity in humans.

Although it appears that progesterone tends to have a disruptive effect on sexuality through inhibitory action on the vagina, this statement must be qualified with respect to pregnancy. Pregnant female chimpanzees often display irregular genital swelling during the early months of gestation. The hormonal basis for the appearance of swelling at this time is unclear, because pregnant chimpanzees have relatively high levels of both progesterone and estrogen (Faiman, Reyes, Winter, & Hobson, 1981; Reyes et al., 1975). Several reports from both the laboratory and the field indicate, however, that genital swelling during pregnancy is accompanied by sexual behavior (Hasegawa & Hiraiwa-Hasegawa, 1983; Nishida, 1979; Tinklepaugh, 1933; Tutin & McGinnis, 1981; van Lawick-Goodall, 1969; Wallis, 1982; Wallis & Lemmon, 1986).

The increase in gestation-related sexual behavior in chimpanzees is caused primarily by heightened attractivity (male initiation) (Wallis & Lemmon, 1986). Reports of human sexual activity during gestation cite the woman, however, as the most frequent initiator (Masters & Johnson, 1966; Morris, 1975). An increased feeling of sexual arousal during pregnancy may be predictable, in light of our previous discussion of possible somesthetic cues from pelvic congestion.

Evolutionary Pressures on Female Sexuality and Hormones

The underlying mechanism involved in the various cultural, individual, and hormonal factors described above lies in evolutionary pressures affecting the social and physiological variables in female primate sexuality. For instance, although monkeys, apes, and humans have very similar hormonal profiles, different social organizations and environmental parameters have led to species-specific mating patterns. We must, therefore, use caution in making comparisons between primate species.

Although various studies report peaks in sexual behavior in women, these peaks are often minor or nonsignificant, and women are considered to be continually receptive. This phenomenon has resulted in so-called concealed ovulation, and a variety of review papers have hypothesized the ultimate mechanisms involved (Alexander & Noonan, 1979; Benshoof & Thornhill, 1979; Burley, 1979; Strassman, 1981; Turke, 1984). One such theory of evolutionary changes resulting in increased human female sexuality lends itself to our discussion of hormonal influence on sexuality. Spuhler (1979) noted that a phylogenetic increase in the relative importance of the central nervous system in sexual behavior is attributable to testosterone levels. As mentioned above, the majority of all androgens (including testosterone) in women come from the adrenal glands, and, in fact, females have larger adrenals than males (Inay, Ruch, Finen, & Fulton, 1940). Spuhler's (1979) thesis is that natural selection for endurance in bipedal running, which requires increased adrenal hormones to catalyze energy in muscles, led to our extremely large adrenal glands. Thus, the evolutionary pressures that resulted in bipedalism may have indirectly affected the pattern of human female sexuality we see today.

Conclusion

This chapter examines the physiological and behavioral parameters that make up female primate sexuality. In general, a particular ratio of the stimulating effect of estrogen and the inhibitory effect of progesterone lead to physical changes in the genitalia, whereas androgens—such as testosterone—are responsible for behavioral correlates of sexuality. Although it is not possible to make direct interpretations between data on the sexuality of nonhuman primates and that of women, it is of interest and importance to note the similarities and differences observed in a comparison of species.

NOTE

We wish to thank Kim Wallen, William McGrew, Jane Lancaster, and Barbara King for helpful comments on an earlier version of this manuscript.

REFERENCES

Abplanalp, J. M., Rose, R. M., Donnelly, A. F., & Livingston-Vaughn, J. (1979). Psychoendocrinology of the menstrual cycle: II. Relationship between enjoyment of activities, moods and reproductive hormones. *Psychosomatic Medicine, 41,* 605–615.

Adams, D., Burt, A., & Gold, A. R. (1978). Rise in female-initiated sexual activity at ovulation and its suppression by oral contraceptives. *New England Journal of Medicine, 299,* 1145–1150.

Alexander, R. D., & Noonan, K. M. (1979). Concealment of ovulation, parental care, and human social evolution. In N. A. Chagnon & W. Irons (Eds.), *Evolutionary biology and human social behavior: An anthropological perspective* (pp. 436–453). North Scituate, MA: Duxbury.

Baum, M. J., Everitt, B. J., Herbert, J., & Keverne, E. B. (1977). Hormonal basis of proceptivity and receptivity in female primates. *Archives of Sexual Behavior, 5,* 173–192.

Bancroft, J., Sanders, D., Davidson, D., & Warner, P. (1983). Mood, sexuality, hormones and the menstrual cycle: III. Sexuality and the role of androgens. *Psychosomatic Medicine, 45,* 509–516.

Beach, F. A. (1976). Sexual attractivity, proceptivity, and receptivity in female mammals. *Hormones and Behavior, 7,* 105–138.

Benshoof, L., & Thornhill, R. (1979). The evolution of monogamy and loss of estrus in humans. *Journal of Social and Biological Structures, 2,* 95–106.

Bielert, C., & Anderson, C. M. (1985). Baboon sexual swellings and male response: A possible operational mammalian supernormal stimulus and response interaction. *International Journal of Primatology, 6,* 377–393.

Billings, J. J., & Billings, E. L. (1973). Determination of fertile and infertile days by the mucus pattern: Development of the ovulation method. In W. A. Urrichio (Ed.), *Proceedings of a Research Conference on Natural Family Planning* (pp. 149–170). Washington, DC: The Human Life Foundation.

Bullock, D. W., Paris, C. A., & Goy, R. W. (1972). Sexual behavior, swelling of the sex skin and plasma progesterone in the pigtail macaque. *Journal of Reproduction and Fertility, 31,* 225–236.

Burley, N. (1979). The evolution of concealed ovulation. *American Naturalist, 114,* 835–858.

Clark, G., & Birch, H. G. (1948). Observations on the sex skin and sex cycle in the chimpanzee. *Endocrinology, 43,* 218–231.

Clutton-Brock, T. H., and Harvey, P. H. (1976). Evolutionary rules and primate societies. In P. P. G. Bateson & R. A. Hinde (Eds.), *Growing points in ethology* (pp. 195–237). Cambridge, England: Cambridge University Press.

Cochran, C. G. (1979). Proceptive patterns of behavior throughout the menstrual cycle in female rhesus monkeys. *Behavioral and Neural Biology, 27,* 342–353.

Coe, C. L., Connolly, A. G., Kraemer, H. C., & Levine, S. (1979). Reproductive development and behavior of captive female chimpanzees. *Primates, 20,* 571–582.

Dixson, A. F. (1983). Observations on the evolution and behavioral significance of "sexual skin" in female primates. *Advances in the Study of Behavior, 13,* 63–106.

Doty, R. L., Ford, M., Preti, G., & Huggins, G. R. (1975). Changes in the intensity and pleasantness of human vaginal odors during the menstrual cycle. *Science, 190,* 1316–1317.

Englander-Golden, R., Chang, H.-S., Whitmore, M. R., & Dienstbier, R. A. (1980). Female sexual arousal and the menstrual cycle. *Journal of Human Stress, 6,* 42–48.

Everitt, B. J., & Herbert, J. (1971). The effects of dexamethasone and androgens on sexual receptivity of female rhesus monkeys. *Endocrinology, 51,* 575–588.

Everitt, B. J., & Herbert, J. (1975). The effects of implanting testosterone propionate into the central nervous system on the sexual behavior of adrenalectomized female rhesus monkeys. *Brain Research, 86,* 109–120.

Everitt, B. J., Herbert, J., & Hamer, J. D. (1971). Sexual receptivity of bilaterally adrenalectomized female rhesus monkeys. *Physiology and Behavior, 8,* 409–415.

Faiman, C., Reyes, F. I., Winter, J. S. D., & Hobson, W. C. (1981). Endocrinology of pregnancy in apes. In C. E. Graham (Ed.), *Biology in the great apes: Comparative and biomedical perspectives* (pp. 45–68). New York: Academic Press.

Gillman, J., & Gilbert, C. (1946). The reproductive cycle of the chacma baboon (*Papio ursinus*) with special reference to the problems of menstrual irregularities as assessed by the behavior of the sex skin. *South African Journal of Medical Sciences, 11,* 1–54.

Girolami, J. (1985). Steroid hormone influences on the mating behavior of vervet monkeys (*Cercopithecus aethiops*). *Hormones and Behavior, 19*, 1-13.

Goldfoot, D. A., Kravetz, M. A., Goy, R. W., & Freeman, S. K. (1976). Lack of effect of vaginal lavages and aliphatic acids on ejaculatory responses in rhesus monkeys: Behavioral and chemical analyses. *Hormones and Behavior, 7*, 1-27.

Goodall, J. (1986). *The chimpanzees of Gombe: Patterns of behavior*. Cambridge, MA: Belknap, Harvard University Press.

Gordon, T. P. (1981). Reproductive behavior in the rhesus monkey: Social and endocrine variables. *American Zoologist, 21*, 185-195.

Graham, C. E. (1976). The chimpanzee: A unique model for human reproduction. In T. Antikatzides, S. Erichsen, & A. Spiegel (Eds.), *The laboratory animal in the study of reproduction* (pp. 29-38). New York: Gustav Fischer Verleg.

Graham, C. E. (1981). Menstrual cycle of the great apes. In C. E. Graham (Ed.), *Reproductive biology of the great apes: Comparative and biomedical perspectives* (pp. 1-43). New York: Academic Press.

Graham, C. E. (1982). Ovulation time: A factor in ape fertility assessment. *American Journal of Primatology* (Suppl. 1), 51-55.

Graham, C. E., Collins, D. C., Robinson, H., & Preedy, J. R. K. (1972). Urinary levels of estrogens and pregnanediol and plasma levels of progesterone during the menstrual cycle of the chimpanzee: Relationship to the sexual swelling. *Endocrinology, 91*, 13-24.

Guerraro, R., Aso, T., Brenner, P. F., Cekan, Z., Landren, B.-M., Hagenfeldt, K., & Diczfalusy, E. (1976). Studies on the patterns of circulating steroids in the normal menstrual cycle. *Acta Endocrinologica, 81*, 133-149.

Hafez, E. S. E. (1971). Reproductive cycles. In E. S. E. Hafez (Ed.), *Comparative reproduction of nonhuman primates* (pp. 160-204). Springfield, IL: Thomas.

Harcourt, A. H. (1981). Inter-male competition and the reproductive behavior of the great apes. In C. E. Graham (Ed.), *Reproductive biology of the great apes: Comparative and biomedical perspectives* (pp. 301-318). New York: Academic Press.

Hart, R. D. A. (1960). Monthly rhythm libido in married women. *British Medical Journal, 1*, 1023-1024.

Hasegawa, T., & Hiraiwa-Hasegawa, M. (1983). Opportunistic and restrictive matings among wild chimpanzees in the Mahale Mountains, Tanzania. *Journal of Ethology, 1*, 75-85.

Hasegawa, T., & Hiraiwa-Hasegawa, M. (1990). Sperm competition and mating behavior. In T. Nishida (Ed.), *The chimpanzees of the Mahale Mountains: Sexual and life history strategies* (pp. 115-132). Tokyo: University of Tokyo Press.

Herbert, J. (1966). The effect of oestrogen applied directly to the genitalia upon the sexual attractiveness of the female rhesus monkey. *Excerpta Medicus International Congress, 3*, 212.

Herbert, J. (1970). Hormones and reproductive behavior in rhesus and talapoin monkeys. *Journal of Reproduction and Fertility* (Suppl. 11), 119-140.

Herbert, J. (1974). Some functions of hormones and the hypothalamus in the sexual activity of primates. *Progress in Brain Research, 41*, 331-348.

Hess, D. L., & Resko, J. A. (1973). The effects of progesterone on the patterns of testosterone and estradiol concentrations in the systemic plasma of the female rhesus monkey during the intermenstrual period. *Endocrinology, 92,* 446–453.

Hrdy, S. B., & Whitten, P. (1987). The patterning of sexual activity. In B. Smuts, D. Cheney, R. Seyfarth, R. Wrangham, & T. Struhsaker (Eds.), *Primate societies* (pp. 370–384). Chicago: University of Chicago Press.

Hrdy, S. B. (1988). The primate origins of human sexuality. In R. Bellig & G. Stevens (Eds.), *The evolution of sex* (pp. 101–136). San Francisco: Harper & Row.

Inay, M., Ruch, T. C., Finen, S., & Fulton, J. F. (1940). The endocrine weights of primates. *Endocrinology, 27,* 58.

James, W. H. (1971). The distribution of coitus within the human intermenstruum. *Journal of Biosocial Science, 3,* 159–171.

Jensen, G. D., & Sassenrath, E. (1977). Sexual chemistry in monkeys: The effect of vaginal secretions on male sexuality. In R. Gemme, & C. C. Wheeler (Eds.), *Progress in sexology* (pp. 345–349). New York: Plenum Press.

Keith, L., Stromberg, P., Krotoszynsk, B. K., Shah, J., & Dravnieks, A. (1975). The odors of the human vagina. *Archives Gynokologica, 220,* 1–10.

Kinsey, A. C., Pomeroy, W. B., Martin, C. E., & Gebhard, P. H. (1948). *Sexual behavior of the human female.* Philadelphia, PA: Saunders.

Kling, O. R., & Westfahl, P. K. (1978). Steroid changes during the menstrual cycle of the baboon (*Papio cynocephalus*) and human. *Biology of Reproduction, 18,* 392–400.

Loy, J. (1987). The sexual behavior of African monkeys and the question of estrus. In E. Zucker (Ed.), *Comparative behavior of African monkeys* (pp. 175–195). New York: Alan R. Liss.

Masters, W. H., & Johnson, V. E. (1966). *Human sexual response.* Boston: Little Brown.

Matteo, S., & Rissman, E. F. (1984). Increased sexual activity during the midcycle portion of the human menstrual cycle. *Hormones and Behavior, 18,* 249–255.

McCauley, E., & Erhardt, A. A. (1976). Female sexual response: Hormonal and behavioral interactions. *Primary Care, 3,* 455–476.

Michael, R. P., Herbert, J., & Welegalla, J. (1967). Ovarian hormones and the sexual behavior of the male rhesus monkey (*Macaca mulatta*) under laboratory conditions. *Journal of Endocrinology, 39,* 81–98.

Michael, R. P., & Keverne, E. B. (1970). Primate sex pheromones of vaginal origin. *Nature, 225,* 84–85.

Money, J. (1961). Sex hormones and other variables in human eroticism. In W. C. Young (Ed.), *Sex and internal secretions* (Vol. 2, pp. 1383–1400). Baltimore, MD: Williams and Wilkins.

Morris, N. M. (1975). The frequency of sexual intercourse during pregnancy. *Archives of Sexual Behavior, 4,* 501–507.

Morris, N. M., & Udry, J. R. (1978). Pheromonal influences on human sexual behavior: An experimental search. *Journal of Biosocial Science, 10,* 147–157.

Nadler, R. D., Graham, C. E., Gosselin, R. E., & Collins, D. C. (1985). Serum levels of gonadotropins and gonadal steroids, including testosterone, during the menstrual cycle of the chimpanzee (*Pan troglodytes*). *American Journal of Primatology, 9,* 273–284.

Nadler, R. D., Herndon, J. G., & Wallis, J. (1986). Adult sexual behavior: Hormones and reproduction. In J. Erwin (Series Ed.), G. Mitchell, & J. Erwin (Vol. Eds.), *Comparative primate biology: Vol. 2A. Behavior, conservation, and ecology* (pp. 363–407). New York: Alan R. Liss.

Nishida, T. (1979). The social structure of chimpanzees of the Mahale Mountains. In D. A. Hamburg, & E. R. McCown (Eds.), *The great apes* (pp. 73–121). Menlo Park, CA: Benjamin Cummings.

Palmer, J. D., Udry, J. R., & Morris, N. M. (1982). Diurnal and weekly, but no lunar rhythms in human copulation. *Human Biology, 54*, 111–121.

Persky, H., Lief, H. I., O'Brien, C. P., Strauss, D., & Miller, W. (1977). Reproductive hormone levels and sexual behavior of young couples during the menstrual cycle. In R. Gemme & C. C. Wheeler (Eds.), *Progress in sexology* (pp. 293–310). New York: Plenum Press.

Persky, H., Lief, H. I., Strauss, D., Miller, W. R., & O'Brien, C. P. (1978). Plasma testosterone level and sexual behavior of couples. *Archives of Sexual Behavior, 7*, 157–173.

Reyes, F. I., Winter, J. S. D., Faiman, C., & Hobson, W. C. (1975). Serial serum levels of gonadotrophins, prolactin, and sex steroids in the non-pregnant and pregnant chimpanzee. *Endocrinology, 96*, 1447–1455.

Salmon, U. J., & Geist, S. H. (1943). Effect of androgens upon libido in women. *Journal of Clinical Endocrinology and Metabolism, 3*, 235–238.

Sanders, D., & Bancroft, J. (1982). Hormones and the sexuality of women: The menstrual cycle. *Clinics in Endocrinology and Metabolism, 11*, 639–659.

Schreiner-Engel, P., Schiavi, R. C., Smith, H., & White D. (1981). Sexual arousability and the menstrual cycle. *Psychosomatic Medicine, 43*, 199–214.

Scott, L. M. (1984). Reproductive behavior of adolescent female baboons (*Papio anubis*) in Kenya. In M. F. Small (Ed.), *Female primates: Studies by women primatologists* (pp. 77–100). New York: Alan R. Liss.

Sherfey, M. J. (1972). *The nature and evolution of female sexuality.* New York: Random House.

Spuhler, J. N. (1979). Continuities and discontinuities in anthropoid-hominid behavioral evolution: Bipedal locomotion and sexual receptivity. In N. A. Chagnon & W. G. Irons (Eds.), *Evolutionary biology and human social organization* (pp. 454–461). North Scituate, MA: Duxbury.

Strassman, B. I. (1981). Sexual selection, paternal care, and concealed ovulation in humans. *Ethology and Sociobiology, 2*, 31–40.

Studd, J. W. W., Collins, W. P., Chakravarti, S., Newton, J. R., Oran, D., & Parsons, A. (1977). Estradiol and testosterone implants in treatment of psychosexual problems in postmenopausal women. *British Journal of Obstetrics and Gynaecology, 84*, 314–315.

Tinklepaugh, O. L. (1933). Sex cycles and other cyclic phenomena in a chimpanzee during adolescence, maturity, and pregnancy. *Journal of Morphology, 54*, 521–547.

Turke, P. W. (1984). Effects of ovulatory concealment and synchrony on protohominid mating systems and parental roles. *Ethology and Sociobiology, 5*, 33–44.

Tutin, C. E. G. (1980). Reproductive behavior of wild chimpanzees in the Gombe

National Park, Tanzania. *Journal of Reproduction and Fertility* (Suppl. 28), 43–57.

Tutin, C. E. G., & McGinnis, R. P. (1981). Sexuality of the chimpanzee in the wild. In C. E. Graham (Ed.), *Reproductive biology of the great apes: Comparative and biomedical perspectives* (pp. 239–264). New York: Academic Press.

Udry, J. R., & Morris, N. M. (1968). Distribution of coitus in the menstrual cycle. *Nature, 220,* 593–596.

Utian, W. H. (1972). The true clinical features of post-menopause and oopherectomy and their response to oestrogen therapy. *South African Medical Journal, 46,* 732.

van Lawick-Goodall, J. (1968). The behavior of free-living chimpanzees in the Gombe Stream Reserve. *Animal Behavior Monographs, 1,* 161–311.

van Lawick-Goodall, J. (1969). Some aspects of reproductive behavior in a group of wild chimpanzees, *Pan troglodytes scheinfurthii,* at the Gombe Stream Reserve, Tanzania, East Africa. *Journal of Reproduction and Fertility* (Suppl. 6), 353–355.

Wallen, K., Winston, L. A., Gaventa, S., Davis-DaSilva, M., & Collins, D. C. (1984). Periovulatory changes in female sexual behavior and patterns of ovarian steroid secretion in group-living rhesus monkeys. *Hormones and Behavior, 18,* 431–450.

Wallis, J. (1982). Sexual behavior of captive chimpanzees *(Pan troglodytes):* Pregnant vs. cycling females. *American Journal of Primatology, 3,* 77–88.

Wallis, J. (1985). Synchrony of estrous swelling in captive group-living chimpanzees *(Pan troglodytes). International Journal of Primatology, 6,* 335–350.

Wallis, J. (1986). *The interrelationship of socio-sexual behavior and changing steroid levels in captive adult chimpanzees (Pan troglodytes).* Unpublished doctoral dissertation, University of Oklahoma, Norman.

Wallis, J., King, B. J., & Roth-Meyer, C. (1986). The effect of female proximity and social interaction on the menstrual cycle of crab-eating monkeys *(Macaca fascicularis). Primates, 27,* 83–94.

Wallis, J., & Lemmon, W. B. (1986). Social behavior and genital swelling in pregnant chimpanzees *(Pan troglodytes). American Journal of Primatology, 10,* 171–183.

Waxenberg, S. E., Drellich, M. G., & Sutherland, A. M. (1959). The role of hormones in human behavior: I. Changes in female sexuality after adrenalectomy. *Journal of Clinical Endocrinology and Metabolism, 19,* 193–203.

Zuckerman, S. (1932). *The social life of monkeys and apes.* London: Routledge and Kegan Paul.

12

Psychological Correlates of Normal and Abnormal Menstrual Cycle Length

Stephanie A. Sanders and June M. Reinisch

Little psychological research has been conducted on menstrual cycle length, irregular cyclicity (oligomenorrhea), and the absence of menses (amenorrhea) (Sommer, 1980). In fact, empirical studies of abnormal menstrual cycle length and duration have been conducted almost exclusively by medical researchers. The relative paucity of psychological research on amenorrhea and irregular cycling is curious for two reasons. First, anecdotal data suggest an intimate association between periods of psychic stress and amenorrhea (see Ihalainen, 1975; Wentz, 1978). Psychogenic factors are most commonly cited as an etiological basis of secondary amenorrhea (see Mazzaferri, 1980), particularly among college students (Osofsky & Fisher, 1967; Siegel, Johnson, & Saranson, 1979). Second, experiencing abnormal menstrual cycles or premenopausal cessation of menses is likely to have psychological impact on a woman's self-concept, her attitudes about her body, her assessment of her femininity, and may itself result in psychological stress.

However, it was not until the recognition of so-called "war amenorrhea" that scientists became interested in the role of emotional factors in menstrual disorders (Ihalainen, 1975). For example, as a cause of war amenorrhea, fear and anxiety rather than malnutrition are now thought to be the major factors in ovarian suppression in concentration camp prisoners (Bass cited in Drew, 1961; Greenhill, 1956; Ihalainen, 1975; Loeser, 1943; Mitani, 1956; Wentz, 1978; Whitacre & Barrera, 1944).

According to psychiatric reports, psychogenic conflicts, periods of stress, depression, and fear may be associated with both primary and secondary amenorrhea (Coldsmith, 1979; Drew, 1972; Goldfarb, 1972; Sandler, 1958, 1961; Wentz, 1978). Psychological disturbance ranging from acute psychic trauma (rape or death of a loved one) to chronic emotional stress (internment, attending medical school) can disrupt the menstrual cycle. Events that might otherwise seem inconsequential (travel, examinations, a change of schools) can alter the timing of ovulation and menstrual flow (Matsumoto, Igarashi, & Nagaoka, 1968). Psychological factors including the desire to win in competitions and the emotional stress of training may contribute to the development of "sports amenorrhea." Amenorrhea is a concomitant of anorexia nervosa (self-starvation), a psychiatric disorder related to struggle for autonomy and control, fear of sexuality, and distorted body image (see Bruch, 1973, for review; Wentz, 1978, 1980). Therefore, both chronic and acute stress, moderate to severe, can cause transient or enduring disruption of menstrual cyclicity. Thus, oligomenorrhea and amenorrhea may represent a psychosomatic reaction to stressful situations.

Not all women seem equally susceptible, however, to developing irregular cycles or amenorrhea in such situations. Are there certain personality or temperament types that are related to vulnerability to menstrual disorders as a response to stress or that lead to stress reactions to normal life events?

Most of the literature regarding personality as it relates to amenorrhea derives from psychoanalytic theory. Amenorrhea in the absence of an organic explanation is often thought to be caused by a desire to avoid the adult female sexual role; conflict regarding pregnancy; rejection of femininity; sexual fears, guilt, and trauma (Deutsch, 1944; Gill, 1943; Jacobs, 1972; Mozley, 1969). Accordingly, secondary amenorrhea is thought to be a defense mechanism protecting the young woman from the perceived responsibilities of womanhood. In general, these psychiatrists have described amenorrheics as more neurotic, specifically as being more infantile and inhibited, with conflicts about their femininity. Some have even reported higher levels of masculine behavior among amenorrheics (see Ihalainen, 1975).

Others disagree with the emphasis on psychosexual conflict and report that most amenorrheics are not psychiatrically disturbed (e.g., Drew, 1972; Goldfarb, 1972). Ihalainen (1975) found significantly less psychiatric symptomology among 114 women with psychogenic amenorrhea compared with neurotic controls. Amenorrheic patients "reacted more productively to environmental stimuli," and "showed less 'pronounced' external and internal locus of control"; they were more dependent on their parents, had more changes in weight, were more dissatisfied with their weight, had participated more in sports, and "more often demonstrated difficulties in accepting the feminine role and image of their own self than the neurotic patients" (Ihalainen, 1975, p. 33). Compared with both neurotic and normal controls, amenorrheics were older at first coitus and enjoyed intercourse less. They started masturbating at a younger age than neurotics and masturbated more frequently than did normal controls. Overall, amenorrheics differed little from normal controls. In addition, more amenorrheics were in the highest occupational class and social strata.

Because anovulation associated with irregular cyclicity and amenorrhea may lead to difficulty conceiving, psychological data on infertile women is relevant. Several reports found infertile women to be more neurotic, dependent, anxious, conflicted over femininity, fearful of reproduction, and more stressed (Ford et al., 1953; Morris & Sturgis, 1959; Nesbitt, Hollender, Fisher, & Osofsky, 1968; Sandler, 1958, 1961; Sturgis, Taymor, & Morris, 1957). However, a double-blind study (Bos & Cleghorn, 1958) failed to differentiate women who were infertile due to somatic reasons from those for whom no organic cause could be found (assumed psychogenic infertility). Seibel & Taymor (1982) concluded that the emotional problems describing infertile women are more often the result of, rather than a cause of, infertility. Only prospective studies can distinguish etiological from consequential factors associated with amenorrhea or infertility.

One prospective study (Osofsky & Fisher, 1967) of an entering class of nursing students reported that the less the woman's "definiteness" of her body-image boundaries and the lower her body "awareness," the more likely she was to develop menstrual irregularity. These variables were thought to be related to lower adaptability to stress and lower femininity. Another study (Shanan, Brzezinski, Sollman, & Sharon, 1965) examined American girls 17–22 years of age who moved to Israel for a year of study. Those subjects who subsequently developed amenorrhea (22% of the group) were characterized by the authors based on the Thematic Apperception Test and Draw-A-Person Test as having a more "active-manly" coping style in response to the novel situation.

Overall, the empirical data suggest a consistent association between stress reactions and menstrual disruption, with less support for the psychodynamic view of amenorrhea as a symbolic symptom of psychosexual conflict. Personality research has demonstrated a correlation between a number of traits and the development of psychosomatic illness (Cattell, Eber, & Tatsuoka, 1970; Karson & O'Dell, 1976; Sheaffer, 1982). These psychological tendencies may mediate a psychosomatic response (e.g., menstrual disruption) to stressful situations. Thus, although amenorrheic women may not be more neurotic, they may have subtle differences in personality such as higher achievement motivation, less interest in the traditionally feminine role, and perhaps less self-satisfaction in terms of both self-esteem and body image, which may correlate with the development of irregular cyclicity.

Method

The possibility that certain personality or temperament traits correlate with the development of abnormal cyclicity was explored (Sanders, 1984). The findings are briefly summarized with emphasis given to a number of important methodological considerations and conceptual issues relevant to investigations of psychological correlates of menstrual patterns.

Sample

Women with various cycle lengths were specifically recruited for this study.[1] Seventy-eight unmarried female university students (ages 17–21 years, $M = 20.8$) completed psychological and medical/menstrual questionnaires.[2] Menstrual calendars were maintained for two complete cycles or 3 months, whichever came first. Standard gynecological convention (e.g., Bachmann & Kemmann, 1982; Mazzaferri, 1980) was used to classify these women by cycle length as follows: 2 polymenorrheic (cycles < 25 days apart); 49 normal (cycle length 25–34 days); 17 oligomenorrheic (cycle length 35–90 days); and 10 amenorrheic (cycles > 90 days apart). Meaningful numerical values for cycle length and relative variability could not reasonably be estimated for 11 subjects; one was at the extreme end of the oligomenorrheic category and 10 were amenorrheic. For the remaining subjects, the mean cycle length was 34.36 days ($SD = 12.23$), with a mean range (longest-shortest cycle) of 11.72 days ($SD = 13.66$).[3]

Procedure

The psychological and biophysical attributes of each subject were assessed (Table 1). Menstrual disruption can be conceptualized in terms of deviance from the 29-day statistical norm and of individual cycle-to-cycle variation. Thus, two menstrual parameters, cycle length and relative variability, were evaluated as dependent variables related to both biophysical and psychological factors. Cycle length was defined as the number of days from the first day of one menstrual period until the day before the onset of the next flow. The longest and shortest cycles reported by each subject for the preceding year in the medical/menstrual histories or documented by calendar dates were used as the best estimate of the degree to which each woman's cycle varied.[4] The midpoint between the longest and shortest cycle lengths was used as the measure of *cycle length.* It should be noted that midpoint scores are highly correlated with reported mean cycle length ($r = .9205$, $p = .001$) and thus, in general, do not differ substantially from subject reports. Range was defined as the difference between the longest and shortest cycle lengths. The ratio of range/cycle length was calculated for each subject and used as the measure *relative variability.* This ratio represents the proportion of range relative to individual's own cycle length; for example, a 6-day range around a 28-day cycle length represents proportionately more variability than does 6 days around a 40-day cycle length. This measures the degree to which a woman's cycle length varied from cycle to cycle.

Table 1.
Psychological and Biophysical Dimensions Assessed in the Study

Dimension	Test	Source
Psychological		
Personality	Cattell 16 Personality Factors (16 PF)	Cattell, Eber, & Tatsuoka (1970)
Temperament	New York Longitudinal Study Adult Temperament Questionnaire (NYLS)	Thomas & Chess (1977)
Sex role	Extended Personal Attributes Questionnaire (EPAQ)	Spence, Helmreich, & Holahan (1979)
Locus of control	Nowicki-Strickland Internal-External Locus of Control Scale (ANS-IE)	Nowicki & Duke (1974)
Self-esteem	Texas Social Behavior Inventory (TSBI)	Spence & Helmreich (1978)
Achievement motivation	Work and Family Orientation Questionnaire (WOFO III)	Spence & Helmreich (1978)
Body image	Body Image Questionnaire (BIQ)	Sanders revision of Secord & Jourard (1953)
Menstrual attitudes	Menstrual Attitudes Questionnaire (MAQ)	Brooks-Gunn & Ruble (1980)
Biophysical[a]		
Age at menarche		
Body weight/height		
Change in body weight over the last year		
Amount of exercise		
Medical history: hospitalization, surgery, medical problems, psychosomatic illnesses, self-ratings of general health		
Type of diet: vegetarian, calorie reduced, regular		
Consumption of substances: alcohol, caffeine, cigarettes, medications		
Sexual activity		
Contraceptive usage: past, present		

[a]Data obtained from Medical/Menstrual Questionnaire.

Analysis

Two levels of analysis were applied to the data. The first compared biophysical and psychological measures across four groups classified according to medically defined cycle lengths: polymenorrhea, normal, oligomenorrhea, and amenorrhea. The second level of analysis consisted

of correlation procedures relating biophysical and psychological dimensions to cycle length measured in days and relative variability. In the
current sample as in others (e.g., Bachmann & Kemmann, 1982; Chiazze,
Brayer, Macisco, Parker, & Duffy, 1968; Treolar, Boynton, Behn, &
Brown, 1967; Vollman, 1977), distributions of menstrual cycle length and
variability were negatively skewed. Thus, log transformations of cycle
length and relative variability were used to linearize functions of interest
and expand the capacity to examine subtle, but perhaps psychologically
meaningful differences in menstrual parameters. These latter procedures
take advantage of the continuous nature of cycle length and variability
measurements and increase sensitivity to variation within the more normal
range over that provided by analyses of variance (ANOVAs) that were used
to compare discrete cycle length groups.

Psychological variables and menstrual cycle parameters may be related
in a number of ways. In some cases, a linear relationship exists between
the psychological dimension and menstrual deviance (longer cycle lengths
and greater variability). Figure 1 (panels a, b) depicts such theoretical relationships for positive and negative correlations, respectively. Nonlinear
relationships may also exist in which deviance on psychological dimensions (represented by extreme scores at either end of the distribution—
high or low scores) is associated with menstrual deviance. Figure 1 (panels
c, d) represents theoretical positive and negative relationships of this kind.
In such cases, absolute values of z-scores can be used for the psychological
data, capturing relative deviance regardless of direction. The term deviance
on psychological dimensions is used in the statistical sense and refers to
scores falling toward the ends of the distribution for the current sample.
In this way, deviance in menstrual parameters can be correlated with
deviance in psychological scores yielding a linear relationship.

Results

Cycle Length Differentiation

When the four cycle-length groups were compared, menarcheal age was
the only differentiating factor. Consistent with other reports (e.g.,
Bachmann & Kemmann, 1982; Ihalainen, 1976), age at menarche was significantly higher among oligomenorrheic and amenorrheic women
compared with normal cyclers, $F(3, 83) = 4.788$, $p = .004$, Student-
Newman-Keuls $p < .05$. Mean menarcheal age was 12.00 years for polymenorrheic women, 12.39 for normomenorrheics, 13.32 for oligomenorrheics, and 13.90 for those with amenorrhea. Age at menarche
accounted for 12% of the variance in cycle length (*Multiple R* = .3601,
$F(1, 75) = 11.17$, $p = .001$), but only approximately 4% of the variance in
relative variability (n.s.).

None of the remaining biophysical factors nor any of the psychological

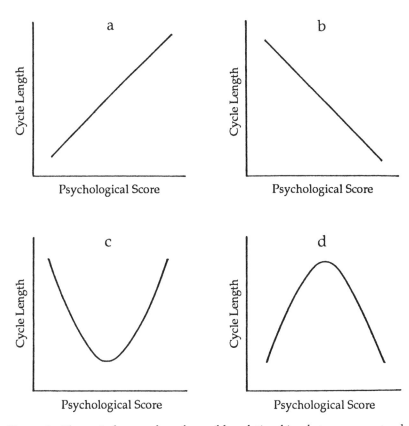

Figure 1. Theoretical examples of possible relationships between menstrual parameters and psychological scores: (a) represents a positive linear relationship; long cycle length is associated with a high psychological score; (b) represents a negative linear relationship; long cycle length is associated with a low psychological score; (c) represents a relationship between long cycle length and deviance from the sample norm on a psychological dimension; and (d) represents an association between short cycle length and deviance from the sample norm on a psychological dimension.

factors differentiated among the four groups. This finding differs from studies stressing the importance of changes in body weight or fat/lean ratio (e.g., Bachmann & Kemmann, 1982; Wentz, 1978, 1980) and athletics (e.g., Bachmann & Kemmann, 1982; Carlberg, Buckman, Peake, & Riedesel, 1983; Erdelyi, 1962; Faiman, Blankstein, Reyes, & Winter, 1981; Shangold, 1982) in the etiology of menstrual disruption, but is consistent with others that have also failed to confirm simple relationships between menstrual disruption and these variables (e.g., Baker, Mathur, Kirk, & Williamson, 1981; Brooks, Sanborn, Albrecht, & Wagner, 1984; Lev-Ran,

1974). This study did not focus on testing the limits of biophysical parameters. However, the homogeneity across cycle length groups obviated their use as covariates in the analyses of psychological data.

Psychological Dimension Correlates

Only when the continuous distributions of menstrual parameters were the focus of *correlational* analyses were systematic relationships between psychological dimensions and either cycle length or relative variability revealed. Stepwise multiple regressions identified psychological variables which, combined with age at menarche, accounted for 76% of the variance in cycle length: *Multiple R* = .8733, *p* < .001 (see Table 2); and 60% of the variance in relative variability: *Multiple R* = .7776, *p* < .001 (see Table 3). It should be noted that significant correlational relationships

Table 2.
Multiple Regression Predicting Cycle Length from Psychological and Physical Variables

Step	Factor	*Multiple R*	R^2	β	*F*	*p*
1	Approach/withdrawal	.3620	.1310	-.8614	8.45	.005
2	Age at menarche	.5220	.2724	.3477	10.30	.000
3	Ability to bind anxiety (Q3)*	.6428	.4132	.3493	12.68	.000
4	Mood*	.7094	.5032	.3061	13.42	.000
5	Activity*	.7456	.5559	.3124	13.02	.000
6	Group conformity (G)*	.7707	.5939	.3692	12.43	.000
7	Self-esteem (TSBI)	.7947	.6315	.6157	12.24	.000
8	Stimulus threshold*	.8179	.6689	-.1677	12.37	.000
9	Femininity (F+)	.8389	.7036	-.2837	12.66	.000
10	Work orientation*	.8571	.7346	.2521	13.01	.000
11	Superego*	.8733	.7626	-.3073	13.43	.000

*Denotes absolute value of z-scores.

Table 3.
Multiple Regression Predicting Relative Variability from Psychological and Physical Variables

Step	Factor	*Multiple R*	R^2	β	*F*	*p*
1	School achievement*	.3527	.1244	.2556	7.82	.007
2	Free-floating anxiety (Q4)*	.4658	.2169	.2198	7.48	.001
3	Age at menarche	.5520	.3047	.3188	7.74	.000
4	Mood*	.6298	.3966	.1564	8.55	.000
5	Stimulus threshold*	.6775	.4590	-.2558	8.65	.000
6	Persistence	.7143	.5102	.0792	8.68	.000
7	Adaptability	.7429	.5518	-.1160	8.62	.000
8	Group conformity*	.7776	.6047	.2646	9.18	.000

*Denotes absolute value of z-scores.

between psychological factors and the parameters of menstrual deviance were found despite the fact that variance on biophysical and psychological dimensions was limited, all scores falling within normal range.

Long cyclers were found to be more withdrawn, less moderate in activity level (i.e., more lethargic or more active), less rhythmic (less predictable in daily patterns such as sleeping and eating), and less stereotypically feminine (as indicated by femininity, self-esteem, and work-orientation scores). It should be noted that such temperamental differences can be viewed as behavioral predispositions (Thomas & Chess, 1977) that (a) can be measured in infancy as early as 4–8 weeks; (b) remain relatively stable over time; and (c) may be highly influenced by the biology of the developing organism.

Cycle length and relative variability shared approximately 25% of their variance. Examination of the constellation of psychological variables that correlate with these menstrual parameters revealed a core common to both. Both cycle length and relative variability were related to difficulty in modulating both anxiety levels and quality of mood within the framework of apparently normal stimulus responsiveness. Women with longer and more variable cycles also appeared to have deviant scores on group conformity. That older age at menarche related to menstrual deviance is consistent with the view that there is some disruption of the underlying physiological "clock(s)" controlling the timing of ovarian cycles.

Around this core there were two divergent satellite clusters of psychological factors that corresponded to either cycle length or relative variability. Figure 2 provides a schematic summarization of the findings. Cycle length was related to temperament and personality traits which are more internalized and less susceptible to environmental influence. Relative variability, on the other hand, was related to more externalized factors involving environmental control and achievement. This distinction suggests that cycle length may be more related to organismic or trait factors, and variability may be relatively more dependent on environmental or state factors.

A test was conducted to assess the usefulness of the prediction equations generated by the stepwise multiple regressions for cycle length and relative variability in distinguishing abnormal cyclers from those within the normal range. ANOVA was used to compare the predicted values for these menstrual parameters across cycle length groups. Compared with normal cyclers, oligomenorrheic and amenorrheic subjects had significantly greater predicted cycle lengths, $F(3, 52) = 8.213$, $p = .0001$, Student-Newman-Keuls $p < .05$, and relative variability, $F(3, 58) = 3.825$, $p = .0144$. Although amenorrheics were not distinguished from oligomenorrheics, both groups were distinguished from normals. This finding is particularly impressive as the amenorrheic women were not included in the regression analyses because their cycle lengths could not be estimated accurately.

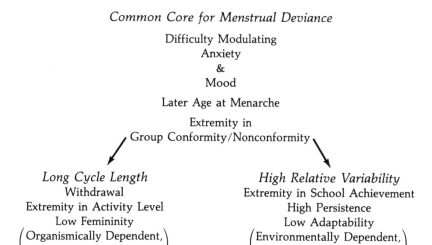

Figure 2. The common core and divergent clusters of factors related to cycle length and relative variability in cycle length. Cycle length appeared to be related to organismic or intrinsic factors, whereas relative variability was related to more environmentally dependent or extrinsic factors.

Therefore, the relationship of psychological variables and age at menarche to menstrual cycle parameters could be thought of as having been "validated" on a "second" sample.

Discussion

As a whole, there appears to be a generalized organismic character to the factors specifically associated with cycle length. Several considerations support this characterization. The age of menarche contributed more strongly to cycle length than to relative variability. The trait variable, ability to bind anxiety, is associated with cycle length, whereas the state variable, free-floating anxiety, is associated with relative variability. It should be noted that data from other sources indicate that predispositions for both certain aspects of behavioral development and menstrual cyclicity may be affected by the prenatal hormonal milieu. Exposure to androgenic substances during early critical periods for sexual differentiation has been shown to delay onset of puberty and increase cyclic dysfunction and even result in cessation of cyclicity in monkeys (Resko, 1974), and humans with adrenogenital syndrome (Money & Schwartz, 1977). Such exposure also has the potential to masculinize or defeminize behavior in humans as well as other animals (see Reinisch & Sanders, 1984a, b; Sanders & Reinisch, 1985). This is not to suggest that longer cycles in the current sample reflected prenatal androgenization, but rather to suggest the type of biological mechanisms which could be involved in both altering behavioral predispositions and shifting cycle length out of the normal range. Thus, the hypothesis that cycle length is more highly related to organismic or trait variables than to environmental or state variables seems consistent with both the current findings as well as those of other researchers.

High relative variability, on the other hand, was related to deviance on the personality factors associated with school achievement, high persistence, and low adaptability. This finding may give some support to the notion that it is the stress of college that leads to slightly higher rates of menstrual irregularity in college women (Osofsky & Fisher, 1967; Shanan et al., 1968). In light of the core difficulties regarding anxiety, as discussed above, those women who, based on personality traits, seemed to be less likely to do well in school may have experienced high levels of anxiety because they may have been testing their scholastic limits with college-level material. On the other hand, high scorers on school achievement may have placed a premium on doing well in school, and as such may have been more anxious regarding their performance than those with more moderate scores. High persistence and low adaptability scores further suggest that women with more variable cycle lengths were less likely to respond adaptively to environmental situations and were perhaps more persistent in their maladaptive responses. These women may have some difficulty in dealing effectively with the perturbations of everyday life. If environmental stimuli can be assimilated, in the Piagetian sense, the woman can happily persist in her behavioral patterns. But should environmental situations require an alteration of behavior (accommodation), this type of person could find it difficult to adjust and might be more disrupted, in some general sense, by the environmental change. Among many possible sequelae of such maladaptation to environmental change, a woman with this constellation of qualities might be more susceptible to menstrual disruption (as a psychosomatic reaction). The psychological dimensions associated with relative variability appear to be more related to susceptibility to environmental change or state factors than to internal/organismic factors.

The distinction between cycle length and relative variability suggests that chronic and transient amenorrhea/oligomenorrhea may represent disruption of distinct but related underlying physiological mechanisms. The literature (reviewed earlier) clearly documents that stress associated with environmental or behavioral change can disrupt menstrual cyclicity, with normal menses resuming upon removal of the stressor or adjustment to it. Thus, transient changes in menstrual pattern may reflect deviance on the dimension of relative variability. Chronic amenorrhea/oligomenorrhea appears to be internally/organismically controlled and may reflect deviance on the cycle length dimension. Bachmann and Kemmann (1982) reported that for the majority of women with chronic amenorrhea or oligomenorrhea, menstrual irregularity developed immediately after menarche and apparently was not related to life stress. Thus, there are data reported in the literature that provide external support for the postulate regarding relative degrees of organismic and environmental control of cycle length and relative variability.

In conclusion, it appears that standard gynecological categorizations of polymenorrhea, normal cycling, oligomenorrhea, and amenorrhea based on mean menstrual cycle length may not be psychologically meaningful because they lack sensitivity in two ways: (a) They utilize artificial boundaries, emphasize group distinctions, and do not take advantage of the continuous nature of cycle length data (e.g., a woman with a 34-day cycle would be classified with a 28-day cycler and not in the same group as a 35-day cycler); and (b) they do not distinguish between cycle length and relative variability which are oblique dimensions. Further, a distinction between chronic and transient amenorrhea/oligomenorrhea seems warranted, because these may reflect disruption of distinct underlying physiological mechanisms related to cycle length and relative variability, respectively. A common core of psychological traits predominantly involving modulation of anxiety and mood appears to be shared by both menstrual parameters. Beyond this common core, cycle length appears to be more related to internal/organismic traits, whereas relative variability is more related to state variables and factors that suggest higher susceptibility to environmental influences.

NOTES

The data reported here were part of my doctoral thesis for the Department of Psychology, Rutgers–The State University of New Jersey, New Brunswick. Support was provided, in part, by The Kinsey Institute for Research in Sex, Gender, and Reproduction at Indiana University, Bloomington, where the writing and data analysis were conducted. I thank Donald Rubin, Department of Statistics, Harvard University, for statistical consultation.

1. I thank Gloria Bachmann and Dorothea Sved for their assistance in recruiting subjects.

2. Five subjects reported previous pregnancies, but none indicated that they had children. Oral contraceptive users were not accepted for the sample except in one case in which the medication was being used for menstrual regulation and five cases in which pill use was just beginning. All of these women provided docu-

mentation of nonhormonally regulated menstrual cycle length.

3. It should be noted that subjects with abnormal cycle lengths were specifically recruited for this study, and therefore the distribution of cycle lengths was not representative of the college population in general. Compared with a survey conducted at the same university 3 years earlier (Bachmann & Kemmann, 1982), the sample reported here had twice as many oligomenorrheics and four times as many amenorrheics.

4. The use of subjects' reports of their longest and shortest cycle length in conjunction with calendar dates was deemed necessary in determining cycle length variability because no more than three cycles were documented for this study and these data alone would be likely to underestimate variability in some cases.

REFERENCES

Bachmann, G. A., & Kemmann, E. (1982). Prevalence of oligomenorrhea and amenorrhea in a college population. *American Journal of Obstetrics and Gynecology, 144,* 98–102.

Baker, E. R., Mathur, R. S., Kirk, R. F., & Williamson, H. O. (1981). Female runners and secondary amenorrhea: Correlation with age, parity, mileage, and plasma hormonal and sex-hormone-binding globulin concentrations. *Fertility & Sterility, 36,* 183–187.

Bos, C., & Cleghorn, R. A. (1958). Psychogenic sterility. *Fertility & Sterility, 9,* 84–95.

Brooks, S. M., Sanborn, C. F., Albrecht, B. H., & Wagner, W. W. (1984). Diet in athletic amenorrhoea [Letter]. *Lancet, 1,* 559–560.

Brooks-Gunn, J., & Ruble, D. N. (1980). The menstrual attitude questionnaire. *Psychosomatic Medicine, 42,* 503.

Bruch, H. (1973). *Eating disorders: Obesity, anorexia nervosa and the person within.* New York: Basic Books.

Carlberg, K. A., Buckman, M. T., Peake, G. T., & Riedesel, M. L. (1983). Body composition of oligo/amenorrheic athletes. *Medicine and Science Sports Exercise, 15,* 215–217.

Cattell, R. B., Eber, H. W., & Tatsuoka, M. (1970). *Handbook for 16 PF.* Champaign, IL: Institute for Personality and Ability Testing.

Chiazze, L., Brayer, F. T., Macisco, J. J., Parker, M. P., & Duffy, B. J. (1968). The length and variability of the human menstrual cycle. *Journal of the American Medical Association, 203,* 377–380.

Coldsmith, D. (1979). "Symbolic" amenorrhea-emotional factors in secondary amenorrhea. *Medical Aspects of Human Sexuality, 9,* 95–112.

Deutsch, H. (1944). *The psychology of women* (Vol. 1). New York: Grune & Stratton.

Drew, F. L. (1961). The epidemiology of secondary amenorrhea. *Journal of Chronic Disorders, 14,* 396.

Drew, F. L. (1972). Commentary on "Secondary amenorrhea and sexual conflicts." *Medical Aspects of Human Sexuality, 6,* 97–102.

Erdelyi, G. J. (1962). Gynecological survey of female athletes. *Journal of Sports Medicine and Physical Fitness, 2,* 174–179.

Faiman, C., Blankstein, J., Reyes, F. I., & Winter, J. S. D. (1981). Endorphins and the regulation of the human menstrual cycle. *Fertility & Sterility, 36,* 267–268.

Ford, E. S. C., Forman, I., Wilson, J. R., Char, W., Mixon, W. T., & Scholtz, C. (1953). A psychodynamic approach to the study of infertility. *Fertility & Sterility, 4,* 456.

Gill, M. M. (1943). Functional disturbances of menstruation. *Bulletin of the Menninger Clinic, 7,* 6–14.

Goldfarb, A. F. (1972). Commentary on "Secondary amenorrhea and sexual conflicts." *Medical Aspects of Human Sexuality, 6,* 87–96.

Greenhill, J. (1956). Emotional factors in female infertility. *Obstetrics & Gynecology, 7,* 602–606.

Ihalainen, O. (1975). Psychosomatic aspects of amenorrhea. *Acta Psychiatrica Scandinavica,* Suppl. 262, 1–139.

Jacobs, T. J. (1972). Secondary amenorrhea and sexual conflicts. *Medical Aspects of Human Sexuality, 6,* 87–102.

Karson, S., & O'Dell, J. W. (1976). *A guide to the clinical use of the 16 PF.* Champaign, IL: Institute for Personality and Ability Testing.

Lev-Ran, A. (1974). Secondary amenorrhea resulting from uncontrolled weight-reducing diets. *Fertility & Sterility, 25,* 459–462.

Loeser, A. A. (1943). Effect of emotional shock on hormone release and endometrial development. *Lancet, 1,* 518.

Matsumoto, S., Igarashi, M., & Nagaoka, Y. (1968). Environmental anovulatory cycles. *International Journal of Fertility, 13,* 15–23.

Mazzaferri, E. L. (Ed.). (1980). *Endocrinology: A review of clinical endocrinology* (2d ed.). New York: Medical Examination Publishing Co.

Mitani, Y. (1956). The effect of the atomic bomb on menstruation. *International Journal of Fertility, 1,* 281–292.

Money, J., & Schwartz, M. (1977). Dating, romantic and nonromantic friendships, and sexuality in 17 early-treated adrenogenital females aged 16–25. In P. A. Lee, L. P. Plotnick, A. A. Kowarsky, & C. J. Migeon (Eds.), *Congenital adrenal hyperplasia.* Baltimore, MD: University Park Press.

Morris, T. A., & Sturgis, S. H. (1959). Practical aspects of psychosomatic sterility. *Clinical Obstetrics and Gynecology, 2,* 890.

Mozley, P. D. (1969). Forced femininity: Opening Pandora's box. *Obstetrics & Gynecology, 34,* 414–417.

Nesbitt, R. E. L., Hollender, M., Fisher, S., & Osofsky, H. J. (1968). Psychological correlates of the polycystic ovary syndrome and organic infertility. *Fertility & Sterility, 19,* 778.

Nowicki, S., & Duke, M. P. (1974). A locus of control scale for noncollege as well as college adults. *Journal of Personality Assessment, 38,* 136–137.

Osofsky, H. J., & Fisher, S. (1967). Psychological correlates of the development of amenorrhea in a stress situation. *Psychosomatic Medicine, 29,* 15–22.

Reinisch, J. M., & Sanders, S. A. (1984a). Hormonal influences on sexual development and behavior. In M. F. Schwartz, A. S. Moraczewski, & J. A. Monteleone (Eds.), *Sex and gender: A theological and scientific inquiry* (pp. 48–64). St. Louis, MO: The Pope John Center.

Reinisch, J. M., & Sanders, S. A. (1984b). Prenatal gonadal steroidal influences on gender-related behavior. In G. J. de Vries, J. P. C. De Bruin, H. B. M. Uylings, & M. A. Corner (Eds.), *Sex differences in the brain: Relation between structure and function. Progress in Brain Research* (Vol. 61, pp. 407–416). Amsterdam, The Netherlands: Elsevier Science.

Resko, J. A. (1974). The relationship between fetal hormones and the differentiation of the central nervous system in primates. In W. Montagna & W. A. Sadler (Eds.), *Reproductive behavior.* New York: Plenum Press.

Sanders, S. A. (1984). *Psychological correlates of menstrual cycle length and variability.* Unpublished doctoral dissertation, Rutgers, The State University of New Jersey, New Brunswick.

Sanders, S. A., & Reinisch, J. M. (1985). Behavioral effects on humans of progesterone-related compounds during development and in the adult. In D. Ganten & D. Pfaff (Eds.), *Current topics in neuroendocrinology: Actions of progesterone on the brain* (Vol. 5, pp. 175–205). Heidelberg: Springer-Verlag.

Sandler, B. (1958). Emotional stress and infertility. *British Journal of Clinical Practice, 13,* 328–330.

Sandler, B. (1961). Infertility of emotional origin. *Journal of Obstetrics and Gynecology of British Commonwealth, 68,* 804–815.

Secord, P. R., & Jourard, S. M. (1953). The appraisal of body-cathexis: Body-cathexis and the self. *Journal of Consulting Psychology, 17,* 343–347.

Seibel, M. M., & Taymor, M. L. (1982). Emotional aspects of infertility. *Fertility & Sterility, 37,* 137–145.

Shanan, J., Brzezinski, A., Sollman, F., & Sharon, M. (1965). Active coping behavior, anxiety, and cortical steroid excretion in the prediction of transient amenorrhea. *Behavioral Science, 10,* 461–465.

Shangold, M. M. (1982). Brief guide to office counseling: Exercise-related menstrual irregularity. *Medical Aspects of Human Sexuality, 16,* 40A–40K.

Sheaffer, M. (1982). *Life after stress.* New York: Plenum Press.

Siegel, J. M., Johnson, J. H., & Saranson, I. G. (1979). Life changes and menstrual discomfort. *Journal of Human Stress, 5,* 41–46.

Sommer, B. (1980). Cognitive behavior and the menstrual cycle. In R. C. Friedman (Ed.), *Behavior and the menstrual cycle* (pp. 101–107). New York: Marcel Dekker.

Spence, J. T., & Helmreich, R. L. (1978). *Masculinity and femininity: Their psychological dimensions, correlates and antecedents.* Austin: University of Texas Press.

Spence, J. T., Helmreich, R. L., & Holahan, C. K. (1979). Negative and positive components of psychological masculinity and femininity and their relationship to self-reports of neurotic and acting out behaviors. *Journal of Social and Personality Psychology, 37,* 1673–1682.

Sturgis, S. H., Taymor, M. L., & Morris, T. (1957). Routine psychiatric interviews in a sterility investigation. *Sterility & Fertility, 8,* 521.

Thomas, A., & Chess, S. (1977). *Temperament and development.* New York:
Brenner/Mazel.

Treolar, A. E., Boynton, R. E., Behn, B. G., & Brown, B. W. (1967). Variation
of the human menstrual cycle through reproductive life. *International Journal
of Fertility, 12,* 77–126.

Vollman, R. F. (1977). *The menstrual cycle.* Philadelphia: W. B. Saunders.

Wentz, A. C. (1978). Psychogenic amenorrhea and anorexia nervosa. In J. R.
Givens (Ed.), *Endocrine causes of menstrual disorders* (pp. 87–113). Chicago:
Year Book Medical Publishers.

Wentz, A. C. (1980). Body weight and amenorrhea. *Obstetrics & Gynecology,
56,* 482.

Whitacre, F. E., & Barrera, B. (1944). War amenorrhea: A clinical and laboratory
study. *Journal of the American Medical Association, 124,* 399.

13

Menstrual Migraine Headache

Patricia Solbach

The word migraine is a French mutation of the Greek word *hemikrania* which translates as "half a head," referring to its most distinguishing feature, unilaterality. Migraine attacks are preceded by constriction of the cranial arteries followed by vasodilation. The throbbing, pulsating pain is commonly associated with nausea, or vomiting or some gastrointestinal upset, photophobia, and irritability. There is usually a familial history.

Headache is as old as humankind. Thousands of Neolithic skulls bear the mark of trephination, surgery often done without anesthesia, which involved making a hole in the victim's skull with a sharp tool, thereby supposedly releasing the pain. The Greeks believed that headaches were caused by evil spirits; the Romans contributed the belief that headaches were inflicted by gods upon those who incurred divine displeasure. Their Latin word for pain, *poena*, literally means a penalty or punishment (Friedman, 1972).

Many of today's treatments for headache have roots from the past. A Greek physician in A.D. 77 compiled a list of 600 herbal remedies for various ailments, including headache (Murphy, 1982). The seventeenth century American Indians found a successful remedy for headache still in use today. Their concoction made from the sex glands of male beavers contained salicylate, a chemical contained in aspirin.

Migraine occurs primarily in women. That adult females are most often the victims of migraine was confirmed by the findings of the National Center for Health Statistics in a survey of prevalence of headaches among American adults (Murphy, 1982). Indeed, the migraine rate rises from a ratio of 1:1 in boys and girls to a ratio of 3:1 in favor of females after puberty (Epstein, Hockaday, & Hockaday, 1975). This difference in prevalence indicates that female hormones play a role in migraine occurrence.

It is estimated that 60% to 70% of all women seen for migraine report some portion of their attacks occurring around the menstrual period (Diamond & Dalessio, 1978; Lance & Anthony, 1956). Frequently, these women report an absence or decrease in migraine activity during pregnancy and after menopause.

It is theorized that a different kind of internal fluctuation triggers the menstrual migraine compared with migraines occurring at other times. Those migraines occurring at times other than with the menses are often described as less severe and disabling and more easily controlled with drugs or the use of biofeedback.

The one-sided head pain occurring with the menses is possibly triggered by the cyclical production of estrogen, specifically, its decline or depletion approaching the 28th day or just before the onset of the next cycle. In any one cycle, the attack may occur at the time of menstruation as well as at ovulation, but it more frequently coincides with menstruation. When it occurs with menstruation, it appears just prior to or during the period. The headache may occur only in some months around the menses or every month at that time.

Few published reports in the literature focus on menstrual migraine. One of the earliest studies involving 720 female migraineurs showed highly significant differences between those with menstrual migraine and those with nonmenstrual migraine (Nattero, 1982). Differences were found in headache patterns, familial background, premenstrual stress, relationship of menstruation and pregnancy, frequency, duration, location, and accompanying symptoms.

Somerville's work (1972, 1975a, 1975b) on estrogen withdrawal is probably the most complete study on the role hormones play in migraine. Menstrual cycles of women with menstrual migraine were experimentally manipulated with estrogen or progesterone. Falling estrogen levels appeared to precipitate an attack; estrogen was hypothesized to prime the vessels, making them more susceptible to other factors. Somerville noted that the rarity of ovulatory migraine suggests that a period of several days of exposure to high estrogen levels may be necessary before estrogen withdrawal precipitates migraine.

Welch, Darnley, and Simkins (1984) in a thorough review of studies in clinical and basic science hypothesized that estrogen exerts its influence by modulating sympathetic control of the cerebral vasculature. They believe that measurements of cerebrovascular reactivity at different stages in the menstrual cycle with correlation to blood estrogen levels, alpha-2 receptor function in platelets, and indices of sympathetic activity are needed to further understand the role estrogens play.

Studies on the role progesterone plays in menstrual migraine have shown conflicting results, with several showing progesterone to be effective in preventing migraines. Somerville (1972) found the administration of progesterone to women with prolonged high exposure to estrogen did not initiate attacks, supporting the view that progesterone withdrawal is not a precipitant for menstrual migraine.

Treatment Studies of Menstrual Migraine

Study 1

There is no universally effective treatment for menstrual migraine (Solbach, Sargent, & Kennedy, 1986). Thermal biofeedback, or hand-warming, which produces an increase of blood flow in the hands at will, has become the treatment of choice for migraine headache. Its effectiveness has been demonstrated in numerous clinical and research studies (Sargent, Solbach, Coyne, Spohn, & Segerson, 1986).

A study of menstrual migraine headache and biofeedback was conducted in which menstrual migraines were identified in 193 migraineurs (Solbach, Sargent, & Coyne, 1984). Of 114 females who completed the study, 83 (73%) had migraines associated with the menstrual period. Menstrual migraine in this study was defined as any migraine headache occurring during the time 3 days prior to, during, or 3 days following the flow.

Subjects were required to participate for 36 weeks and to maintain daily records of headache frequency, intensity, duration, degree of disability, medication usage, and symptoms. During this period, subjects participated in 22 laboratory sessions in which hand temperature and frontalis electromyographic measurements were taken. The 36-week period was divided into three phases: I. Baseline, 4 weeks; II. Training, 8 weeks; III. Follow-up, 24 weeks (Figure 1).

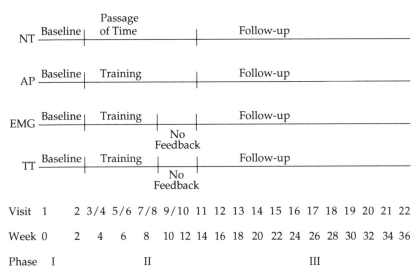

NT = no treatment; AP = autogenic phrases; EMG = electromyographic biofeedback; TT = thermal biofeedback.

Figure 1. Trial design of Study 1.

Subjects were randomly assigned to one of four independent groups over the 36 weeks: no treatment, autogenic phrases, electromyographic biofeedback, and thermal biofeedback. All subjects except those in the no-treatment group were required to practice daily for 15 min at home.

The no-treatment group charted their headache activity daily and participated in the 22 laboratory sessions. The autogenic phrases group also kept daily records, participated in the 22 laboratory sessions, and used autogenic phrases (e.g., my hands feel warm) to help encourage relaxation and increase blood flow in the hands. The electromyographic biofeedback group kept daily records, underwent 22 laboratory sessions, used the autogenic phrases, and received electromyographic feedback from the frontalis area. The thermal biofeedback group maintained daily records, had 22 laboratory sessions, used autogenic phrases, and received skin temperature feedback from the right hand.

The mean age of the sample was 31 years. On the average, headache onset began at 19 years. The majority, 58 (70%), were married; 63 (76%) worked outside the home. A history of headache in the family was reported by 63 (76%) with 35 (42%) identifying their mother as being affected. In this sample 20 (24%) were identified in the physical examination as obese; 19 (23%) reported allergies; 9 (11%) also had irritable colon; 4 (5%) had sinus trouble; and 3 (4%) had hypertension.

The 83 subjects showed a reduction in menstrual migraine frequency, $F=3.679$, $df=75$, $p<.001$; intensity, $F=3.363$, $df=75$, $p<.002$; disability, $F=3.73$, $df=75$, $p<.001$; and symptoms, $F=3.964$, $df=75$, $p<.001$, over the 36-week period. Significant differences among groups were not found.

Study 2

An examination was made of the effectiveness of a nonsteroidal anti-inflammatory drug, naproxen sodium (Anaprox); a well-known migraine prophylactic, propranolol hydrochloride (Inderal); and a placebo drug for menstrual migraine (Sargent et al., 1985). This double-blind, placebo-controlled, parallel-treatment study lasted 17 weeks.

Patients were randomly assigned to one of three regimes: propranolol hydrochloride 40 mg t.i.d., naproxen sodium 550 mg b.i.d., or a placebo. The trial consisted of four phases: Phase I, a 2-week washout period when all patients received placebo; Phase II, a 2-week period when patients randomized to the propranolol group received 40 mg b.i.d., patients on the naproxen sodium regimen received the full dosage (550 mg b.i.d.), and the third group continued to receive placebo; Phase III, a 12-week period when patients received full dosage of all drugs (propranolol hydrochloride 40 mg t.i.d., naproxen sodium 550 mg b.i.d., or placebo); Phase IV, a 1-week taper-off period for propranolol hydrochloride when patients again received 40 mg b.i.d., and subjects in the other two groups continued to receive their Phase III dosages (Figure 2).

Of the 170 patients who entered this multicenter study, 161 entered Phase I, 149 entered Phase II, and 129 had valid data for analysis. Thirty-six patients with valid efficacy data recorded menstrual dates during the 17-week study period. Data were analyzed for 30 patients who reported at least two menstrual periods. Menstrual migraine was defined as unilateral head pain occurring during the 7 days before the start of the menses and the 7-day period after the start.

Subjects receiving placebo had more frequent and severe headaches during the week before menses than after its onset. Subjects in the two active-treatment groups had fewer and less severe headaches during the premenstrual week than during the week after the onset.

When pre- and postmenstrual weeks were compared for headache frequency, pairwise comparisons were of borderline statistical significance for naproxen sodium/placebo ($p = .07$) and not statistically significant for propranolol hydrochloride/placebo ($p = .22$). A comparison of pre- and postmenstrual weeks for headache severity showed that naproxen sodium was more effective than either placebo ($p = .01$) or propranolol hydrochloride ($p = .054$).

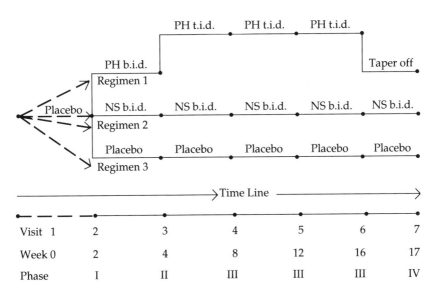

PH = propranolol hydrochloride 40 mg; NS = naproxen sodium 550 mg.

Figure 2. Drug trial design of Study 2.

Discussion

Menstrual migraine headache has been identified only recently as a distinct clinical entity. Previously, it was generally assumed that treatments for migraine would also be effective for menstrual migraine, but researchers and clinicians are reporting the latter more difficult to treat (Edelson, 1985).

The biofeedback study reported here showed a total group reduction of headache activity due probably to nonspecific effects, such as the subject's expectancy to improve and the focus of attention by the subject and research staff on the subject's headache activity. But no specific treatment effects could be found in the biofeedback-trained groups.

After that study was conducted, similar findings showing that non-pharmacological treatment has a lesser impact on menstrually associated headaches emerged in a study comparing relaxation-biofeedback behavior therapy and person-centered insight therapy (Szekely et al., 1986). Neither the behavioral treatment nor the insight treatment had a significant effect on reduction of menstrual headache, even though the behavioral group demonstrated a learning effect in the physiological measures and the insight group rated their therapist very highly.

Significant biochemical and clinical differences have been documented between menstrual migraine sufferers and those with nonmenstrual migraine (Nattero, 1982). Menstrual migraine appears to be based more on biochemical factors although the role of stress probably has some influence.

In the drug study, women treated with naproxen sodium experienced the greatest decrease in headache severity as well as some decrease in frequency during the premenstrual period. Other drug studies have indicated some effectiveness of nonsteroidal anti-inflammatory agents in controlling menstrual migraine (Baskin, Rapport, Weeks, & Sheftell, 1985; Diamond, 1984). These results indicate that additional studies are warranted using naproxen sodium and similar drugs because other prophylactic and analgesic drugs have had no impact.

Indications of a possible relationship between premenstrual stress and menstrual migraine are hinted at in several headache studies. Nattero (1982) found an absence of premenstrual tension in 54% of his female subjects sampled in a comprehensive study of 2,000 headache sufferers. Epstein et al. (1975) found menstrual migraine was more likely to be reported by migraineurs whose periodic menstrual syndrome included both fluid retention and breast discomfort. More research is needed in this area.

Studies are also needed to replicate other researchers' findings that those patients whose migraine onset coincided with the beginning of the first menstrual period were subsequently more likely to have menstrually related migraine and to have relief of their migraine during pregnancy (Epstein et al., 1975). Finally, few clinical studies have examined the effects of menopause on migraine, and research in this area is long overdue. Recognition of menstrual migraine and increased understanding of the mechanisms behind this disorder should lead to improved treatment.

REFERENCES

Baskin, S., Rapport, A., Weeks, R., & Sheftell, F. (1985, June). *The effect of naproxen sodium on menstrual migraine.* Paper presented at the meeting of the American Association for the Study of Headache, New York.

Diamond, S. (1984). Menstrual migraine and non-steroidal anti-inflammatory agents. *Headache, 24,* 52.

Diamond, S., & Dalessio, D. (1978). *The practicing physician's approach to headache.* Baltimore, MD: Williams & Wilkins.

Edelson, R. N. (1985). Menstrual migraine and other hormonal aspects of migraine. *Headache, 25,* 376–379.

Epstein, M. T., Hockaday, J. M., & Hockaday, T. D. R. (1975). Migraine and reproductive hormones throughout the menstrual cycle. *Lancet, 1,* 543–547.

Friedman, A. P. (1972). The headache in history, literature and legend. *Bulletin of the New York Academy of Medicine, 48,* 661–681.

Lance, J. W., & Anthony, M. (1956). Some clinical aspects of migraine. *Archives of Neurology, 15,* 356.

Murphy, W. (1982). *Dealing with headaches.* New York: Time-Life Books.

Nattero, G. (1982). Menstrual headache. *Advances in Neurology, 33,* 215–226.

Sargent, J., Solbach, P., Coyne, L., Spohn, H., & Segerson, J. (1986). Controlled, experimental outcome study of non-drug treatment for the control of migraine headaches. *Journal of Behavioral Medicine, 9,* 291–323.

Sargent, J., Solbach, P., Damasio, H., Baumel, B., Corbett, J., Eisner, L., Jessen, B., Kudrow, L., Mathew, M., Medina, J., Saper, J., Vijayan, N., Watson, C., & Alger, J. (1985). A comparison of naproxen sodium to propranolol hydrochloride and a placebo control for the prophylaxis of migraine headache. *Headache, 24,* 320–324.

Solbach, P., Sargent, J., & Coyne, L. (1984). Menstrual migraine headache: Results of a controlled, experimental, outcome study of non-drug treatments. *Headache, 24,* 75–78.

Solbach, P., Sargent, J., & Kennedy, K. (1986). Migraine headaches associated with menstruation. *IM-Internal Medicine for the Specialist, 7,* 93–103.

Somerville, B. W. (1972). The role of estradiol withdrawal in etiology of menstrual migraine. *Neurology, 22,* 355.

Somerville, B. W. (1975a). Estrogen-withdrawal migraine I. Duration of exposure required and attempted prophylaxis by premenstrual estrogen administration. *Neurology, 25,* 239–244.

Somerville, B. W. (1975b). Estrogen withdrawal migraine II. Attempted prophylaxis by continuous estradiol administration. *Neurology, 25,* 245–250.

Szekely, B., Botwin, D., Eidelman, B. H., Becker, M., Elman, N., & Schemm, R. (1986). Nonpharmacological treatment of menstrual headache: Relaxation-biofeedback therapy and person-centered insight therapy. *Headache, 26,* 86–92.

Welch, K. M. A., Darnley, D., & Simkins, R. (1984). The role of estrogen in migraine: A review and hypothesis. *Cephalalgia, 4,* 227–236.

14

Perimenstrual Symptoms and the Health-Seeking Process: Models and Methods

Nancy F. Woods, Martha J. Lentz, Ellen S. Mitchell, Kathryn Lee, Diana Taylor, and Nitsa Allen-Barash

Perimenstrual symptoms (PS) occur immediately before and during menstruation and may include irritability, mood swings, depression, tension, anxiety, fatigue, cramps, backache, weight gain, painful or tender breasts, and swelling, among others. Although labeled "premenstrual syndrome" by some, these symptoms occur in multiple configurations of negative affect, water retention, and discomfort and are not confined to the premenstruum (Abplanalp, Haskett, & Rose, 1980; Halbreich, Endicott, Schach, & Nee, 1982; Haskett, Steiner, Osmun, & Carroll, 1980; Moos, 1968; Woods, Most, & Dery, 1982b). One of the most striking characteristics of perimenstrual symptomatology is its variability, reflected both in the wide range of symptoms women experience and in the large variation in the prevalence of these symptoms from one population to another (Bergsjo, Jenssen, & Vellar, 1975; O'Rourke, 1983; Sheldrake & Cormack, 1976; Taylor, 1979; Van Keep, 1979; Woods et al., 1982a).

Despite extensive research on the etiology and treatment of PS, what accounts for these symptoms remains unclear. Most studies of a single biological or behavioral mechanism have been inconclusive. Moreover, controlled clinical trials of pharmacologic agents such as progesterone (Sampson, 1979); antiprostaglandins (Budoff, 1980; Jakubowicz, Godard, & Dewhurst, 1984; Wood & Jakubowicz, 1980); bromocriptine (Andersch, 1983; Elsner, Buster, Schindler, Nessim, & Abraham, 1980); spironolactone (Hendler, 1982, 1984; O'Brien, Craven, Selby, & Symonds, 1979); pyridoxine (Abraham & Hargrove, 1980; Harrison, Endicott, Rabkin, & Nee, 1984); magnesium (Abraham & Lubran, 1981); tryptophan (Harrison, Endicott, Rabkin, & Nee, 1984); and gonadotropin releasing hormone (GNRH) (Muse, Cetel, Futterman, & Yen, 1984) have found that medical treatment with these agents has been no more effective than placebo therapy.

Another line of investigation has addressed the influence of the social environment on symptom formation. Theories related to socialization include those linking individual differences in expectations about menstruation to symptoms (Brooks, Ruble, & Clarke, 1977). Socialization in a traditional feminine role has been linked to menstrual symptoms in some studies (Paige, 1973) but not in others (Brown & Woods, 1987).

The influence of social stressors on symptoms has been demonstrated for major life events (Siegel, Johnson, & Sarason, 1979; Wilcoxon, Schrader, & Sherif, 1976; Woods, Dery, & Most, 1982) and daily hassles (Woods, Longenecker, & Most, 1985). Moreover, there is evidence for differential effects of stressors given the nature of the symptoms, with the major influence seen on negative affect (Woods, 1985).

To date, most research has been devoted to defining and measuring PS as well as seeking its etiology and treatment. No published work has addressed perimenstrual symptoms as "symptoms" rather than as a discrete disease entity or has studied PS from the theoretical perspective of the health-seeking process. Moreover, little is known about the relationship between the nature of the symptoms women experience and the effects of symptoms on their lives.

Our early work explored the influence of socialization and stressful social milieu (Woods, 1985) on three classes of PS (negative affect, water retention, and pain), disability, and menstrual attitudes. In a sample of 179 women 18 to 35 years of age, exposure to a stressful milieu was useful in explaining negative affect, but not other symptoms. Of all the symptom clusters, negative affect was the most important cause of perimenstrual disability, defined as "lowered school or work performance" and "take naps or rest in bed." Traditional socialization as a woman, intense negative affect symptoms, and symptom-related disability, in turn, all influenced attitudes toward menstruation as debilitating (Woods, 1985).

Based on these earlier results, this study was designed to increase our understanding of women's experiences of symptoms rather than to identify the etiology of a disease entity; to increase our knowledge of women's experience with PS from the perspective of health-seeking processes; and to evaluate the application of a model of health-seeking processes in relation to episodes of cyclical recurrent symptoms.

This chapter presents a model to account for women's perimenstrual symptom experiences from the perspective of the health-seeking process and describes the approaches being used to test the model in an ongoing research program.

Model of PS and Health-Seeking Processes

The concept of health-seeking processes accounts for people's experiences in response to symptoms and links these experiences to their social and cultural context (Chrisman, 1977). Mechanic (1962) advanced the idea that an individual's definitions of illness are shaped by three factors: bodily sensations that are labeled as symptoms or feelings that differ from the ordinary; cognitive definitions suggesting some hypothesis about what the individual is feeling; and the environment, particularly social stress. Mechanic viewed reporting symptoms as part of a pattern of illness behavior shaped by socialization and responsive to personal stress and the occurrence of bodily dysfunction. Perception and evaluation of symptoms and response to symptoms constituted core elements of illness behavior. In the current study, perception of symptoms refers to whether women notice a change from their usual feelings or experiences during the perimenstruum. Some women may perceive changes in how they feel as pleasant, whereas others may perceive these changes as unpleasant or disruptive. Still others may perceive no change at all during the perimenstruum.

Chrisman (1977) introduced the concept of symptom definition — the cognitive categorization and evaluation of perceived changes. A complex set of factors influences whether the symptom is categorized or defined as illness. Among these are the severity, frequency, and visibility of the changes people experience (Mechanic, 1962). Culturally based explanatory models include professional, lay, or idiosyncratic categories that allow an individual to ascribe meaning to the symptom experience (Chrisman & Kleinman, 1983). Symptom definition precedes the evaluation of threat posed by the symptoms, including associated danger and disability (Chrisman, 1977).

In the current study, the meanings women ascribe to perimenstrual symptoms reflect the cultural norms conveyed to women through socialization processes, expectancies regarding menstruation and symptoms, attitudes and beliefs about menstruation and its effects on one's life, and aspects of behavior to attribute to the perimenstruum.

Mechanic (1962) linked symptom definition to the current social context, emphasizing the influence of a stressful life. In the current study, the dimensions of women's social environment included supports as well as stressors.

Symptom definition precedes response to symptoms. Indeed, individuals may participate in a series or combination of responses, such as self-care efforts including rest or diet change, and seeking help or advice from a social network or health professional. Responses to symptoms are influenced by socialization as well as by the current social context (Maunz & Woods, 1988; Woods, 1980; Woods & Hulka, 1979). The proposed relationships are illustrated in Figure 1.

Testing the Model

Testing the proposed model of perimenstrual symptom and health-seeking processes presented multiple challenges with respect to research

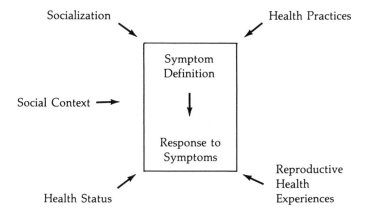

Figure 1. Relationship of socialization, social context, health status, health practices, reproductive health experiences, and health-seeking processes (symptom definition and response to symptoms).

methods. These included (a) assuring the representativeness of women's experiences; (b) accurately assessing women's symptom experiences; and (c) reflecting the dynamic nature of women's perimenstrual symptom experiences. The methods we chose to deal with these challenges follow.

Assuring Accurate Representation of Women's Experiences
   To assure an accurate representation of the range of women's experiences, we developed a complex sampling strategy that would maximize the likelihood of including black and Asian women as well as white women of comparable social class. First, census block groups (fractions of census tracts) in which 40% or more of the population reported an income between $12,999 and $39,900 were identified from the 1980 census data from King County, WA. Subsequently, those block groups meeting the initial income criterion were sorted to identify those in which 10% or more of the population was black or Asian. The number of eligible block groups resulting from applying this criterion was reduced from 901 to 119. On the basis of data from the 119 block groups, the number of potential respondents from which to select 200 to 300 of each racial-ethnic group was estimated to be 2,500 blacks and 2,600 Asians. For each ethnic group in each of these 119 block groups, we generated profiles of the number of women between the ages of 15 and 59 (these are the age bands employed in reporting census data) and educational status (completion of more than elementary school). The most suitable block groups from the standpoint of age, ethnicity, and educational status were then identified by the research team. The street segments of the selected block groups were then

identified and randomly ordered with a computer program. The numbers of the street segments within block groups provided the link between this initial set of criteria and a city directory of all addresses in Seattle, from which the sampling units (telephone numbers of all potential participants) were chosen.

This approach generated a sample of women consisting of 103 Asians, 149 blacks, 374 white, and 30 Native American, Hispanic, and others. The women were 18 to 45 years of age ($M = 32.7$). They reported a mean educational level of 14.2 years and a mean income range from \$29,000 to \$30,999.

Accurately Assessing Women's Perimenstrual Experiences

This assessment involved focusing on symptoms rather than syndromes, using concurrent as well as retrospective reports of symptoms, and triangulating measurement approaches.

We used a hybrid design involving cross-sectional, prospective, and retrospective elements. After we identified eligible women, we invited them to complete an in-home interview, and a 90-day health diary. We invited some ($n = 50$) to participate in a food diary component of the study. After completing the 90-day diary and in some cases the food diary, all women were asked to complete a telephone interview.

Our orientation to understanding women's experiences of symptoms rather than a syndrome or disease entity led us to ask women to describe their symptoms in several ways. First, women completed a daily health diary in which they responded to an enumeration of common symptoms and listed additional symptoms they experienced. Second, women participated in a telephone interview at the end of the 90-day period, rating their symptoms retrospectively over the last three menstrual cycles. In addition, they described those symptoms they found most distressing and clustered them as they experienced them. Although others have developed instruments to classify women with respect to a typology of premenstrual syndromes (Halbreich, Endicott, Schacht, & Nee, 1982; Moos, 1968), we emphasized the naturalistic clustering of symptoms rather than diagnostic classification of syndromes. We used factor analysis to group the symptoms women reported in the daily diaries and during the telephone interview. We named the factors using emic terms (i.e., the person's own words) rather than biomedical terms. For example, the cluster of symptoms that included anxiety and irritability we labeled *turmoil* rather than depression or negative affect. After clustering the symptoms, we used cluster analysis to group women according to their symptom experiences. Using this approach, we discovered one group of women who experienced moderately severe disturbed sleep during the perimenstruum with only mild or no symptoms of other types. Had we used a priori categories of premenstrual syndrome, we would have obscured the group of women having difficulty sleeping.

We used daily records of symptom experience as well as retrospective recall of symptoms to identify those symptoms women experienced as most distressing. The daily recordings provided an evaluation of symptoms for a 24-hr period, whereas the retrospective rating spanned three menstrual cycles, characterizing the patterns of symptoms women perceived. Of interest is that daily diary ratings placed the most distressing symptoms during menses, whereas retrospective reports placed them in the premenstruum. Despite the difference in timing of distress across methods, women consistently rated turmoil symptoms as most distressing.

Finally, we triangulated measurement approaches to enhance accuracy (Mitchell, 1986). We used open-ended interviewing to learn women's perceptions of their symptoms as well as the daily diary recording and retrospective recall of symptoms included in the diary. The use of multiple approaches confirmed women's concurrence that turmoil symptoms were most distressing. Quantitative ratings of symptoms in the diary and in the telephone interview agreed with qualitative analysis of women's responses to open-ended questions such as "Which of these is most distressing to you?" In addition, women described the effects of their symptoms on daily living, their presumed treatability, explanatory models for the symptoms, and their perceptions of themselves as ill or not ill when they experienced symptoms. They also completed the Menstrual Attitudes Questionnaire (Brooks-Gunn & Ruble, 1980), indicating the extent to which they viewed menstruation as natural, debilitating, and so forth. Women also recorded their response to symptoms in the daily health diary and described in the telephone interview what alleviated or exacerbated their symptoms. As a result, we were able to collect multiple indicators of women's symptom definition and response from multiple data-collection methods.

Dynamic Nature of Women's Perimenstrual Symptom Experiences

Our recognition of the dynamic nature of women's perimenstrual experiences led us to select measures that supported the recognition of patterns occurring over time. Women recorded their symptom experiences, as well as other life experiences, in a health diary for 90 days (see Table 1). Daily recordings support planned intra-individual as well as between-group analyses. Lentz and Lee (1985) characterized patterns of symptom experience using intra-individual analysis of daily reports of sleep disruption symptoms over 90 days of data. Plots of daily symptom levels allowed the identification of patterns in symptom level. Symptom-level patterns were suggestive of both weekly and seasonal cycles as well as menstrual cycle. Autocorrelations of a woman's reported symptoms provided further evidence for cyclic patterns of symptom experiences.

Daily symptom reports used in between-groups repeated measures analyses provide a dynamic view of difference in symptom experience across the menstrual cycle by comparing symptoms at four phases of the menstrual cycle — postmenses, ovulatory, premenses, and menses. In addition to testing for differences in levels between groups at each phase, repeated measures allow for testing between-group difference in the slope or the pattern of change in symptoms across the menstrual cycle.

Table 1.
Daily Health Diary

		ID No.			
		Date		/	
Daily Experiences List		*Month*		*Day*	

Please read the list of feelings and behaviors. Please fill in the blank with the number that best describes how you felt today.

0	1	2	3	4
not present	minimal	mild	moderate	extreme

1. abdominal pain, discomfort _____	21. difficulty making decisions _____
2. anger _____	22. dizziness or lightheaded-
3. anxiety _____	ness _____
4. awakening during the night _____	23. early morning awakening _____
5. backache _____	24. fatigue or tiredness _____
6. bloating or swelling of	25. feelings of guilt _____
abdomen _____	26. feelings of well-being _____
7. blurred or fuzzy vision _____	27. forgetfulness _____
8. bursts of energy or activity _____	28. general aches and pains _____
9. confusion _____	29. headache _____
10. cramps — uterine or pelvic _____	30. hostility _____
11. craving for specific foods	31. hot flashes or sweats _____
or tastes _____	32. impatient, intolerant _____
12. craving for alcohol _____	33. impulsiveness _____
13. decreased appetite _____	34. in control _____
14. decreased food intake _____	35. increased activity _____
15. decreased sexual desire _____	36. increased appetite _____
16. depression (feel sad or	37. increased food intake _____
blue) _____	38. increased sensitivity to
17. desire to be alone _____	cold _____
18. diarrhea _____	39. increased sexual desire _____
19. difficulty concentrating _____	40. increased sleeping _____
20. difficulty in getting to	41. intentional self-injury _____
sleep _____	42. irritable _____

Continued on next page

Table 1—Continued

43. lonely	_____	51. restlessness or jitteriness	_____
44. lowered coordination or clumsiness	_____	52. sensation of weight gain	_____
45. lowered desire to talk or move	_____	53. skin disorders	_____
46. nausea	_____	54. suicidal ideas or thoughts	_____
47. nervousness	_____	55. swelling of hands or feet	_____
48. out of control	_____	56. tearfulness, crying easily	_____
49. painful or tender breasts	_____	57. tension	_____
50. rapid mood changes	_____	58. anything else? (please describe) _____	
		_____	

59. Please describe *what you did*, if anything, about the experiences you had today.
   For example: backache—back exercises; heating pad
               headache—Motrin; went to the doctor
               restlessness—talked to a friend

60. Please list any medications, vitamins, or minerals you took today (other than those listed in item #59). Please give name and amount taken.

61. Did your health keep you from carrying on your normal activities today?
   _____ no
   _____ yes → Did you:
               _____ cut down your activity
               _____ stay home from work or other outside activities
               _____ stay in bed
               _____ other (please specify)

62. How physically active were you today?
   _____ strenuous exercise (e.g., jogging, swimming, tennis)
   _____ mild exercise (e.g., walking, bowling)
   _____ basic activities (e.g., housework, work, school)
   _____ not even basic activities

63. Please mark an X to show:
   a. how healthy you felt today

   Not at all healthy   Extremely healthy
   b. how happy you were today

   Not at all happy   Extremely happy
64. a. Did anything upset you today? Please describe.

   b. Please describe *what you did*, if anything, about it.

Table 1 — Continued

65. a. Please check any tastes you craved (had a strong desire for) today.
   _____ no taste cravings today (skip to #66)
   _____ sweet _____ sour _____bitter _____salty _____ other (please specify)
   BE SURE TO RATE ITEM 11
   b. Please describe anything *you ate or drank* in response to these cravings.

   c. Please describe anything else *you did* in response to cravings.

66. Please mark an X to show:
   a. how much *control* you felt over what you ate today

   No control   Complete control
   b. was the *kind of food* you ate _____ typical _____ unusual (please describe)

   c. was the *way you ate* today (e.g., speed, frequency, amount at one time)
   _____ typical _____ unusual (please describe)

67. a. Are you having your menstrual period today?
   _____ yes _____ no
   b. Do you think you ovulated today?
   _____ yes _____ no _____ cannot tell
   c. If yes, how could you tell?

COMMENTS. Please feel free to comment on anything else you experienced today.

Summary

In summary, the model of viewing perimenstrual symptoms from the perspective of the health-seeking process mandated methods that accurately presented women's symptom experiences, reliably assessed women's experiences, and documented women's experiences as dynamic rather than static. These strategies can be applied to other research on the menstrual cycle.

REFERENCES

Abplanalp, J., Haskett, R., & Rose, R. (1980). The premenstrual syndrome. *Psychiatric Clinics of North America, 3,* 327–347.
Abraham, G., & Hargrove, J. (1980). Effect of vitamin B_6 on premenstrual symptomatology in women with premenstrual tension: A double-blind cross-over study. *Infertility, 3,* 155–165.

Abraham, G., & Lubran, M. (1981). Serum and red cell magnesium levels in patients with premenstrual tension. *American Journal of Clinical Nutrition, 34,* 2364–2366.

Andersch, B. (1983). Bromocriptine and premenstrual symptoms: A survey of double-blind trials. *Obstetrics and Gynecology, 38,* 643–646.

Bergsjo, P., Jenssen, H., & Vellar, O. (1975). Dysmenorrhea in industrial workers. *Acta Obstetrica Gynecologica Scandinavica, 54,* 355–359.

Brooks-Gunn, J., & Ruble, D. (1980). The menstrual attitude questionnaire. *Psychosomatic Medicine, 42,* 503–512.

Brooks, J., Ruble, D., & Clarke, A. (1977). College women's attitudes and expectations concerning menstrual related changes. *Psychosomatic Medicine, 39,* 288–298.

Brown, M., & Woods, N. (1986). Sex role orientation, sex typing, occupational traditionalism, and perimenstrual symptoms. *Health Care for Women International, 7,* 25–30.

Budoff, P. (1980). Zomepirac sodium in the treatment of primary dysmenorrhea syndrome. *New England Journal of Medicine, 307,* 714–717.

Chrisman, N. (1977). The health seeking process: An approach to the natural history of illness. *Culture, Medicine and Psychiatry, 1,* 351–377.

Chrisman, N., & Kleinman, A. (1983). Popular health care, social networks, and cultural meanings: The orientation of medical anthropology. In D. Mechanic (Ed.), *Handbook of health care and health professions* (pp. 569–590). New York: Free Press.

Elsner, C., Buster, J., Schindler, R., Nessim, S., & Abraham, G. (1980). Bromocriptine in the treatment of premenstrual syndrome. *Obstetrics and Gynecology, 56,* 723–736.

Halbreich, U., Endicott, J., Schacht, S., & Nee, J. (1982). The diversity of premenstrual changes as reflected in the premenstrual assessment form. *Acta Psychiatrica Scandinavica, 62,* 177–180.

Harrison, W., Endicott, J., Rabkin, J., & Nee, J. (1984). Treatment of premenstrual dysphoric changes: Clinical outcome and methodological implications. *Pharmacologic Bulletin, 20,* 118–122.

Haskett, R., Steiner, M., Osmun, J., & Carroll, B. (1980). Severe premenstrual tension: Delineation of the syndrome. *Biological Psychiatry, 15,* 121–139.

Hendler, N. (1982). Effects of spironolactone in the treatment of PMS. *Journal of the American Medical Association, 247,* 1295–1298.

Hendler, N. (1984). Premenstrual symptoms and aldosterone inhibition. *Female Patient, 5,* 17–19.

Jakubowicz, D., Godard, E., & Dewhurst, Sir J. (1984). The treatment of premenstrual tension with mefenamic acid: Analysis of prostaglandin concentrations. *British Journal of Obstetrics and Gynecology, 91,* 78–94.

Lentz, M., & Lee, K. (1985, June). *Sleep disturbance symptom patterns across the menstrual cycle.* Paper presented at the meeting of the Society for Menstrual Cycle Research, Galveston, TX.

Maunz, E., & Woods, N. F. (1988). Self-care practices among young adult women: Influences of symptoms, employment, and sex role orientation. *Health Care for Women International, 9,* 29–41.

Mechanic, D. (1962). The concept of illness behavior. *Journal of Chronic Disease, 15,* 189–194.

Mitchell, E. (1986). Multiple triangulation: A methodology for nursing science. *Advances in Nursing Science, 8,* 18–26.

Moos, R. H. (1968). The development of a menstrual distress questionnaire. *Psychosomatic Medicine, 30,* 853–867.

Muse, F., Cetel, N., Futterman, L., & Yen, S. (1984). The premenstrual syndrome: Effects of medical ovariectomy. *New England Journal of Medicine, 311,* 1345–1348.

O'Brien, P., Craven, D., Selby, C., & Symonds, E. (1979). Treatment of premenstrual syndrome by spironolactone. *British Journal of Obstetrics and Gynecology, 86,* 142.

O'Rourke, M. (1983). Subjective appraisal of psychological well-being and self-reports of menstrual and nonmenstrual symptomatology in employed women. *Nursing Research, 32,* 288–293.

Paige, K. (1973). Women learn to sing the menstrual blues. *Psychology Today, 7,* 41–46.

Sampson, G. (1979). Premenstrual syndrome: A double-blind controlled trial of progesterone and placebos. *British Journal of Psychiatry, 135,* 209–215.

Sheldrake, P., & Cormack, M. (1976). Variations in menstrual cycle symptom reporting. *Journal of Psychosomatic Research, 20,* 169–177.

Siegel, J., Johnson, J., & Sarason, I. (1979). Life changes and menstrual discomfort. *Journal of Human Stress, 5,* 41–46.

Taylor, J. (1979). The timing of menstrual related symptoms assessed by a daily symptom rating scale. *Acta Psychiatrica Scandinavica, 60,* 87–105.

Van Keep, P. (1979). *The premenstrual syndrome.* Geneva: International Health Foundation.

Wilcoxon, L., Schrader, S., & Sherif, C. (1976). Daily self-reports on activities, life events, moods, and somatic changes during the menstrual cycle. *Psychosomatic Medicine, 38,* 399–417.

Wood, C., & Jakubowicz, D. (1980). The treatment of premenstrual symptoms with mefanamic acid. *British Journal of Obstetrics and Gynecology, 87,* 627–630.

Woods, N. (1980). Women's roles and illness episodes: A prospective study. *Research in Nursing and Health, 3,* 137–145.

Woods, N. (1985). Social context, socialization, and perimenstrual symptoms. *Nursing Research, 34,* 145–149.

Woods, N., Dery G., & Most, A. (1982). Stressful life events and perimenstrual symptoms. *Journal of Human Stress, 8,* 23–31.

Woods, N., & Hulka, B. (1979). Symptom reports and illness behavior among employed women and homemakers. *Journal of Community Health, 5,* 36–45.

Woods, N., Longenecker, G., & Most, A. (1986). Major life stressors, daily hassles and perimenstrual symptoms. *Nursing Research, 34,* 263–267.

Woods, N., Most, A., & Dery, G. (1982a). Prevalence of perimenstrual symptoms. *American Journal of Public Health, 72,* 1257–1264.

Woods, N., Most, A., & Dery, G. (1982b). Toward a construct of perimenstrual distress. *Research in Nursing and Health, 5,* 123–136.

PART THREE

Menopause

The six chapters in the menopause section focus from various angles on the normal phenomenological experience of menopause. Several papers contrast cultural stereotypes or clinical views with women's lived experiences of normal menopause, and take the health care system to task for remaining ignorant of the bias in available information.

The section begins with Beyene's report (chap. 15) of her extensive field work with rural Mayan Indian and rural Greek women. She contrasts the positive views of menopause among 107 Mayan interviewees with the more negative views of 96 Greek women, and identifies several aspects of their lives that may contribute to variations in menopausal experience. In cross-cultural comparisons, she suggests the importance of dietary variables, fertility patterns, and genetic background, as well as cultural values and social conditioning. Next, Jackson (chap. 16) presents a survey of 120 urban Afro-American climacteric women, documenting their experiences with menarche and menopause. She notes that few studies have included black women, even as a subgroup, and points out both similarities and differences in relation to literature on white menopausal women. Her identification of areas of concern for black women is especially useful, for both health care providers and researchers. Another group, Mexican-American women, is the subject of the chapter by Kearns and Christopherson (17) on perceptions of menopause. In understanding the experience of this rural, Spanish-speaking sample, the authors emphasize the integration of menopause as a natural process into differing cultural contexts. The normal experience of menopause is specifically contrasted with medical views in the chapter by DeLorey (18). She utilizes attribution theory to explore the meaning of midlife and menopause to 120 midlife women and 52 of their physicians. Findings indicate that menopause is a far more salient problem in physicians' minds than it is for the women, and the analysis of this discrepancy points to different information sources and role definitions.

After these rich explorations of menopause experience in a variety of ethnic and cultural contexts, two chapters present important methodological information for future research on menopause. Bowles reports the development of a useful, valid, and reliable measure of attitude toward menopause (chap. 19). Her instrument is especially well suited to cross-cultural comparisons and to inclusion in multivariate studies, because of its brevity and uncomplicated format. Mansfield and Jorgensen (chap. 20) discuss a variety of methodological issues in longitudinal research on menopausal change. They focus on valid documentation of normal patterns of menstrual change in women approaching menopause, suggesting data-gathering techniques and innovative statistical analyses. Pilot data are presented to illustrate the usefulness of the proposed methods. Like other authors in this section, Mansfield and Jorgensen challenge current health care practices for midlife women, and emphasize the need for research from the perspectives of women at this stage of life.

15

Menopause: A Biocultural Event

Yewoubdar Beyene

In anthropological literature early life has been given careful investigation: Infancy, childhood, and the adult years have all received meticulous ethnographic attention. However, ethnographic reports covering menopause and findings related to the phenomenon are rare, anecdotal, inconsistent, or peripheral to other major topics of study. Menopause as a topic of interest in anthropology is a recent phenomenon. We know very little, therefore, about the menopausal transition of women in non-Western societies to compare with menopausal transition in Western women.

The few existing cross-cultural reports on the menopausal experiences of women suggest that in some non-Western societies, women experience few, if any, of the physiological and psychological symptoms of which Western women commonly complain in connection with menopause (Dowty, Maoz, Antonovsky, & Wijsenbeek, 1970; Flint, 1975; Maoz, Antonovsky, Apter, Wijsenbeek, & Datan, 1977). Some social scientists attribute these differences to the fact that menopause precipitates a positive role change for women in many non-Western cultures (Flint, 1975; Griffen, 1977, 1982). A change from high to low status is assumed to correlate with circumstances in which menopause is experienced as negative and disabling. Where menopause is associated with freedom from the cultural taboos associated with childbearing years, women are reported to have positive or indifferent attitudes to this event and fewer symptomatic complaints.

Such authors make associations between menopausal symptoms and events such as "empty nest" syndrome and marriage crisis, that may or may not occur simultaneously with the menopause. Moreover, a change in role and gain in status by women in non-Western societies does not necessarily correlate with or depend on menopausal age. The analysis of the scanty cross-cultural data on menopause is inadequate, and the explanations are reflections of middle-class, Western cultural values, expressing a tacit notion that new roles for women, such as participation in male activities (mentioned by Flint, 1975; Griffen, 1977, 1982), are a universal measure of status gain for all women. In fact, women in some societies do not necessarily consider male activities to be superior to female roles. Attempts to make a distinction of menopausal experiences of women based on social and cultural factors alone result in misleading conclusions. On the other hand, if menopause is principally a hormonal event, one would expect that women throughout the world would experience symptoms in the same way.

The data presented below were obtained from a 3-year extended ethnographic work that investigated and compared the natural history of the menopausal experiences of women in two non-industrialized cultures where there is no hormonal therapy for the physical and emotional changes said to occur.

Design and Methodology

Members of two cultures were studied: rural Mayan Indians living in Yucatan, Mexico, and rural Greek women living on the island of Evia, Greece. The field work was conducted utilizing a systematic ethnographic approach. This involved informal and formal interviews and direct observation and participation in everyday activities of women for 12 months in each of the cultures. Participant observation was a very important part of the research methodology, enabling me to win the confidence of the villagers. Because the topic of menstruation is a very personal issue and is not freely discussed with strangers, it was necessary to spend a good part of the research time building friendships with the women in the communities. I presented myself as someone who wanted to study the lives of women. Thus, women in both cultures took an interest in teaching me how to cook and allowed me to participate in their everyday activities. Furthermore, participating in such activities gave me the opportunity to engage in general conversation with them on different topics including menstruation, menopause, and the status of older women, attitudes toward aging, and related areas.

The study involved 107 Mayan and 96 Greek women, who were classified in three categories: premenopausal, menopausal, and postmenopausal (Table 1). They were interviewed regarding general life history, including pregnancy, health, experience and attitudes toward menstruation, menopause, and aging. In addition, unstructured interviews were conducted with key informants such as older women, traditional healers, midwives (among the Mayans), and medical personnel in the health services and clinics that served the villagers. I conducted all interviews personally in either Spanish or Greek.

Results and Discussion

Comparison of the data from these two groups indicates both similarities and marked differences between women in the two cultures. Women in both locales are concerned much more with menstruation and factors related to childbirth than with menopause. They also share common taboos and restrictions related to menstruation and childbearing. The average reported age for onset of menarche for both cultures is approximately the same: 13 for Mayan women and 14 for Greek women. Both groups use a variety of herbs to treat different illnesses, including menstrual pain and discomfort and problems related to fertility.

Women in both Yucatan and Evia perceive menopause as a life stage free of taboos and restrictions, offering increased freedom to participate in many activities such as going to church and visiting friends. Both groups reported that they felt relief from the fear of unwanted pregnancy, as well as from the monthly menstrual flow, which they considered bothersome.

The data also indicate that in both cultures the roles of "good" mother, housekeeper, and hard worker are highly valued. In both societies old age is associated with increased power and respect. However, a woman's status in these cultures does not depend on her chronological age alone. Rather, it is a result of an interrelation of factors such as her age, marital status, and the marital status of her sons; these factors are independent of the onset of menopause.

There were marked differences, however, between the Mayan and Greek women in relation to experience of menopause, diet, childbearing patterns, and aspects of their ecological niche.

The average reported age for onset of menopause was 42 for the Mayan women and 47 for the Greek women. The age categories for onset of menopause show striking differences between the two groups (Table 2). The Mayan women cluster in the age categories of 36 to 45 and the Greek women 41 to 55.

Menopause and Mayan Women

Menopause in the Mayan culture is unrecognized except as marking the end of menstruation and childbearing. Mayan women perceive meno-

Table 1.
Comparison of Distribution of Menstrual Stages of Mayan and Greek Women

Menstrual stages	Mayan women (N=107)		Greek women (N=96)	
	n	%	n	%
Premenopausal	36	33.6	30	31.3
Menopausal	36	33.7	31	32.2
Postmenopausal	35	32.7	35	36.5

Table 2.
*A Comparison of the Distribution of Age at Onset of Menopause
for Mayan Women and Greek Women*

Age at onset (years)	Mayan women (N=71)[a]		Greek women (N=66)[b]	
	n	%	n	%
30–35	5	7.0	2	3.0
36–40	25	35.3	6	9.1
41–45	30	42.2	19	28.8
46–50	8	11.3	25	37.9
51–55	3	4.2	14	21.2

[a]M=42.0 years. [b]M=47.0 years.

pause as an event that occurs when a woman has used up all her menstrual blood. Thus, they believe that the onset of menopause occurs early for those women who have had many children because they had used up their blood by giving birth often. Because women get married at 13 to 14, it was not uncommon to find women of 35 to 40 who were already grandmothers. Therefore, the loss of fertility at menopause is usually not lamented, because a woman feels she has already produced enough children.

Women were asked what their husbands felt now that they were menopausal, and most said that their husbands did not care one way or another. One Mayan woman said that it did not matter to him because they already had enough children. Another woman said, "What more was he to think, he is not the one who menstruates."

I asked all women in the study sample to describe what they anticipated at menopause, their attitude toward menopause, how they perceived the experiences of women in their communities, and what behavior was particularly associated with menopausal women. In addition, menopausal and postmenopausal women in the study were asked about their own experiences of menopause, the symptoms associated with menopause, how they felt, and what they believed their health status was before and after menopause. Their responses indicated that Mayan women did not associate menopause with physical or emotional symptomatology. Among the Mayan women menopause is welcomed and expressed with such phrases as "being happy," "free like a young girl again," and "content and good health." No Mayan woman reported having hot flashes or cold sweats or other symptoms of discomfort associated with menopause. Anxiety, negative attitudes, health concerns, and stress for Mayan women are associated with the childbearing years, not with menopause. For Mayan women, menopause is not a negatively perceived event. Women are pleased to get rid of their periods; thus premenopausal women in the study look forward to the onset of menopause.

Menopause and Greek Women

On the other hand, menopausal experiences among rural Greek women seem to bear more resemblance to menopausal experiences of American women described in the medical literature. Even though the postmenopausal and menopausal women reported being relieved from the taboos and restrictions of childbearing years at menopause, overall it is perceived negatively by the premenopausal women. Premenopausal women expressed anxiety and anticipated possible health problems with menopause and were not looking forward to its onset.

Although there is respect and status gain for older women in Greek culture, getting old is perceived by some Greek women as tantamount to dropping out of the mainstream of life. Thus some Greek women, particularly the premenopausal group, associated menopause with growing old, diminution of energy, and a general downhill course in life. In striking contrast to the Mayan women, Greek premenopausal women reported anxiety and a negative affect in association with menopause.

The Greek menopausal and postmenopausal women reported hot flashes and some cold sweats similar to such reports by American women. However, Greek women differed from American women in their perception and management of menopausal hot flashes. I would like to emphasize that the Greek women in my study *do not* perceive hot flashes as a disease symptom and do not seek medical intervention. Although they have a variety of herbs to treat menstrual pain and discomfort, there are none for hot flashes. They regarded it as a natural phenomenon causing a temporary discomfort that would stop with no intervention. When asked what they did when they had hot flashes, women replied: "You pay no attention to it. . . . You go outside the house and take fresh air. . . . If it is during the night, you take the covers off of you." The Greek women's explanation for hot flashes is that the retained menstrual blood in a woman's body "boils up" so that a menopausal woman has a sensation of heat.

Even though symptoms such as irritability, melancholia, and emotional problems are not expected in the normal process of menopause, these symptoms were reported in association with "off-time" menopause (i.e., when menopause occurs before the age of 40). Because Greek village women believe that menstruation cleans their blood, late onset of menopause is preferred. With "off-time" menopause, they feared a negative health effect because the cleansing was stopped before its time.

Differences Between Mayan and Greek Women

Women in the two cultures also differ in their patterns of childbearing. For Mayan women pregnancy is viewed as a stressful experience. They do not use any birth control methods, and many were pregnant at regular 2-year intervals. The average number of pregnancies for women in the

Mayan sample was seven, with an average of 4.7 children surviving the first year of life. They marry early and continue having children until menopause. They all breastfeed their children for 1.5 to 2 years. It is rare for Mayan women to have a steady menstrual cycle, because successive pregnancies and long periods of amenorrhea due to lactation are so common. For example, one woman in the study said that she had not had her period for 15 years because she was pregnant or lactating.

Unlike the Mayan women, the Greek women have few pregnancies; they marry in their late twenties or early thirties; use birth control methods, and plan their family size. The average number of pregnancies for women in the Greek sample was 2.9 with an average of 2.3 children surviving the first year of life. They breastfeed only 6 to 9 months, and they tend to have steady menstrual cycles.

Another striking difference between the two cultures is diet. The Mayan diet consists of mainly carbohydrates, little animal protein, and no milk products. My information from medical personnel serving the Mayan villages indicated that the Mayans have a high incidence of vitamin deficiency and anemia. Greeks, on the other hand, have a wide variety of nutrients, including enough animal protein and milk products.

Although both groups are agrarian, the two cultures differ in their environment, subsistence economy, and the levels of technological development.

This comparison indicates that perception and experience of menopause vary in different cultures. However, the comparison also suggests that the presence or absence of physiological symptoms cannot be accounted for simply by role changes at middle age or by the removal of cultural taboos. Although the Mayan's positive attitude toward menopause and aging may account for the lack of psychological symptoms in the Mayan women, the lack of physiological symptoms such as hot flashes calls for explanations beyond social and cultural factors. If menopausal hot flashes are phenomena induced by hormonal changes, research must investigate factors that could affect hormone production in a woman's body.

Conclusions

The data from this study suggest that the following factors may be implicated in the variation of onset of menopause and how menopause is experienced.

1. It has been documented that nutrition plays a role in reproduction, affecting conception, fetal mortality, the health of the newborn, and the length of postpartum amenorrhea. The onset of menarche is related to nutritional status, and menstrual activity continues to be affected by nutritional factors throughout a woman's reproductive life (Eveleth & Tanner, 1976; Frisch, 1980; Hill et al., 1980). Moreover, differences in hormone

production between populations have been partly accounted for by differences in diet. Dietary factors, such as dietary fat intake, are also reported to influence the hormone profile in women (Hill, Chan, Cohen, Wynder, & Kuno, 1977; MacMahon et al., 1974). However, the process whereby these factors affect onset of menopause and presence or absence of menopausal symptoms is unknown.

Diet does vary dramatically between Mayan and Greek women. The cultural practices of nutritional intake and ecological as well as economic limitations are major factors in the differences in diet between these two cultures. If diet is known to affect growth and development as well as hormone production, it is possible that malnutrition can be identified as one of the factors for the relatively early onset of menopause for Mayan women. However, the effect of diet on menopausal symptomatology is unknown and needs further investigation.

2. Another striking difference between the Mayan and Greek women is their fertility patterns. The Mayan fertility pattern is typical of most nonindustrialized, traditional societies. For example, data from present day !Kung hunters and gatherers in the Kalahari Desert suggest that given the fertility patterns of traditional societies, during her reproductive life a woman would experience about 15 years of lactation amenorrhea, and just under 48 menstrual cycles. In contrast, the woman in industrialized societies with her family size of two, and little or no breast feeding, can expect about 35 of her average of 37 reproductive years to have consistent menstrual cycles (Short, 1978).

Furthermore, repeated pregnancies are known to lead to frequent interruption in cyclic ovarian function (Neville, 1983). Studies on lactation and hormone levels also indicate that prolactin levels of lactating women are high where breast milk forms all or a substantial portion of the infants' diet (Konner & Worthman, 1980; Madden, Boyan, MacDonald, & Porter, 1978). Moreover, studies on cancer rates in parous and nulliparous women (Cole, Brown, & MacMahon, 1976) suggest that parity and age at first pregnancy may alter the estrogen ratio. This raises questions about the extent to which frequent interruption in cyclic ovarian function, due to successive childbearing, and prolonged amenorrhea affect the production of reproductive hormones. In addition, the degree to which amenorrhea may affect age at onset of menopause and the presence or absence of hot flashes is also uncertain.

3. Genetic factors are known to affect rate of growth and development and age at menarche (Golub, 1983). Correlations are found between twin sisters, mother-daughter, and sister-sister regarding age at onset of menarche and patterns of menstrual flow (Chern, Gatewood, & Anderson, 1980; Shields, 1962; Tanner, 1978). However, we do not know to what extent genetic factors affect menopause.

4. Finally, the differences in management and attitudes toward hot flashes between rural Greek women and American women draw attention to the importance of cultural values and social conditioning. This may account for the seemingly low discomfort threshold and overtreatment of menopause experienced by some American women.

Menopause is going through another transformation in the Western biomedical system: from a disease to a disease-causing agent. Menopausal hot flashes are no longer the focus for estrogen replacement therapy (ERT). At present, menopause is considered a syndrome causing osteoporosis. Low estrogen at menopause is assumed to cause loss of calcium, thereby giving a new rationale to legitimize long-term use of ERT. A recent ad for participants in an osteoporosis study put out by one of the medical establishments in San Francisco referred to osteoporosis as a "national epidemic" affecting some 15 to 20 million American women ("Woman Volunteers," 1985).

Menopause is a universal biological phenomenon. If osteoporosis is a result of low estrogen due to menopause, one would predict the rate of such a condition to be higher in cultures where the menopausal age of women is relatively early (e.g., the Mayan women). However, my information from medical personnel and from my own observation indicates that there is no problem of bone fracture associated with Mayan women. This could be attributed to the mineral content of the nutrients consumed as well as to their daily activities. Mayans have a high intake of calcium from tortillas and their drinking water. Hormonal factors alone cannot explain the incidence of osteoporosis. Cross-cultural studies are needed to untangle menopause from other factors, such as environment and life styles, which may play a significant role in the incidence of osteoporosis.

Like other developmental events, menopause is a biocultural experience. Therefore, this study proposes that research on menopause should consider biocultural factors such as environment, diet, fertility patterns, and genetic differences which could affect the production and equilibrium of hormones in a woman's body. To do so, comparisons are needed between menopausal experiences of women from different nonindustrialized societies, as well as from various industrialized societies. With such an increased data base, comparisons between several major cultures can yield important new perspectives.

NOTE

This research was supported in part by the National Institutes of Health, National Institute on Aging Grant R01 AG02622.

REFERENCES

Chern, M., Gatewood, L., & Anderson, V. (1980). The inheritance of menstrual traits. In A. Dan, E. Graham, & C. Beecher (Eds.), *The menstrual cycle* (Vol. 1, pp. 25–34). New York: Springer.

Cole, P., Brown, J., & MacMahon, B. (1976, September 18). Estrogen profiles of parous and nulliparous women. *Lancet,* pp. 596–599.

Dowty, N., Maoz, B., Antonovsky, A., & Wijsenbeek, H. (1970). Climacterium in three cultural contexts. *Tropical and Geographical Medicine, 22,* 77–86.

Eveleth, P., & Tanner, J. (1976). *World wide variation in human growth.* Cambridge, England: Cambridge University Press.

Flint, M. (1975). The menopause: Reward or punishment? *Psychosomatics, 16,* 161–163.

Frisch, R. (1980). Fatness, puberty and fertility. *Natural History, 89,* 16–27.

Golub, S. (1983). Menarche: The beginning of menstrual life. In S. Golub (Ed.), *Lifting the curse of menstruation* (pp. 17–36). New York: Haworth Press.

Griffen, J. (1977). A cross-cultural investigation of behavioral changes at menopause. *Social Science Journal, 14*(2), 49–55.

Griffen, J. (1982). Cultural models for coping with menopause. In A. Voda, M. Dinnerstein, & S. O'Donnell (Eds.), *Changing perspective on menopause* (pp. 248–262). Austin: University of Texas Press.

Hill, P., Chan, P., Cohen, L., Wynder, E., & Kuno, K. (1977). Diet and endocrine-related cancer. *Cancer, 39,* 1820–1826.

Hill, P., Garbaczewski, L., Helman, P., Huskisson, J., Sporangisa, E., & Wynder, E. (1980). Diet, lifestyle, and menstrual activity. *American Journal of Clinical Nutrition, 33,* 1192–1198.

Konner, M., & Worthman, C. (1980). Nursing frequency, gonadal function, and birth spacing among !Kung hunter-gatherers. *Science, 207,* 788–791.

MacMahon, B., Cole, P., Brown, J., Aoki, K., Lin, T., Morgan, R., & Woo, N.-C. (1974). Urine estrogen profiles of Asian and North American women. *International Journal of Cancer, 14,* 161–167.

Madden, J. D., Boyar, R. M., MacDonald, P. C., & Porter, J. C. (1978). Analysis of secretory patterns of prolactin and gonadotropins during twenty-four hours in a lactating woman before and after resumption of menses. *American Journal of Obstetrics and Gynecology, 4,* 436–441.

Maoz, B., Antonovsky, A., Apter, A., Wijsenbeek, H., & Datan, N. (1977). The perception of menopause in five ethnic groups in Israel. *Acta Obstetrica et Gynecologica Scandinavica, 65*(Suppl. 8), 35–40.

Neville, C. M. (1983). Regulation of mammary development and lactation. In M. C. Neville & M. R. Neifert (Eds.), *Lactation: Physiological, nutritional, and breast-feeding* (pp. 103–140). New York: Plenum Press.

Shields, J. (1962). *Monozygotic twins.* London: Oxford University Press.

Short, R. V. (1978). Healthy infertility. *Upsala Journal of Medical Science, 22*(Suppl. 4), 23–26.

Tanner, J. (1978). *Foetus into man.* Cambridge, MA: Harvard University Press.

Woman volunteers to participate in an osteoporosis study. (1985, April 3). *San Francisco Progress.*

16

Black Women's Responses to Menarche and Menopause

Beryl B. Jackson

Although many studies suggest the importance of culture and ethnicity in determining variations in menopausal experience, few studies have documented response to menopause among black women. Of the 84 studies on menopause and postmenopause reported by McKinlay and McKinlay (1973), none involved black climacteric women as a subgroup in the United States, nor has the situation changed much since that article was written. Only Frere (1971) of South Africa considered race as a potential variable in his study of white and Bantu menopausal women. That the role of culture is an important factor in moderating response to menopause has been well demonstrated (Beyene, 1986; Flint, 1975; Goldstein, 1987; Griffin, 1977; Moaz, Dowty, Antonovsky, & Wijsenbeek, 1970; van Keep & Kellerhals, 1974; Wright, 1982). All of these studies investigated nonblack ethnic groups of women. Their findings suggested that marked differences existed among the women's responses and attitudes toward menopause, and that these differences were primarily a result of ethnicity and culture.

What is known about the climacteric experience for American women is applicable for the most part to white women. Because women's experiences differ in meaning as well as in the timing and manifestation of the midlife markers, black American women should be investigated in relation to their social environment, life style, and culture. Therefore, scientific information is needed to provide knowledge and understanding about black women's adjustments to the menarcheal and menopausal transitions.

This chapter describes the responses of black climacteric women to two significant female developmental stages: menarche (the beginning of the reproductive cycle) and menopause (the end of the reproductive cycle). Black climacteric women are defined as African American women between the ages of 40 or 60 who were born and raised in the United States.

The literature indicates that satisfactory physical and social adjustments during the menopause and postmenopause are dependent upon the quality of prior experiences (Brooks-Gunn & Ruble, 1980; Shainess, 1961). These prior experiences may include (a) menarche, (b) current social experiences with friends, (c) relationships with male companions, (d) children and relatives, (e) experiences with church and volunteer organizations, (f) the quality of responses to intimate and personal changes at menopause, and (g) socioeconomic status (Jackson, 1982/1983). I will focus on the responses of black climacteric women to menarche and menopause in this chapter.

Menarche

Both the empirical and clinical literature suggest that when prepubertal girls were prepared for menstruation within a loving, caring, and accepting relationship by the mothering person, their response to the first menstruation experience was not traumatic or anxiety ridden. Studies also indicated that such girls were able to manage menstruation, and later, menopause, with fewer physiological and psychological symptoms (Bardwick, 1971; Benedek, 1950; Brooks-Gunn & Ruple, 1980; Chadwick, 1932; Deutsch, 1945; Durham, 1979; Ladner, 1971; Shainess, 1961). In contrast, girls who received no prepubertal preparation, or were subjected to rejecting, negative, and even hostile responses from the mothering person were found to respond poorly to the demands of the menstrual cycle and later, to menopausal changes (Shainess, 1961).

The quality of the interpersonal relationship between mother and daughter at the onset of the first menstruation is of importance to the psychological adjustment not only at menarche but also at menopause when the mature body recapitulates the reoccurring experiences of menarche (Benedek, 1950, 1952; Shainess, 1961). On the one hand, Benedek (1952) believed that for most girls, menstruation is accepted with ambivalence and that girls will be able to accept menstruation only if psychological maturity accompanies the process. The menarcheal stage is characterized as especially narcissistic, and the girl requires much love and acceptance from the mothering figure for her to be able to proceed successfully to other stages of her adult development (Deutsch, 1945). On the other hand, other researchers have argued that the sociocultural environment in which menarche is experienced also influences acceptance of the menarcheal experience and adjustment to it.

Menopause

Menopause is one of the most identifiable biophysiological stages of the female developmental life span. It signifies the end of a woman's reproductive ability and is identified as the beginning of the female aging process (Lichtendorf, 1982; Notman, 1979). The female menopause has been studied from different theoretical orientations (Benedek, 1950; Deutsch, 1945; Flint, 1975; Griffin, 1977; Neugarten, 1973; Neugarten & Kraines,

1965; Voda, 1982). Most of these authors found that some women were able to go though menopause without overwhelming fear, without disabling physiological and psychological disruption, without negative and unrealistic attitudes about menopause, and without holding that menopause changes are permanent. Other authors, however, found from empirical and clinical investigations and observations that the majority of women in their samples reported increased physiological and psychological difficulties at menopause resulting in much of the negative attitude associated with menopause (Bungay, Vessey, & McPherson, 1980; Gavan, 1981; Neugarten & Datan, 1974; van Keep & Kellerhals, 1974).

Feminist researchers have reported that menopausal difficulties were primarily the result of restrictive cultural norms, role expectations, sociocultural conditions, stereotyping of the aging female, and lack of respect and sensitivity among some practicing male gynecologists, who are the primary health care providers for the majority of middle-aged women (Bart & Grossman, 1976; Flint, 1975; Griffin, 1977; Lichtendorf, 1982; Marieskind, 1980; Posner, 1979; Voda, 1982). Goodman (1980), from the perspective of her cross-cultural investigations of menopausal women, suggested that the medical model of menopause as endocrine failure should be rejected and replaced with a new model of menopause, which includes variables such as race and culture. Although menopausal studies are voluminous, it is the paucity of empirical information on the menopausal experiences in black women that formed the motivation for this study. The experiences of black women surveyed in the chapter should contribute to the baseline information that is needed.

Method

Sample

The final convenience sample consisted of 120 women with no history of psychiatric hospitalizations or hysterectomies; they could read sufficiently well to complete the questionnaires. These subjects were obtained from a larger survey sample of 209 black climacteric women between the ages of 40 and 60 and included 89 who had had hysterectomies (this latter group is described in Jackson, 1985). Subjects were recruited from an ambulatory care clinic in a health center, a community health care clinic, a black sorority organization, the private practice of two black gynecologists, and from educational institutions, community organizations, and several black churches, all located in an urban center.

Individual respondents to the questionnaire were asked to participate voluntarily. A letter introducing the investigator was sent to each participant with information about the need for the study and the importance of her participation. A consent form was enclosed along with assurances that all information would be held in strict confidence.

Coded sets of questionnaires were mailed to each participant with two self-addressed stamped envelopes, one for the return of the signed consent form and the other for the return of the completed questionnaires. In this way, signatures were separated from protocols, thus providing a further degree of confidentiality. This was an ex post facto design.

Instrument

The instrument, constructed by the author, was a questionnaire that had been pretested and piloted on a sample of 32 black climacteric women between the ages of 40 and 60. It was revised, and only those items were considered that displayed sufficient variability and at least minimum correlations with the subscales for which they were written. The final scales comprised 141 items, categorized as developmental, social, familial, socioeconomic, and personal. In this report, only responses to the developmental scales of response to menarche and menopause are described. The items on these scales are presented below.

Menarcheal Scale

1. How much were you told about menstruation before it started?
2. How expectant of your first menstrual period were you?
3. How did you feel about yourself when you first started to menstruate?
4. How did you experience your menstrual pattern in the early years? (scanty, flooded, regular, irregular, comfortable, in pain, well, sick)
5. During the first 2–3 years of your menstruation, how much of your usual activities did you have to give up? (all, most, some, a few, none)
6. Rate the extent to which information provided by family members and teachers was helpful in preparing you for menstruation.
7. Identify the sources from which you received information about menstruation.
8. During the first 2–3 years of your menstrual periods, how many days did you menstruate?

These items were evaluated using a Semantic Differential Scale with values of 1–7, as well as a Likert Scale with values of 1–5. The Cronbach alpha coefficient was .80.

Menopause Scale

Some menopausal women experience hot flashes during the day and/or at night.
1. How much difficulty did you have with hot flashes and sweats during your menopause?
2. How much difficulty did you experience or are you experiencing with sleep due to menopause?
3. Have you experienced or are you experiencing increased irritability during menopause?

4. Have you experienced or are you experiencing any mood changes such as depression or feeling blue during menopause?

5. In general, how would you say your health is at the present time?

6. How old were you when your menstrual period ceased?

7. How did your menstrual period cease — suddenly, gradually, regular/irregular?

8. How strong is or was your wish for your menopause to be completed?

The Cronbach alpha coefficient was .70. These items were evaluated using a Likert Scale.

A subscale of the menopausal scale examined the changes a woman perceived in her social and sexual life attributable to menopause and the degree of relief experienced at menopause.

a. Rate the amount of change you feel the menopause brings about in a woman's social life.

b. Rate the amount of change you feel menopause brings about in a woman's sexual life.

c. Rate the amount of relief you feel the woman experiences after the menopause is over.

Responses ranged from no relief at all to considerable relief, on a 5-point Likert Scale. The Cronbach alpha coefficient was .72.

Menopausal Open-Ended Question

An open-ended question was presented at the end of the questionnaire to which a small proportion of the women voluntarily responded. The question was: Is there anything else you would like to add because you think it is important and would help me to understand more about the menopause and postmenopause periods as they relate to the lives of black women?

Findings

The major findings of the study are presented in terms of the two developmental stages: menarche and menopause. They raise many questions and reinforce the need for research on differences among racial and ethnic groups in their experiences of puberty and the climacteric.

Menarcheal Scale

Previous knowledge. One of the major findings of this study relates to previous knowledge of menarche. In this sample of black climacteric women ($N=120$), 33% of the women were knowledgeable and prepared for menstruation before it actually started. These women described the knowledge they had as accurate, complete, adequate, and extensive. Among the 67% who reported that they were neither prepared nor knowledgeable about menstruation, responses ranged from limited, incomplete, inaccurate, to none at all.

Expectancy. In response to how expectant the women were of their first period, only 41% indicated that they were anticipatory of the event and that they were calm and confident. In contrast, 59% of the women reported that they were surprised, fearful, and anxious when their first period started.

Feelings at menarche. Responding to how they felt about themselves when their first period started, the women's responses were categorized into three groups. The first group of women (*n*=33, 27.5%) felt good about themselves. They felt the experience was a normal one, and they were happy, proud, and satisfied to have reached that stage of their maturing womanhood. The second group (*n*=55, 46%) was less positive. They felt that to menstruate was normal, but they were neither happy nor sad over it. The third group (*n*=32, 27%) described their feelings about having started to menstruate in negative terms, such as sad, ashamed, and dissatisfied.

Menstrual patterns. Surprisingly, when asked to describe how they physically responded to their menstrual patterns during the early years, 51% of the women reported in the following terms: always irregular, sick, and in pain. However, 49% described themselves as regular, well, and comfortable during those early years.

Activities. About half the sample (51%) reported that they did not have to give up or curtail any of their usual activities, and the rest (49%) replied that they had to give up a few to almost all of their activities while they were menstruating.

Information. In response to how helpful the information provided by family members and teachers was in preparing for their first period, 50% of the women (*n*=60) indicated that it was considerably helpful or moderately helpful to fairly helpful; 38% (*n*=32) said that the information helped very little or not at all; 12% (*n*=10) of the women replied that no one had told them about menstruation before it actually started.

Sources. When asked to identify sources from which they received information, the majority of the women (66%) identified mothers or guardians first but included other sources. Next, teachers were identified by 33% of the women plus other sources. Friends ranked third (22.5%) as informational sources along with others, and three of the women identified friends as their only source of information. Books and other reading materials, as well as sisters and other relatives, were cited as informational sources by 40% of the sample.

Days of flow. Finally, in response to the number of days the menstrual flow lasted during the first 2 to 3 years, 44% indicated 3–4 days; 50% indicated 5–6 days; 2% indicated over 7 days; and 4% did not answer.

Menopausal Scale

The findings relating to the concept of menopause are presented from the menopausal scale, the menopausal subscale, and the open-ended question on the questionnaire to which a small proportion of the women voluntarily responded.

In the sample of black climacteric women, 85 (71%) indicated that they were definitely menopausal or postmenopausal. The remaining 29% of the women reported that they had not completed menopause.

Hot flashes. The first question asked was How much difficulty did you have with hot flashes and sweats during your menopause? Only 78 of the 85 women responded to this item: 13% reported considerable difficulty, 23% moderate, 21% fair, 15% very little difficulty, and 28% reported no difficulty.

Sleep. The question relating to difficulty with sleep during the menopause was answered by 92% of the women: 30% of these women reported moderate to fair amounts of difficulty with sleep; 35% experienced very little, and 35% none at all.

Irritability. There were 78 women who responded to the question Have you experienced or are you experiencing increased irritability during menopause? Only one reported a considerable amount, 15% a moderate amount, 14% a fair amount, 34% very little, and 34% none at all.

Mood changes. The percentages of women who reported degrees of depression or mood change during menopause ranged from considerable (6%), moderate or fair (11%), very little (38%), to none at all (27%).

Health. The majority of the women (70%) indicated they were in good to excellent health.

Age. The women experienced menopause at these ages: the largest group (36%) were between 46 and 49 years of age; 29% between 40 and 45; 25% between 50 and 53; and the other 10% between 54 to 58.

Cessation. Of the 69 menopausal or postmenopausal women who responded to the question How did your menstrual periods cease? 32% reported that it was a sudden cessation; for 68% of the women, their menstrual periods ceased gradually, and in some cases were also irregular.

Desire for cessation. Finally, when reporting how strong the wish was for menopause to be completed, 39% indicated that the wish was not strong at all. But for 33% the wish was moderately strong, and fairly strong for 13%.

Menopausal Subscale

Social life. The women were asked to rate the amount of change menopause brings about in a woman's social life. Over 40% indicated very little change, and 21% indicated no change at all. However, some women experienced moderate (15%) to fair (15%) amounts of change; only 5%

reported considerable amounts of change.

Sexual life. In response to changes that menopause brings about in a woman's sexual life, 13% indicated that menopause caused a considerable amount of change, 14% a moderate amount, 17% a fair amount, 30% very little change, and 24% no change.

Relief. When asked to rate the amount of relief they felt that women experience after the menopause is over, over half reported considerable relief. For 28% of them the relief was moderate, for 19% it was just fair, and for 10% there was very little or no relief.

Adjustment to Menopause

Four major categories of the responses to the open-ended question were determined. The categories and selected quotes follow:

Satisfactory Adjustment

> Speaking for myself, my life at the time was good. After the doctor told me I was going through menopause, I knew I had to go through it, so I just programmed myself to accept it as one of life's periods. So I didn't accept any medication and it was easy.

> Premature menopause was my experience. Estrogen products made menopause more comfortable.

> In the past eight months I have experienced reduction in frequency and duration of hot flashes. I had much discomfort. Black women have given me tremendous support during the menopause — a feeling of kinship that I can't measure.

> I went through the menopause without complications. The sweats were embarrassing. When my periods became irregular, I had a D&C.

Need for Information

> I really don't know for sure if I am going through the menopause periods or not. But I have not had a menstrual period for the past four years.

> Need more information on the different signs of postmenopause or menopause. What kind of symptoms to look for in postmenopause? Black women do not have much knowledge about menopause and postmenopause periods.

> Is change of life and menopause all the same? I see little difference in my sex life, but my whole problem is my husband, who has not much time or feelings for sex with his wife. I feel strange when he avoids me sexually.

> I think some schooling or instruction should be made so that Black women will know what to expect and the kinds of changes her body will be going through. Some form of help should be made available so we will have somewhere to call or go to for help with special problems as a result of menopause.

Experiences and Coping Strategies

The major complaint that other women have expressed to me is: 1) vaginal dryness, and 2) pain with intercourse. Personally, I find the need to use a lubricant when engaging in sexual activity.

For most black women, oftentimes families are doubled up because of the housing shortage which causes a lot of problems for the person that is going through menopause because you need a lot of time for yourself and a lot of understanding.

Other Responses

Many black women are not open about their true sexual feelings. Black women have always been very private about their real selves. They behave as though no one ever except them experienced menopause.

Psychologically, the advent and continuation of menopause starts one to thinking about approaching old age, even though being aged is many years away.

Discussion

This chapter describes experiences of menarche and menopause in a sample of 120 African American climacteric women between the ages of 40 and 60 who responded to a mailed questionnaire. These women indicated lack of preparation (67%) or anticipation of menarche (59%), as well as negative (27%) or ambivalent (46%) feelings toward menstruation in adolescence. Hot flashes and sweats were the most frequently reported symptom of menopause, with 13% experiencing considerable difficulty and 28% experiencing no difficulty with this symptom. Other menopausal changes reported included difficulty with sleep patterns, mood changes, depression, irritability, and changes in social or sexual lives.

Some of the findings of this study are consistent with Ladner's (1971) menarche study. Ladner investigated black adolescent girls regarding their knowledge of menstruation and found that the girls considered the onset of menstruation a serious and often fearful time of their lives, causing them to be filled with misgivings, frustration, and ambivalence. Our findings suggest that differences exist in terms of preparation that black and white women receive for menarche. Previous findings for white women indicated that 50% (Shainess, 1961) and 33% (The Tampax Report, 1981) had no preparation prior to menarche. In contrast, only 33% of black women in this study were knowledgeable and prepared for menstruation. This finding, then, indicates that approximately twice as many black women had no premenarcheal preparation, a factor that might have influenced their poor adjustment to the menarcheal and menopausal experiences. It is also highly probable that other factors such as low socioeconomic status, sociocultural influences, and race could be implicated in the overall adjustment process of the menarcheal and menopausal experiences in this sample of black women.

Despite the universality of the female phenomena of menarche and menopause, the major findings of this study highlight similarities and differences between the responses for black women and those documented for white women in relation to menopause. First, in terms of similarities, the findings of this study support previous findings for white menopausal women which stated that mothers were the primary source of information about menarche (Brooks-Gunn & Ruple, 1980; Dunham, 1978). The majority of menopausal women experienced some degree of difficulty with hot flashes, sleep disturbances, mood changes, depression, and irritability (Green & Cooke, 1982; Kaufert & Syrotuik, 1981; Neugarten & Kraines, 1965; McKinlay & Jeffreys, 1974; Voda, 1982). Some studies found that some women were able to make satisfactory adjustments and to cope with menopausal changes (Beyene, 1986; Flint, 1975; Griffen, 1977; Lock, 1986; McKinlay, McKinlay, & Bramhilla, 1987); other studies found that some women experienced increased difficulties, for a variety of reasons, which resulted in negative attitude toward menopause (Bungay, Vessey, & McPherson, 1980; Hunter, Battersby, & Whitehead, 1986; Lennon, 1982; Neugarten & Datan, 1974).

The answers to the open-ended question provided information in three areas: (a) satisfactory adjustment to menopausal changes, (b) need for information to help women better understand what is actually happening to their bodies at menopause and to help those whose experiences are stressful to be able to cope with the changes, and (c) coping strategies that the women have used and were willing to offer as suggestions to help other black women manage their menopause.

Implications for Research, Clinical Practice, and Education

The findings of this study have implications for research, clinical practice, and health education. First, it is important that researchers continue to investigate black women's responses to menarcheal and menopausal experiences. To what extent do lack of preparation for the menarche, the inadequacy of information about menarche and menopause, sociocultural factors, and socioeconomic status influence attitude and the amount of symptomatology experienced from menarche to postmenopause? To what extent do these factors impact the perception of the overall experience?

Second, health care providers could utilize the findings of this study in the clinical settings when they encounter black preadolescents, adolescents, and middle-aged women who are concerned or distressed about physical changes occurring in their bodies that they do not understand.

Black women usually access all areas of the health care delivery system, and are often in need of anticipatory guidance in matters of health and illness. Clinical nurses are in a unique position to intervene by providing factual information about menarche and menopause. Because some women in the study indicated considerable difficulty talking about personal matters, health care providers could help to facilitate more self-disclosure.

Third, health care educators could utilize these findings both at the undergraduate and graduate levels of health care education. Students at both levels should be knowledgeable and sensitive to the sociocultural differences of their female patients or clients. Most important, health care providers need to be empowered in awareness of the key role they can play in implementing therapeutic primary prevention strategies to assist black women make satisfactory adjustment to developmental changes in their lives.

In conclusion, this descriptive survey study on the responses to menarche and menopause by black climacteric women has provided long-overdue information which will begin to close the gaps in research about black women. However, one must be particularly careful in interpreting and making generalizations about black menopausal women based on this small sample. While we await the findings of future studies on black women as a subgroup on all aspects of the menstrual cycle, these findings can be utilized to generate hypotheses for further research.

NOTE

This study was supported by the American Nurses Association, Ethnic/Racial Minority Fellowship Programs (#5TOIMH ISI55), and assisted by a research grant from Sigma Theta Tau, Eta Chapter, Pittsburgh, and by the School of Nursing Alumni Association, University of Pittsburgh, PA.

REFERENCES

Bardwick, J. M. (1971). *Psychology of women.* New York: Harper & Row.

Bart, P. (1971). Depression in middle-aged women. In V. Gormick & B. Moran (Eds.), *Women in a sexist society* (pp. 99–117). New York: Basic Books.

Bart, P., & Grossman, M. (1976). Menopause. *Women & Health, 1*(3), 3–11.

Benedek, T. (1950). Climacterium: A developmental phase. *Psychoanalytic Quarterly, 19,* 1–27.

Benedek, T. (1952). *Climacterium: Psychosexual functions in women.* New York: Ronald Press.

Beyene, Y. (1986). Cultural significance and psychological manifestations of menopause: A biocultural analysis. *Cultural Medicine and Psychiatry, 10,* 47–70.

Brooks-Gunn, J., & Ruple, D. (1980). Menarche: The interaction of physiological, cultural, and social factors. In A. Dan, C. Graham, & C. Beecher (Eds.), *The menstrual cycle: Synthesis of interdisciplinary research* (pp. 141–159). New York: Springer.

Bungay, G., Vessey, M. P., & McPherson, C. K. (1980). Study of symptoms in middle life with special reference to the menopause. *British Medical Journal, 281,* 181–184.

Chadwick, M. (1932). *The psychological effects of menstruation.* New York: Nervous and Mental Disease.

Deutsch, H. (1945). *The psychology of women* (Vol. 2). New York: Grune & Stratton.

Durham, F. (1979). Timing and source of information about attitudes toward menstruation among college students. *Journal of Genetic Psychology, 117,* 205–207.

Flint, M. (1975). The menopause: Reward or punishment. *Psychosomatics, 16,* 161–163.

Frere, G. (1971). Mean age at menopause in South Africa. *South African Journal of Medical Science, 16,* 21–24.

Gavan, J. A. (1981). Why the menopause? *American Journal of Physical Anthropology, 54,* 224–230.

Goldstein, M. (1987). Aspects of gender and ethnic identity in menopause: Two Italian-American women. *Journal of the American Academy of Psychoanalysis, 15,* 383–394.

Goodman, M. (1980). Toward a biology of menopause. *Signs: Journal of Women in Culture and Society, 5,* 739–753.

Greene, J., & Cooke, D. (1982). Psychological factors in women during the climacterium: A community study. In C. Main (Ed.), *Clinical psychology and medicine: A behavioral perspective* (pp. 131–152). New York: Plenum Press.

Griffin, J. (1977). A cross-cultural investigation of behavioral changes at menopause. *Social Science Journal, 14*(2), 49–55.

Hunter, M., Battersby, R., & Whitehead, M. (1986). Relationship between psychological symptoms, somatic complaints, and menopausal status. *Maturitas, 8,* 217–236.

Jackson, B. B. (1982/1983). Life satisfaction in black climacteric women in relation to specific life events. (Doctoral dissertation, University of Pittsburgh, 1982) *Dissertation Abstracts International, 43,* 8305585a.

Jackson, B. B. (1985). Role of social resource variables upon life satisfaction in Black climacteric hysterectomized women. *Nursing Papers Perspectives EN Nursing, 17*(1), 4–21.

Kaufert, P., & Syrotuik, J. (1981). Symptom reporting at the menopause. *Social Science and Medicine, 15,* 173–184.

Ladner, J. A. (1971). *Tomorrow's tomorrow.* New York: Doubleday.

Lennon, M. (1982). The psychological consequences of menopause: The importance of timing of life stage event. *Journal of Health and Social Behavior, 23,* 353–366.

Lichtendorf, S. (1982). *Eve's journey: The physical experiences of being female.* New York: Putnam.

Lock, M. (1986). Ambiguities of aging: Japanese experience and perception of menopause. *Culture, Medicine, and Psychiatry, 10,* 23–46.

Marieskind, H. (1980). *Women in the health system.* St. Louis, MO: Mosby.

McKinlay, S. M., & McKinlay, J. B. (1973). Annotated bibliography of selected studies of the menopause. *Journal of Biosocial Science, 5,* 533–555.

McKinlay, J., McKinlay, S., & Bramhilla, D. (1987). The relative contributions of endocrine changes and social circumstances to depression in middle-aged women. *Journal of Health and Social Behavior, 28,* 345–363.

Moaz, B., Dowty, N., Antonovsky, A., & Wijsenbeek, H. (1970). Female attitudes to menopause. *Social Psychiatry, 5,* 35–40.

Neugarten, B. L. (1973, April). A new look at menopause. The female experience. *Psychology Today,* pp. 39–44.

Neugarten, B., & Datan, N. (1974). The middle years. In S. Ariette (Ed.), *American handbook of psychiatry* (2d ed., Vol. 1, pp. 602–606). New York: Basic Books.

Neugarten, B., & Kraines, R. (1965). Menopausal symptoms in women of various ages. *Psychosomatic Medicine, 27,* 266–273.

Notman, M. (1979). Midlife concerns of women: Implications of the menopause. *American Journal of Psychiatry, 136,* 1270–1274.

Posner, J. (1979). It's all in your head: Feminist and medical models of menopause: (Strange bedfellows). *Sex Roles, 5,* 179–181.

Shainess, N. (1961). A re-evaluation of some aspects of femininity through a study of menstruation. *Comprehensive Psychiatry, 2,* 20–26.

The Tampax report: Summary of survey results. (1981, June). New York: Research Forecasts, Inc.

van Keep, P., & Kellerhals, J. M. (1974). Impact of socio-cultural factors on symptom formation. *Psychotherapy and Psychosomatics, 23,* 251–263.

Voda, A. (1982). Menopausal hot flashes. In A. M. Voda, M. Dinnerstein, & S. R. O'Donnell (Eds.), *Changing perspectives on menopause* (pp. 136–159). Austin: University of Texas Press.

Wright, A. (1982). Variations in Navajo menopause: Toward an explanation. In A. M. Voda, M. Dinnerstein, & S. R. O'Donnell (Eds.), *Changing perspectives on menopause* (pp. 84–99). Austin: University of Texas Press.

17

Mexican-American Women's Perceptions of Menopause

Jean Ruley Kearns and Victor A. Christopherson

Although often perceived as an event, menopause is more accurately viewed as a process, guided by a gradual decline in estrogen production that eventually leads to a last menses. The symbolic meaning of this time of life is thought to be more significant than the physiological symptoms accompanying the process. Indeed, as investigators have pointed out, the only symptom reliably associated with menopause is the so-called "hot flashes" (Mikkelsen & Holte, 1982). Other often-associated symptoms, such as headaches, fatigue, irritability, loss of orientation, and depression, are apparently common in the menopausal period, but the association is not as firmly established (Wood, 1979).

Because menopause does affect the lives of women in a pronounced way, namely by ending menstruation and the ability to conceive, it seems both predictable and logical that menopause should take on special significance in the specific cultural traditions in which the process takes place. Some evidence indicates that menopause is regarded as a natural part of life and that middle-aged women see little reason for seeking the help of medical practitioners (McKinlay & McKinlay, 1985). This suggests that menopause tends to be perceived not as an unrelated event, but as an integrated cultural element and a natural process in the life cycle. This does not mean, however, that menopause has a standard meaning from culture to culture. Weideger (1976) states that "it is the cultural attitudes toward older women, not the biological realities of menopause, that are responsible for the meaning attached to menopause and aging" (p. 207). Thus there seems to be variation both among and within societies in terms of how menopause is viewed. In the United States, of course, this is not surprising. We still retain a number of ethnic, hence, subcultural groups. The Mexican-Americans are one of our principal examples.

The proximity of the Mexican border in southeastern Arizona where this study took place facilitates a large and constant emigration from Mexico. There is both less pressure to assimilate and less opportunity to do so in rural communities, and this can result in the maintenance of ethnic culture and traditions. Beyene (1986) suggests that it is fruitful to look at cross-cultural studies to differentiate the sociocultural from the physiological aspects of menopause. Although, strictly speaking, Mexican-Americans in Arizona do not constitute a context in which a legitimate cross-cultural study can be undertaken, the cultural isolation in many of the small rural communities of southeastern Arizona comes reasonably close to approximating the cross-cultural condition. Only one study was found to deal specifically with Latin attitudes toward menopause, and this study was confined to Columbian rather than Mexican-American women (de Munoz, Munoz, Rozo, & de Aguirre, 1982). These researchers found no significant differences between young and old women with regard to their attitudes toward menopause.

In light of the apparent dearth of information regarding menopause among Mexican-American women, a study was undertaken to address such questions as the following: What do Mexican-American women believe about menopause? Is menopause perceived in a way that highlights its culturally unique aspects among this group? What are the primary information sources about menopause for women of the Mexican-American cultural group? And what is their belief about the necessary information to be transmitted to young females who have not yet gone through the process?

Method

The data were gathered by two trained interviewers who were master's degree candidates of Mexican-American descent, bilingual, and native to southeastern Arizona, the region in which the study took place. An interview instrument, which had been developed by Kearns (1982) in a previous study of menopause perceptions among Papago Indian women, was adapted for this study. The interviews were conducted in the subjects' homes or in the home of a relative. Each interview was initiated only after the women understood the purpose of the study, the interviewer had determined that the subject was comfortable with the subject matter, the anonymity of the responses had been assured, the respondent had agreed to participate, and the interviewer thought that enough time was available to complete the questions. The characteristics of the participants are listed in Table 1.

Results

The questions asked covered the following areas: terminology, meaning of menopause, normative aspects of menopause, symptoms associated with

Table 1.
Characteristics of Women Responding to the Interview on Menopause (N=100)

Characteristic	No. of women
Age (years)	
20–49	91
50–89	9
Residence	
Rural	100
Urban	0
Place of birth	
United States	71
Mexico	29
Employed outside home	30
40 hr/week	7
Less than 40 hr/week	23
Unemployed outside home	70
Marital status	
Single	20
Married	75
Widowed or divorced	5
Women married, widowed, and divorced by number of children	
No children	9
1–5	54
6–9	19
16	1

menopause, general knowledge, sources of information, and informing children about menopause.

Terminology

Approximately three-fourths of the 100 women in this study used the term *cambio de vida*, literally "change of life," to denote menopause. Nineteen used "menopause," and the remainder did not know an appropriate term for the process. Related to the terminology used for menopause was the acceptability of the topic as a subject of conversation: 48 respondents said that women freely talk about menopause without undue embarrassment, 33 that women seldom speak of it, and 17 that it was almost never discussed.

The Meaning of Menopause

The responses to questions in this category were predictably both literal and symbolic: 36 women said that menopause meant no more monthly periods, 21 indicated that it was a change in life, and 18 associated the term or process with aging and lack of ability to bear any more children. Other responses were generally accurate and reflected some aspect or combination of these ideas. For example, in the discussions such statements as the following were made:

> We were very poor and had no way to get birth control method – didn't know where to go or could afford to buy. So I was glad no more babies. (44-year-old woman)

> It was as sign of me getting old. But it was a relief not have to deal with babies or husband. I was not afraid to lose husband then. (46-year-old woman)

> Was glad it was all over. Of course it means I am getting old but we have to get old some day. I was prepared to face *cambio de vida* cause my Mom gave me a lecture right after I had my first baby. Before then she wouldn't talk to me about it. (46-year-old woman)

Normative Aspects of Menopause

The women who had not yet experienced menopause were asked at what age they expected the process to occur. Another question asked all respondents their opinion of when menopause takes place among Mexican-American women. The answers were generally the same, namely, between 40 and 50 years of age. No response suggested that Mexican-American women go through menopause at a different time or rate than non-Mexican-Americans. When asked if they felt that Mexican-American women deal with menopause differently than other women, 93 said there was no difference, and one indicated she thought there was a difference. Six responded that Mexican-Americans take better care of themselves than do non-Mexican-Americans. For example, one respondent stated, "Mexican women wear more warm clothes and don't eat as many sour things as other women."

When asked how long the "change of life" takes from beginning to end, 4 women indicated that it took only 2 days! The longest estimate was 5 to 10 years, 27 women had no idea, and the rest gave intermediate answers, from 1 to 5 years.

Symptoms

Inasmuch as there is lack of agreement among the medical profession concerning the physical symptoms associated directly with menopause, it was not unexpected to find a good deal of variation among the subjects' responses on the matter. When asked to discuss whether they had experienced or would experience pain during the change of life, 26 said no, 19 did not know, 24 said that it depended on the individual, and 31 were certain that pain was one of the symptoms accompanying menopause. Other frequently experienced symptoms included hot flashes (22%), dizziness (16%), backache and headache (16%), and nervousness (11%). Less frequent answers included cramps, fever, swollen stomach, heavy flowing, "total wrecked feeling," body swelling, and mental distress. Some specific responses were "Woman has hot flashes and woman is kind of like dogs in heat and that is why women get pregnant"; "Woman looks like she is going to have a baby"; "Woman feels like drinking a lot of liquid"; and "Some women end up in the hospital." Although certain outcomes of the menopause seem generally well understood and predictable, the associated symptoms appear to be one of the most highly variable aspects.

General Knowledge

The majority of Mexican-American women had the necessary and practical knowledge about *cambio de vida.* There was considerable variation about details, but the main truths about the condition were familiar: the cessation of menstruation, the inability to conceive, and the signaling of a change of life including the signs of aging. Even so, 14% said that it was possible to have children after menopause. Seven of these respondents claimed they had known such cases to have happened. The respondents who thought that menopause signaled the end of childbearing, gave as the reason that the woman's reproductive system or parts thereof ceased to function.

When asked if women could conceive during the time of menopause but prior to the last menstrual period, 71 said it was possible, 12 responded negatively, and 17 did not feel firm enough in their knowledge to have an opinion. Of those who thought it possible to conceive during the change but prior to its completion, such comments as the following were offered: "The woman is still in heat"; "She must be careful during the change"; "Children born then may be defective"; and "The 'ovum' still releases eggs."

It is interesting to note that throughout the discussions involving childbearing or birth control, at no time was any responsibility for preventive measures attributed to the husband.

Sources of Information

The general consensus (64%) was that the girl's or woman's mother should be the individual to provide information both about menstruation and menopause. However, 24% said the schools should be the primary source of information for girls. These responses might serve as a commentary on the difference between the "ideal" and the "real." When the respondents were asked whether they had sought or would seek help during the change of life process, 94 answered affirmatively. They often wanted information about what was happening to them and sought such help from a doctor. Approximately one-quarter of the respondents also indicated that an unrelated older woman had been a source of information for them.

Informing Children About Menopause

Although 64 respondents believed that the mother should provide information about menopause to the young girl or woman, only 7 believed that the mother should be the information source for boys. According to 42 of the women, the boys' fathers should provide the necessary information about menopause, and the rest believed the school or older friends should take care of it. There appears to be a rather sharp division along gender lines as to what information is considered appropriate for males and females in terms of orientation about menopause.

Summary and Discussion

Basically the responses by Mexican-American women to questions asked of them concerning their perceptions of menopause revealed that their basic knowledge was both generally accurate and functional. Although their responses were often phrased differently from those that might be expected from an Anglo sample, the content was similar. Saunders (1961) characterized Spanish-speaking people in terms of their reactions to illness and disease: "Resist the temptation to equate cultural or subcultural differences in behavior or attitude with ignorance or lack of intelligence. Failure to behave as we might in a given situation does not necessarily imply either lack of knowledge or stupidity. It may mean that the person has access to a different body of knowledge, a different set of values, a different set of standards from those provided by our own cultural conditioning" (p. 71).

Saunders' cautionary note is well advised. Another caveat when working with Spanish-speaking individuals is to realize that they are not a homogeneous group. Each location, each degree of rurality, length of residence in the United States, age, and other factors all affect the degree of acculturation Mexican-Americans will reflect. Perhaps if a comparable study were done in another location, the results might be somewhat different. At any rate, the principal findings of this study were as follows:

1. Mexican-American women were not noticeably different from non-Mexican-American women in the ways they deal with or face the menopause.

2. The women who had completed menopause felt that it was a relief to have finished that phase of life.

3. The respondents generally agreed that women cannot have children after menopause, but they can have children during the process.

4. There was no consensus on the time necessary to complete the change of life.

5. There was great variation concerning the symptoms that the women associated with the process of menopause.

6. The majority of women felt that menopause was a subject that could

be discussed without undue embarrassment; however, a significant number felt somewhat uncomfortable with the subject.

7. The principal source of information concerning menopause was the mother; other sources were the school, older relatives, and nonrelatives.

8. The majority of respondents believed that both boys and girls should be informed about menopause. There was, however, a sharp division along gender lines as to the appropriate source of information. They believed that the mothers and the school should inform the girls, and that the fathers and the school should inform the boys.

Future research on menopause might explore the attitudes of Mexican women in the interior of Mexico to compare how acculturation has affected the attitudes and perceptions of Mexican-American women. The findings from this study suggest that in spite of the relative isolation of the Mexican communities in rural southeastern Arizona, a good deal of acculturation has taken place regarding the perception of menopause.

REFERENCES

Beyene, Y. (1986). Cultural significance and physiological manifestations of menopause: A biocultural analysis. In A. Kleinman (Ed.), *Culture, medicine and psychiatry* (Vol. 10, pp. 47–71).

de Munoz, J. G., Munoz, A., Rozo, R. E., & de Aguirre, M. S. (1982). Attitudes de las mujeres hacia la menopausia [Attitudes of women toward menopause]. *Revista Latinoamerica de Psicologia, 14,* 397–404.

Kearns, B. J. R. (1982). Perceptions of menopause by Papago women. In A. Voda, M. Dinnerstein, & S. O'Donnell (Eds.), *Changing perspectives on menopause* (pp. 70–83). Austin: University of Texas Press.

McKinlay, S., & McKinlay, J. (1985). The menopausal syndrome. *British Journal of Preventative Social Medicine, 28,* 108–115.

Mikkelsen, A., & Holte, A. (1982). A factor-analytic study of climacteric symptoms. *Psychiatry and Social Science, 2,* 35–39.

Saunders, L. (1961). Some suggestions for working with Spanish-speaking patients. In P. P. Coulter (Ed.), *Report of Southwestern Conference on Cultural Influences on Health Services and Home Economics Programs* (pp. 70–72). Tucson: University of Arizona.

Wood, C. (1979). Menopausal myths. *Medical Journal of Australia, 1,* 496–499.

Weideger, P. (1976). *Menstruation and menopause: The philosophy and psychology, the myth and the reality.* New York: Knopf.

18

Differing Perspectives of Menopause: An Attribution Theory Approach

Catherine DeLorey

By the year 2000, there will be 58 million midlife women (aged 40 to 60 years) in the United States, accounting for 20% of the total population. Even though this group is the fastest growing segment of the population, little is known of their health concerns or if their health care is adequate and appropriate.

Menopause and midlife are significant experiences for all women. They often occur simultaneously, and each comes laden with its own stereotypes. This can prejudice women's expectations and can lead their physicians to see them as menopausal/midlife women rather than as individual women at midlife, who coincidentally may also be experiencing menopause.

Except for anecdotal reports, little is known of the concerns and experiences of midlife women, or how they view the experience of menopause. Additionally, we have little information on how physicians view midlife women or menopause. In view of this, I decided to investigate perceptions of a representative group of midlife women and of their physicians concerning the health of midlife women. I chose a sample of 120 women randomly from the residence lists of the wards and precincts of the city of Boston, Massachusetts, stratified in 5-year increments. In addition, I interviewed physicians of these women to determine their views of midlife women. I have used attribution theory to explain the differing perceptions of women and physicians, the salience of factors that influence causation, and how cognition or awareness influences interpretation.

Attribution Theory

Research, begun in the 1960s, demonstrated that a particular physiological response could be the basis for different emotional responses and interpretations, depending on cues from the environment (Schachter & Singer, 1962). This original explanation led subsequently to the development of attribution theory, the delineation of factors that influence our perception of causation, and the development of models to explain how causation is assigned to events (Deaux, 1984; Harvey, 1976; Jones & Nisbett, 1972; Kelley, 1971; Shaver, 1971).

One aspect of attribution theory, especially relevant to the focus of this chapter, concerns the roles of *actor* and *observer*. Actors attribute actions to the situation requirements, whereas observers attribute actions to trait characteristics of the actor. Actors who do not fit the stereotype are rejected as deviant, and those who fit the stereotype reinforce the observer's belief in it (Jones & Nesbitt, 1972).

Examining the stereotypes attributed to menopause, while seeing the woman experiencing menopause as an actor, permits us to propose how these stereotypes are formed. The observers in this study are the physicians of women in midlife.

Although this study looks at midlife women in examining the attributions assigned to menopause, not all women at menopause are also at midlife. A number of younger women experience menopause, both naturally and artificially. This makes it imperative that we understand menopause not just as an experience of midlife women but also as an event itself.

In addition to divergent perspectives of actor and observer, another factor that influences our perception of causality is information bias. Information processing biases are the usual dispositions people bring to dealing with information. Because of differences in the information available and because its salience is unique for each party, the events and the behaviors in a given situation have different significance for the actor and the observer. One limitation is that the observer inevitably sees the actor in a restricted number of roles. Another limitation is the generally recognized human need to maintain consistency in our view of others. This is referred to as "maintenance of cognitive balance." A further limitation is that the observer sees the behavior of the actor as the focus of the situation and may not be aware of stimuli that preceded the behavior.

These factors and limitations lead the observer to see the actor as a "trait package" rather than as an individual, and tend to reinforce and confirm previously held stereotypes about the actor. When we add to this the stereotypic assumptions about women in general, potential differences between women's descriptions of their experiences and the perceptions of their physicians are not surprising.

To explore the usefulness of attribution theory, the perceptions of midlife women and their physicians were examined to assess and compare their attitudes.

Method

This study utilized a random community sample of 120 women, ages 40 to 60 years, and 52 physicians, who were their primary health care providers. Women identified by the stratified random sampling procedure received letters requesting their participation, and data was obtained in their homes by trained interviewers. The physicians identified by these women also received letters requesting their participation, including endorsements of the research by a prominent dean and by the state medical society. Physicians were then contacted and interviewed by telephone by trained interviewers. The sample of women was 65% white, 70% had at least a high school education, and 57% were employed outside the home. Physicians were 37 to 62 years of age ($M = 43$). They were predominantly white (85%) and male (89%). Comparisons of male and female physicians yielded no significant differences in attitudes or perceptions.

In this study, physicians were not asked to comment on specific women; in fact, they were not told which woman had designated them. Physicians were asked all questions in reference to midlife women in general, *not women experiencing menopause.*

In addition, a measure of subjective health experiences based on Neugarten and Kraines's (1965) symptom check list was administered. Women indicated if they experienced each symptom, whereas physicians estimated the proportion of midlife women who experienced each symptom.

Health attitude was measured by a 37-item scale that included statements relating to perceived health status, perceptions of health care, and attitudes relating to midlife and aging.

Results

Women's responses to general questions concerning health care and their physicians were positive. Health attitude questions concerning satisfaction with health care, time spent with their physicians, and satisfaction with care each achieved a score of 80 on a scale of 0–100, with 100 being most positive.

How do the responses of women and physicians compare? Both women and physicians were asked to name the major health problem of midlife women. Not one woman responded with menopause, whereas 21% of the physicians indicated that menopause was the major health problem of midlife women. Even when women were provided with a list from which to select major issues, only 5% selected menopause.

When all items concerning health care were dichotomized to agree/disagree, the physicians were in accord with the women 58% of the time. When only those items relating to menopause were considered, this agreement dropped to 50%. The most dramatic item was the statement, "Menopause is of *no concern* to midlife women." Whereas 60% of the women supported this statement, only 17% of the physicians thought it true.

A comparison of responses to the health items as expressing either a positive or a negative attitude revealed that women were more positive than physicians 5% of the time. However, when items relating specifically to menopause were compared, women were more positive 71% of the time.

As a whole, the measures for which the physicians had the least awareness of women's perceptions were related to menopause. These can be summarized by saying that physicians see menopause as both more important *and* more negative than women do.

The subjective symptom list contained many symptoms often ascribed to menopause, ranging from constipation and diarrhea to headaches and rheumatic pains. On 75% of the items, physicians' estimates of incidence differed from women's reports of symptoms by more than 10 percentage points. From this list, those symptoms most consistently associated with menopause were selected for analysis: hot flushes/flashes, cold sweats, and vaginal dryness. The proportion of women who report experiencing each symptom and the physicians' estimation of that proportion are shown in Table 1.

The physicians either underestimated or overestimated women's reported experiences, suggesting that physicians do not have an accurate core of information from which they can perceive the individual midlife woman.

Table 1.
Proportion of Women Experiencing Menopausal Symptoms Compared With Physicians' Estimates

Symptom	Women ($n=120$)	Physicians ($n=52$)	χ^2	p
Hot flushes	45%	31%	2.48	.12
Cold sweats	28%	21%	.63	.43
Vaginal dryness	1%	29%	30.50	.001

Discussion

Although women in this study indicated they were satisfied with their health care and physician when asked to assess each, further exploration indicates relevant differences in perceptions of women and physicians.

Various aspects of attribution theory provide us with a useful explanation for the perpetuation of misinformation and stereotypes about midlife women and menopause. One example of the influence of cognition on a state of physiological arousal concerns midlife women and the subjective experience of hot flushes. Hot flushes have been described as being unpleasant, uncomfortable, or even embarrassing. Each woman's experience is unique; for some women the intensity and quantity of hot flushes may be uncomfortable, but this is not necessarily so for all women (Voda, 1982). One explanation for the negative connotation of hot flushes is that their interpretations may be more significant than the experience itself. In explanatory interviews with women, as well as in literature written by women, it becomes obvious that hot flushes are viewed not just as physiological signs of menopause but as social symbols of aging as well.

These data demonstrate various discrepancies in the perceptions of menopause between affected women and their physicians. The physician/ observer and the woman/actor approach the whole issue differently, as the core of the theory would suggest. One way to account for these differences is by the use of various aspects of attribution theory:

1. *Available information.* The physicians' primary source of information is medical school education and current medical literature, both of which address menopause as a pathological process or problem (Buchsbaum, 1983; Kerzner, 1983; McCrea, 1983). Women use their own experience and that of their contemporaries as their primary source of information. As a result, 21% of the physicians saw menopause as a major health problem, whereas none of the women listed menopause as a primary health problem. Even when presented with a list of possible major problems which contained menopause, only 5% of women checked that item.

2. *Restricted number of roles.* Physicians saw women in only one role: patient. The woman who has problems will be the one to discuss this with her physician, not the woman with no concerns. This produces a distorted sample for inferences.

3. *Cognitive balance.* Having formed an opinion on available information, and given the restriction of roles, to avoid cognitive dissonance, the physician excludes information that is inconsistent with previously formed views. This is illustrated by the finding that 60% of women indicated that menopause is "of no concern" to midlife women, but only 17% of physicians considered it "of no concern."

4. *Differential salience.* To the observer/physician, menopausal woman is the object of observation, whereas to the actor/woman, she is an individual with the entire complexity of her life.

5. *Focus of the situation.* To the physician/observer, menopause is considered a pathological entity and becomes the focus of observation to the exclusion of other events. The woman, on the other hand, is aware of her history and her current situation and focuses on the stimuli which led to her contact with the physician.

6. *Trait package.* As illustrated in Figure 1, one characteristic of the

observer is to see the actor as a trait package, that is, as embodying a group of characteristics rather than seeing each actor as a discrete entity (Mitchell, 1985). Thus, each woman is seen as a representative of midlife woman rather than as woman who happens to be at midlife or experiencing menopause.

Seeing a midlife woman as a menopausal trait package then defines and explains all her behaviors. Information-processing biases can inhibit disconfirmation of prior perceptions by denying behaviors that contradict the trait package.

Model of Attribution

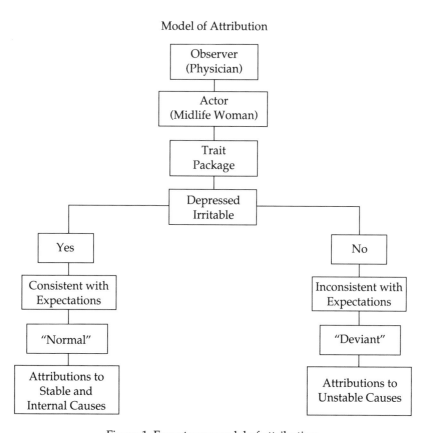

Figure 1. Expectancy model of attribution.

Conclusion

Both midlife and menopause are varied experiences for all women with some similarities among them. If physicians and other observers do not have an accurate view of midlife women or menopause, what can be done? It is important to recognize that the explanation offered by attribution theory does not "blame" physicians, but illustrates the processes by which they may come to have inaccurate views of women at midlife.

Physicians have a distorted perception of menopause because their information sources are distorted. These distorted sources of information include medical advertisements that present midlife women in negative terms, medical literature that presents menopause as a pathology, and medical education that neglects to present midlife as a totality (Cowan, Warren, & Young, 1985; McCrea, 1983).

One way to attenuate the process of informational bias is to provide the same information on events and history to the observer and the actor so that similar perceptions can emerge. In the actor/observer interaction of woman/physician, if the physician is to have the same information and history as the woman, an investment of time is needed. Because only 53% of women have a private physician and only 25% of physician visits are more than 15 min long (Drury, 1978; Koch, 1978; Lawrence & McLemore, 1983), this needed investment of time does not seem realistic.

To provide appropriate health care for midlife women, both the structure of existing health care services and the dearth of accurate information need to be addressed. This can be accomplished by implementing the following priorities:

1. Support environments in which women are empowered to take control of their own health care and can develop realistic expectations about midlife health issues, as is being done in many midlife and menopausal self-help groups.

2. Establish priorities of health care that address women's priorities, derived from their own experiences.

3. Establish an information base that considers precursors of health at midlife, derived from the sociological and behavioral sciences, not just biomedical sciences.

4. Present a more realistic, nonpathological view of midlife women to health care providers.

5. Redefine research priorities so that nonclinical and prospective studies are conducted that give a more accurate assessment of midlife.

Midlife is an important stage of women's lives, but from the perspective of health, the domination of menopause has obscured our understanding of the totality of women's experiences. Only when we look at all the facets of midlife experience can we begin to make valid statements and assessments relating to the health of midlife women.

NOTE

The author wishes to acknowledge the contribution of Dr. Paul Rosenkrantz to the preparation of this chapter. The chapter is based on a presentation coauthored by Dr. Rosenkrantz, who is now deceased.

REFERENCES

Buchsbaum, H. J. (1983). *The menopause*. New York: Springer-Verlag.

Cowan, G., Warren, L. W., & Young, J. L. (1985). Medical perceptions of menopausal symptoms. *Psychology of Women Quarterly, 9,* 1–14.

Croxton, J. S., & Morrow, N. (1984). What does it take to reduce observer bias? *Psychological Reports, 55,* 135–138.

Deaux, K. (1984). From individual differences to social categories: Analysis of a decade's research on gender. *American Psychologist, 39,* 105–116.

Drury, T. F. (1978). *Access to ambulatory health care.* (*AdvanceData*, Report No. 17). Washington, DC: National Center for Health Statistics. (PHS No. 78-2250)

Harvey, J. (1976). *New directions in attribution research*. Hillsdale, NJ: Erlbaum.

Jones, E. E., & Nisbett, R. E. (1972). The actor and the observer: Divergent perceptions of the causes of behavior. In E. E. Jones, D. E. Kanouse, H. H. Kelley, R. E. Nisbett, S. Valins, & B. Weiner (Eds.), *Attribution: Perceiving the causes of behavior* (pp. 79–94). Morristown, NJ: General Learning Press.

Kelley, H. H. (1971). *Attribution in social interaction.* Morristown, NJ: General Learning Press.

Kerzner, L. J. (1983). Physical changes after menopause. In E. W. Markson (Ed.), *Older women* (pp. 299–311). Lexington, MA: Lexington Books.

Koch, H. (1978). *National ambulatory medical care survey.* (*AdvanceData*, Report No. 30). Washington, DC: National Center for Health Statistics. (PHS No. 78-1250)

Lawrence, L., & McLemore, T. (1988). *National ambulatory medical care survey.* (*AdvanceData*, Report No. 88). Washington, DC: National Center for Health Statistics. (PHS No. 83-1250)

McCrea, F. B. (1983). The politics of menopause: The discovery of a deficiency disease. *Social Problems, 31,* 111–123.

Mitchell, T. E. (1985). Actor observer differences in attributions to morality. *Journal of Social Psychology, 125,* 475–477.

Neugarten, B. L., & Kraines, R. J. (1965). Menopausal symptoms in women of various ages. *Psychosomatic Medicine, 27,* 266–273.

Schachter, S., & Singer, J. E. (1962). Cognitive, social and physiological determinants of emotional state. *Psychological Review, 69,* 379–399.

Shaver, H. (1978). *Introduction to attribution processes.* Cambridge, MA: Winthrop.

Voda, A. M. (1982). Menopausal hot flash. In A. M. Voda, M. Dinnerstein, & S. R. O'Donnell (Eds.), *Changing perspectives on menopause* (pp. 136–159). Austin: University of Texas Press.

19

The Development of a Measure of Attitude Toward Menopause

Cheryl Bowles

Menopause has received very little attention in the past, particularly with regard to valid research studies. Actually, little is known about the whole female midlife developmental period of which the menopausal experience is only a part.

Menopause has been stereotyped as the dominant factor in midlife development, yet many misconceptions exist about the nature and extent of symptomatology directly attributable to the menopause. Multiple physiological and psychological problems are assumed to be associated with menopause; however, clear empirical support for this assumption is lacking (Parlee, 1981).

It has been suggested that behavioral research on the menopause requires a multidisciplinary approach because of the multivariate nature of the menopausal experience. This approach includes exploration of the biological, psychological, social, and cultural factors that interact to determine women's experiences and behavior (Parlee, 1981). Literature regarding the study of the menstrual cycle and menopause reveals that attitudes are an important dimension of this approach (Ruble, Brooks-Gunn, & Clarke, 1980).

Attitudes regarding menopause are important not just from the standpoint of the women who are experiencing it. Cultural attitudes and beliefs, as well as attitudes of significant others toward menopause, may have an important influence on the expectations and menopausal experiences of women. Ruble and Brooks-Gunn (1982) pointed out that there is a particular need to study the role of expectation in the formation of symptoms related to menopause. This can be done only when valid and reliable measures of women's attitudes and beliefs about menopause are available.

Recent studies have investigated attitudes toward menopause, often in conjunction with assessment of associated symptoms. These studies have used several measures of attitude toward menopause. The most widely used instrument is the Attitude Toward Menopause Scale (ATM), developed by Neugarten, Wood, Kraines, and Loomis (1963). This instrument has not been assessed for reliability or validity in any study which has used it. Other types of attitude assessment tools have included interviews and several short semantic differential scales. These techniques were also not evaluated for reliability or validity.

The lack of a valid and reliable measure of attitudes toward menopause poses problems in the ability to build on findings of previous studies and frequently renders the data unsuitable for comparison. The existing literature consists largely of fragmented research where findings have not been replicated using consistently reliable and valid assessment tools (Bowles, 1986a).

For results of studies concerning attitude toward menopause to be comparable, a valid and reliable assessment tool needed to be developed. Additionally, given the multivariate nature of menopause, the attitude instrument should be short and provide a more general assessment of attitude so that it could be used in conjunction with assessments of other variables related to menopause without overassessing subjects. This assessment tool could then be used in a variety of studies related to menopause which would provide an additional appraisal of attitude in conjunction with whatever other variables were being studied. This might include, for example, assessment of attitude as part of a study to look at the effect of biofeedback on hot flashes or assessment of attitude as part of a descriptive study on the effects of stressful life events occurring during menopause.

The semantic differential model was chosen because it is a highly acceptable and frequently used measure of attitude, requires a short time to complete, and provides a general assessment in an uncomplicated approach. This versatile model can be used with a variety of populations and has also been used successfully in cross-cultural studies. The semantic differential appeared to offer a suitable format for identifying attitude toward menopause as well as lending itself to statistical techniques for validation. Therefore, this study was designed to construct and validate a measure of attitude toward menopause using the semantic differential model.

Method

Participants were from the northern Illinois area and included women 18 to approximately 85 years of age. None had undergone a total hysterectomy. Women were recruited from hospital volunteer services, women's fraternal and business organizations, church groups, social clubs, senior citizens' centers, and the faculty, staff, and students from a large state university. The subjects were predominantly white (93%), Catholic (42%), or Protestant (41%) women who were employed outside the home (69%).

Sixty-nine percent had a yearly family income of $20,000 or more; 75% had some college education or advanced degrees. Most women had no, one, or two children. Forty-five percent were married, 42% single, and 13% divorced or widowed. Sixty-six percent of the subjects were premenopausal, 6% were menopausal, and 28% were postmenopausal (Bowles, 1986a). The volunteer sample was divided into two groups: (a) 504 women used for the initial pilot testing of the instrument; (b) 419 women used for the validation study of the revised instrument which included factor analysis and assessments of test-retest reliability, internal consistency reliability, and convergent and discriminant validity.

All the women completed a face sheet which requested the following information: age, race, religion, education, occupation, employment status, marital status, number of children, family income, amount of time since last menstrual period, whether the woman had had a hysterectomy, and self-assessment of menopausal status and health status. Women who reported having had a total hysterectomy were excluded because the study focus was on natural menopause.

The initial pilot instrument consisted of 45 bipolar adjective scales. These 7-point scales were used to rate how a woman feels during menopause. The scale point positions were identified as *extremely, quite, slightly,* with the center position indicating both polar adjectives equally. The concept of menopause was presented by the lead-in phrase "During menopause a woman feels." This particular phrase was chosen because many of the relevant adjectives described the woman rather than the term menopause.

Pilot Study

The instrument was administered to the first sample of 504 women, who were asked to comment on the clarity of the instructions and the scales as well as to indicate any scales they felt were not relevant to the concept. The results of a principal components factor analysis of the scores on the 45-scale instrument revealed one main factor from which 20 of the scales with the highest factor loadings were selected. A second factor analysis of these 20 scales produced one factor which accounted for 60.4% of the total variance for the 20 scales.

Second Validation Sample

The revised 20-scale instrument was called the Menopause Attitude Scale (MAS).[1] The MAS was administered to a second sample of 419 women. A factor analysis was performed on the MAS scores and revealed one factor with all 20 scales loading on this factor. The factor accounted for 61.5% of the variance for the 20 scales. The Cronbach alpha reliability coefficient was .966, and the test-retest reliability coefficient for 39 subjects was $r = .872$.

Three previously developed instruments were used to estimate construct validity in the form of convergent and discriminant validity as described by Campbell and Fiske (1967). *Convergent validation* is confirmation of a positive relationship by independent measurement procedures. *Discriminant validation* refers to demonstration that measures of different but related constructs have a much lower correlation than correlations between separate measures of the same construct.

The sample of 419 women was randomly divided into three groups. One subsample ($n = 138$) was asked to complete the Neugarten (1963) Attitudes Toward Menopause Scale (ATM) as well as the MAS to assess convergent validity. The correlation coefficient was $r = .639$ for the MAS scores with the ATM scale.

The second subsample ($n = 135$) was asked to complete the Kogan (1961) Attitudes Toward Old People Scale (OP) as well as the MAS to assess discriminant validity. The correlation coefficient was $r = .420$ for the MAS scores with the OP scale. This correlation was significantly lower ($p < .02$) than the correlation for convergence obtained with the ATM scale.

The third subsample ($n = 146$) was asked to complete the Attitudes Toward Women Scale (AWS) developed by Spence, Helmreich, and Stapp (1973) as well as the MAS as a second assessment of discriminant validity. The correlation coefficient was $r = -.047$ for the MAS scores with the AWS scale.

A multiple regression analysis was also done with the data from the second sample. This analysis assisted in examining the instrument's ability to distinguish differences in attitude toward menopause among sample subjects with regard to demographic variables. This analysis identified age, marital status, number of children, family income, and menopausal status as potential explanatory variables for variance of the MAS scores. The two significant explanatory variables were age and menopausal status.

Additional analyses were done to examine the attitude toward menopause further. A one-way analysis of variance (ANOVA) was performed on the MAS scores for each of the explanatory variables identified by the multiple regression analysis. Table 1 provides frequency distributions, mean attitude scores, and the results of the ANOVA analyses for the second sample by age, marital status, number of children, and menopausal status.

Women in the various age groups showed a significant difference in attitude toward menopause ($p < .0001$). As the women grew older, the attitude toward menopause became more positive. This agrees with similar findings from other studies. The youngest age group (18–25) had the lowest mean score (68), and the oldest age group (65 and over) had the highest

Table 1.
Frequency Distribution, Mean Attitude Scores, and One-way ANOVA *for Menopause Attitude Scale (MAS) Scores for the Second Sample by Age, Marital Status, Number of Children, and Menopausal Status (N=419)*

Variable	Frequency	%	Mean MAS score	F	p
Age (years)				14.77	.0001
18–25	98	23.4	68.12		
26–35	73	17.4	77.98		
36–45	68	16.2	86.47		
46–55	77	18.4	87.09		
56–65	42	10.0	91.36		
Over 65	61	14.6	93.34		
Marital status				20.08	.0001
Single	137	32.7	73.72		
Married	215	51.3	84.07		
Divorced or widowed	67	16.0	94.21		
Number of children				8.68	.0001
None	176	42.0	74.82		
1–2	120	28.6	87.32		
3–4	94	22.4	86.87		
Over 4	28	6.7	92.57		
Menopausal status				47.83	.0001
Premenopausal	240	57.3	76.13		
Menopausal & postmenopausal	179	42.7	90.59		

mean score (93). The 26–35-year group did not differ significantly in attitude from the 18–25-year group (mean score, 77), but the 18–25-year group differed significantly from the four succeeding age groups (36–45, 46–55, 56–65, and 65 years and older). The significance of the individual group differences was assessed by the Scheffé post hoc test. This is the most conservative post hoc test, requiring a large difference in mean scores to be significant at the $p < .05$ level.

There was also a significant difference in attitude in terms of marital status. Single women had the lowest mean score, married women the next lowest, and widowed and divorced women the highest. Post hoc analyses revealed a significant difference in attitude scores between all three of these groups ($p < .05$).

Mean attitude scores also showed significant differences according to the number of children the women had. The group with no children had a mean score significantly lower than that of the other groups (1 or 2 children, 3 or 4, more than 4).

Because the size of the menopausal group was small, it was combined with the postmenopausal group and their mean attitude score was compared with that of the premenopausal group. The difference between these two groups was significant ($p < .0001$).

One factor that must be kept in mind about these differences is that the sample covered a wide age range from 18 years to approximately 85 years. With a sample covering such a wide age range, many of the demographic variables considered are related to age, such as marital status, number of children, and menopausal status. Interpreting the findings for these variables in this sample is more difficult than in a sample more homogeneous for age. It therefore will be important to sample various age groups separately for characteristics such as occupation, education, marital status, number of children, and other related variables.

Based on the results of this study, the MAS appears to be a valid and reliable measure of general attitude toward menopause for an adult female population in northern Illinois. It has been proposed in the literature that attitudes toward menopause are significantly related to women's expectations and experiences associated with menopause. At the present time, however, this relationship is not understood. A valid and reliable measure of attitude toward menopause permits the exploration of this relationship and should also provide needed information for a more thorough understanding of menopause and its relationship to other aspects of women's midlife experiences. This knowledge will in turn offer clearer directions for the promotion of women's health during this time of life.

Recommendations

Both of the samples in this study had very small groups of women who were classified as menopausal, and it is recommended that menopausal women be studied more specifically using the MAS. Also, because of the limited population of women sampled, other populations of women with different racial, ethnic, religious, educational, socioeconomic, and occupational backgrounds should be studied. This would further validate the MAS with regard to variables considered important for differentiating between groups of women.

It is recommended that significant others be studied in relation to attitudes toward menopause. A study conducted by the author (Bowles, 1986b) in the Las Vegas, Nevada, area to examine attitudes toward menopause of 180 middle-aged men, indicated that these men viewed menopause negatively. A comparison of the average attitude score for the male sample with the sample of women discussed in this report showed a significant difference between the attitudes of the men versus the women, with the men being more negative. The men's attitudes were also significantly more negative than the attitudes of the sample subgroup of young women (18–25 years). It would also seem important to assess attitudes of health care providers such as physicians and nurses.

Studies that attempt to translate the MAS into other languages are recommended so that cross-cultural comparisons of attitudes toward menopause can be made. This would also validate the MAS for further cross-cultural studies. Finally, it is recommended that the MAS be used in multivariate studies because this instrument provides information on only one of many interrelated variables that are part of menopause and other midlife experiences of women.

NOTE

1. Copies of the Menopause Attitude Scale (MAS) may be obtained from Cheryl Bowles, Graduate College, University of Nevada, Las Vegas, 4505 Maryland Parkway, Las Vegas, NV 89154.

REFERENCES

Bowles, C. (1986a). Measure of attitude toward menopause using the semantic differential model. *Nursing Research, 35,* 81–85.

Bowles, C. (1986b). *Men's attitudes toward menopause: A preliminary study.* Unpublished manuscript.

Campbell, D., & Fiske, D. (1967). Convergent and discriminant validation by the multitrait-multimethod matrix. In M. Fishbein (Ed.), *Attitude theory and measurement* (pp. 100–122). New York: Wiley.

Kogan, N. (1961). Attitudes toward old people: The development of a scale and an examination of correlates. *Journal of Abnormal Social Psychology, 62,* 44–54.

Neugarten, B., Wood, V., Kraines, R., & Loomis, B. (1963). Women's attitudes toward the menopause. *Vita Humana, 6,* 140–151.

Parlee, M. (1981). Gaps in behavioral research on the menstrual cycle. In P. Komnenich, M. McSweeney, J. Noack, & N. Elder (Eds.), *The menstrual cycle: Vol. 2. Research and implications for women's health* (pp. 45–53). New York: Springer.

Ruble, D., & Brooks-Gunn, J. (1982). Expectations regarding menstrual symptoms: Effects on evaluation and behavior of women. In A. Voda, M. Dinnerstein, & S. O'Donnell (Eds.), *Changing perspectives on menopause* (pp. 209–219). Austin: University of Texas Press.

Ruble, D., Brooks-Gunn, J., & Clarke, A. (1980). Research on menstrual-related psychological changes: Alternative perspectives. In J. Parsons (Ed.), *The psychobiology of sex differences and sex roles* (pp. 227–243). New York: McGraw-Hill.

Spence, J., Helmreich, R., & Stapp, J. (1973). A short version of the attitude toward women scale (AWS). *Bulletin of the Psychonomics Society, 2,* 219–220.

20

Menstrual Pattern Changes in Middle-Aged Women

Phyllis Kernoff Mansfield and Cheryl M. Jorgensen

Despite its centrality in women's lives, menopause has been a widely neglected research topic, largely because of the social stigma associated with menstruation and its cessation; menopause makes us uncomfortable, even frightened (McKinlay & McKinlay, 1973; Selby, Calhoun, Vogel, & King, 1980). A second reason for the relative lack of attention paid to menopause research may be that only within this century has the average life expectancy of women exceeded the average age of menopause (Selby et al., 1980; World Health Organization, 1981). There may have been too few menopausal women to generate scientific interest in this life stage.

A particular weakness of the existing menopause literature has been its failure to characterize adequately the normal menstrual cycle changes women can anticipate as they approach menopause (Asso, 1983). Indeed, ignorance of the normal body changes that occur during the menopausal transition has been described by women as the worst aspect of their menopause experience (Golloway, 1975; Perlmutter & Bart, 1982) and may explain at least in part the finding by Kahana, Kiyak, and Liang (1980) that premenopausal women expected menopause to be a more stressful event than postmenopausal women actually found it to be.

A serious shortcoming of previous research efforts has been their failure to document precise *patterns* of change during the transition to menopause. Instead, most studies have reported *average* menstrual cycle characteristics (cycle length, cycle variability) at different ages (Burch, Macisco, & Parker, 1967; Chiazze, Brayer, Macisco, Parker, & Duffy, 1968; Collette, Wertenberger, & Fiske, 1954; Cutler, Garcia, & Krieger, 1979; Fluhman, 1934; Geist, 1930; Goldzieher, Henkin, & Hamblen, 1947; Gunn, Jenkin, & Gunn, 1937; Matsumoto, Nogami, & Ohkuri, 1962; Treloar, Boynton, Behn, & Brown, 1967; Vollman, 1956).

From such studies, we learn, for example, that with advancing age the *average* menstrual cycle changes by first becoming shorter, then longer, and increasingly more variable, as complete cessation approaches (Presser,

1974; Treloar et al., 1967). However, such aggregate data obscure variability, with the result that women and their physicians may interpret patterns other than "average" as abnormal and therefore pathological (Ballinger, 1976).

Methodological shortcomings such as these have resulted in misunderstandings that might adversely affect the well-being of middle-aged women in at least two important ways. First, because few norms exist to inform women about the variety of menstrual cycle changes that they might experience in the decade or so prior to menopause, any changes that do occur may be interpreted as signs of pathology, causing alarm and fear. For instance, Ballinger (1976) reported that premenopausal women who notice changes in their bleeding patterns often interpret these as signs of cancer. Several physicians have documented visits from women in their late thirties and early forties, wondering whether the menstrual conditions they were noticing were caused by the "change of life" (McEwan, 1973; Selby et al., 1980).

Likewise, physicians who lack scientific data concerning the variety of normal changes women may experience prior to menopause may order unnecessary and sometimes dangerous drug or surgical interventions. For example, even though 51% of premenopausal women in one study reported that unusually heavy menstrual flows characterized their later-life menstrual cycles, their physicians nonetheless interpreted this symptom as an indication of pathology (Neugarten & Kraines, 1965; see also DeLorey, chap. 18, this volume).

There may be a tendency to label natural but poorly documented changes as "dysfunctional uterine bleeding" (DUB), a poorly defined clinical term often used to justify the need for a D&C (dilation and curettage) (Finck, 1979) or hysterectomy (Finck, 1979; Kasper, 1985; Morgan, 1984). In fact, in recent years, the considerable number of hysterectomies performed because of dysfunctional uterine bleeding has given rise to a warning from the Centers for Disease Control that DUB is a "questionable" indication for a hysterectomy (Morgan, 1984).

A Study of Menstrual Pattern Changes: Three Phases

Since 1985, a multiphased study of menstrual pattern changes designed to address the shortcomings of previous research has been in progress. The objectives of this study are

1. to close significant gaps in our knowledge of menstrual cycle changes prior to menopause that have arisen from general inattention to the subject as well as from serious methodological shortcomings in those studies already performed;

2. to identify and describe a field of patterns of age-related changes in menstrual cycle characteristics, using innovative, multidisciplinary approaches including those suggested by learning theorists and econometricians;

3. to make significant methodological improvements over prior studies in these ways: selection of a nonclinical sample of adequate size; daily instead of retrospective reporting; inclusion of positive as well as negative symptomology to maximize respondents' options and avoid researcher bias; and an interactive perspective of menstrual cycle events that recognizes the bidirectional influences of biological events and social-psychological contextual factors (Koeske, 1982);

4. to analyze the relationships between identified change patterns and relevant demographic and contextual variables;

5. ultimately, to improve the well-being of middle-aged women by adding to their knowledge of normal, healthy premenopausal changes while dispelling harmful myths (Barnett & Baruch, 1978; Bart & Grossman, 1976; Frey, 1981; Mansfield & Boyer, 1990).

Study Design

The overall research project comprises three phases: the first and second, a pair of pilot studies conducted in 1985 and 1986, respectively, and the third, a 5-year longitudinal study that began in early 1990. The pilot studies will be described first.

Pilot Studies

Two pilot studies were performed to (a) develop a valid and reliable instrument for collecting menstrual cycle, demographic, and contextual data; (b) determine the feasibility of daily reports by subjects; and (c) identify the appropriate statistical techniques for menstrual pattern analysis.

Pilot Study 1. The first pilot, conducted in the summer of 1985, was a feasibility study and a test of instruments for collecting daily mood and menstrual cycle data. A convenience sample of 10 women agreed to participate in a 2-month study requiring daily reports of their moods (positive and negative) and menstrual cycle activity (whether they were menstruating, and amount of flow). Two styles of monthly calendars were tested by each participant, one each month, in a counterbalanced order.

The first format was a standard calendar, with the codes for 18 moods and physical symptoms as well as five levels of menstrual flow. Subjects were permitted to list up to five symptoms they experienced per day; in addition, they indicated whether they were menstruating by placing an *M* in the corner of each day's box, along with a code number describing the amount of flow.

The second format was adapted from Harrison's (1983) design for charting the course of premenstrual syndrome. Days of the month were listed down the left, and columns afforded space for respondents to record daily up to three symptom codes, menstrual activity, and amount of flow. Because this study tested instruments and procedure, no attempt was made to conceal its true nature; subjects were aware that their menstrual cycles were of primary interest to the researchers.

Results of this study confirmed the anticipated difficulties of collecting detailed written reports from women over an extended period of time. First, 3 of the 10 subjects dropped out because of loss of interest or personal concerns that interfered with participation. Second, although the instructions emphasized the importance of daily reports, several subjects reported that they sometimes forgot, and provided retrospective reports instead.

Neither monthly reporting form was overwhelmingly preferred by subjects; in fact, they were equally preferred (even by the researchers!). Some respondents preferred the calendar because it reminded them of "real time," and others preferred the chart because it seemed easier to use and was better organized. That the chart method restricted daily responses to three symptoms was not an issue; three seemed sufficient.

These results suggested that any study requiring prolonged data collection of daily reports would require some incentive to minimize the drop-out rate, and some method of monitoring daily reports to avoid retrospective reporting. The second pilot study attempted to remedy these problems.

Pilot Study 2. (See Mansfield, Hood, & Henderson, 1989, for a full description of this study.) This 3-month study, which took place in the spring and early summer of 1986, asked 12 women and their spouses to phone in their daily reports of "well-being" to a telephone answering machine. Spouses were included to obscure the focus on the menstrual cycle and to examine partner and gender effects. Calls were monitored daily to ensure same-day reports; any subject failing to call was prompted with a reminder call.

Subjects were asked to report how much *more or less than usual* (on a 7-point scale) they experienced 10 positive and negative mood items: *sad, nervous, friendly, depressed, alert, irritable, sensual, overwhelmed, energetic,* and *capable.*

Subjects also reported whether they experienced each of 10 somatic symptoms that day, and if so, how much *more or less bothersome than usual,* on a 7-point scale, the experience was. These symptoms were *headache, bloating, menstrual cramps, weight gain, tiredness, dizziness, menstrual flow, sudden sweating, breast pain,* and *backache.*

Menstrual cycle questions were embedded in the list to keep subjects naive about the true nature of the study. A financial incentive of $120 per couple, paid in three instalments, was offered to participants who remained in the study.

Results showed the importance of daily prompting; our monitors had to make some reminder calls nearly every day. Even though a phone call probably has more salience for subjects than a calendar entry, we experienced some difficulty in getting subjects to remember to report daily data over a period of time.

The financial incentive appeared to be highly effective; there were no drop-outs over the 3-month study (the personal contact with the monitor may have helped also). The incentive seemed to become increasingly important to subjects as the study moved into its final month (unfortunately, the beginning of summer). Implications for the costliness of a major study with a large number of participants cannot be ignored.

This study also provided a setting for testing the ability of a variety of statistical approaches to identify patterns of menstrual cycle characteristics. One of these was P-technique factor analysis (Cattell, 1963; Nesselroade & Ford, 1985), used to determine patterns of intraindividual changes in symptoms. Employing this method, we first correlated the 20 items on our Daily Well-Being Form across occasions separately for each participant. Items showing no day-to-day variation were eliminated from further analysis for that subject. The intercorrelation matrix for each woman was then factor analyzed, with from two to five factors per subject emerging. These factors represent, in effect, groups of variables, or dimensions, that change in concert over time (Nesselroade & Ford, 1985).

To determine the overall factors that best represented the commonalities among the subjects, we included only those items with factor loadings over 0.60 or those which loaded on the same factor for at least half of the subjects. The result was two factors that appeared consistently across subjects: a Negative Mood factor, comprising four items (sad, nervous, depressed, irritable) and an Arousal or Energy factor, with three items (alert, energetic, capable). Two menstrual items from our list, menses and menstrual cramps, loaded onto a third factor; however, their obvious association with menstrual phase resulted in their elimination. It is interesting that no other physical factors emerged; the other physical items loaded onto either the Negative Mood or the Arousal factors for different subjects, with little consistency as to which symptoms fell into which factors.

Two other techniques will be explored, using this data set, to determine their applicability in the large-scale longitudinal study. Tucker's (1966) generalized learning curve analysis is one approach for determining cycle-related changes in patterns of menstrual bleeding characteristics. This technique permits the identification of a field of learning curves, each one representing a class of individual learning curves rather than a single general learning curve. Tucker argues that if one average curve is considered as the learning law for all subjects, then variations are treated as errors of observation. Similarly, in menstrual cycle research, when a single generalized age-related change pattern is reported as the norm, deviations are interpreted as signs of pathology. Utilization of learning curve analysis, then, may be fruitful for providing aging women and their physicians with a variety of "normal" patterns of menstrual changes. This approach would also appear to have promise in the description of within-bleeding-episode changes, such as day-by-day changes in bleeding flow and menstrual symptomology.

Patterns of changes in blood loss and other symptoms reported daily will require special techniques, because we are interested in describing both intra- and intercycle changes. The few researchers who have attempted to describe daily changes in blood flow (within one cycle) have provided qualitative (e.g., bleeding shape A, B, etc.) but not quantitative classifications (Matsumoto et al., 1962; Snowden & Christian, 1983). Our analysis of blood flow data will include attempts to represent these daily changes within a cycle in quantifiable form and then attempt descriptions of trends across menstrual cycles.

Conclusions from Pilot Studies 1 and 2

Certain conclusions emerge from these two studies. First, it will be a challenge to retain a large sample of women willing to provide daily information over several years concerning their menstrual cycles and other experiences. Pilot Study 1 had a substantial drop-out rate; Pilot Study 2 was highly successful in achieving 100% retention, but only at great financial cost (large financial incentives and same-day reminder calls to subjects forgetting to make reports).

Second, P-technique factor analysis has been shown to be a useful tool. It permitted us to determine two common factors (Negative Mood, Arousal) comprising seven items with strong loadings that appeared consistently across subjects. This technique, in permitting the extensive investigation of interindividual differences in intraindividual change, will be useful in the identification of individual patterns of symptom experiences over time as well as commonalities among respondents in these patterns.

These findings give rise to the design adopted for the final phase of this project, the long-term longitudinal study of premenopausal menstrual pattern changes.

5-Year Longitudinal Study

The final phase of our project, begun in early 1990, is being conducted by the first author in collaboration with Ann Voda, head of the Tremin Trust Reproductive Health Research Program. We will collect data reported by premenopausal women for at least 5 years and will employ a variety of innovative statistical techniques to describe patterns of menstrual cycle changes and the relationships of these patterns to demographic and other contextual variables.

Sample Selection

Subjects for this study were recruited from the more than 700 women between the ages of 35 and 55 years who are already enrolled in the Tremin Trust Reproductive Health Research Program headed by Dr. Ann Voda at the University of Utah. This program was initiated in 1934 by Dr. Alan Treloar, who upon retirement in 1984, offered the program to the University of Utah's School of Nursing. The original participants were 2,350 University of Minnesota women students who volunteered during 1934–1963. The daughters and granddaughters of these women continue to participate (Voda, undated). A second sample is comprised of women graduating from Douglass College (Rutgers University) in 1963.

Participation is limited to women over the age of 35 who are still menstruating and are not taking hormonal drugs. Both anecdotal and scientific evidence (Asso, 1983; Chiazze et al., 1968; Cutler, Garcia, & Edwards, 1983; Kopera, 1979; Treloar et al., 1967) suggest that, on average, changes in the menstrual cycle begin up to a decade or more before actual cessation at age 50–51 (Asso, 1983; Flint, 1979; Frommer, 1964; Jaszmann, vanLith, & Zaat, 1969; McKinlay, Jefferys, & Thompson, 1972). Selecting a sample with the lower age limit of 35 permits an opportunity to study menstrual cycle characteristics across the entire premenopausal transition period. The selection of a nonclinical sample represents a major methodological improvement over many previous menopause studies (Fluhmann, 1934; Geist, 1930) that incorrectly used clinical samples to represent normal, healthy aging women (Christie-Brown & Christie-Brown, 1976; Goodman, 1982).

Instrumentation

Each January, Tremin Trust respondents receive (a) a menstrual cycle reporting card on which they designate prospectively each day of menses throughout the year and (b) a detailed 9-page Health Report Form collecting demographic, medical, and menstrual information. Both are returned at the end of the year. Beginning in 1990, all respondents will receive an additional form each year requesting daily reports of 20 emotional and physical experiences (from a precoded list), reports of the amount of blood flow (using designated codes) on each day of menses throughout the year, and reports of noticeable changes in menstrual flow, emotional or physical experiences, and so on.

The original selection of symptom experiences for Pilot Study 2, though guided by the menstrual cycle and menopause literatures, was complicated by the lack of consensus among researchers concerning the existence of a true menstrual or menopausal syndrome. Mood states and menopausal symptoms, for instance, once believed to be hormonally determined, now are popularly viewed more as sociocultural and psychological phenomena than as evidence of a biologically determined syndrome of events (Abplanalp, Donnelly, & Rose, 1979a, 1979b; Ballinger, 1975; Christie-Brown & Christie-Brown, 1976; Donovan, 1951; Flint, 1979; Goodman, Stewart, & Gilbert, 1977; McKinlay & Jefferys, 1974; Ruble, 1977; Selby et al., 1980; Wood, 1979). Symptom selection has been complicated further by the absence of any previous research on pattern analysis to guide the present researchers in their investigation of relationships between particular patterns of age-related changes and the presence of certain symptoms.

The proposed 20-item symptom list is based in part on the findings of Pilot Study 2 and includes the mood items *sad, nervous, friendly, depressed, alert, irritable, sensual, overwhelmed, energetic,* and *capable,* and the somatic symptoms *headache, bloating, menstrual cramps, weight gain, tiredness, dizziness, breast pain, backache, hot flashes,* and *vaginal dryness.* The inclusion of both positive and negative symptoms is important in avoiding the creation of negative stereotypes about menstrual events that can influence responses (Kahana et al., 1980; Kaufert & Syrotuik, 1981; Koeske, 1980; Parlee, 1980). Hot flashes and vaginal dryness are the only two menopausal symptoms that the literature consistently associates with declining estrogen levels during the climacteric (Asso, 1983; Reitz, 1977; Seaman & Seaman, 1977).

The *amount of blood flow* for each bleeding day is measured subjectively by the Mansfield-Jorgensen-Voda Menstrual Bleeding Scale, in terms of the amount of protection needed, following the suggestion of Snowden (1977) and others to operationalize the definition. This 6-point scale follows:

1. *spotting* — few drops of blood, not enough to require sanitary protection

2. *very light bleeding* — just enough bleeding to require minimal protection; feels like menstrual flow has not really begun yet, or is really just about over; need to change *least absorbent* tampon or pad once or twice during the day

3. *light bleeding* — need to change *low* or *regular absorbency* tampon or pad 2–3 times a day

4. *moderate bleeding* — need to change *regular* tampon or pad every 3–4 hours

5. *heavy bleeding* — need to change *high-absorbency* tampon or pad every 3–4 hours

6. *very heavy bleeding (gushing)* — sanitary protection hardly works at all, flow is so heavy; feels like the day revolves around menstrual flow; need to change *highest-absorbency* tampon and/or pad every hour or two

Although objective quantitative measurements might enhance the validity of this variable, they exceed the resources of this study. In any case, our primary interest here is with intraindividual events (changes within and across bleeding episodes for each person); the reliability of the measures of blood flow thus becomes critical, and is enhanced by our utilization of explicit standards for describing blood loss.

Contextual variables to be measured include those demographic, sociocultural, and psychological phenomena currently believed by researchers to influence women's moods and menopausal symptomatology: socioeconomic (SES), marital, family, and employment status, and attitudes toward menopause (Christie-Brown & Christie-Brown, 1976; Flint, 1979; Selby et al., 1980). Other contextual variables to be measured, especially health-related factors such as smoking, contraceptive use, parity, height, and weight, are of special interest because of their possible link to age of menopause. Aside from the consistent link between smoking and early menopause (Hill, 1982; Jick, Porter, & Morrison, 1977), few other variables are known to bear a strong relationship to age of cessation. Most of this information will be available from the annual Health Report Form sent to all Tremin Trust subjects.

We are interested also in subjects' interpretations of noticeable menstrual cycle changes, because the meaning women attach to biological events may alter those very events (Dan, Graham, & Beecher, 1980; Flint, 1979; Koeske, 1980; Parlee, 1980) and may provide important clues as to which events influence women's perceptions of themselves as they age.

The normal menstrual cycle changes that middle-aged women experience during the menopausal transition have been a neglected research topic. As a result of the limited understanding of these changes, premenopausal women may look upon normal changes as symptoms of disease and become alarmed; in addition, their health care providers, also lacking normative data, may tend to call for interventions that are unnecessarily invasive. To begin to close this knowledge gap, we have undertaken a multiphased research project that will describe patterns of changes in menstrual cycle characteristics of women during the menopausal transition (from age 35 until actual cessation of menses).

In addition, we have suggested that the contexts of women's lives, their perceptions about menopause and the changes in their menstrual cycle characteristics that predate menopause, are interrelated. This study will add to our understanding of these complex relationships, and, ultimately, to an easier transition into menopause for midlife women.

NOTE

Without the important contributions of Dr. Ann Voda, director of the Tremin Trust Reproductive Health Research Program at the University of Utah, this chapter and the research described herein would not have been possible.

REFERENCES

Abplanalp, J. M., Donnelly, A. F., & Rose, R. M. (1979a). Psychoendocrinology of the menstrual cycle: I. Enjoyment of daily activities and moods. *Psychosomatic Medicine, 41,* 587–604.

Abplanalp, J. M., Donnelly, A. F., & Rose, R. M. (1979b). Psychoendocrinology of the menstrual cycle: II. The relationship between enjoyment of activities, moods, and reproductive hormones. *Psychosomatic Medicine, 41,* 605–615.

Asso, D. (1983). *The real menstrual cycle.* Chichester, England: Wiley.

Ballinger, C. B. (1975). Psychiatric morbidity and the menopause: Screening of general population sample. *British Medical Journal, 3,* 344–346.

Ballinger, C. B. (1976). Psychiatric morbidity and the menopause: Clinical features. *British Medical Journal, 1,* 1183–1185.

Barnett, R., & Baruch, G. (1978). Women in the middle years: A critique of research and theory. *Psychology of Women Quarterly, 3,* 187–191.

Bart, P. B., & Grossman, M. (1976). Menopause. *Women and Health, 1,* 3–10.

Burch, T. K., Macisco, J. J., Jr., & Parker, M. P. (1967). Some methodological problems in the analysis of menstrual data. *International Journal of Fertility, 12,* 67–76.

Cattell, R. B. (1963). The structuring of change by P- and incremental R-technique. In C. Harris (Ed.), *Problems in measuring change.* Madison: University of Wisconsin Press.

Chiazze, L., Jr., Brayer, F. T., Macisco, J. J., Jr., Parker, M. P., & Duffy, B. J. (1968). The length and variability of the human menstrual cycle. *Journal of the American Medical Association, 203,* 89–92.

Christie-Brown, J. R. W., & Christie-Brown, M. E. (1976). Psychiatric disorders associated with menopause. In R. J. Beard (Ed.), *The menopause: A guide to current research and practice* (pp. 58–79). Baltimore: University Park Press.

Collett, M. E., Wertenberger, G. E., & Fiske, V. M. (1954). The effect of age upon the pattern of the menstrual cycle. *Fertility and Sterility, 5,* 437–448.

Cutler, W. B., Garcia, C. R., & Edwards, A. M. (1983). *Menopause: A guide for women and the men who love them.* New York: Norton.

Cutler, W. B., Garcia, C. R., & Krieger, A. M. (1979). Sexual behavior frequency and the menstrual cycle length in mature premenopausal women. *Psychoneuroendocrinology, 4,* 297–309.

Dan, A. J., Graham, E. A., & Beecher, C. P. (Eds.). (1980). *The menstrual cycle* (Vol. 1). New York: Springer.

Donovan, J. C. (1951). The menopausal syndrome: A study of case histories. *American Journal of Gynecology, 62,* 1281–1291.

Finck, K. S. (1979). The potential health care crisis of hysterectomy. In D. K.

Kjervik & I. M. Martinson (Eds.), *Women in stress: A nursing perspective* (pp. 276–302). New York: Appleton-Century-Crofts.

Flint, M. P. (1979). Sociology and anthropology of the menopause. In P. A. van Keep, D. M. Serr, & R. B. Greenblatt (Eds.), *Female and male climacteric* (p. 73). Baltimore: University Park Press.

Fluhmann, C. F. (1934). The length of the human menstrual cycle. *American Journal of Obstetrics and Gynecology, 27,* 73–78.

Frey, K. A. (1981). Middle-aged women's experience and perceptions of menopause. *Women and Health, 6,* 25–36.

Frommer, D. J. (1964). Changing age of the menopause. *British Medical Journal, 11,* 349–361.

Geist, S. (1930). The variability of menstrual rhythm and character. *American Journal of Obstetrics and Gynecology, 20,* 320–323.

Goldzieher, J. W., Henkin, A. E., & Hamblen, E. C. (1947). Characteristics of the normal menstrual cycle. *American Journal of Obstetrics and Gynecology, 54,* 668–675.

Golloway, K. (1975). The change of life. *American Journal of Nursing, 75,* 1006–1011.

Goodman, M. J. (1982). A critique of menopause research. In A. M. Voda, M. Dinnerstein, & S. R. O'Donnell (Eds.), *Changing perspectives on menopause* (pp. 273–288). Austin: University of Texas Press.

Goodman, M. J., Stewart, C. J., & Gilbert, F., Jr. (1977). A study of certain medical and physiological variables among Caucasian and Japanese women living in Hawaii. *Journal of Gerontology, 32,* 291–298.

Gunn, D. L., Jenkin, P. M., & Gunn, A. L. (1937). Menstrual periodicity: Statistical observations on a large sample of normal cases. *Journal of Obstetrics and Gynecology of the British Empire, 44,* 839–879.

Harrison, M. (1983). *Self-help for premenstrual syndrome.* Cambridge, MA: Matrix Press.

Hill, J. (1982). Smoking, alcohol and body mass relationships to early menopause. In A. M. Voda, M. Dinnerstein, & S. R. O'Donnell (Eds.), *Changing perspectives on menopause* (pp. 160–169). Austin: University of Texas Press.

Jaszmann, L., vanLith, N. D., & Zaat, J. C. A. (1969). The age at menopause in the Netherlands. *International Journal of Fertility, 14,* 107–117.

Jick, H., Porter, J., & Morrison, A. S. (1977). Relation between smoking and age of natural menopause. *Lancet, 1,* 1354–1355.

Kahana, E., Kiyak, A., & Liang, J. (1980). Menopause in the context of other life events. In A. J. Dan, E. A. Graham, & C. P. Beecher (Eds.), *The menstrual cycle* (Vol. 1, pp. 167–178). New York: Springer.

Kasper, D. S. (1985). Hysterectomy as social process. *Women and Health, 10,* 109–127.

Kaufert, P., & Syrotuik, J. (1981). Symptom reporting at the menopause. *Social Science and Medicine, 15,* 173–184.

Koeske, R. K. D. (1980). Theoretical perspectives on menstrual cycle research. In A. J. Dan, E. A. Graham, & C. P. Beecher (Eds.), *The menstrual cycle* (Vol. 1, pp. 8–25). New York: Springer.

Koeske, R. K. D. (1982). Toward a biosocial paradigm for menopause research: Lessons and contributions from the behavioral sciences. In A. M. Voda, M. Dinnerstein, & S. R. O'Donnell (Eds.), *Changing perspectives on menopause* (pp. 3–23). Austin: University of Texas press.

Kopera, H. (1979). Effects, side effects, and dosage schemes of various sex hormones in the peri- and post-menopause. In P. A. van Keep, D. M. Serr, & R. B. Greenblatt (Eds.), *Female and male climacteric.* Baltimore: University Park Press.

Mansfield, P. K., & Boyer, B. (1990). The experiences, concerns, and health care needs of women in the menopausal transition. *Annals of the New York Academy of Sciences, 592,* 448–449.

Mansfield, P. K., Hood, K. E., & Henderson, J. (1989). Women and their husbands: Mood and arousal fluctuations across the menstrual cycle and days of the week. *Psychosomatic Medicine, 51,* 66–80.

Matsumoto, S., Nogami, Y., & Ohkuri, S. (1962). Statistical studies on menstruation: A criticism of the definitions of normal menstruation. *Journal of Medical Science, 11,* 294–318.

McEwan, J. A. (1973). Menopause: Myths and medicine. *Nursing Times, 69,* 1483–1484.

McKinlay, S. M., & Jefferys, M. (1974). The menopausal syndrome. *British Journal of Preventative Social Medicine, 28,* 108–115.

McKinlay, S., Jefferys, M., & Thompson, S. (1972). An investigation of the age of menopause. *Journal of Biosocial Science, 4,* 161–173.

McKinlay, S. M., & McKinlay, O. B. (1973). Selected studies of the menopause. *Journal of Biosocial Science, 5,* 533–555.

Morgan, S. (1984). Hysterectomy: Current treatment. In K. Weiss (Ed.), *Women's health care: A guide to alternatives* (pp. 103–111). Reston, VA: Reston.

Nesselroade, J., & Ford, D. (1985). P-technique comes of age. *Research on Aging, 7,* 46–80.

Neugarten, B. L., & Kraines, R. J. (1965). Menopausal symptoms in women of various ages. *Psychosomatic Medicine, 27,* 266–273.

Parlee, M. B. (1980). Changes in moods and activation levels during the menstrual cycle in experimentally naive subjects. In A. J. Dan, E. A. Graham, & C. P. Beecher (Eds.), *The menstrual cycle* (Vol. 1, pp. 247–263). New York: Springer.

Perlmutter, E., & Bart, P. B. (1982). Changing views of "The Change." In A. M. Voda, M. Dinnerstein, & S. R. O'Donnell (Eds.), *Changing perspectives on menopause* (pp. 187–199). Austin: University of Texas Press.

Presser, H. B. (1974). Temporal data relating to the human menstrual cycle. In M. Ferin, F. Halberg, R. M. Richart, & R. Van de Wiele (Eds.), *Biorhythms and human reproduction* (pp. 145–160). New York: Wiley.

Reitz, R. (1977). *Menopause — a positive approach.* Middlesex, England: Penguin.

Ruble, D. N. (1977). Premenstrual symptoms: A reinterpretation. *Science, 197,* 291–292.

Seaman, B., & Seaman, G. (1977). *Women and the crisis in sex hormones.* New York: Bantam.

Selby, J., Calhoun, L. G., Vogel, A. V., & King, H. E. (1980). *Psychology and human reproduction.* New York: Free Press.

Snowden, R. (1977). The statistical analysis of menstrual bleeding patterns. *Journal of Biosocial Science, 9,* 107–120.

Snowden, R., & Christian, B. (Eds.). (1983). *Patterns and perceptions of menstruation.* New York: St. Martin's Press.

Treloar, A. E., Boynton, R. E., Behn, B. G., & Brown, B. W. (1967). Variation of the human menstrual cycle through reproductive life. *International Journal of Fertility, 12,* 77–127.

Tucker, L. R. (1966). Learning theory and multivariate experiment: Illustration by determination of generalized learning curves. In R. B. Cattell (Ed.), *Handbook of multivariate experimental psychology* (pp. 476–501). Chicago: Rand McNally.

Voda, A. (undated). *The Tremin Trust research program.* Salt Lake City: University of Utah, College of Nursing.

Vollman, R. F. (1956). The degree of variability of the length of the menstrual cycle through reproductive life. *International Journal of Fertility, 12,* 77–127.

Wood, C. (1979). Menopausal myths. *Medical Journal of Australia, 1,* 496–499.

World Health Organization. (1981). A cross-cultural study of menstruation: Implications for contraceptive development and use. *Studies in Family Planning, 12,* 3–15.

PART FOUR

Contextual Issues for Menstrual Health

While several chapters in the previous section emphasized the cultural context for understanding menopause, other aspects of context are also important to menstrual health. This section is especially multidisciplinary, recognizing that menstrual phenomena are not only biological, but also interact with social, environmental, historical, political, and spiritual aspects of life.

In the first chapter (21), Cayleff, a feminist historian, presents an analysis of nineteenth- and early-twentieth-century medical views of women and menstruation, and shows how they still influence discourse today. She provides a superb illustration of the historical use of menstrual function as a rationale to restrict women's roles, noting the distortion of "health care" through such myths and misinformation. Next (chap. 22), Ulman explores how the event of menarche changes family activities and the meaning of family relationships. Through survey questionnaires and interviews with 205 pre- and postpubertal girls, their mothers, and fathers, she reveals the complexities of biological events in the context of close relationships.

C. Graham and McGrew (chap. 23) examine menstrual synchrony and explore the ways in which social interaction, common environment, and the use of deodorants and perfume affect this phenomenon. They document that closeness of relationship was the significant factor in producing more synchronous menstrual cycles. Seasonal variability in menstrual patterns among Alaskan Eskimo women is the focus for the chapter (24) by E. Graham, Stewart, and Ward. They found that increased incidence of amenorrhea was correlated with the length of darkness during the winter months. They suggest the possibility that seasonal affective disorders may be related to similar mechanisms, indicating another potential area of relationship between mood and reproductive function.

The final two chapters of this book represent the special commitment of the Society for Menstrual Cycle Research to make connections with the political and personal implications of our work. These chapters are written by activist-researchers who are engaged in processes of social change, trying to learn from efforts to correct the distortions identified by Cayleff and others. Rome and Wolhandler present a policy study of the various interests concerned with tampon safety in the United States (chap. 25). They document the involvement of government, business, and consumer groups over the last 15 years, with commentary on the effectiveness of trying to influence regulation of tampon manufacturing. The emergence of toxic shock syndrome as a serious threat to women's health makes this a particularly significant area for consumer action.

Culpepper, a radical theologian, takes another approach to creating change (chap. 26). In her report on menstrual consciousness-raising, she shares her methods of reaching out to women through workshops on menstruation. Her approach is very personal, focusing on experience as it is lived by women. She describes her encounters with Hebrew and Zoroastrian menstrual taboos in divinity school, and uses examples from the experiences of black and white women, including women of the Jewish faith. Although some may find Culpepper's work shocking, she points out the need to create an open and nonjudgmental atmosphere for discussion of menstrual rituals, customs, habits, stories, and health concerns.

Menstrual health research does not happen only in universities. It happens when women are free to validate their own experience, when determined feminists challenge business as usual. How can we untangle "the knot patriarchy has made of this basic life experience" (Culpepper, p. 282)? We believe the answer lies in helping to create a context that is not oppressive to women.

21

She Was Rendered Incapacitated by Menstrual Difficulties: Historical Perspectives on Perceived Intellectual and Physiological Impairment Among Menstruating Women

Susan E. Cayleff

> Miss D＿＿ went to college in good physical condition. During the four years of her college life, her parents and the college faculty required her to get what is properly called an education. Nature required her, during the same period, to build and put in working-order a large and complicated reproductive mechanism. . . . She naturally obeyed the requirements of the faculty. . . . The stream of vital and constructive force evolved within her was turned steadily to the brain, and away from the ovaries and their accessories. The result of this sort of education was, [the ovaries] began to perform their functions with pain . . . next, to set up once a month a grumbling torture that made life miserable; and, lastly, [Miss D＿＿] became neuralgic and hysterical.
> —Clarke, 1873/1972, pp. 83–84

Edward H. Clarke chronicled the demise of Miss D＿＿ in his slim 1873 volume, misleadingly entitled *Sex in Education; Or, A Fair Chance for the Girls.* The steady yet inevitable withering of this patient "furnished another text for the often repeated sermon on the delicacy of American girls" (p. 85). The widespread popularity of Clarke's interpretation of menstrual dangers is evidenced in the 17 editions *Sex in Education* went through in 13 years. Two medical historians, Bullough and Voght (1973), recount speculation that Clarke wrote this book to nullify the chance for women to be admitted to Harvard. Theorists who came after Clarke were far more virulent than he: Clarke advocated a 5-hour class day for girls; those who followed him argued, at times, for *no* education for girls.

Clarke's views, although the best known on the subject of the incompatibility of education and proper physiological development for girls, were demonstrative of a widely held nineteenth-century medical belief which posited that women's entire system was built around, and relentlessly affected by, her ovaries. As John Wiltbank, a medical instructor, succinctly surmised in 1853: "Women's reproductive organs are pre-eminent. They exercise a controlling influence upon her entire system, and entail upon her many painful and dangerous diseases. They are the source of her peculiarities, the centre of her sympathies, and the seat of her diseases. Everything that is peculiar to her, springs from her sexual organization" (cited in Smith-Rosenberg, 1974, p. 24).

Medical experts were in agreement, then, as to the ovarian origins of women's "peculiarities" although there was considerable debate as to the etiology of menstruation itself. Theories that explained menstruation included these: It was connected with ovulation; it was the effect of the moon upon women; the fetus formed from the menstrual flow; and it was the casting out of excess blood which would have nourished the embryo if pregnancy had occurred. A widely debated issue revolved around whether menstruation was induced by the ovaries, the uterus, or the fallopian tubes. Other theories held that menstruation was pathological, and proof of the inactivity and threatened atrophy of the uterus; the cause of gonorrhea in men; and the result of nervous stimulation (Bullough & Voght, 1973, p. 67; see also George, 1878; Girdwood, 1842–43; Goodman, 1877, 1878; King, 1875–76; Martin, 1893; Montgomery, 1904; Studley, 1875).

Although physicians may have been divided among themselves as to the physiological basis of menstruation, they largely agreed as to the proper management of menstruating women. Puberty, seen as a critical physiological turning point, necessitated that all of the energy in a girl's body be focused on the proper and full development of her uterus and ovaries (Smith-Rosenberg, 1974, p. 27; see also Delaney, Lupton, & Toth, 1976). To this end, physicians enlisted the invaluable influence of mothers to ensure that pubescent girls curtailed all activities outside the home, avoided strong emotions, got sufficient fresh air, rest, unstimulating foods, moderate exercise, and avoided down beds, corsets, liquors, and stimulating beverages. In short, the only safe tasks were routinely domestic. If not shepherded through this critical juncture, medical theorists claimed, "disease, insanity, and even death would surely follow" (Smith-Rosenberg, p. 27; see also Goodell, 1882; Gray, 1872).

Intellectual pursuits for women came under increasing attack as the most damaging distraction from proper physiological development. This rationale was, in fact, the theoretical mainstay in the argument used by the opponents of education for women in late nineteenth- and early twentieth-century America. Dr. A. F. A. King, speaking before the Washington, DC, Obstetrical and Gynecological Association in 1895 said, "any drain upon the nervous powers of whatever character, was liable to unfavorably influence menstruation in girls. And the method of education in the schools was a large factor in producing menstrual disorders" (cited in Cook, 1895b, p. 571).

Notes from the conference went on to summarize the opinions expressed by the physicians present. "We were all agreed," the statement recounts, "that there was much fault in the education of girls" (Cook, 1895b). Among the evils enumerated in 1905 were the stooping position assumed by one who studies, which constricts blood vessels and interferes with circulation; the necessity to reduce the number of studies; and "The sedentary life adopted by girl students, which . . . weakens the body and arrests the natural development of the pelvis, while the same causes enlarge the fetal head because of the increased size of the child's brain" (Van Dyke, 1905, p. 297).

Another physician, writing in the *American Journal of Obstetrics* in 1881, tells of an even more dramatic case of a patient of his who experiences delirium during her menstrual cycle as a result of her studies. But rather than manifest her ovarian-induced mental incapacitation in the more commonly observed expressions of ill-temper, angry outbursts, and mood alterations, this girl "could not be made to recognize [her doctor]. . . . She talked vehemently in French; while her mind was wandering back to a residence in Algiers some four years before. . . . As the menses disappeared, the delireum [*sic*] gave way to long quotations from Shakespeare, especially Ophelia" (Fothergill, p. 43). Whether this girl was suffering from delirium, or was simply an excellent, if somewhat eccentric student, is left to historical conjecture.

These medical conferences, case histories, and prescriptive tracts reveal a deeply imbedded cultural ambivalence toward women's intellectual pursuits and activities outside of the domestic realm. In fact, menstruation was invoked as proof positive that women's ties to home and hearth were biologically determined and thus socially justified and immutable. The real contribution and place of women was not to master the sciences, language, or music. Women's ordained role was to produce healthy offspring and remain the nurturant, untarnished influence within the home. As one physician exclaimed in an 1895 essay, the subjects offered in school to a girl at puberty were not only dangerous, but unnecessary: "With an over-stimulated brain and a weakened body, what, if any, progeny is to be expected from her, to say nothing of the misery she is laying up for herself" (Cook, 1895a, p. 535).

This physician, like many of his colleagues, perpetuated and created "scientific theories" that kept women inextricably linked to reproduction and domesticity to the exclusion of all else. As R. W. Parsons argued in the *New York Medical Journal* in 1907, "What earthly use to the ordinary woman is a smattering of Latin, Greek, the higher mathematics, music, and all such branches of learning. . . . Nature has ordained that the vast majority of women shall become wives and mothers, and if they are exhausted mentally as well as physically, how is it possible to keep the race strong and healthy?" (p. 116). Can a girl thus educated, the essay continues, "becom(e) acquainted with the mysteries of housekeeping, or . . . acquire a general knowledge of plain sewing and cookery. . . . Can it be reasonably expected that such a girl would be capable of creating a happy home or of becoming a help mate in the truest sense of the term?" (p. 118). The resounding rhetorical response was an emphatic no.

Intellectual pursuits and physiological destiny were mutually exclusive at the turn of the century. In fact, Hill (1904) cites statistics that claim the sterility rate at more than twice as high among college-educated women as among the general populace, proof of the incompatibility of the two pursuits.

Medical theorists continued to perpetuate such beliefs and "scientific findings" despite the availability of evidence to the contrary. As early as 1883, a study by W. LeC. Stevens, entitled "The Admission of Women to Universities," was conducted that revealed that "Most women are more vigorous at their graduation than on their admission" (cited in Hollingworth, 1914, p. vi). This, from a questionnaire sent to the presidents of coeducational colleges. Similarly, Martha Carey Thomas, president of Bryn Mawr College, commented in 1905 that these theories of menstruation were "sickening sentimentality" and pseudoscientific (cited in Bullough & Voght, 1973, p. 78). In 1886 a complementary thesis was statistically proven by one investigator, who found that "female graduates of our colleges and universities do not seem to show, as a result of their college studies and duties, any marked difference in general health from . . . women engaged in other kinds of work" (Dewey, 1886, p. 606).

Despite this evidence, proscriptive definitions affected perceived physical as well as mental capabilities of women. The "weakened condition" caused by menstruation played a prominent yet dubious role in the securing of protective labor legislation for women in the early twentieth century (Cayleff, 1982; Delaney et al., 1976, pp. 47–56), again, despite evidence to the contrary. Jacobi (1886/1978) argued that forced rest for women during menstruation was a result of custom and men's wishes — not physiological necessity.

As the invoking of what one historian has called "menstrual politics" in the protective legislation campaigns for working-class women reveals, such theories of physical frailty as they related to the menstrual cycle were taken to apply across class lines — unlike more class-specific "female ailments" such as hysteria or neurasthenia (chronic nervous debility) which existed essentially only among the upper classes. In short, popular descriptions portrayed *all* women as "rendered incapacitated by menstrual difficulties."

Summarily, a number of society's leading arbiters of public opinion in late nineteenth- and early twentieth-century America viewed women's menstrual cycles as times of illness during which women were "ruled" by their ovaries and rendered mentally and physically incapacitated. Physiological impairment resulting from mental work served as the rationale for the opponents of education for women and perpetuated "appropriate" sex-role-specific aspirations and pursuits.

Beliefs and superstitions promulgated in this era continue to affect cultural perceptions of menstruating women and women's perceptions of themselves. For example, a 1960 study by Dalton that looked at "Effects of Menstruation on Schoolgirls' Weekly Work" found that menstruation impaired scholastic performance. This prompted the researcher to conclude, "While zealots campaign assiduously for equality of the sexes, Nature refuses to grant equality even in one sex" (p. 328). Similarly, E. F. Berman, a physician speaking in 1970, when commenting upon women's possibly dangerous mood shifts and their ability to make decisions during menstruation proclaimed: "If you had an investment in a bank, you wouldn't want the president of your bank making a loan under those raging hormonal influences at that particular period" (cited in Cox, 1976, p. 27). Continuing on with one example too many, the physician concludes, "Suppose we had a menopausal woman President who had to make the decision of the Bay of Pigs, which was, of course, a bad one. . . ."

In our own era, we are witnessing a resurgent belief in the incapacitating effects of menstruation. Although the physiological manifestations of premenstrual syndrome are a clinically valid diagnosis for certain women, the larger implications of this new form of "ovarian rule" are profound indeed. Once again, menstruation is invoked as a prime determinant of emotional, physical, intellectual, and behavioral impairment, as witnessed by its successful use as a defense in British murder trials at which its "sufferers" were found not responsible for their actions. Although this provides a dubious vindication for those experiencing the syndrome, it casts an insidious shadow over all women whose *normal* physiological fluctuations are now deemed suspect as excessive or incapacitating in nature. In an era where the majority of women work outside the home, in many markets that compete with men, and where a struggle for equality in personal relations between the sexes concerns us, this illness labeling serves to reinforce perceived disparities between the normative/unimpaired "rational" male physiology and its erratic/uncontrollable female counterpart. This damaging dichotomy once again casts women as the "social opposite" precisely when they seek parity in the personal and social realms.

Finally, then, at present we see this historical use of illness labeling and its consequent social proscription, although modified in content, still affecting culturally held perceptions of women's mental and physical competence. Illuminating both for the historical and contemporary issues raised, the experts' view of menstruating women continues to influence the acceptable parameters of women's social roles. Contemporaneously, the descriptive language and scientific understanding of the physiological processes are more sophisticated, but a similar message is still implicit: women's physiology is a "natural" impairment to true cultural and institutional equality between the sexes.

REFERENCES

Bullough, V., & Voght, M. (1973). Women, menstruation, and nineteenth-century medicine. *Bulletin of the History of Medicine, 47*(1), 66–82.

Cayleff, S. E. (1982). *Protective labor legislation, 1894–1931: An American response to the woman worker.* Unpublished manuscript.

Clarke, E. H. (1972). *Sex in education; Or, A fair chance for the girls.* New York: Arno Press and New York Times. (Original work published 1873)

Cook, G. W. (1895a, November 1). Some disorders of menstruation. *American Journal of Obstetrics, 33,* 532–537, 570–572.

Cook, G. W. (1895b, November 1). Transactions of the Washington Obstetrical and Gynecological Society. *American Journal of Obstetrics, 33,* 570–572.

Cox, S. (1976). *Female psychology: The emerging self.* Chicago: Science Research Associates.

Dalton, K. (1960, January 30). Effects of menstruation on schoolgirls' weekly work. *British Medical Journal, 5169,* 326–327.

Delaney, J., Lupton, M. J., & Toth, E. (1976). *The curse: A cultural history of menstruation.* New York: Signet. [Rev. ed., Urbana: University of Illinois Press, 1988]

Dewey, J. (1866). Health and sex in higher education. *Popular Science Monthly, 28,* 606.

Fothergill, J. M. (1881). Systematic relations of the menstrual week. *American Journal of Obstetrics, 14,* 38–47.

George, G. A. (1878, March 9). The rationale of the menstrual flow. *Lancet, 1,* 346.

Girdwood, G. F. (1842–43). Theory of menstruation. *Lancet, 1,* 825–830.

Goodell, W. (1882). Clinical notes on the extirpation of the ovaries for insanity. *American Journal of Insanity, 38,* 294–302.

Goodman, J. (1877). The menstrual cycle. *Transactions, 2,* 650–662.

Goodman, J. (1878, October). The cyclical theory of menstruation. *American Journal of Obstetrics and Diseases of Women and Children, 11*(4), 673–694.

Gray, J. P. (1872, October). Thoughts on the causation of insanity. *American Journal of Insanity, 29*(2), 264–283.

Hill, R. S. (1904, September 24). Some causes of menstrual disorders in the girl. *New York Medical Journal, 30,* 594–597.

Hollingworth, L. S. (1914). *Functional periodicity: An experimental study of the mental and motor abilities of women during menstruation.* New York: Columbia University Press.

Jacobi, M. P. (1978). *The question of rest for women during menstruation.* New York: Center for Policy Research. (Original work published 1886, New York: Putnam)

King, A. F. A. (1875-76). A new basis for uterine pathology. *American Journal of Obstetrics, 8,* 242-243.

Martin, C. (1893, October 25). The nerve theory of menstruation. *Medical Press and Circular, 4*(1), 420-421.

Montgomery, E. E. (1904, October 29). The disturbances of menstruation and their significance. *New York Medical Journal, 80,* 820-823.

Parsons, R. W. (1907, January 19). The American girl versus higher education, considered from a medical point of view. *New York Medical Journal, 85,* 115-119.

Smith-Rosenberg, C. (1974). Puberty to menopause: The cycle of femininity in nineteenth-century America. In M. Hartman & L. Banner (Eds.), *Clio's consciousness raised* (pp. 23-35). New York: Harper & Row.

Studley, W. H. (1875). Is menstruation a disease? *American Journal of Obstetrics, 8,* 487-512.

Van Dyke, F. W. (1905, February 25). Higher education a cause of physical decay in women. *Medical Record, 67,* 296-298.

22

The Impact of Menarche on Family Relationships

Kathleen H. Ulman

Adolescence and puberty historically have been considered important stages of psychological development. However, women psychoanalysts and anthropologists such as Deutsch (1944) and Benedict (1934, 1954) were among the first social scientists to present menarche as a significant event in the psychological development of woman.

Helene Deutsch (1944) addressed in detail the psychological impact of menarche on a young girl. Based on observations drawn from her clinical work with women, she maintained that the impact of menarche and menstruation was so important that it merited study as the "psychology of menstruation." She expanded the earlier psychoanalytic idea that the psychological reaction to blood was tied to the female castration complex, but also maintained that girls' reactions to menstruation were in part based on what they had consciously learned in their culture. She expanded anthropological observations on the menstrual taboo in primitive cultures and applied them to civilized societies, maintaining that the menstrual taboo existed in the unconscious of Western cultures and thus it operated unconsciously in modern Western women. As an example she pointed to the mother's concealment of her menstruation from her daughter and the girl's resistance to learning about it from her mother because she has experienced her mother's menstruation as "unclean and disgusting."

Deutsch (1944) described women's psychological reactions to menarche as having a common root of anxiety "in which the approaching adulthood and sexuality are experienced as a threatening danger" (p. 156). She explained the postmenarcheal depression that some girls experience as a disappointment that they were not magically changed by the event. "All observations suggest that, whether or not the girl is given intellectual knowledge even when she has the best possible information about the biologic aspects of the process, and despite its wish-fulfilling character, the first menstruation is usually experienced as a trauma" (p. 157). She also stated that with menarche, conflict between reproductive functions and sexuality came to the forefront for women. In sum, Deutsch saw the experience of menarche as inevitably traumatic and as being influenced by primitive unconscious ideas that menstruation was dangerous, unclean, and to be avoided, and by unconscious anxiety related to its symbolic representation of approaching dangers of female sexuality and reproductive ability.

Other clinicians and theorists also addressed the impact of menarche on women. Thompson (1942) described menarche as traumatic because of real effects of loss of freedom, power, and spontaneity. In contrast, Kestenberg (1961, 1967) and Blos (1962) presented menarche as a potentially positive point in a girl's development. Kestenberg pointed to the girl's sense of intellectual and emotional preparedness as one of the most important factors in influencing the experience of menarche.

Cultural anthropologists such as Mead (1949, 1952) and Benedict (1934, 1954) depicted menarche as stressful and potentially traumatic because of the discontinuities between the cultural expectations for prepubertal and pubertal girls, the implications of the "menstrual taboo" which operates in our culture, and the lack of well-defined rituals surrounding menarche.

Recently, menarche has become the subject of thoughtful and well-designed research with nonclinical populations. Retrospective studies as well as clinical observation (Deutsch, 1944; Kestenberg, 1961, 1967; Koff, Rierdan, & Sheingold, 1980; Whisnant & Zegans, 1975) indicate that menarche is most often remembered as an emotionally important event. For some, the outstanding affect remembered is excitement, for others it is fear and upset, and for others it is a mixture of feelings. Whatever the emotional tone, menarche is remembered as a highly salient event in a woman's life. Nevertheless, our culture still treats this pivotal event in female development with secrecy and denial. Many, including young girls and women, do not know what the term *menarche* means.

Recent research has shown that menarche influences a girl's body image (Koff, Rierdan, & Silverstone, 1978), sense of femininity (Rierdan & Koff, 1980), menstrual attitudes (Brooks-Gunn & Ruble, 1980; Clarke & Ruble, 1978), amount of sleep (Danza, 1983), interests (Stone & Barker, 1937, 1939), and mood (Ulman, 1984). In addition, the timing of menarche has been demonstrated to be an important influence on the experience of menarche.

Petersen's (1980) biopsychosocial model for development at puberty emphasizes the interactive nature of events surrounding puberty and encourages investigation of both direct and indirect factors that might influence puberty. However, at present we understand little about the context in which menarche takes place, that is, the attitudes and behavior of those around the menarcheal girl and how these interact with the girl's reaction to her own menarche.

Little information is available on the influence of attitudes toward menarche by those around the pubertal girl or the ways in which these attitudes may influence the relationships with the girl, but some studies have looked at the influence of menarche on a girl's view of her relationship with her parents. Whisnant and Zegans (1975), Koff, Rierdan, and Jacobson (1981), and Danza (1983) all found that postmenarcheal girls expressed an increased sense of closeness and dependence on their mothers and a withdrawal from or increased distance from their fathers. In addition, Danza (1983) found that postmenarcheal girls reported more conflict with their parents and less comfort in discussing emotionally charged subjects such as love, sex, drugs, and alcohol with their mothers. She also found that postmenarcheal girls had experienced more developmental changes, such as wearing make-up and shaving legs, than had premenarcheal girls. Danza concluded that menarche had a significant impact on the family life cycle and served as a nodal point for change in parent-child relations.

To explore further the relationship between menarche and family relations, the current study investigated daughters' and parents' views of their relationships.

Method

Subjects

Subjects were 205 white girls from a middle-class suburban school system. Approximately 40 girls were in Grades 6, 7, 8, 9, and 10, respectively. The girls were 11 to 17 years of age ($M = 13.22$). There were 176 mothers and 146 fathers participating in the study. Parents of every girl did not participate in the study.

Procedure

The girls were given questionnaires in a group at school. They filled out a personal data sheet (a modified version of that used by Koff, Rierdan, & Silverstone, 1978) asking for routine personal data including age at menarche. They also filled out a Family Relationships Questionnaire designed by the author to assess their comfort in discussing a variety of issues with their parents such as "a bad grade in school," "anger," and "feelings of sadness." At home, the parents filled out the same personal data sheet completed by the girls and two scales designed by the author. The first, the Relationship with Daughter Questionnaire, was the same questionnaire filled out by the daughters but with the questions reworded to ask the parents how comfortable they felt in discussing particular issues with their daughters. The second, the Activities with Daughter Questionnaire, was a 10-item Likert scale designed to assess the amount of time spent with daughters in specific activities. Parents also answered a one-sentence completion item: "The biggest change in my daughter in the past year was. . . ."

Fifteen families, solicited from the larger sample, were individually interviewed regarding the daughter's menarche (or expected menarche). The mother, father, and daughter were each interviewed separately.

Grouping of Subjects

Subjects were divided into two menarcheal groups: premenarcheal (81 girls) and postmenarcheal (124 girls). For some statistical analyses, the postmenarcheal girls were then divided into two further groups: postmenarcheal I — less than 2 years postmenarcheal (64), and postmenarcheal II — more than 2 years postmenarcheal (60). Each girl's menarcheal status was based on a comparison of the mother's and the daughter's reports of menarcheal age. If the reports differed by less than 6 months, the daughter's report of her menarcheal age was used; if the reports differed by more than 6 months, the reports of the menarcheal ages were averaged. Each subject's age was rounded off to years with those 15 years and over being grouped together. The classification of the girls by grade and menarcheal group is shown in Table 1.

Table 1.
Number of Girls in Each Grade and Each Menarcheal Status Group

	Grade				
Group	6	7	8	9	10
Premenarcheal	36	27	10	6	2
Postmenarcheal I	4	11	24	20	5
Postmenarcheal II	0	4	8	15	33
Total	40	42	42	41	40

Note. Postmenarcheal I = less than 2 years postmenarcheal; Postmenarcheal II = more than 2 years postmenarcheal.

Results

A principal components analysis with varimax rotation was done on each relationship scale and both activities scales. Items with a factor loading of .50 or less were not included in any factor. For each scale (i.e., mothers with daughters, fathers with daughters, daughters with fathers, or daughters with mothers) slightly different factors were found. For the Daughter's Relationship with Mother Scale, there were three factors: (a) Impersonal Issues, (b) Intimate Feelings, and (c) Affection. For the Daughter's Relationship with Father Scale, two factors were found: (a)

Impersonal Issues and Affection and (b) Intimate Feelings. In contrast, for the Mother's Relationship with Daughter Scale two factors were identified: (a) Personal and Initimate Feelings and (b) Impersonal Issues; and for the Father's Relationship with Daughter Scale three factors were found: (a) Intimate Issues, (b) Intimate Feelings, and (c) Impersonal Issues. For the Activities with Daughter Scale, two factors were identified for both mothers and fathers: (a) Out-of-Home Activities and (b) Home-Based Activities.

Two analyses of variance (ANOVAS) were done on all scores by grade and menarcheal group. The first was a 3×2 design with two grade groupings (7th and 8th; 9th and 10th) and three menarcheal groups (premenarcheal, postmenarcheal I, and postmenarcheal II). Grade 6 was dropped because there were too few postmenarcheal subjects to fill the cells. They were not added to the Grades 7 and 8 group because it was thought that the age span of the younger group would then become too wide, which could significantly influence the scores. The second ANOVA was a 2×2 design with two menarcheal groups (premenarcheal and postmenarcheal) and two grade groupings (7th and 8th; 9th and 10th). Both ANOVAS were performed on every score.

For daughters, two factors differed according to menarcheal status (Figure 1). The scores on the Initmate Feelings factor on the Relationship with Mother Scale showed that the premenarcheal girls experienced more

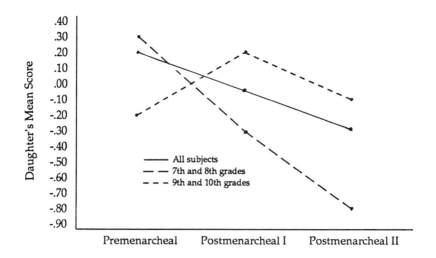

Figure 1. Daughters' mean scores on Intimate Feelings factor with mother (postmenarcheal I= less than 2 years postmenarcheal; postmenarcheal II=more than 2 years postmenarcheal).

comfort in discussing intimate feelings with their mothers than did the girls who were more than 2 years postmenarcheal ($p < .05$). When the scores were examined by grade, there were no significant differences according to menarcheal status for the girls in Grades 9 and 10. In contrast, for girls in Grades 7 and 8, the differences were in the same direction but more marked than for the whole group. The postmenarcheal I girls showed significant decreases in comfort in discussing intimate feelings with their mothers when compared with premenarcheal girls. Also the two postmenarcheal groups were significantly different from each other.

For the Impersonal Issues and Affection factor on the Relationship with Father Scale, the postmenarcheal I girls showed more comfort in discussing impersonal issues and in showing and receiving affection from their fathers than did the postmenarcheal II girls ($F = 3.179$, $p < .05$). For the Fathers' Relationship with Daughter Scale, no factors differed according to menarcheal status.

For the Mothers' Relationship with Daughter Scale, there were significant menarcheal status effects on the Intimate Feelings factor and the Impersonal Issues factor. Mothers of postmenarcheal girls reported more comfort in discussing intimate feelings with their daughters than did mothers of premenarcheal girls ($F = 4.261$, $p < .05$). In contrast, for the Impersonal Issues factor, mothers of premenarcheal girls reported more comfort in discussing impersonal issues than did mothers of all postmenarcheal girls (Figure 2).

For the Parents' Activities with Daughter Scale, there were no menarcheal status effects for fathers. For the Out-of-Home Activities factor, mothers of postmenarcheal girls reported more time spent together than did mothers of premenarcheal girls.

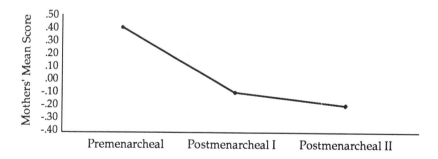

Figure 2. Mothers' mean scores on Impersonal Issues factor (postmenarcheal I = less than 2 years postmenarcheal; postmenarcheal II = more than 2 years postmenarcheal).

Discussion

The finding that premenarcheal girls reported more comfort discussing intimate issues with their mothers than did girls who had gone through menarche several years before and that this difference was most marked in girls in Grades 7 and 8 appears to contradict earlier findings (Danza, 1983; Koff, Rierdan, & Sheingold, 1980; Whisnant & Zegans, 1975) that girls expressed an increased sense of closeness with their mothers after menarche. However, perhaps the overall sense of feeling closer to someone is not the same as sharing intimate feelings with that person. These results indicate a pulling away of the daughter from the mother in terms of decreased comfort in discussing particular feelings and in keeping these feelings more private. During the interview, some of the girls reported that they felt closer to their mothers since they had begun to menstruate. Some of these same girls also reported that they had discussed menstruation with their mothers but did not mention their feelings about it. The response of the parents of the postmenarcheal I girls to the sentence-completion item supports the daughters' views of their relationships with their mothers. More parents of postmenarcheal I daughters indicated that their daughters were increasingly emotionally distant from them than did parents of postmenarcheal II or premenarcheal girls.

Perhaps one way of understanding this distance is to look at the developmental tasks facing a girl at this age — tasks which pose a seemingly contradictory demand on young menarcheal girls. On the one hand, as she enters adolescence a young girl must begin slowly to develop an independent identity separate from her parents. To do this, she first has to pull away from her parents in some area. On the other hand, menarche with its dramatic and concrete aspects forces her to begin to deal with her femininity and precipitates a need to have a more experienced woman, in most cases her mother, available to help her master this new task. However, as much as she needs her mother for support, she also needs to figure out how to be a woman different from her mother (Chodorow, 1978).

In contrast to their daughters, the mothers of postmenarcheal girls reported an increase in comfort in discussing intimate feelings with their daughters when compared with mothers of premenarcheal girls. Interview data also indicated that most mothers felt closer to their daughters after menarche. They stated that it gave them something in common. The mothers' reports of increased activities outside of the home with their daughters indicates that they spent more time in shared activities by choice and supports the mothers' view of increased closeness with daughters.

It may be that for the mothers, their daughters' menarche served to increase their sense of identity with their daughters by (a) stirring up their feelings about their own menarche and (b) concretely defining their daughters as women. This transition to womanhood may have allowed the mothers to feel that their daughters now needed to be protected less from adult feelings and could be included in "women's talk." Anthropological literature (Mead, 1949, 1952) has pointed out that in many societies menarche puts young girls in a group with other menstruating women in terms of specific prohibitions and privileges. Perhaps without realizing it, the mothers saw their menarcheal daughters as joining "the society of women," and therefore certain emotions that were previously shared only with other women could now be shared with their daughters.

That mothers of postmenarcheal girls reported less comfort in discussing impersonal issues with their daughters may be a reflection of the mothers' responses to the daughters' increased distance and need for independence and privacy. The mothers may have given the daughters more distance and independence in areas that felt less personal.

Rierdan (1983), Kestenberg (1961, 1967), and Deutsch (1944) emphasized the importance of mothers to daughters at the time of menarche. The current research supports that view and presents a picture of postmenarche as a time when girls are struggling with issues of being a woman and beginning to develop some independence from their families while at the same time needing to turn to their mothers for support and advice. Mothers appear to respond to this change in their daughters with an increased sense of closeness and a sense of freedom to share intimate feelings they may not have shared before. In other words, the mothers begin to enjoy a more mutual relationship with their daughters.

Mothers must balance their enjoyment of having another adult woman in the family with whom they can share their feelings with their daughters' needs for independence and distance as well as support. This requires a flexible stance on the part of the mother, one that is acutely sensitive to the needs of the daughter and not dominated by the mother's own need for closeness with other women or by competition.

We are only beginning to understand this complex relationship between a girl's reaction to her menarche and the reaction of her parents. We know little about how changes in postmenarcheal girls' body image, sense of femininity, and mood influence their parents' reactions to them. Further research needs to be done on the roles of birth order and parents' developmental stages in determining a family's reaction to menarche. The influence of such things as handicaps, chronic illness, socio-economic status, and ethnicity on menarche is almost totally unexplored.

REFERENCES

Benedict, R. (1934). *Patterns of culture.* Boston: Houghton-Mifflin.
Benedict, R. (1954). Continuities and discontinuities in cultural conditioning. In

W. E. Martin & C. B. Stendler (Eds.), *Readings in child development* (pp. 123–147). New York: Harcourt, Brace, and World.

Blos, P. (1962). *On adolescence.* New York: Free Press.

Brooks-Gunn, J., & Ruble, D. (1980). Menarche: The interaction of physiological, cultural, and social factors. In A. J. Dan, E. A. Graham, & C. P. Beecher (Eds.), *The menstrual cycle: Synthesis of interdisciplinary research* (pp. 141–159). New York: Springer.

Chodorow, N. (1978). *The reproduction of mothering: Psychoanalysis and the sociology of gender.* Berkeley: University of California Press.

Clarke, A. E., & Ruble, D. (1978). Young adolescents' beliefs concerning menstruation. *Child Development, 49,* 231–234.

Danza, R. (1983). Menarche: Its effect on mother-daughter and father-daughter interactions. In S. Golub (Ed.), *Menarche: The transition from girl to woman* (pp. 99–105). Lexington, MA: Lexington Books.

Deutsch, H. (1944). *The psychology of women: A psychoanalytic interpretation* (Vol. 1). New York: Grune and Stratton.

Faust, S. (1960). Developmental maturity as a determinant in prestige of adolescent girls. *Child Development, 31,* 173–184.

Kestenberg, J. S. (1961). Menarche. In S. Lorand & H. I. Schneer (Eds.), *Adolescents: Psychoanalytic approach to problems and therapy* (pp. 19–50). New York: Harper and Row.

Kestenberg, J. S. (1967). Phases of adolescence. *Journal of the American Academy of Child Psychiatry, 6,* Pt. 1, 426–463, Pt. 2, 577–611.

Koff, E., Rierdan, J., & Jacobson, S. (1981). The personal and interpersonal significance of menarche. *Journal of the American Academy of Child Psychiatry, 20,* 148–158.

Koff, E., Rierdan, J., & Sheingold, K. (1980, April). *Memories of menarche: Age and preparedness as determinants of subjective experience.* Paper presented at the annual meeting of the Eastern Psychological Association, Hartford, CT.

Koff, E., Rierdan, J., & Silverstone, E. (1978). Changes in representation of body image as a function of menarcheal status. *Developmental Psychology, 14,* 635–642.

Mead, M. (1949). *Male and female.* New York: Morrow.

Mead, M. (1952). Adolescence in primitive and in modern society. In G. E. Swanson, T. M. Newcomb, & E. L. Hartley (Eds.), *Readings in social psychology* (pp. 76–82). New York: Holt.

Petersen, A. C. (1980). Biopsychological processes in the development of sex-related differences. In J. E. Parsons (Ed.), *The psychobiology of sex differences and sex roles* (pp. 31–55). Washington, DC: Hemisphere.

Rierdan, J. (1983). Variations in the experience of menarche as a function of preparedness. In S. Golub (Ed.), *Menarche: The transition from girl to woman* (pp. 119–125). Lexington, MA: Lexington Books.

Rierdan, J., & Koff, E. (1980). Representation of the female body by early and late adolescent girls. *Journal of Youth and Adolescence, 9,* 339–396.

Stone, C. P., & Barker, R. G. (1937). Aspects of personality and intelligence in postmenarcheal and premenarcheal girls of the same chronological age. *Journal of Comparative Psychology, 23,* 439–455.

Stone, C. P., & Barker, R. G. (1939). The attitudes and interests of premenarcheal and postmenarcheal girls. *Journal of Genetic Psychology, 54,* 27–72.

Thompson, C. (1942). Cultural pressures in the psychology of women. *Psychiatry, 5,* 331–339.

Ulman, K. (1984, August). *Impact of menarche on self-image and mood in adolescent girls.* Paper presented at the annual meeting of the American Psychological Association, Toronto, Canada.

Whisnant, L., & Zegans, L. (1975). A study of attitudes toward menarche in white, middle-class American adolescent girls. *American Journal of Psychiatry, 132,* 809–814.

23

Social Factors and Menstrual Synchrony in a Population of Nurses

Cynthia A. Graham and William C. McGrew

Synchronization of menstrual cycling among women is said to occur when their dates of onset of menstruation shift progressively closer together in time. Menstrual synchrony was first described by McClintock (1971), who found that in all-female groups the cycles of college roommates became increasingly synchronized over a 7-month period. Recent studies have confirmed these findings and extended them to mixed-sex communities in Europe and North America (Graham & McGrew, 1980; Quadagno, Shubeita, Deck, & Francoeur, 1981; Triedman, 1980). The phenomenon has also been documented in an Indian population, where 127 hostel residents had menstrual cycles timed more closely than nonresident subjects (Skandhan, Pandya, Skandhan, & Mehta, 1979). There are anthropological accounts of menstrual synchrony occurring among the Yurok Indians (Buckley, 1982). However, there has also been one report of a lack of synchrony among roommates and close friends (Jarett, 1984).

As McClintock (1983) has observed, the parameters of menstrual synchrony are similar across these studies. Synchronization of menstrual cycles occurred only among women who spent time together, usually after 3 to 4 months. Jarett (1984) identified psychosocial and biological factors that predicted individual differences in menstrual synchrony (e.g., the use of sanitary napkins, long menstrual flow). Whether the amount of time spent together determines the extent of synchrony between close friends has not been established. Triedman (1980) found that roommates spending fewer than 8 hours per day together showed no significant trend toward synchrony.

If olfactory communication between individuals is involved in menstrual synchrony, then women who wear strong (masking?) deodorants or perfume may not show the effect. Other studies to date have not investigated this possibility. In Russell, Switz, and Thompson's (1980) study, a "donor" female, who induced synchronous menstrual cycles in a group of subjects, did not use deodorants or perfume. Schleidt (1980) also reported that women using neither deodorants nor perfume had greater olfactory acuity than a group who did use them.

The mechanisms underlying menstrual synchrony have not yet been identified. In an attempt to elucidate these mechanisms, the present study focused on specific variables that might influence the tendency toward synchronization. The aim was to determine whether any relationship exists between the degree of menstrual synchrony evidenced and (a) the amount of time spent together by close friends, or (b) the use of deodorants and perfume. Because documentation of synchrony has been restricted to student populations, we decided to investigate the effect in a sample of resident nurses.

Method

Subjects

Subjects were 80 female nurses (18–29 years of age, $M = 20.9$) living at two hospitals in central Scotland. Seventy of the nurses lived in nine blocks of flats within a large residential complex housing 250 persons. Each block contained seven all-female flats which comprised two to four bedrooms and a communally used kitchen and bathroom. The remaining 10 subjects lived in a small nurses' home that housed about 60 residents. All subjects had single bedrooms. Two of the blocks of flats studied contained three flats with only male residents, and the nurses' home housed male residents in separate corridors.

Procedure

Permission was obtained from the nursing administration of two hospitals to recruit resident nurses. In the first stage of the study, 150 nurses were asked to take part in a study on the menstrual cycle. Notice was given at a residents' meeting that approval for the study had been granted but that participation was voluntary. Only women to be resident over the 4 months of the study (February–May) were included. Before the beginning of February, the 80 volunteers who fulfilled this criterion were given a chart on which to record the date of onset and duration of menstrual flow. Charts were collected monthly.

In February, a questionnaire was administered to all subjects asking them to rank up to three of their closest female friends living in the residential complex and to name the two women whose rooms were nearest to their own. Close friends were defined as in McClintock's (1971) study as being "those women who you see most often and with whom you spend the most time and not necessarily those with whom you feel the closest." Subjects also disclosed (a) the approximate amount of time spent daily with their closest friend and with males, (b) the frequency with which perfume and underarm deodorants or antiperspirants was used, (c) the regularity and variation of menstrual cycle timing, (d) the degree of pain experienced during menstruation, (e) whether they used oral contraception, and (f) their awareness of the timing of their closest friends' menstrual cycles.

Subjects were told that the aim of the study was to learn more about variations in the menstrual cycle and that their responses would be kept confidential. In June, a letter explaining the purpose and results of the study was given to all participants.

Techniques of Measurement

For each subject, her closest (i.e., highest ranking) friend and the woman living nearest to her room were chosen to form two pairs: close friends, and neighbors. For inclusion in the group of close-friend pairs, it was necessary that each woman list the other as a close friend. In 53% of the close-friend pairs, a subject's highest ranking friend was also cited as being one of the women whose rooms were nearest to her own; in these cases a different subject was chosen to form a neighbor pair. Although women living in adjacent rooms often did not spend a lot of time together, women living near to one another would still be expected to see each other more often than women living in separate residences. Subjects were therefore randomly paired and tested for synchrony to allow for the possible effects of the common environment affecting all the nurses (e.g., similar lifestyle, common eating habits, etc.). Women using oral contraception (19 of 80) were included in the synchrony analyses because although their cycles were fixed and uniform, they may have influenced the timing of others' cycles.

In February, the date of menstrual onset of one arbitrarily chosen member of a pair was compared with the closest onset date of the other.[1] In calculating the March difference, the onset date of the next consecutive cycle for each subject was chosen. The mean differences in menstrual onset dates in each cycle were compared for four types of pairing: (1) close friends ($n = 42$); (2) neighbors ($n = 36$); and (3) randomly chosen subjects ($n = 80$).

Results

Temporal Characteristics of the Menstrual Cycle

Over half of the sample (54%) estimated that they spent at least 4 hours daily in the company of males. The mean cycle lengths of subjects who estimated that they spent fewer than 4 hours each day with males ($n = 28$) were compared with those who reported spending more than 4 hours per day with males ($n = 30$). Women using oral contraception ($n = 19$) and those for whom menstrual data was incomplete ($n=3$) were excluded from this comparison. Using Student's t test, no significant difference was found ($t=0.5$, $p \geq .05$, one-tailed), indicating that there was no relation between menstrual cycle length and the amount of time spent with males.

Concerning regularity in the menstrual cycle, 77% of the subjects not using oral contraception reported "very regular" or "quite regular" cycles, which generally indicated a variation in length of less than 4 days. The other 23% described their cycles as "very irregular" or "quite irregular," corresponding to a variation in timing from 4 days to more than 7 days. These findings are much like those of a large-scale study of students in Scotland (Sheldrake & Cormack, 1976). However, a few ($n=4$) of the self-defined "regular" women in our sample had cycles that varied by over 5 days, while conversely 2 subjects whose cycles varied by only 1 or 2 days described their cycles as "quite irregular." This suggests that self-description in menstrual studies should not be accepted without confirmatory data.

The mean cycle length of the subjects not using oral contraception ($n=61$) was 29.4 ± 0.42 (SE) with a range of 21–44 days, and the mean duration of menstruation was 5.1 days ± 0.14 (SE).

Menstrual Synchrony

The mean menstrual differences between onset dates in each of the 4 months for groups of close friends, neighbors, and randomized pairs are shown in Table 1. Overall comparison of the means shows that there is a significant difference between the mean onset dates of close friends, neighbors, and random pairs (Friedman two-way analysis of variance [ANOVA], Siegel, 1956), $n=4$; $k=3$; $\chi^2=7.13$; $p=.042$. Post hoc comparisons revealed a significant difference between close friends and random pairs, $p=.03$; no other significant differences were found.

Table 1.
Mean Differences ($\pm SE$) in Menstrual Onset Dates (Days) Over 4 Months for Close Friends, Neighbors, and Random Pairs

Pairs	February	March	April	May
Close friends	9.0	8.3	8.7	9.2
($n=42$)	(1.06)	(0.94)	(1.08)	(1.07)
Neighbors	10.5	11.1	10.3	10.8
($n=36$)	(1.17)	(1.4)	(1.39)	(1.59)
Random	11.4	11.1	12.9	13.1
($n=80$)	(0.76)	(0.8)	(1.01)	(1.01)

Over half (58%) of the subjects reported spending at least 4 hours each day with their closest female friend. Pairs of close friends were divided into two groups: those who estimated that they spent more than 4 hours each day together ($n=20$) and those who reported spending fewer than 4 hours in daily interaction ($n=22$). The menstrual onset differences in February for these two groups were compared by means of Student's t test, and no significant differences were found, $t=.33$, $p \geq .05$, one-tailed.

Pairs of close friends were divided on the basis of the frequency with which they used deodorants or antiperspirants and perfume, and the following comparisons were made: (a) Pairs who reported using deodorants or antiperspirants more than once a day on average ($n=24$) were compared with pairs who indicated that they used deodorants or antiperspirants only once a day ($n=18$); (b) pairs who reported using perfume at least once a day ($n=21$) were compared with pairs who used perfume less than once daily ($n=21$). Using Student's t test, no significant differences were found in the size of menstrual onset discrepancies related to use of deodorants, $t=1.26$, $p \geq .05$, one-tailed, or perfume, $t=.15$, $p \geq .05$, one-tailed.

Discussion

These data provide further evidence that menstrual synchrony depends on interaction between individuals and not on common environmental variables. The cycles of close friends were significantly more synchronized than the cycles of neighbors or randomly chosen, paired subjects. In contrast to our previous findings (Graham & McGrew, 1980), "neighbors" in this study exhibited an intermediate degree of synchrony between close friends and randomized pairs. The large majority of subjects (88%) in the present study lived in flats housing 2 to 4 nurses who shared a communal kitchen and a bathroom with other residents. It seems likely that this setting gave more opportunity for interaction between neighbors than did halls of residence, where most of the subjects in the earlier study lived. This may explain why the size of menstrual onset differences was intermediate between those of close friends and randomized pairs.

No relationship was found between the time spent with close friends and the degree of menstrual synchrony shown. However, this does not disconfirm suggestions that the time spent together between individual females is the important factor. There may be a critical threshold for amount of time spent together that facilitates the development of synchrony, but any additional hours spent together may have no further effect. In the present study, unfortunately, only a small percentage (10%) of subjects spent fewer than 2 hours each day with their closest friends, so our data cannot shed light on this threshold hypothesis.

The proportion of subjects (24%) who were aware of their friends' menstrual cycles was higher than in our previous study (16%) and closer to that of McClintock's (1971) sample (28%). Awareness might be partly a function of length of time spent living together, because subjects had been resident within the hospital prior to the beginning of this study.

No relationship was observed between the frequency with which deodorants and perfume was used and the degree of synchrony between close friends. However, the extensive use of deodorants and perfume in the sample precluded an accurate test of this hypothesis. It remains to be seen whether a group of women who did not use deodorants or perfume would show a greater degree of synchronization. It is also possible that use of a strong deodorant might disrupt preestablished synchrony occurring between close friends; this too awaits testing.

One of the possible explanations for lack of synchrony is that atypical samples may include a high proportion of irregular cycles (Jarett, 1984). She hypothesized that the many long, irregular cycles in her sample (mean cycle length was 35.1 days) might account for the discrepant findings. The average cycle length in the current sample was 29.4 days, which is consistent with that of other studies (Cutler, Garcia, & Krieger, 1979). A limited proportion of irregular cycles in a sample may reflect a move toward synchrony, but a large variation in cycle lengths may obscure the synchronization effect (McClintock, 1983). Very long cycles tend to be anovulatory (Cutler et al., 1979). If menstrual synchrony reflects synchrony of ovulation (McClintock, 1978), then one would expect less synchrony in women showing long and irregular cycles.

We found no relationship between cycle length and the amount of interaction with males. McClintock (1971) observed that subjects who frequently associated with males had significantly shorter cycles than those who had minimal contact with males. Recent studies have not supported these findings, but most subjects had opportunities for daily social interaction with males (Graham & McGrew, 1980; Quadagno et al., 1981). Cutler, Garcia, and Krieger (1980) showed that women engaging in a high frequency of sporadic heterosexual activity showed a higher incidence of unusually long or short cycle lengths. Although McClintock (1971) did not assess the degree of sexual contact, it is interesting to note that in her sample, males were only present in the dormitory on weekends. It is possible that the pattern of interaction rather than the overall amount of time spent with males is the key factor in lengthening the menstrual cycle.

Many questions in the area of menstrual synchrony remain unanswered. It is not yet known whether synchrony occurring in a group of females is "led" by one individual or is the result of a mutual shift in timing (McClintock, 1981). It seems likely that the cycles of certain individuals will be more susceptible to modification than those of others, but cycle-lengths would have to be monitored before and after the emergence of synchrony to establish this. More work is needed on identifying variables that influence the tendency toward synchronization and the characteristics of those groups who fail to synchronize. Further evidence relating to these questions would shed light on the mechanisms involved in mediating the effect.

NOTES

This work was supported by a Greater Glasgow Health Board Scholarship. We thank the Department of Psychological Medicine, Glasgow, and the nurses who took part in the study.

1. Re-analysis of the data using a different selection method that chose the closest onset dates for a pair, irrespective of calendar month, showed virtually identical results. McClintock (personal communication, September 19, 1983) reported finding similar results with both methods.

REFERENCES

Buckley, T. (1982). Menstruation and the power of Yurok women: Methods in cultural reconstruction. *American Ethnologist, 9,* 47–60.

Cutler, W. B., Garcia, C. R., & Krieger, A. M. (1979). Sexual behavior frequency and menstrual cycle length in mature pre-menopausal women. *Psychoneuroendocrinology, 4,* 297–309.

Cutler, W. B., Garcia, C. R., & Krieger, A. M. (1980). Sporadic sexual behavior and menstrual cycle length in women. *Hormones and Behavior, 14,* 163–172.

Graham, C. A., & McGrew, W. C. (1980). Menstrual synchrony in female undergraduates living on a coeducational campus. *Psychoneuroendocrinology, 5,* 245–257.

Jarett, L. R. (1984). Psychosocial and biological influences on menstruation: Synchrony, cycle length and regularity. *Psychoneuroendocrinology, 6,* 21–28.

McClintock, M. K. (1971). Menstrual synchrony and suppression. *Nature, 229,* 244–245.

McClintock, M. K. (1978). Estrous synchrony and its mediation by airborne chemical communication. *Hormones and Behavior, 10,* 264–276.

McClintock, M. K. (1981). Social control of the ovarian cycle and the function of estrous synchrony. *American Zoologist, 21,* 243–256.

McClintock, M. K. (1983). Pheromonal regulation of the ovarian cycle: Enhancement, suppression and synchrony. In J. G. Vandenbergh (Ed.), *Pheromones and reproduction in mammals* (pp. 113–143). New York: Academic Press.

Quadagno, D. M., Shubeita, H. E., Deck, J., & Francoeur, D. (1981). Influence of male social contacts, exercise and all-female living conditions on the menstrual cycle. *Psychoneuroendocrinology, 6,* 239–244.

Russell, M. J., Switz, G. M., & Thompson, K. (1980). Olfactory influences on the menstrual cycle. *Pharmacology, Biochemistry, & Behavior, 13,* 737–738.

Schleidt, M. (1980). Personal odor and nonverbal communication. *Ethology and Sociobiology, 1,* 225–231.

Sheldrake, P., & Cormack, M. (1976). Variations in menstrual symptom reporting. *Journal of Psychosomatic Research, 20,* 169–177.

Siegel, S. (1956). *Nonparametric statistics for the behavioral sciences.* New York: McGraw-Hill.

Skandhan, K. P., Pandya, A. K., Skandhan, S., & Mehta, Y. B. (1979). Synchronization of menstruation among intimates and kindreds. *Panminerva Medica, 21,* 131–134.

Triedman, K. E. (1980). *On the existence and importance of human pheromones: Social interaction effects on the human menstrual cycle.* Unpublished manuscript, Brown University, Providence, RI.

24

Seasonal Cyclicity: Effect of Daylight/Darkness on the Menstrual Cycle

Effie Graham, Martha Stewart, and Penelope Ward

As a public health nurse at an Eskimo village at the Arctic Circle, one of the authors of this chapter discovered that many clients experienced a cessation of menstruation during the winter months. Her observation prompted a review of 2 years of clients' clinic records in a village in northwest Alaska. The findings of this preliminary study have led to a larger data analysis plan that we hope will clarify the question of a possible relationship of the menstrual cycle to daylight and darkness variability.

As public health nurse and program manager for the public health nursing clinic, Martha Stewart noted the apparent high incidence of nonpregnancy-related secondary amenorrhea among health center clients in winter months compared with summer months. The relationship was noted when concerned women came to the clinic requesting pregnancy tests.

Secondary amenorrhea is defined as the cessation of menstruation in a woman who has already established menstruation. The most common reason is pregnancy, followed by a variety of functional and pathological causes. It is assumed that in most functional cases there is a suppression of the complex pituitary gonadal system to which the occurrence of menstruation is related.

Background

The use of light to regulate menstrual cycles has been reported by Dewan (1967) and Dewan, Menkin, and Rock (1978). They reestablished regularity by the use of artificial light when the women were sleeping. Somewhat more recently, the role of the pineal gland in this relationship was described. Blask (1982) noted that melatonin levels increase during periods of darkness (at night); Mullen (1981), among others, also noted this relationship. Melatonin apparently has an antigonadotrophic action.

Sundararaj, Chern, Gatewood, Hickman, and McHugh (1978) analyzed seasonal variability over a 3-year period in 2,088 women, mostly college students in Minnesota, and found a small but statistically significant difference related to seasons. Cycles in fall and early winter were 2 hr longer than the mean; summer cycles were similarly shorter. Minneapolis is located near 45° latitude where the darkness/daylight contrast is much less pronounced than in the geographic area studied here.

A map of the location of various Alaskan, Canadian, and Siberian communities at various latitudes is shown in Figure 1. The Anchorage area has sunlight for as long as 19+ hr in the summer and as short as 5+ hr in the winter. In Barrow, the sun is below the horizon from mid-November until late January, and above the horizon from May 11 through the end of July.

The gonadal effect of daylight/darkness variation is also useful in explaining the seasonal differences in birthrates frequently reported in northern latitudes. Condon (1981) noted the high incidence of conceptions in summer compared with winter in a Canadian Inuit community. In a study of seasonal differences, this anthropologist noted an increased activity in heterosexual relationships with increasing daylight. He also reported, from a study of birthdates, a relationship of conceptions to spring daylight. In a review of the subject, Leppaluato (1983) noted two conception peaks in Finland. He attributed June-July conceptions to biological

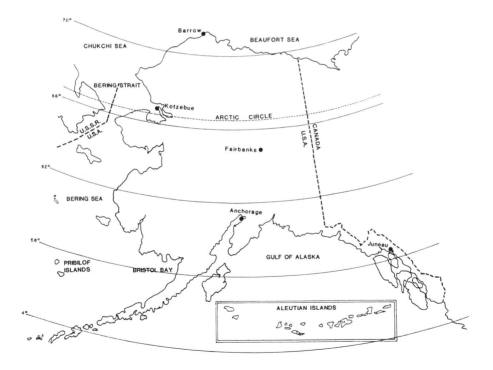

Figure 1. Map of Alaska showing relative latitudes of degrees north.

factors and December conceptions to social factors, such as the Christmas holiday festivities, with increased social mixing and more opportunity for sexual activity. Leppaluato suggested that the lack of monthly variation in conception in more recent years (since 1963) is due to the use of contraceptive pills.

At least two other relevant studies have been done in northern countries. A study of the incidence of secondary amenorrhea in the Upsala area of Sweden considered a variety of external and subject variables; however, amenorrhea was defined as lasting longer than 3 months and seasonal relationships were not studied (Pettersson, Fries, & Nillius, 1973). Shvareva and Tkachev (1984) in the U.S.S.R. studied three groups of immigrant and two groups of indigenous women in the Anadyr area of Siberia. Winter (but not summer) blood levels of cortisol, LH, and FSH varied among these groups. The most important finding was the relatively high levels of blood cortisol in the Eskimo women. The incidence of amenorrhea was not studied; all women studied had "normal cycles."

Jongbloet (1983) notes the "historical remnants of ancestral reproductive biology that have had adaptive values throughout millions of years" and states that "a seasonal recurrent disruption of the ovulatory pattern can be interpreted as nature's 'concession' to abandoning the lunar cycle in favor of seasonal light-dark periodicity" (p. 530).

The Retrospective Eskimo Village Study

Method

We analyzed the records of pregnancy testing for clients reporting to the health center in this village of 2,500 persons (Eskimo and other) located between 66° and 67° latitude. The primary reason these clients requested the test was the absence of menstruation. Most clients were Inuit Eskimo. The center was the only site for pregnancy testing in the village.

Permission was received from the board of directors of the agency to use the de-identified data. The files from 2 full calendar years were complete, including records of total numbers of cases and the results of pregnancy testing. The periods studied were October 1980 through September 1981 and March 1982 through February 1983. Data from the intervening months were missing. Negative pregnancy reports were double-checked for positive pregnancy tests in the next month in the event the original tests showed false negatives. Data were grouped according to months of the calendar year. During the 2 years, 135 cases of pregnancy-related amenorrhea and 138 cases of nonpregnancy-related amenorrhea were observed.

Because of the predicted relationship of these data to seasonal darkness, tables of sunrise and sunset times for this community were secured from the U.S. Naval Observatory. The number of daily hours of darkness present on the 15th day of each month was selected as the norm for that month.

A statistical analysis using rank-order correlation was computed between the hours of darkness on the 15th day of a month and the number of cases of negative pregnancy tests ranked by month. It was also computed for the number of positive pregnancy tests, ranked by month. We hypothesized that the incidence of nonpregnancy-related amenorrhea would be higher in dark months and that pregnancy-related amenorrhea would be higher in months with more daylight.

Results

There was a positive relationship ($rho = 0.733$, $p < .05$) between hours of darkness on the 15th day and the number of cases of nonpregnancy-related secondary amenorrhea ranked by month (Figure 2). Months are ranked by hours of darkness.

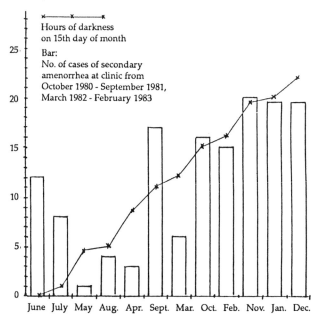

Figure 2. Relationship of monthly incidence of cases of nonpregnancy-related secondary amenorrhea and hours of darkness on 15th day of the month. (Health clinic located between 66° and 67° latitude in northwestern Alaska.)

A comparative analysis for number of positive pregnancy tests showed a positive (*rho*=0.371) correlation with darkness. This was not statistically significant; also it did not have the predicted negative relationship. Numbers of conceptions showed an irregular pattern with a slight increase in December and January, a confirmation of the "social factors" mentioned earlier.

Figure 3 illustrates the two groups of clients compared with the darkness curve. The curve for the nonpregnancy-related amenorrhea is slightly in advance of the darkness curve, but the close relationship is otherwise apparent.

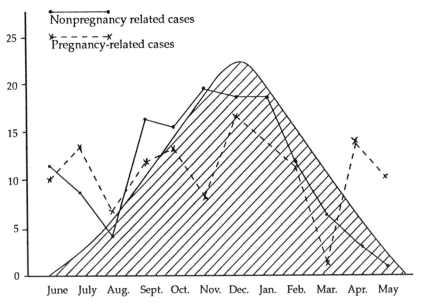

Figure 3. Monthly incidence of pregnancy-related and nonpregnancy-related secondary amenorrhea plotted against darkness curve (hours of darkness in village located between 66° and 67° latitude).

Discussion

The results of this study lend support to only one aspect of the two-part hypothesis. It may be that social factors relating to increased (e.g., holidays) and decreased (e.g., taboos) opportunity for sexual activity, as well as the advent of better birth control methods, confounds the linking of conceptions to physiological factors. The incidence of nonpregnancy-related cases of amenorrhea appears to be more related to increased darkness, yet these data are not entirely reliable. Certainly most women experiencing only one missed period or a delayed period will not seek pregnancy testing.

The seasonal variability of menstrual patterns, in general, appears to be a more promising area for research. Conversations with women who are currently living or who have lived in villages above the Arctic Circle have resulted in many personal anecdotes of menstrual variability, particularly increased length of winter cycles. These women expect this as a normal variation. This is clearly an area that needs more investigation.

Alaska provides a natural field area for research of this type because it lies between 56° and 72° north latitude. Recent linkages of the University of Alaska with the U.S.S.R. to study health issues in polar areas offer the possibility of studying this question on cross-national populations.

A promising source for the exploration of this question of light-related menstrual variability already exists, namely, a data set of over 1,000 women who kept menstrual calendars and who lived in Barrow, Bethel area villages, and in Anchorage. These data are housed in the Tremin Trust at the University of Utah. However, data from the Anchorage Municipal Family Planning Clinic, reviewed for a period of 2 years by Graham, did not reveal any significant seasonal variation in amenorrhea patterns.

Any exploration of this question must, in the end, study hormonal levels, which are the basis of this phenomenon. These may include repeat measures on the same individuals or measures on randomized sets of women at the various seasons of the year.

The clinical implications of this research area became apparent when this proposal was presented for approval to the board of directors of the Eskimo health clinic. The women on the board agreed that if there is a general pattern of irregularity in menstrual cycles of a seasonal type which tends to be self-correcting, then such information would be important in reassuring clients and reducing their anxiety.

It is also logical that this reproductive area (and its associated hormones) interfaces with the area of seasonal depression and mood change. Brody (1984) described a conference of the New York Academy of Sciences on seasonal affective disorder (SAD). Elucidation of the pineal/melatonin/gonadotrophic relationship was described as essential to our understanding of this problem. One researcher noted that "Now only a small number of investigators are working on this area, but as recent findings become more widely known, we expect this community of researchers to enlarge, and our knowledge to be greater" (Sec. 5, p. 1).

REFERENCES

Blask, D. E. (1982). Potential role of the pineal gland in the menstrual cycle. In A. Voda, M. Dinnerstein, & S. O'Donnell (Eds.), *Changing perspectives on menopause* (pp. 124–135). Austin: University of Texas Press.

Brody, J. (1984, December 16). Scientists begin to discover positive effects of sunlight. *Anchorage Daily News*, Sec. 5, p. 1. (Reprinted from *New York Times*)

Condon, R. G. (1981). *Inuit behavior and seasonal change in the Canadian Arctic.* Ann Arbor: University of Michigan Research Press.

Dewan, E. M. (1967). On the possibility of a perfect rhythm method of birth control by periodic light stimulation. *American Journal of Obstetrics and Gynecology, 99,* 1016–1019.

Dewan, E. M., Menkin, M. F., & Rock, J. (1978). Effect of photic stimulation on the human menstrual cycle. *Photochemistry and Photobiology, 27,* 581–585.

Jongbloet, P. H. (1983). Menses and moon phases, ovulation and seasons, vitality and month of birth. *Developmental and Child Neurology, 25,* 527–539.

Leppaluato, J. (1983). Seasonal variations of human reproductive functions (Report No. 36). *Nordic Council for Arctic Medical Research,* pp. 527–539.

Mullen, P. E. (1981). The endocrinology of the human pineal. *British Journal of Hospital Medicine, 25,* 248–256.

Pettersson, F., Fries, H., & Nillius, S. J. (1973). Epidemiology of secondary amenorrhea: 1. Incidence and prevalence rates. *American Journal of Obstetrics and Gynecology, 117,* 80–86.

Shvareva, N. V., & Tkachev, A. V. (1979). Gonadotropic hormones and cortisol levels in women during adaptation to polar conditions. *Abstracts of Scientific Proceedings of the 4th All-Union Biochemical Congress* (p. 205). (Translated from *Fiziologiya Cheloveka,* 1983, *9*(4). New York: Plenum)

Sundararaj, N., Chern, M., Gatewood, L., Hickman, L., & McHugh, R. (1978). Seasonal behavior of human menstrual cycles: A biometric investigation. *Human Biology, 50,* 15–31.

25

Can Tampon Safety Be Regulated?

Esther R. Rome and Jill Wolhandler

Although tampons are classified as "medical devices," subject to regulation by the Food and Drug Administration (FDA), tampon regulation only became a major concern following recognition that the fatal occurrence of toxic shock syndrome (TSS) had been associated with tampon use (Radetsky, 1985). In this chapter, we report on our experience with the regulation process, analyze the forces involved in the process, and recommend ways for consumers to have some impact on this policy making.

Since 1976, the FDA has been required by law to classify and regulate safety and performance of medical devices. Tampons were assigned to Class II, the middle-risk category. Although the FDA is legally required to develop and enforce minimum product standards for tampons, it does not plan to do so.

In 1980, however, widespread public concern about TSS forced the agency to take some action regarding tampons. It negotiated with Proctor and Gamble to remove from the market its popular new superabsorbent tampon, Rely, which was heavily linked with TSS. It persuaded the other companies to put a TSS warning on or in tampon boxes. It notified menstrual sponge distributors, mostly small woman-owned businesses, to stop distributing their product for menstrual purposes. In 1982, the agency finally required a TSS warning to include the advice to use the lowest absorbency necessary, either on the box or as a package insert. Companies that had been putting warnings on the box immediately moved them to the insert. Unfortunately, the advice to use the least absorbent tampon necessary was meaningless because there was no way to compare the absorbencies of different brands of tampons in the absence of uniform absorbency labeling.

Under pressure to take further action, the FDA tried to move the responsibility for writing a tampon standard onto the private sector. The FDA requested the American Society for Testing and Materials (ASTM) to convene a group consisting of tampon manufacturers, consumers, the FDA, and other interested parties to write a private, voluntary tampon standard (letter from F. Alan Andersen to Patrick G. Laing, July 13, 1981).

This was consistent with FDA policy during the Reagan administration to minimize government regulation of business. Andersen stated that the purpose of the task force was "to develop a standard which would include performance requirements, disclosure requirements, and appropriate labeling to control, to the extent possible, the mechanical and material properties of tampons. . . . Performance standards are necessary to control the biocompatibility, absorbency, and leachability of the materials that are used in these devices. . . . We [the FDA] also believe that a performance standard should address the smoothness and mechanical operation of the tampon inserter." He further stated that the FDA believed that a performance standard could address the "reports of broken strings, particulates, cleanliness, shredding, sharp edges, allergies, absorption, and mispackaging" that had been reported to the FDA.

At the suggestion of the FDA and the insistence of the manufacturers, all of which were in the midst of lawsuits, TSS was not among the issues the task force would address. Of course, TSS was the reason behind the entire process and colored the discussion of many topics.

ASTM called the first meeting in January 1982, inviting all five manufacturers and only one consumer group. The three major tampon producers were Tampax (now Tambrands), Playtex, and Johnson & Johnson (o.b. tampons). Kimberly Clark (Kotex) and Jeffrey-Martin (Pursettes) each had a negligible part of the market in 1982. Sometime around 1983, DEP Corporation bought Jeffrey-Martin and then discontinued making Pursettes. In 1984, Sentinel started marketing tampons and as yet has an insignificant market share. After the manufacturers agreed to participate on the Tampon Task Force, the National Consumers League recruited other consumer groups to participate. These groups included the Boston Women's Health Book Collective (BWHBC), Woman Health International and the National Women's Health Network in Washington, DC, the Empire State Consumers League in Rochester, NY, and the Coalition for the Medical Rights of Women in San Francisco, CA. The authors represented BWHBC on the task force.

The original plan was for the Tampon Task Force to meet every 6 weeks for about a year to hammer out a standard that would cover performance, safety, and labeling. The manufacturers agreed to provide money to ASTM to fund consumers' travel expenses, conference calls, and technical consultants, but consumer time would not be compensated.

Though many serious issues were explored, the task force remained deadlocked on what to do about them, because consumer and producer interests were polarized. The task force produced a chart of relative tampon absorbencies based on a test method standardized from the manufacturers' methods for measuring absorbency. The test method itself was never approved by ASTM because questions raised by consumers about consistency and statistical reliability of the results were never answered. Although the task force met for over 3 years, it became inactive in April 1985 without producing any kind of standard.

Manufacturer and Consumer Stands on the Issues

From the beginning, it appeared that the manufacturers did not consider the consumers' concerns very important. They said they had to avoid revealing any information to other manufacturers in their highly competitive business, although they did admit to testing competitors' products in their own laboratories. The first year was spent with the manufacturers' getting comfortable working together, belittling the consumer representatives and their concerns, and insisting that all information about their products and about safety testing was proprietary — that is, a trade secret. The consumers later discovered that some of what they wanted to know was already in the public record, because plaintiffs' lawyers in TSS cases had succeeded in getting information introduced as evidence in court.

By working on the task force, the consumer groups became painfully aware of how little is known about the safety of tampons. In some areas, the technology clearly exists to perform tests. In others, it needs to be developed. The manufacturers have consistently claimed that tampons are safe because they have been on the market since the 1930s and TSS is the only major health problem convincingly associated with them. This questionable argument assumes that tampons are still the same relatively low-absorbency cotton products that were sold 50 years ago. But for the last 15 to 20 years tampons have included new superabsorbent materials and have been designed and constructed in different ways. Reports have begun to appear in the medical literature linking tampons with micro-ulcerations and ulcers of the vagina as well as increased risk of TSS. Dr. Philip Tierno, who has testified many times for plaintiffs in TSS cases, believes that the particular constituents of the fibers, differences in oxygen availability, and the selective absorbency of the fibers are some of the factors in tampons that create an environment that promotes TSS (Hanna & Tierno, 1985). He asserts that only the all-cotton fiber is safe.

There is no available research that addresses the safety of new fibers for use inside the vagina. One way to do this is with biocompatibility testing designed to assess the effects of tampons and tampon ingredients on living tissue. Tests can measure such factors as irritation, drying, tissue injury, effects of chemicals which might leach out of tampons during use, effects of repeated long-term use, toxicity, and carcinogenicity.

Most responsible researchers in biocompatibility, a relatively new field, say that a battery of tests is necessary, because each test gives only limited information. Tampon manufacturers, however, refused to consider more than two tests. The consumers believed these two tests alone would give women a false assurance of safety. For instance, these tests would not have discovered problems with polyacrylates or the known problems with micro-ulcerations. Thus, the task force was deadlocked on one of the most crucial safety issues.

Another area of concern is the material tampons shed inside the vagina during use. If you immerse any tampon in a glass of water, you will find that all tampons shed some fibers. The worst tampon material, rayon poly-acrylate, actually turns the water cloudy. In 1985, manufacturers stopped formulating tampons with this ingredient after laboratory tests showed that rayon polyacrylate may enhance the toxin production of *Staphylococcus aureus*, a type of bacteria believed to be responsible for TSS (Mills et al., 1985). Viscose rayon, also associated with TSS, is still in use. Consumers are also concerned about microscopic particles, because theoretically the particles could enter the lymph system through vaginal ulcers or micro-ulcerations and cause problems somewhere else in the body. Yet the manufacturers refused to measure or limit these fibers and particles.

Tampons are not sterile, but tampon manufacturers refuse to divulge how many and what microorganisms are in their products. The companies resisted every effort to include this simple microbiology testing in the standard. Are these microbes in any way related to problems of recurring vaginal infections some women report they experience with tampons? Are the wrappers sufficient to keep the tampons reasonably clean? Once again, the Tampon Task Force reached a dead end.

Labeling requirements are another area of intense interest to the consumers. Two of these issues are absorbency disclosure and a safety warning. Absorbency is a crucial safety factor, because lower absorbency tampons are associated with decreased risk of TSS and other problems. Until 1990, the terms "regular," "super," and "super-plus" meant something different for each brand, and manufacturers changed actual absorbencies at will. In some cases, one brand's "regular" was more absorbent than another's "super" (Reame, Delonis, & Lewis, 1987; see Tables 1 & 2). It became clear that the manufacturers would not agree on any system of uniform absorbency labeling. For this reason, consumer representatives made a formal demand that the FDA remove this issue from the ASTM voluntary process. [Letter from Esther R. Rome (Boston Women's Health Book Collective), Miriam Goodman (Coalition for the Medical Rights for Women), Judith Braiman-Lipson (Empire State Consumer Association), Rebecca Cohen (National Consumers League), Susan Seidler (National Women's Health Network), and Judith Beck (Woman Health International)

Table 1.
1983 Tampon Absorbencies.

Brand and style	Absorbency[a]	Brand and style	Absorbency
Tampax Junior	5	Kotex Security Super	12
Tampax Original Regular	7	Playtex Deodorant Regular	13
Tampax Slender Regular	7	o.b. Super	13
Kotex Stick Regular	8	Playtex Nondeodorant Regular	13
Kotex Security Regular	9	Playtex Nondeodorant Super	16
Tampax Super	9	Playtex Deodorant Super	16
Pursettes Regular	10	Tampax Super Plus	16
o.b. Regular	11	o.b. Super Plus	17
Kotex Stick Super	11	Playtex Nondeod. Super Plus	17
Pursettes Super	12	Playtex Deodorant Super Plus	17

Note. From *Tampons: Are They Safe?* Copyright 1986 by the Boston Women's Health Book Collective. Adapted by permission.
[a]Grams of salt water absorbed in laboratory tests.

Table 2.
1987 Tampon Absorbencies.

Brand and style	Absorbency[a]	Brand and style	Absorbency
Tampax Junior	5	Tampax Super	9
Playtex Slender Regular	6	Tampax Super Petal	9
Playtex Slender Regular		o.b. Regular	11
Deodorant	6	Playtex Super	11
Tampax Regular Petal	6	Playtex Super Deodorant	11
Tampax Slender Regular	6	Playtex Super Plus Deodorant	11
Kotex Regular Stick	7	Sentinel Super	11
Tampax Original Regular	7	Tampax Super Plus Petal	11
Kotex Regular Security	8	Kotex Super Security	12
Kotex Super Stick	9	Playtex Super Plus	12
Playtex Regular	9	Tampax Super Plus	12
Playtex Regular Deodorant	9	o.b. Super	13
Sentinel Regular	9	o.b. Super Plus	16

Note. From *Tampons: Are They Safe?* Copyright 1987 by the Boston Women's Health Book Collective. Adapted by permission.
[a]Grams of salt water absorbed in laboratory tests. Tampons with the same absorbency number are listed alphabetically. This does not imply any endorsement.

to Dr. Mark Novitch, Acting Commissioner, FDA, April 16, 1984.] Ultimately, this is the only area in which the FDA has taken any action.

In addition, the consumers believe that the tampon box ought prominently to warn a woman that if she experiences itching, irritation, unusual discharge, or unusual bleeding, she should remove her tampon immediately and see a health practitioner if symptoms persist. The manufacturers categorically refused to include this safety warning, because consumers could not offer extensive published scientific and medical studies proving that tampons can be associated with any vaginal problems.

The Role of the Federal Government

The FDA has the authority to regulate tampons in several ways, but its regulatory functions are hampered by inadequate funding, government policy, and potential staff conflicts of interest. FDA actions in the ASTM Tampon Task Force indicated a strong desire to achieve some sort of private, voluntary standard, regardless of its content. Consequently, the agency frequently sided with the manufacturers to overrule consumer concerns, to avoid tie votes, and to create the appearance that the task force was making progress.

The FDA also changed its position on a number of important issues. Originally the agency presented to the task force an excellent absorbency labeling proposal, including both a uniform absorbency number system (similar to sunscreen rating numbers) and standardization *or* elimination of the terms "regular," "super," and "super-plus." Playtex and Johnson & Johnson lobbied hard for each manufacturer to be allowed to use the absorbency terms in its own way and to *add* an absorbency number. This system would have allowed a "Regular-13" that is more absorbent than a "Super-9," a situation the consumers strongly opposed.

In fall 1983, outside the ASTM Tampon Task Force, the FDA extracted an agreement from the manufacturers to put on the outside of tampon packages the advice to use the lowest absorbency needed (National Center for Devices and Radiological Health, 1983). Of course, lack of uniform absorbency labeling meant it was still impossible to follow this advice. In addition, the size and placement of this advice were not specified. Manufacturers embedded this warning in the promotional literature on the box where it was easy to miss. More important, it was not linked with information about TSS or other health problems so there was no reason for women to take it seriously. Two examples from 1985 of this practice follow:

> Designed in three absorbencies for various flow needs, each with or without deodorant. Playtex makes Regular absorbency for lighter flows and Super and Super Plus absorbencies for heavier flows. Use the least absorbent size needed to control your menstrual flow.

> *Designed in three sizes to meet various absorbency needs.* Use the least absorbent size needed to control your menstrual flow. Try o.b. Regular for average or light flow. You may need o.b. Super for heavier flow. Super Plus is for exceptionally heavy flow.

This information was presented as if convenience were the only reason to choose a lower absorbency. The industry has vetoed any information that might alert the consumer that there is cause for concern.

In September 1984, in an effort to prod the FDA into action, Woman Health International petitioned the FDA to develop a safety standard for tampons. The FDA held a hearing on the petition at the end of August 1985, but nothing came of it directly.

Under pressure from media attention, letters from consumers, a Public Citizen Health Research Group petition, a highly critical Congressional Report, and the demand from the consumer representatives of the ASTM Tampon Task Force, the FDA agreed to mandate an absorbency disclosure rule early in 1985.

In the spring of 1988, the Public Citizen Health Research Group filed a lawsuit in federal district court to force the FDA "to issue a regulation requiring all tampon manufacturers to print, on the outside of every box, the numerical absorbency of the tampon along with the information that high absorbency puts women at higher risk of the often-fatal toxic shock syndrome" (Tampons and Toxic Shock, 1988). The case was finally heard in the summer of 1989. The judge ruled that the FDA had to publish a final regulation by October 31, 1989.

In the meantime, the FDA had proposed a labeling requirement in September 1988 that unfortunately involved a dual-labeling system — a standardized A through F rating which also allowed each manufacturer to apply any definition it wanted to the terms "regular," "super," etc. Later, the Boston Women's Health Book Collective discovered through OMBwatch, a Washington, DC, public interest organization, that the FDA had been stymied in its attempts to produce a straightforward labeling system by the Office of Management and Budget (OMB), which must approve all executive branch regulations under the Paperwork Reduction Act.

In the fall of 1988, BWHBC mounted a letter-writing campaign to the FDA to support standardizing the common terminology already on the tampon boxes. There were about 270 letters from all parties to the FDA regarding this rule. Approximately 90% of the comments were a result of the BWHBC consumer alert. Because this agency rarely hears from the public, even a few hundred letters have an impact in counteracting the influence of industry lobbying.

The FDA indicated it would issue a final rule in the spring of 1989. Instead, in June 1989, under pressure from OMB, it proposed another rule with a different dual-labeling system. At this time the FDA indicated it did not want to receive more letters from consumers. During the summer of 1989, several congressional committees were holding hearings on the Paperwork Reduction Act, which was up for renewal. BWHBC testified that OMB not only delayed regulation of tampons but had insisted on a labeling system that was confusing and contradictory.

The Collective also suggested to one of the manufacturers that supported the same absorbency labeling system as the consumers that it join with BWHBC in writing one common letter to the FDA. In the end all of the manufacturers except Johnson & Johnson wrote a joint consumer/ manufacturer letter in support of the standardization of existing terms (letter signed by Esther R. Rome for BWHBC, National Women's Health Network, Consumer Federation of America, National Consumers League, Public Voice, Tambrands, Inc., Kimberly-Clark Corp., and Sentinel Consumer Products, Inc., to Frank Young, FDA Commissioner, August 7, 1989).

OMB decided not to continue to block sensible tampon absorbency labeling. Consequently, the final rule favored consumers. The final rule, issued October 26, 1989, includes labeling regulations that standardize the existing terms (see Appendix). At last, any brand of "regular" tampons is less absorbent than any brand of "super," which is less absorbent than any "super plus." The labeling must also "prominently and legibly" include information linking absorbency to TSS risk and advising using the tampon "with the minimum absorbency needed to control menstrual flow" (*Federal Register*, Vol. 54, p. 43771). The confluence of consumer and manufacturer interests allowed standardized, noncontradictory labeling to take effect in the spring of 1990, 10 years after the recognition that tampons are associated with TSS.

The FDA has jurisdiction over tampons apart from standard setting and rule making. Unfortunately, these procedures are insignificant in their impact on tampon safety. The agency requires that major changes in the products be reported to it, and copies of these notifications of changes [called a 510(k) application] can be obtained through the Freedom of Information Act. At the request of the manufacturers, however, the FDA blacks out all the substantive information, including any testing that might have been done.

The FDA also maintains records of all complaints it receives about tampons in its Device Experience Network (DEN). The public can receive a report listing these complaints. Although anyone can report a problem, tampon users and most medical practitioners do not even know that DEN exists, nor do they realize the importance of having a public record of tampon-associated problems. In fact, the majority of TSS cases are not even reported. Despite this near-total obscurity, DEN reports make horrifying reading. The Collective continues to urge both lay women and medical practitioners to report any problems that might be related to tampon use to DEN (DEN Reports, Food and Drug Administration, 5600 Fishers Lane, Rockville, MD 20857) and to BWHBC (Boston Women's Health Book Collective, P.O. Box 192, West Somerville, MA 02144). Write what happened and which tampons were used. Tampon users should report directly to both even if they have seen a doctor about the problem. Only through public records will it be possible to determine the extent of problems with tampons. This information is necessary to increase public awareness in order to create pressure for safer tampons.

Every 2 years, the FDA is legally required to conduct inspections of tampon factories. The inspectors, however, only examine whether the plant looks clean and whether the company seems to be following some sort of quality control program. There are no specific requirements for tampon manufacturing and testing, although the FDA does have the authority to require uniform testing and quality control measures.

What Power Do Consumers Really Have?

What are the minimum conditions necessary for consumers to achieve their objectives in a group with manufacturers and government representatives? The bottom line, of course, is how power is distributed in a working group, the rules of procedure. In this instance, the ASTM process allowed either side final veto power. Numbers of industry and consumer groups represented, numbers of people participating on each side, and resources of time and money are also critical. The power of industry includes money, technical and legal expertise, and ongoing relationships with government officials and agencies. Among tampon manufacturers are multinational corporations and a major drug company in frequent contact with the FDA and OMB. The power of consumer advocates is drawn from their constituencies, their organizing skills, and their access to media. Listening to the experiences of their constituency enables them to identify important safety issues. Knowing the facts and advocating for better health and safer products engender respect and credibility and help gain media access. In regard to tampons, a feminist analysis helped them make sense of the issues and of the dynamics of the ASTM Tampon Task Force.

Consumers need to be careful that their participation does not legitimate a process or outcome that they do not endorse. We felt this most profoundly in regard to whether a standard with incomplete safety testing was better than one with no safety testing. The consumers did not want women to be falsely reassured that tampons were safe because there was some standard testing. In addition, the existence of any official standard that included any safety testing could be used by manufacturers in court as a defense against product liability lawsuits brought by women who believed they were harmed by using tampons.

Consumers need to evaluate their very limited resources. It is important to decide if the possible outcome warrants the expected amount of time and effort to do a good job on the project. Because the various consumer groups involved in the task force had different politics and expectations, some became inactive after 2 years. This task force continued much longer

than originally planned and required *much* more work for effective participation than we anticipated. Funding that the manufacturers promised
to give to ASTM to pay for technical consultants was canceled. Without
expert consultation, it is impossible for consumers to evaluate many areas.
In fact, the Tampon Task Force finally dissolved itself in 1985 for this very
reason. If consumer representatives are forced to work as unpaid volunteers, as the authors were, their time and energy must of necessity be
extremely limited. We have repeatedly asked ourselves, "Is this task force
really a good use of our resources?"

The ASTM Tampon Task Force had much more consumer representation and power than is usual in voluntary standards organizations. The
public spotlight on tampons and TSS, the FDA request for consumer participation, the tampon industry's agreement to put up money for travel
expenses, and the choice of genuine, well-informed consumer activists who
were not docile—these factors magnified consumer power. Yet, in terms
of the product standard the task force was commissioned to develop, the
main consumer achievement was preventing ASTM from issuing the ridicu-
lously inadequate standard desired by industry and supported by the FDA.

After the task force ended, one of the authors committed herself to
following the progress of the FDA labeling requirement. Without the institutional base of the BWHBC to provide facilities and a name for fund-
raising for the project, this monitoring would have been far more difficult. Many issues, particularly those involving government regulation,
require a sustained interest over many years time. Trying to understand
political forces acting both outside and inside an organization enables consumers to make more effective decisions. In addition, it is necessary to
pay close attention to the technical rules of procedure.

Our experiences have led us to the conclusion that neither a voluntary
standard nor FDA action will adequately address tampon safety. Consumer groups on the task force have identified areas where information
is either inadequate or nonexistent. Tampons cannot be effectively regulated until there is much more research. But funds for thorough, independent research are not forthcoming. Because women's health issues are
not a research priority and because the FDA is limited in its effectiveness,
product liability lawsuits will continue to be the single most effective way
to make public results of manufacturers' proprietary research and to get
questionable products off the market. This is why legislation to limit
product liability awards is not in the public interest.

The effect of product liability on profits motivated industry behavior.
The manufacturers wanted only enough government regulation or the
imprimatur of a recognized voluntary standard to protect them in court.
They needed to show they had sufficiently warned consumers of the known
danger, TSS. The warning would then shift the legal liability for damage

from the manufacturer to the consumer. High absorbency is the one TSS risk factor the government considers provable in court. Thus it was no accident that both the FDA and the ASTM Tampon Task Force narrowed their final scope to absorbency disclosure.

Although manufacturers vehemently denied any association between tampons and TSS, they started to lower the absorbency of their products in the early 1980s. All of the highest absorbency tampons were off the market by the end of the decade. In fact, by 1984, the incidence of TSS appeared somewhat reduced. Researchers noted that the drop correlated with the reduction of average tampon absorbencies (Berkley, Hightower, Broome, & Reingold, 1987).

Moreover, publicity about consumers suffering serious harm or death is damaging to corporate image or public confidence in the product. Such publicity is a very effective way of alerting consumers that a product may be dangerous. In fact, tampon sales did decrease in the wake of media attention to TSS.

Grassroots support and the power of the market place were important hidden forces in tampon absorbency labeling regulation. BWHBC worked during the process of developing the rule to educate the public directly and through the media as much as its resources allowed. It certainly will continue in this effort in distributing its brochure and other information on tampons.

Although we can explain why the mission to write a comprehensive product standard failed, we cannot be sure which were the deciding factors in achieving the relatively good absorbency disclosure requirement. It was a complex political situation with many people, groups, and special interests. In addition, much decision making and negotiation happened behind closed doors that often shut out the consumers. When the authors ask ourselves if it was worth it, our answer is a qualified yes.

Appendix. The following paragraphs are the labeling requirements excerpted from the *Federal Register* [October 26, 1989, *54*(206), 43771].

   — The labeling of menstrual tampons shall contain the following consumer information prominently and legibly, in such terms as to render the information likely to be read and understood by the ordinary individual under customary conditions of purchase and use:

   — The risk of TSS to all women using tampons during their menstrual period, especially the reported higher risks to women under 30 years of age and teenage girls, the estimated incidence of TSS of 1 to 17 per 100,000 menstruating women and girls per year, and the risk of death from contracting TSS;

   — The advisability of using tampons with the minimum absorbency needed to control menstrual flow in order to reduce the risk of contracting TSS;

—Avoiding the risk of getting tampon-associated TSS by not using tampons, and reducing the risk of getting TSS by alternating tampon use with sanitary napkin use during menstrual periods; and

—The statements required by paragraph (e) of this section shall be prominently and legibly placed on the package label of menstrual tampons in conformance with section 502(c) of the Federal Food, Drug, and Cosmetic Act (the act) (unless the menstrual tampons are exempt under paragraph (g) of this section).

(1) Menstrual tampon package labels shall bear one of the following absorbency terms representing the absorbency of the production run, lot, or batch as measured by the test described in paragraph (f)(2) of this section;

Ranges of absorbency in grams[1]	Corresponding term of absorbency
6 and under	Junior absorbency.
6 to 9	Regular absorbency.
9 to 12	Super absorbency.
12 to 15	Super plus absorbency.
15 to 18	None.
above 18	None.

[1]These ranges are defined, respectively, as follows: less than or equal to 6 grams; greater than 6 grams up to and including 9 grams; greater than 9 grams up to and including 12 grams; greater than 12 grams up to and including 15 grams; greater than 15 grams up to and including 18 grams; and greater than 18 grams.

(2) The package label shall include an explanation of the ranges of absorbency and a description of how consumers can use a range of absorbency, and its corresponding absorbency term, to make comparisons of absorbency of tampons to allow selection of the tampons with the minimum absorbency needed to control menstrual flow in order to reduce the risk of contracting TSS.

REFERENCES

Berkley, S. F., Hightower, A. W., Broome, C. V., & Reingold, A. L. (1987). The relationship of tampon characteristics to menstrual toxic shock syndrome. *Journal of the American Medical Association, 258,* 917–920.

Hanna, B. A., & Tierno, P. M. (1985). The microbiology of toxic shock syndrome. *Clinical Microbiology Newsletter, 7,* 89–91.

Mills, J. T., Parsonnet, J., Tsai, Y.-C., Kendrick, M., Hickman, R. K., & Kass, E. H. (1985). Control of production of toxic-shock-syndrome Toxin-1 (TSST-1) by magnesium ion. *Journal of Infectious Diseases, 151,* 1158–1161.

National Center for Devices and Radiological Health. (1983). Advice on absorbency to appear on outside of all tampon packages. *Medical Devices Bulletin, 1*(3), 1.

Radetsky, P. (1985). The rise and (maybe not the) fall of toxic shock syndrome. *Science 85, 6,* 72–79.

Reame, N. E., Delonis, S., & Lewis, R. (1987). *Menstrual tampons: Changes in absorbency and styles since 1982.* Paper presented at the Seventh Conference of the Society for Menstrual Cycle Research, Ann Arbor, MI.

Tampons and Toxic Shock. (1988). *Public Citizen Health Research Group Health Letter, 4*(7), 11.

26

Menstruation Consciousness Raising: A Personal and Pedagogical Process

Emily Erwin Culpepper

> I am older than this age
> the moon calls forth my blood
> Even as it rules the ocean tides.
> I dream of ancient women
> Who did not apologize
> For their moon-stains
> Or their way of living.
> We pray their like
> Will come on earth again.
> (Lanyere Liggera, "Invocation")[1]

As a basic, frequent experience for many years of most women's lives, menstruating is inextricably connected with our sense of self. Menstruating is the subject of taboo, secrecy, and confused and conflicting information in most societies. Many of us come to our experiences of menstruating with mixed messages, in a social context that is primarily negative. But this is beginning to change. As more and more women and girls talk openly with each other about our periods, we are gradually creating new menstrual attitudes, and with them, new menstrual experiences.

Images and attitudes about menstruating contribute to our total experiences of menstruation, for attitudes can affect our sensations and how we interpret them. This interconnection has often been used against women, promoting theories that menstrual problems are all psychological. Women are keenly aware of this trap, and it is important to acknowledge.

Feminists are especially concerned not to create any new "feminist mystique" that romanticizes menstruation. We are not claiming that attitudes and sensations are simplistically correlated. Rather, women are asserting our desire and right to open up this entire field of inquiry. We are adding the thinking and experiences of multitudes of ordinary women to the selected scientific samples and traditional disciplines of theory on which studies are often based. We are exploring complex interrelated facets of menstruation in new, women-identified ways.

This chapter focuses on emerging new menstrual attitudes as I encounter and utilize them in workshops and classes. By designing these classes to encourage women and girls to explore attitudes, this exploration becomes a catalyst for changing attitudes. The methods I use are drawn from feminist consciousness-raising techniques. My pedagogical approach also grows out of the premise that women's primary tradition has been and still is an oral tradition. Therefore, I specifically elicit storytelling and personal history, identifying this oral tradition as an essential but neglected source of primary information about the realities of menstruating. This chapter, then, is designed to evoke in the reader a sense of participating in such a workshop. I will begin the way I begin a workshop, by telling some menstrual stories of my own. In the workshop, these serve several functions. They demonstrate a willingness to open the door into an intimate and taboo subject and describe a normal, understandable process for getting there. Additionally, these stories trace the path leading to making the film *Period Piece*,[2] introducing the movie (discussed further below), and preparing participants for its explicit images. I invite you to think of your own menstrual stories as an additional primary source while you read this chapter.

In 1972, as a graduate student at Harvard Divinity School, my fascination with menstruation led me to write an article comparing ancient Hebrew attitudes with contemporary attitudes (revised as Culpepper, 1978). Doing this research led to my first experience of what I and other women would call "menstrual power." Surrounded by men in the library basement, I read pages from Leviticus that proclaim "the menstruant" and all she touches as ritually unclean. One day I was menstruating as I read and touched these pages. An exhilarating feeling of strength and freedom from taboo came over me. I almost shouted out in the library, "HA HA! I'm menstruating now!" I did laugh aloud, and went right home to write about this magical experience in my journal and tell my friends.

After preparing a second article on ancient Zoroastrian menstrual taboos (Culpepper, 1973), I realized that I could continue this research forever. Negative attitudes and restrictive customs about menstruation exist in virtually all known cultures. But feminism and the women with whom I was discussing menstruation inspired me to do more. I wanted to help create more positive, health-promoting attitudes. A return to basic inquiry was essential.

I concluded that we needed to look, really look, at menstruation, and see for ourselves what it is. See that it is red . . . it is blood . . . it flows from our vulvas regularly. Remember that we have all heard menstrual folklore. I decided a film was needed to do this, which was alarming since I knew nothing about film making. However, with persistence, luck, and the help of a feminist film instructor and friends, I produced *Period Piece* for my master's thesis.

The response was overwhelming. With *Period Piece* I had tapped a need and energy source greater than I had ever dreamed. The film functioned as a catalyst for opening up a very frank and obviously pro-woman context for women to share our stories, fears, ideas, hopes, and basic information about menstruating.

Let me briefly describe *Period Piece.* The visuals begin by slowly exploring images women might associate with menstruation. On the sound track are first-person stories by four women and one man about menstrual experiences. Gradually the film moves toward two more direct visual encounters: a woman interrupting her work to change her tampon; and my own very first vaginal self-examination while menstruating—showing reflected in a mirror drops of blood emerging from my cervix.

This last scene, which felt so risky to do, turned out to be, as a newspaper reviewer wrote, "inherently dramatic. . . . The final effect has the spontaneity of a home movie; and the shock of seeing a bright red bleeding cervix and realizing it *is* beautiful" (Fenton, 1974). When my cervix appeared on the screen a professor at my Master's Disputation gasped, "It looks like a jewel!" Motivated by these experiences, I have given hundreds of classes, workshops, and lectures in settings ranging from mother-daughter groups at the YWCA to Stanford Medical School. I have learned that the simple "first movie honesty" is part of why this film works as a catalyst for sharing. It is obviously not yet another authoritatively delivered "correct" view. Dogmatic or smugly reassuring presentations silence women, who are made to feel they do not measure up to a norm.

Several important methods foster the atmosphere of openness crucial to these workshops. First, I directly address the issue of norms, stating clearly that the workshop will include a variety of materials reflecting divergent, often contradictory experiences and attitudes. There are women who love their periods, women who hate them, women for whom they are "no big deal" or a "minor hassle." There are women who have serious pain and other difficulties that need to be addressed better than medicine has managed to do so far, women whose menstrual experiences are uncomplicated, women whose experience is ecstatic. Sometimes, these are all the same woman.

Each group decides whether first to discuss attitudes, customs, personal stories, or health information. If the group is small enough, each woman says briefly why she came to a group on menstruation—what did she hope to find? Thus, we start where the women's concerns and energy are, rather than by imposing my agenda. Groups beginning with health issues (e.g., premenstrual syndrome, toxic shock syndrome, cramps) soon intersect with concern about attitudes, because they figure so significantly in how women approach and live with the health issues.

Early in the discussion, women volunteer all the names they can think of for menstruation, and I add others from my collection. The variety is always surprising, and women explain names to each other. Frequently mentioned are falling off the roof, the curse, Aunt Martha's coming to visit, my friend, my red-headed cousin, the bloods, riding the rag, flying baker (a male name, from the air force red flag for danger), my moons, that time of the month, my red-letter day. The list is endless because, as these discussions reveal, women (and men) often create personal or in-group names for our periods.

The naming discussion leads naturally into the diverse attitudes these names reflect, and whether the women and girls present share them. It is at this point that historical and cultural background enters the picture. I bring many interdisciplinary resources to a workshop and quote them as they fit the needs of the group. Only after a variety of information has emerged from within the group do I introduce these references (e.g., Boston Women's Health Book Collective, 1984; Cameron, 1981; Delaney, Lupton, & Toth, 1976; Dores, Siegel, & Midlife and Older Women's Book Project, 1987; Gardner-Loulan, Lopez, & Quakenbush, 1978; Grahn, 1982; Golub, 1985; Harrison, 1982; Lander, 1988; Lorde, 1984; Olesen & Woods, 1986; Rooney, 1975; Shuttle & Redgrove, 1986; Steinhem, 1978; Taylor, 1988; Weideger, 1976).

Every group is different, so I will trace here one example of how a discussion might typically develop. The patriarchal custom of demanding the separation of menstruating women is usually a subject of keen interest. I often contrast two readings.

> When a woman has a discharge of blood which is her regular discharge from her body, she shall be in her impurity for seven days, and whoever touches her shall be unclean until the evening. And everything upon which she lies during her impurity shall be unclean; everything upon which she sits shall be unclean. (Lev. 15:19–20, RSV)

These and other verses from the *Torah* (Pentateuch of the Hebrew Bible or Christian Old Testament) are the *Niddah* laws, which mandate a state of separation for a menstruating woman. The *Niddah* laws are still observed by Orthodox Jewish women. I follow Leviticus with a poem called "Niddah" by a contemporary Jewish feminist. The poem begins:

> I have bled for seven days
>   for seven nights
>   and seven times seventy.
>
> I have bled for centuries

> and the rivers of my blood
> go deep into the earth.

It concludes with its own demand:

> Rabbis take heed:
> your decrees are for naught.
>
> For my blood is both life and death
> and from these there is no
> state of separation.
> (Michal Sharron, "Niddah,"
> *Lilith's Rib*, n.p.)

Following these readings, I invite any Jewish women to share their stories and especially ask if any have experienced the Jewish folk custom of the "menstrual slap." Briefly, the menstrual slap is just that, a slap on the cheek of a girl who has just started her first period, a folk menarche ritual. I had never heard of it until women began telling these stories in my groups. Sometimes, as might be expected from the name, it is a negative experience, a hard slap that hurts. It may come as a total surprise or a girl may have been told in advance or seen it. Diverse reasons for the custom have been given: "This is to let you know you can get pregnant now"; "this will bring blood back to your cheeks"; "this marks the day you have become a woman"; "remember a woman's life is filled with pain"; "this is just something we do—my mother did it to me."

Women also tell stories of the menstrual slap being a love pat, a caress in honor of this important female change in a girl's life. Sometimes it is a private mother-daughter rite, sometimes the occasion for a special family dinner. As more and more versions are shared (and as some Jewish women add their observation that it is not familiar to them), it becomes clear that the meanings of customs and rituals are complex. Context and intention are part of the actual meanings that are experienced. This custom is a thought-provoking example of how the same act can be experienced quite differently. This key point about rituals and customs is best made through exploring diverse accounts rather than by simply asserting differences in experience.

Such a discussion leads easily into stories comparing other religious attitudes, family practices, and secular customs. Eventually this process raises the larger question of whether women want to have special customs and rituals about menstruating. We consider examples of women experimenting with changing customs and inventing new practices. Some feminists are experimenting with choosing to separate ourselves, to take "special personal time" alone during our periods. This idea is guaranteed to be controversial. Is this not just perpetuating patriarchal stereotypes? Does it not reinforce the sexist notion that women are weaker and cannot par-

ticipate fully in social decision making? But then, perhaps it is a necessary balance to a society that is oppressively ordered – that demands a
rigid, overstressed clockwork schedule that allows no time for personal
rhythms of introversion and extraversion. Perhaps men also need periods
of separation? Such conversations highlight the ways standards for judging
behavior are socially constructed and interpreted.

Other new customs show women experiencing pride in our periods.
Some record their flow on lunar calendars. Some have celebrations of their
periods. One woman had a gathering marking the 13th anniversary of
her menarche. Guests were asked to wear red, bring red food and drink,
and come prepared to tell menstrual stories. Many participants were moved
by the unexpectedly deep memories that surfaced during this creative
evening.

Women often confide that they love wearing red during their periods,
as a private sign that they feel good about themselves when menstruating, a talisman against a disapproving climate. There are women who mark
these days by burning a red candle. Some regard their periods as a
reminder: to meditate or exercise; to tune in more closely to their physical, emotional, and intellectual needs; to reward themselves with some
special treat or activity too easily forgotten in the social pressure on women
to be focused first on the needs of others. Many women discover that they
have already developed special habits, but had not fully focused on doing
so. Often, women felt they were the only ones who did this and are
delighted to hear such stories from others.

In a different vein, some women articulate quite directly that they use
their periods as an "okay" time for emotions and behaviors ordinarily
unacceptable in their living situations. Women describing difficult relationships with husbands or others have been surprisingly explicit about
using stereotypes of "menstrual moodiness" or premenstrual syndrome as
a survival strategy. They find their periods are a culturally condoned time
to relieve stress or lighten a heavy work load. Typical comments: "That's
the only time I can get mad at my husband"; or, "the only time he leaves
me alone"; or, "the only time . . ." of whatever she has been unable to
achieve otherwise.

Because the workshop atmosphere is not judgmental, these women feel
free to be frank. Their feeling that they have achieved some small victory
by turning prejudice into a survival tool is validated, even as we go on
to reflect together that such methods are problematic because they rarely
accomplish permanent change and can even become self-perpetuating.
These women are quite aware that this is a stopgap measure. They often
state they would not share such information with very many people,
especially researchers, who are seen as condescending. In this kind of
group, I have seen quite traditional women and radical feminists partici-

pate together in a process that validates all our perceptions as important parts of creating a fuller understanding of menstruation and new menstrual possibilities.

Menstruation and erotic feeling is another topic generating diverse perspectives. Among both lesbians and heterosexual women, there are those who find menstruating is a time of heightened arousal, and others who say they cannot possibly imagine feeling sexual then. There is clearly no one "right" experience here, nor in any of the areas we discuss. Some women want to minimize the attention menstruation demands in their lives, whereas others want to explore and maximize its role.

Increasingly, women make the point that by valuing and trusting their menstrual sensations, they have come to understand and *feel* them in completely new ways. As one participant in a workshop put it: "What I used to think was clumsiness and 'slow reaction time' during my first days, I now realize is better described as feeling a different rhythm, a different drummer. Actually, I'm most likely to write my best poetry then if I listen to those rhythms instead of being impatient and critical of myself. Those poems didn't get written when I used to force myself to conform to the rest of the month. In fact, that's when I'd have more period problems."

Women report discovering that their perimenstrual days are times of greater creative energy, dramatic dreams, or special insights that do not happen when they dismiss their perceptions as "just being too sensitive now." There is an emerging sense that for some women, menstruation is a time when one's body asserts what we need to pay attention to, when usual coping methods cannot so easily cover over things we need to know. For these women, this special "body wisdom" is an asset, an aid to health and well-being.

Such positive feelings about menstruation are certainly not shared by all women. Far too many of us have cramps or the range of uncomfortable and painful symptoms now being called premenstrual syndrome (PMS). A healthy self-image does not, as all too many of us know, just make such pain go away. In workshops, the focus is on what *women* have found to work in alleviating these problems, not only the latest medical theories. Recently, women have discussed concern that PMS is seeming like a fad diagnosis, applied and encouraged for more women than those who have serious physical symptoms. The increase of PMS jokes and the attitudes they reveal are often discussed.

When the workshop context does not blame menstrual problems on attitudes but takes all women seriously, women often report ways in which learning to explore attitudes has helped with cramps and PMS. As a common example, women describe how just being more comfortable with talking about menstruation has helped them to keep a menstrual calendar or journal, recognize eating habits and sources of stress that contribute to the severity of symptoms, and gain greater support from others in their lives.

Sometimes a woman may come to a group because she does not menstruate or does so infrequently. I always bring up this possibility. Other women are often surprised to hear a woman who is not menstruating express feelings of loss. The woman herself may not have expected this sense of loss. Sometimes, the group is the first place she has felt free to express this.

As is obvious by now, each topic leads to many others. Once underway, most women and girls are eager for this kind of thought-provoking discussion. There are other techniques I want to mention but do not have space to describe in detail. A major one is the consciousness-raising method of picking a topic and having each woman speak about it. If the group is too large, the women offer comments for a set amount of time. Many "first time" topics come up: my first period; how I first heard about menstruation; the first time I used a tampon. The groups always come up with fresh topics: my best/worst/funniest menstrual or menopause experience; superstitions I have heard; attitudes of men I've known; family attitudes; fears; childhood jokes; what's most important to me now about menstruation.

Another valuable technique is to lead a guided fantasy centered on menstruation, menarche, or menopause. Guided fantasy is a directed, open-ended meditation focusing on awareness of self-images. Often these release new self-awareness. Some women prefer to keep these feelings private, so there is no pressure or expectation for all to share their discoveries.

Especially in small groups, I may use imaginative drawing, having women draw pictures of menstrual themes and describe them to each other. Very diverse images result from everyone's drawing "how I feel when I have my period," or "how my last period felt." Others are "how my significant person sees my period," or "how I imagine menopause." Girls who have not started to menstruate have responded especially to drawing pictures about "how I think my period will feel." This exercise has led to some wonderful conversations.

Throughout each group, I sprinkle examples of poetry, art, music, humor, and fiction that contain new menstrual images. A new sensibility and aesthetic is clearly emerging among women about our menses. Because poetry is frequently a vehicle for new menstrual imagery, I will conclude with several striking examples which I usually read. In her poem, "New World Coro," Ntozake Shange (1983a) declares:

> our visions are our own
> our truth no less violent than necessary
> to make

> our daughters' dreams
> as real as mensis.

In "We Need a God Who Bleeds Now," Shange (1983b) blends menstrual and birthing blood imagery.

> we need a god who bleeds now . . .
> spreads her lunar vulva & showers us in shades of scarlet
> thick and warm like the breath of her
> . . . . i am
> not wounded i am bleeding to life.

It should not be surprising that goddess and female god imagery is a frequent form for new menstrual visions. Menstrual consciousness-raising goes to the core of the female senses of Self. It often touches a depth of experience that leads to spiritual expression. Untangling the knot patriarchy has made of this basic life experience can help open up joyful assertion of a distinctly female sense of self-worth. This last poem (quoted in full) by Penelope Scambly Schott (1979) always elicits profound response. It voices a still too rare celebration of mother-daughter bonding, creating a rite of affirming menstrual initiation into the circle of women.

> When you phoned from California to tell me it had started
>
> A brilliant globule of blood
> rolled out over the surface of the desert
> up and down the Continental Divide
> through the singing prairies
> parting the Mississippi
> leaping the Delaware Water Gap
> until it spilled into this tall red kitchen
> in Rocky Hill, New Jersey
> where it skittered across the linoleum
> and cracked into hundreds of little faceted jewels.
>
> I will not diminish this day with labeling
> I will not say foolishly
> "now you are a woman"
> I will never tell you
> "don't talk to strangers"
>
> because we are each of us strangers
> one to another
> mysterious in our bodies,
> the connection between us
> ascending like separate stone wells
> from the same dark waters
> under the earth
>
> But tonight you delight me like a lover

so that my thigh muscles twitch
and the nipples of my breasts
rise and remember
your small mouth
until I am laughing to the marrow of my bones
and I want to shout
Bless you, my daughter, bless you, bless you;
I have created the world in thirteen years
and it is good.

Clearly women are creating new and powerful ways of understanding our Selves, and our menses as part of that self-understanding. I do not think feminists are exaggerating when seeing these changes as part of a process that will have, that *is* having, far-reaching implications for women's personal, political, and spiritual lives. Menstrual consciousness-raising is one source of women's liberation.

NOTES

1. This song, "Invocation," by Lanyere Liggera (1976) begins and ends the movie *Period Piece* (see note 2).

2. I created the film *Period Piece* in 1974 at Harvard Divinity School for my master's thesis. It is a 10-minute, color film about attitudes and experiences of menstruation, and is available from Emily Culpepper, Director of Women's Studies, University of Redlands, Redlands, CA 92373-0999. A descriptive flyer is also available.

Lines from the poems "New World Coro" and "We Need a God Who Bleeds Now" by Ntozake Shange are from the book *A Daughter's Geography*, copyright 1983 by St. Martin's Press. The poem "When you phoned from California to tell me it had started" by Penelope Scambly Schott appeared in *Ms.* magazine and in *I'm on My Way Running*, edited by L. Reese, J. Wildinson, and P. S. Koppelman, copyright 1983 by Avon Books, reprinted by permission.

REFERENCES

Boston Women's Health Book Collective. (1984). *The new our bodies, ourselves.* New York: Simon & Schuster.

Cameron, A. (1981). *Daughters of copper woman.* Vancouver, BC: Press Gang.

Culpepper, E. E. (1973). Zoroastrian menstruation taboos: A women's studies perspective. In J. Romero (Ed.), *Women and religion—1973* (pp. 94–102). Tallahassee, FL: American Academy of Religion.

Culpepper, E. E. (1978). Exploring menstrual attitudes. In M. Hennifin & B. Fried (Eds.), *Women look at biology looking at women* (pp. 135–161). Cambridge, MA: Schenkman.

Delaney, J., Lupton, M. J., & Toth, E. (1976). *The curse: A cultural history of menstruation.* New York: Dutton. [Rev. ed., Urbana: University of Illinois Press, 1988]

Doress, P., Siegal, D., & the Midlife and Older Women's Book Project. (1987). *Ourselves growing older.* New York: Simon & Schuster.

Fenton, L. (1974, June 12). Period piece: Bloody but unbowed. *The Real Paper,* Boston, p. 16.

Gardner-Loulan, J., Lopez, B., & Quakenbush, M. (1978). *Period.* San Francisco: New Glide. [Also available in Spanish]

Golub, S. (Ed.). (1985). *Lifting the curse of menstruation: A feminist appraisal of the influence of menstruation on women's lives.* New York: Harrington Park Press.

Grahn, J. (1982). From sacred blood to the curse and beyond. In C. Spretnak (Ed.), *The politics of women's spirituality: Essays on the rise of spiritual power within the feminist movement* (pp. 265–279). Garden City, NY: Anchor Books.

Harrison, M. (1982). *Self-help for premenstrual syndrome.* New York: Random House.

Lander, L. (1988). *Images of bleeding: Menstruation as ideology.* New York: Orlando Press.

Liggera, L. (1976). "Invocation." In Cheney, M. Deihl, & Silverstein (Eds.), *All our lives: A women's song book* (p. 76). Baltimore, MD: Diana Press.

Lorde, A. (1984). *Zami: A new spelling of my name.* New York: Kitchen Table Press.

Olesen, V. L., & Woods, N. F. (1986). *Culture, society, and menstruation.* New York: Hemisphere.

Rooney, F. (1975). Womanblood. In L. Galana & G. Covina (Eds.), *The lesbian reader* (pp. 139–141). Oakland, CA: Amazon.

Schott, P. S. (1979, December). "When you phoned from California to tell me it had started." *Ms.,* p. 113.

Shange, N. (1983a). "New World Coro." In *A daughter's geography* (p. 52). New York: St. Martin's Press.

Shange, N. (1983b). "We need a god who bleeds now." In *A daughter's geography* (p. 51). New York: St. Martin's Press.

Shuttle, P., & Redgrove, P. (1986). *The wise wound: The myths, realities and meanings of menstruation.* New York: Grove Press.

Steinhem, G. (1978, October). If men could menstruate. *Ms.,* p. 110.

Taylor, D. (1988). *Red flower: Rethinking menstruation.* Freedom, CA: Crossing Press.

Weideger, P. (1976). *Menstruation and menopause: The physiology and psychology, the myth and the reality.* New York: Knopf.

Contributors and Editors

NITSA ALLEN-BARASH is a senior fellow in the Department of Epidemiology & Dental Public Health Sciences at the University of Washington. She earned her PhD in epidemiology at the University of Washington in 1988. Her research interests include risk factors for smoking relapse, oral disease prevention, and etiology of pediatric fear.

HOWARD I. BARON, MD, is chief resident in the Department of Pediatrics at the University of Minnesota Health Center. He completed the pediatrics residency at the University of Minnesota in June 1989. In July 1990, he became a fellow in pediatric gastroenterology at UCLA Medical Center.

YEWOUBDAR BEYENE is an assistant research anthropologist in the Medical Anthropology Program at the University of California, San Francisco. She earned her PhD at Case Western Reserve University in 1985. Her book *From Menarche to Menopause: Reproductive Lives of Peasant Women in Two Cultures* was published by SUNY Press in 1989. She is currently principal investigator for "Menopause, Aging & Osteoporosis: Cross-Cultural Inquiry," a study to provide comparative data on patterns of age-related skeletal and hormonal status in Mayan women in southeastern Yucatan, Mexico.

CHERYL BOWLES is associate dean of the Graduate College, and professor of nursing at the University of Nevada, Las Vegas. She received her EdD in educational psychology from Northern Illinois University in 1984. Her research interests include women's midlife development, menopause, stress and coping, and psychosocial aspects of women's health.

SUSAN E. CAYLEFF is associate professor of women's studies at San Diego State University. She earned her PhD at Brown University in 1983. She is the author of *Wash and Be Healed: The Water-Cure Movement and Women's Health*, published by Temple University Press in 1987, and two forthcoming books, *Minority Women and Health: Gender and the Experience of Illness* (edited with Barbara Bair) and *Babe Didrikson Zaharias: Public Triumphs, Private Trials.*

VICTOR A. CHRISTOPHERSON is professor of family studies at the University of Arizona. He received his EdD from Columbia University in 1954. He recently coauthored *Aging and Family Therapy* (Haworth Press), and his research interests include personality continuity throughout the life span, and gerontology. He served as chair of human development at the University of Arizona for 17 years.

RUTH B. CHURCH is a postdoctoral fellow in the Department of Linguistics at the University of Chicago. She earned her PhD in educational psychology at the University of Chicago in 1987. She was awarded the Rosenburger Educational Prize for outstanding doctoral dissertation, 1988. Her research interests include cognitive development, cognitive issues in clinical therapy, and behavioral endocrinology.

EMILY E. CULPEPPER is assistant professor of women's studies and religion at the University of Redlands, and director of women's studies there. She was awarded her doctorate in theology by Harvard in 1983. She produced the film *Period Piece* about menstrual attitudes, and recently published "Are Women's Bodies Sacred? Listening to the Yes's and No's," in *Sacred Dimensions of Women's Experience*, edited by Elizabeth Dodson Gray (Roundtable Press).

ROBERT T. CHATTERTON, JR., PhD, is a professor in the Department of Obstetrics and Gynecology at Northwestern University Medical School, and director of the Reproductive Endocrinology Laboratory. He has published many research papers.

ALICE J. DAN is a professor in the College of Nursing, University of Illinois at Chicago. She was a founder and first president of the Society for Menstrual Cycle Research. She earned her PhD in human development from the University of Chicago in 1976, and received the Cattel Award from the New York Academy of Sciences for her dissertation. Her research interests include menstrual cycle change, self-management for premenstrual syndrome, self-care approaches to women's health, and gender and mental health.

FRANK A. DeLEON-JONES, MD, is a biological psychiatrist interested in affective disorders. He has held the position of chief of research at the Westside VA Hospital in Chicago, and clinical associate professor at the University of Illinois College of Medicine.

CATHERINE DeLOREY is a professor in the graduate school, and director of the Health Services Management Program at Lesley College. She earned her doctorate in public health from Harvard University in 1983. Her research interests include women, health, and aging.

PAULA ENGLANDER-GOLDEN is professor and director, Institute for Studies in Addictions at the University of North Texas. She earned her PhD at the University of Nebraska in 1977. Her current research interests include chemical dependency, health psychology, and human emotions. Her prevention program, "Say It Straight," was cited as a national model for substance-abuse prevention education.

DIANE ESSEX-SORLIE is an associate professor of biometrics in the University of Illinois College of Medicine. She earned her PhD at the University of Illinois, Urbana-Champaign in 1974, with specialization in applied statistics. Her research interest is the application of statistics to medical and biomedical data.

CYNTHIA A. GRAHAM is a senior clinical psychologist in the Department of Psychological Medicine at the Royal Infirmary in Edinburgh, Scotland. She was awarded her PhD in clinical psychology in 1990. Her research interests include premenstrual changes and effects of oral contraceptives on premenstrual symptoms.

EFFIE GRAHAM is now retired. She was formerly a professor of nursing at the School of Nursing of the University of Alaska, Anchorage. She earned her PhD in psychology at Boston University in 1972. She is interested in the relationship of pregnanediol level to cognitive behavior and mood.

CYNTHIA HEDRICKS is a research assistant professor in the College of Medicine, and project director of the Bone Density Research Program in the College of Nursing at the University of Illinois at Chicago. She received her PhD in biopsychology from the University of Chicago in 1985. Her research interests include female reproductive hazards and work, biosocial determinants of female sex roles, and hormones and sexual behavior.

ELIZABETH HENRIK is an associate professor in the Department of Psychology at Concordia University in Montreal, Canada. She earned her PhD in psychology at Tulane University in 1974. Dr. Henrik was born in Hungary and completed her studies in Canada and the United States; she has been a fellow of the Simone de Beauvoir Institute, Montreal, since its founding in 1978. Her research interests include behavioral correlates of the menstrual cycle (sexual behavior, premenstrual syndrome), and health issues of women, particularly reproductive health.

KATHRYN E. HOOD is associate professor of human development and women's studies at Pennsylvania State University. In 1983, she earned her PhD in psychology at Temple University in Philadelphia. Her research interests include observational study of behavior change during the menstrual cycle, husbands' menstrual-related change, and menstrual-related changes of women at work.

GERALD A. HUDGENS, PhD, is a physiological psychologist interested in the impact of stress on performance. He is a research scientist at the U.S. Army Human Engineering Laboratory, Aberdeen, Maryland.

BERYL JACKSON is an associate professor in psychiatric nursing at the University of Pittsburgh. She earned her PhD at the University of Pittsburgh in 1982. Her research interest focuses on health of black women.

CHERYL M. JORGENSEN is assistant professor and project codirector of the Center for Health Promotion and Research at the University of New Hampshire. She received her PhD from Pennsylvania State University. Her expertise is in curriculum design, district-wide systems change, techniques for integrating related services into instructional contexts, and merging the special education curriculum with the general education curriculum.

JEAN RULEY KEARNS is deputy executive director of the Consortium for International Development in Tucson, Arizona. She earned her PhD at the University of Florida in 1966. She was appointed by President Reagan to the Board for International Food and Agricultural Development in 1986 for a four-year term. This seven-person board acts as liaison between the U.S. Agency for International Development and American universities to foster international development work.

KATHRYN LEE is assistant professor in the School of Nursing at the University of California, San Francisco. She received her PhD from the University of Washington in 1986. She has published research on circadian temperature rhythms in relation to menstrual cycle phase. Her research interests include fatigue and sleep patterns in women of childbearing age.

JUDITH LEFEVRE is assistant professor and Brookdale national fellow of the Andrus Gerontology Center at the University of Southern California. She earned her PhD at the University of Chicago in 1986, and she was awarded the Robert J. Havighurst prize for an outstanding dissertation on adult development and aging. In addition to that area, her research interests include hormone-behavior interactions.

MARTHA J. LENTZ is research assistant professor in the School of Nursing at the University of Washington. She earned her PhD at the University of Washington in 1984. She is principal investigator for a grant from the National Center for Nursing Research (NIH), "Circadian Temperature Rhythm, and Sleep: Alterations in Patterns with Aging."

LINDA L. LEWIS is assistant professor in the Department of Physiological Nursing at the School of Nursing of the University of Washington. She received her PhD from the University of Illinois at Chicago in 1987. Postdoctorally, she was awarded the Robert Wood Johnson clinical nurse fellowship at the University of California, San Francisco, from 1987 to 1989. Her research focus is premenstrual syndrome: endocrine and psychosocial variables. She is a member of the board of directors of the Society for Menstrual Cycle Research.

THOMAS B. MACKENZIE is associate professor of psychiatry at the University of Minnesota Health Center. He earned his MD at Harvard in 1970.

SARAH E. MADDOCKS is staff psychologist of the Women's College Hospital in Toronto, Ontario. She earned her PhD in clinical psychology at Queen's University. Her major interests include women's health, in particular the clinical management and research of the menstrual cycle from menarche to menopause and also infertility, postpartum mood disorders, body image disturbance, and eating disorders.

PHYLLIS KERNOFF MANSFIELD is associate professor of health education and women's studies at Pennsylvania State University. She earned her PhD at Pennsylvania State University in 1983. Her research interests include health concerns of midlife women, midlife pregnancy, and the menopause experience.

MARTHA MCCLINTOCK is a professor of psychology at the University of Chicago. She earned her PhD at the University of Pennsylvania in 1976. She began research on menstrual synchrony while an undergraduate at Harvard University, and has published widely in behavioral endocrinology. She received the Distinguished Scientist Award for an Early Career Contribution to Psychology by the American Psychological Association.

WILLIAM C. MCGREW is a senior lecturer in psychology in the Department of Psychology at the University of Stirling, Scotland. He earned his doctorate of philosophy at Oxford in 1970. He serves as European editor of the journal *Ethology and Sociobiology*. His research interests include behavior and ecology of human and nonhuman primates.

ELLEN S. MITCHELL is a research assistant professor in the Department of Parent and Child Nursing at the University of Washington, School of Nursing. She earned her PhD in nursing science at the University of Washington in 1986. Her research interests include menstrual cycle symptom experiences, food cravings and eating control, and cycle variability.

KAREN OSTROV received her PhD in psychology from Marquette University in 1980. She is currently a clinical psychologist in private practice at Affiliated Psychological Resources in Madison, Wisconsin. She specializes in women's health concerns and career and relationship issues.

ROBERT L. REID, MD, is an associate professor and chief of the Division of Reproductive Endocrinology in the Department of Obstetrics and Gynecology at Queen's University in Kingston, Ontario. He was honored as a Scholar of the Medical Research Council of Canada. He has published extensively on premenstrual syndrome.

JUNE M. REINISCH has been director of The Kinsey Institute since 1982 and is one of the nation's leading researchers and educators in human sexuality and sexual and psychosexual development. Since receiving her PhD from Columbia University, she has won numerous federal and private research grants and published many scientific papers in professional and scholarly journals. She is currently a professor in the Departments of Psychology and Psychiatry at Indiana University, and was previously a member of the Departments of Psychology and Psychiatry at Rutgers University. Her internationally syndicated newspaper column, "The Kinsey Report," is read by millions, and she is the author of the recently released book *The Kinsey Institute New Report on Sex: What You Must Know to Be Sexually Literate* (St. Martin's Press, 1990).

ESTHER ROME is a member of the Boston Women's Health Book Collective and has served on the Society for Menstrual Cycle Research Board of Directors. She earned her master of arts in teaching at Harvard University, Graduate School of Education, in 1968. She testified before the Subcommittee on Legislation and National Security of the Committee on Government Operations on the topic of interference by the Office of Management and Budget in Food and Drug Administration rule-making on tampon absorbency labeling. She currently is participating in a Food and Drug Administration-sponsored work group to write booklets for women considering having silicone breast implants for augmentation or reconstruction.

STEPHANIE A. SANDERS is assistant director at the Kinsey Institute for Research in Sex, Gender, and Reproduction at Indiana University. She earned her PhD in psychology at Rutgers University in 1984 and continues to do research on behavioral endocrinology, the role of prenatal hormones and drugs in development, sexual behavior, and factors affecting reproductive cycles.

SUSAN SANDERS is a clinical psychologist. She earned her master of arts in applied psychology at Concordia University in 1984.

PATRICIA SOLBACH is a medical researcher and writer. She earned her doctorate in education at the University of Kansas in 1974. Currently, she is codirector of the Headache and Internal Medicine Research Center at the Menninger Foundation, Topeka, Kansas.

JOHN F. STEEGE is an associate clinical professor in the Department of Obstetrics and Gynecology at Duke University Medical Center, Durham, North Carolina. He earned his MD at Yale University in 1972, and he was awarded a MacArthur Foundation Mid-Career Fellowship. His research interests include premenstrual syndrome, chronic pelvic pain, and operative/laser laparoscopy, and he has been active in the American Society for Psychosomatic Obstetrics and Gynecology.

MARTHA STEWART is currently serving as a professional assistant to Senator Al Adams of Alaska.

ANNA L. STOUT is assistant professor of the division of medical psychology in the Department of Psychiatry and Department of Obstetrics and Gynecology at Duke University Medical Center. In 1980, she earned her PhD in clinical-community psychology at the University of South Carolina-Columbia. Her research interests include hormonal influences on mood and behavior, chronic pelvic pain, sexual functioning, and anxiety disorders. She recently published an article in the *American Journal of Psychiatry* comparing premenstrual symptoms in black and white community samples.

DIANA TAYLOR is an assistant professor and director of the women's health program in the Department of Family Health Care at the University of California, San Francisco. She was awarded her PhD at the University of Washington in 1988. Her research interests include perimenstrual symptoms, perimenstrual turmoil, and health-seeking behavior.

SUZANNE TRUPIN is currently the head and clinical associate professor of the Department of Obstetrics and Gynecology at the University of Illinois College of Medicine at Urbana-Champaign. She has been involved in the delivery of women's healthcare services for many years with Women's Health Practice, a private practice providing care to the downstate Illinois region in obstetrics, gynecology, and infertility, located in Champaign, Illinois. Her research interests include nutrition in pregnancy, exercise in pregnancy, development of contraceptive technology including the cervical cap, the premenstrual syndrome, and menopause. Currently, she is coauthor of a handbook on sexually transmitted diseases, soon to be published by Medical Economics, Inc.

KATHLEEN H. ULMAN is an instructor in psychology at Harvard Medical School. She earned her PhD at Boston University in 1984. She currently works primarily as a clinical psychologist doing psychotherapy. Her clinical interests include treatment of premenstrual syndrome and adult survivors of incest. Research interests include investigation of depression in midlife women and its relationship to social support and gynecological problems. She has served as a member of the board of directors of the Society for Menstrual Cycle Research.

JANETTE WALLIS earned her PhD in psychology, zoology and anthropology at the University of Oklahoma in 1986. She is currently serving as coordinator of chimpanzee research at Gombe Stream Research Centre, Tanzania, under the direction of Jane Goodall. Her research interests focus on reproductive behavior and biology of nonhuman primates.

PENELOPE WARD is assistant professor of nursing at the University of Texas-San Antonio Health Science Center School of Nursing. She earned her MS in nursing at the University of California, San Francisco, in 1972. She is a certified clinical nursing specialist in medical-surgical nursing. She is a commander of the nurse corps in the U.S. Naval Reserve. Her research interests include psychophysiologic response to pain, use of imagery in pain control, and nursing interventions in the body-mind bridge.

KIMERLY WILCOX is a research specialist in the Department of Genetics and Cell Biology at the University of Minnesota. She earned her PhD at the University of Cincinnati in 1982. Her research interests are in human behavioral genetics involving the use of family and twin designs, in particular, epilepsy, menstrual cycle phenomena, and human sexuality.

JILL WOLHANDLER represented the Boston Women's Health Book Collective to the Tampon Task Force of the American Society for Testing and Materials. She is a coauthor of *Our Bodies, Ourselves.*

NANCY F. WOODS is professor and chairperson, Department of Parent and Child Nursing, University of Washington. She received her PhD in epidemiology from the University of North Carolina at Chapel Hill in 1978. She is a fellow of the American Academy of Nursing and a member of the board of directors of the Society for Menstrual Cycle Research. She is principal investigator on a grant from the National Center for Nursing Research to study the biopsychosocial dimensions of perimenstrual symptoms.

Index